BEFORE THEY WERE THE

PACKERS

GREEN BAY'S
TOWN TEAM DAYS

DENIS J. GULLICKSON & CARL HANSON

TRAILS BOOKS
Black Earth, Wisconsin

Library of Congress Control Number: 2004104310
ISBN: 1-931599-44-0

Editor: Stan Stoga
Project Manager: Mike Martin
Assistant Project Manager: Erika Reise
Designer: Colin Harrington

Cover Photo: This 1897 photo is of the first championship team in the history of Green Bay, taken a full 22 years before Curly Lambeau and his "Packers" would take the field. The first man on the left in the second row from the top is Fred Hulbert, who introduced Green Bay to football in 1895. Other key members of the team include the mustachioed T. P. Silverwood (holding the football in the center), a graduate of the UW-Madison Law School who brought his football and organizational skills to the team in 1896. The football in Silverwood's arm indicates that he was that year's team captain. To Silverwood's left is Tom Skenandore, a powerful fullback from Oneida, who, after learning his football at Carlisle Indian School, became the first professional football player in Green Bay. He pulled down a whopping $20 per game—if the team could pay him. C. A. Gross, who later became a prominent Green Bay businessman, is the young mascot with the football doll, front and center. Photo obtained from and used with permission of Elton Cleveland, Oconto Falls, Wisconsin.

Printed in the United States of America.

09 08 07 06   6 5 4 3 2

Trails Books, a division of Trails Media Group, Inc.
P.O. Box 317 • Black Earth, WI 53515
(800) 236-8088 • e-mail: books@wistrails.com
www.trailsbooks.com

To Kathy and Rachel, for believing and waiting,
And Frank, for the wine and wisdom.

—Denis

To Laura: thank you for your patience;
To Megan and Eric: I hope you are proud of your Daddy;
To Benji: welcome aboard!
To Denis: it's been quite a ride, thanks;
To the reader: read, learn, and explore.

—Carl

CONTENTS

PREGAME WARM-UPS

AN INTRODUCTION

In that stretch of time between 1890 and 1950, the approximate beginning and absolute end of the town team era, hundreds of "elevens" came and went across the Midwest. We wanted to learn the stories of as many town teams as we could, especially the story of the town team that mattered to us the most, that of the Green Bay Packers. It wasn't just a study in history, either, because today the best part of the Packer mystique is the fact that they are—in the absolute truest sense of the term—the last remaining town team.

It quickly became clear, even to a couple of slow guys like us, that in order to study the town team phenomenon, we would need to narrow our focus to the football "elevens" in our immediate area: northeastern Wisconsin and the Upper Peninsula of Michigan. We figured that if we were going to gain an appreciation for what made our Packers so unique, we'd better get it from the angle of the towns that had played the early Green Bay teams as well as from a couple of seats in the aluminum bleachers at Lambeau Field.

From there, tracking down information on these teams was an arbitrary and capricious process at best. If we had received $10 every time someone told us, "You guys should have been here 10 years ago," we wouldn't have had to write this book, at least not from the cold and snowy confines of a cottage in northern Wisconsin. Rather, our mantra would have been something like "Another piña colada and some more lotion on my burning back, Tatianna, while I hammer out the rest of this chapter I'm calling 'Bare Hands on a Snowy Gridiron.'"

Way too often, we'd arrive in a town and find that the man we were set to interview had passed away the week before. Extremely few players who had played the game on a town team, even in the 1920s, were around any longer, and no one was available from any earlier years. As a result, most of our information had to come from the descendants of turn-of-the-century players who, themselves, were already in their retirement years. Of course, there were also the scant and sporadic accounts of long-forgotten games we gleaned from crumbling newspapers or rolls of microfilm. While we worked on this project, wrestling with a roll of microfilm frequently was cause enough to drive us to the local drinking establishment at the end of our workday. Often enough, our research continued there.

At our best estimate, there were 60-some towns in this general area with independent teams of various shapes, sizes, and degrees of organization at widely disparate times; the stories of their appearance and disappearance were fascinating. A pocket of football could spring up and burn red-hot for a year to a decade and then fade like a cooling ember. Teams that, the year before, were touted as strapping champions would, the next year, be swept under the rug of history. Three years later, they might, on the heels of some blustery barroom banter, suddenly reappear on the gridiron.

Local newspapermen were good for pumping up rivalries between teams that had never before faced one another as well as failing to show up at a championship game that everyone was yakking about. These pulpmen were far more interested in sensation than sensibility, and facts were useful as long as they didn't throw up any hurdles in a good story line. Glowing descriptions of a ball player's gridiron prowess could flow for a paragraph without ever suggesting his name.

While we were initially aiming for a definitive history of every team in every one of our target towns, it quickly became clear that this was not going to happen. Sometimes, there was no local newspaper to cover the results of these early games. But even when there had been a tabloid, we ran into plenty of problems. Shoddy reporting and shoddy follow-through on the part of the early "scribes" were the most common. Occasionally, we had to face the lack of written records caused by long-ago newspaper-building fires. It was also pretty evident that the terms *football player* and *scribe* were anything but synonymous. The men who actually played football did not often record their games, won-lost records, or statistics. Some of these facts may have been scratched out on a barroom napkin, but then tossed out with the dead beer glasses. Instead of executing our original game plan, we found ourselves "taking what the defense would give us" and telling our story in a way that was dependent on the time, materials, and human resources available.

One thing we did discover was that the game, as it was played at the end of the nineteenth century and the beginning of the twentieth century was especially violent; players were injured and some even died. We spent plenty of hours coming to grips with a sport that featured an annual death toll and the dementia of the men who insisted on playing it. Orville Anderson told us that his father, who had played with Curly Lambeau in 1918, cautioned him against playing the brutal sport. "I'm going to tell you something," his father said. "You won't listen to me. But if you want to play football, play. But when you play football you're gonna hurt in your later years like I am." We did not run across a single account of a father warning his son against the dangers of that other popular town team sport, baseball.

So, after miles on the road and hours at the keyboard, here is our best attempt to relay the story of Green Bay's earliest football teams, including the first years of the Packers. It is our hope that Packer fans (as well as saner individuals who simply stare aghast and wonder at exactly what ails Packer fans) will put this book down with an even greater appreciation of what makes this team so unique.

In closing, we want to thank the countless individuals along the way who have helped us turn guesses into truths and gaps into bridges. Consider this a work in progress with an open invitation to every reader to straighten out the curves where they might see them and fill the long, open stretches with more information. Finally, and most importantly, this book is dedicated to the other town teams that brushed elbows with the greatness of the Green Bay Packers, either directly on the gridiron or in destiny as kindred spirits.

ACKNOWLEDGMENTS

This book is a pure and simple labor of love, nearly a decade in the making. To start, a confession is in order: the authors are unabashed and unashamed Packer fans. As a result, the pages will gush with enthusiasm for the Green and Gold. If you can't stand that heat, get out of this fire while you still can!

We set out to put some kind of name to our fanaticism. We wanted to know why we woke up every morning thanking the Supreme Being that we were born Packer fans and lamenting those poor souls destined to root for other teams. We found out that it all began back in the days of the town team, back in the dimly lit shadows of football history when men were first taking to the game. In learning about the town teams, we learned much about what makes our Packers sacred.

This project began innocently enough, on a whim. From there, it spun completely out of control. I was perusing a book on Packer history, *Packer Legends in Facts*, by Eric Goska, when I noticed the game schedules and results from 1919 and 1920. Listed in both years was the name *Stambaugh*. Now, I knew of a Stambaugh town in Michigan's Upper Peninsula, where I made many ski trips with family and friends over the years. That Stambaugh was right next to Iron River. I confess that I am not a "Yooper," one of those hardy souls from Michigan's U. P., and so, having only read the name on road signs, I was still saying—logically, but erroneously—"Stam-baw."

That's the point at which Carl jumped into the fray. First things first, Carl, who is a proud Yooper, taught me to say *Stambaugh* the way the natives do: "Stam-bo." But no matter how you say it, we agreed that there was no way that the Stambaugh in question could be the same one listed in Goska's book. After all, what were the mighty Green Bay Packers, under the direction of Earl "Curly" Lambeau, doing on the same field as a team from *that* Stambaugh? It had to be "Stambaugh,

BEFORE THEY WERE THE PACKERS

Pennsylvania," or "Stambaugh, Ohio," right? Those were the states producing the independent football powerhouses in the early part of the last century. Curiosity thoroughly tweaked, we embarked on our epic journey to unearth the truth of the town teams and the story of football's earliest days in "Titletown, USA."

Upon further review and a little investigation, it turned out that the Stambaugh listed right there next to the name *Green Bay Packers* was indeed that same little town in Michigan. It also turned out that the Packers had even traveled to Stambaugh for their 1919 contest. Better yet, the Stambaugh boys gave Lambeau and his crew a good run for their money in all three of the games the two teams played over those two years.

We agreed. We had to find out more. But we couldn't just let it go at that. Once in Stambaugh, we learned of teams scattered all across northern Wisconsin and Michigan's U. P. Then we came to understand how the game of football had really come out of the colleges and subsequently found its way to the towns—so many towns, in fact, it was amazing! As the town team story unfolded, we were able to trace football in Green Bay back to its roots in the mid-1890s.

It was one great road trip. The by-product is this book and, perhaps, another one in the future that will turn the spotlight directly on the teams from the other towns. After all, they were the "elevens," which gave our beloved Packers and their predecessors a run for their money back in those early years.

Along the way, we've encountered countless individuals who have helped. They usually began with "I don't know much about it" and proceeded to give us a ton of information. Some of these people worked in the local libraries and museums, while others educated us right in their living rooms or at their kitchen tables.

Before we acknowledge those individuals, however, there are a handful of key people who have to get a nod of appreciation. The first of these is Mary Jane Herber, Local History and Genealogy Librarian at the Brown County Library in Green Bay. Mary Jane persisted in finding out some of the most obscure details we asked of her, and her efforts are truly appreciated. Sometimes it turned into a sport of its own to see if we could stump her. The fact was, we never did; we'd throw up a challenge and she'd call on her infinite resources to meet it.

Then there is Lee Remmel, who has an official role as the Team Historian of the Green Bay Packers, but is actually more like the embodiment of the Packers. His wit, his charm and, above all, his memory and sense of history put Lee in a unique class of people. Also, thanks to Art Daley who read through our manuscript and was gracious enough to give us his blessing despite that pain in the neck we likely caused him. Like Lee, Art represents the class of the human race as well as the National Football League.

When we arrived out of the blue in Stambaugh one day, we were wonderfully greeted and assisted by Harold and Marcia Bernhardt. In a way, they were the midwives who attended the birth of this project; they represent the savoir faire of Michigan's Upper Peninsula.

Also of great help on Green Bay town team and Packer history were Nubs Pigeon and Ray Drossart. With the two of them and Ray's son, Dan, we found and "toured" the White City Grounds on Green Bay's northeast side. Both men are gone now, and the ranks of Packer fans are poorer for their loss. Likewise, we gained great insight from Orville Anderson into the pre-Packer years as well as into Green Bay high school and semipro football.

Howie Levitas was another wealth of information on the early Packer years as well as on early Packer player Nate Abrams. Likewise, Howie's cousin, Janice Abrohams, shared many of her early memories of the Packers when they played at Hagemeister Park and were so much a part of the color of downtown Green Bay. Both Howie and Janice helped debunk the myth that Nate Abrams actually founded the Packers but was denied acknowledgment because of his ethnicity.

Judith Silverwood-Sharp was wonderful in sharing information on her grandfather and early Green Bay football stalwart T. P. Silverwood. Paul De Tennis came through with some great information on the 1897 championship team. Ruth Hudson was also gracious in her stories about her father, Harry Hanrahan, a member of the early Green Bay city teams. Nancy Leicht was a great help for information on Curly and for arranging a visit with Marguerite Lambeau. Russell Mott helped us understand the "gridograph" or "pictograph," which relayed early away games to the people back home, and he shared some great stories about that colorful chronicler of early Packer years, George Whitney Calhoun. Lorraine Redhail and Jesse Peron helped fill in some blanks on Tom Skenandore, the Oneida man who defined the skilled footballers of the days of "King Football." Of tremendous help in learning about the Grandfather of Green Bay Football, Fred Hulbert, were his niece, Ethel Evrard, and his granddaughter, Nancy McCue. Elton Cleveland gave us access to a copy of an original photograph of the first championship team in Green Bay. Likewise, Adeline Vincent, Chuck Giordana, and Jim Jameson helped us with other photographs. Several staffers at the Green Bay Packer Hall of Fame were also helpful, especially Tom Murphy.

Members of the media helped us get our story out there and, as a result, aided in getting information from others. These include Ray Barrington of the *Green Bay News-Chronicle*; Jean Peerenboom, Tom Perry, and Nathan Phelps of the *Green Bay Press-Gazette*; Michele Cheplich and Preston Rudie of Channel 26 TV; Charles Leroux of the *Chicago Tribune*; and Ed Erickson III and Peter Nocerini of the *Iron County Reporter*.

Key to getting information from the towns was Karen Kuhn of the Oneida Nation Library. Then, there were the individuals who helped us piece together the story of particular college or town teams. Some of these stories are told in the sidebars scattered throughout the book. These individuals include Art "Snowy" Hendrickson, Caspian; Louie Leiberg, De Pere; Robert E. Billings, Clintonville; Tony Carlotto and Malcolm McNeil, Crystal Falls; Jim Livermore, Escanaba; David Wright, Fall River; Matt Houhle, Gladstone and Escanaba; Marino "Muzz" Pucci, Iron Mountain; Dr. Donald J. Jacobs, Fred Jacobs, and Marcia and Harold Bernhardt, Iron River; Carol J. Butz, archivist at Lawrence University; Loretta Metoxen, Oneida Nation Cultural Heritage Department; John Groat, New London Museum; Sue Cross, Oconto; Mike Manci, Niagara; Mark Boucher, archivist at Ripon College; Donald L. Pieters, archivist at Saint Norbert College; Harold Anderson, Vic Shepich, and Sally Brzezinski, Stambaugh; and Valerie Rops, Wayland Academy.

Finally, when it comes to help on the story of town team football, one person emerges as a contributor of inestimable importance, Frank Shepich. It was Frank, after all, who gave us exclusive insight into the saga of the Stambaugh All-Stars, one of the all-time great town teams. Better yet, as a player, coach, and manager of a town team, Frank was able to take us to the very heart of the town team story. Under his tutelage, we gained a far greater appreciation of how fragile the life of a town team was and, as a result, just how precious it is for Green Bay to still have and hold its Packers, the quintessential town team.

It was probably because of his firsthand knowledge of the trials and tribulations of town team football that Frank was such a staunch Packer fan himself. It was in his kitchen in Stambaugh that I once asked Frank what he thought of another pretty decent footballer, Brett Favre. Frank never batted an eye. "Hell," he said, "Ya gotta love Favre. He just doesn't care. He's gonna give you all he's got on every play. I think if he wasn't a family man and if times got tough again in this country and they couldn't pay him, he'd play football for a pinch of snuff and an orange at halftime like we used ta."

We knew then that, as Frank watched Favre lay out a linebacker with a block on a reverse or get in the face of some would-be sacker with a hundred pounds on him or heave a 30-yard bullet while he was being gang tackled, he didn't see a multi-million-dollar superstar. Instead, Frank saw a rough-and-tumble guy with a chilly autumn afternoon attitude who could have easily lined up with the All-Stars against another crew of miners and done some serious football damage.

Frank's graciousness, charm, and delightful sense of humor were icing on the cake, as was his great homemade wine. It is with great regret that this project was finally completed after Frank's passing. His wit, even in the matter of death, was amazing. I remember stopping at his house once to see if he would be home the following weekend. I wanted him to draw up some of the plays he ran with the All-Stars.

"Are you going to be around next weekend?" I asked him.

"I'm an old man," he said, "what are you trying to say?" A big smile crawled across his weathered face and he snickered at me, a wonderful rascality racing across his eyes.

I caught on. "You know what I mean. Are you going to be home?"

"Well," he said, "if I'm not around, I won't be home." Now he was just playing.

"Okay, let me try this again," I said. "Do you have anything going on next Saturday?"

"You mean like dying?" he teased. "No. I don't think that's on my schedule yet." He was chuckling.

"Well don't pencil anything in until you've heard from me," was all I could come back with.

Frank Shepich was a man who lived life a lot like he played football. He knew that you had to learn the rules of the game and the obligations of your position first, and then, once you understood them, you could have a great deal of fun. Though Carl and I met him late in his life, it is so very clear that Frank was a tremendous talent at both football and life.

After this kind of road trip, is there the slightest chance that we forgot someone? Just in case, to all those individuals who played a key role in the completion of this book and to those who have yet to help us bridge the gaps and straighten out the curves, thank you!

—Denis Gullickson

FIRST HALF
CELEBRATING THE PACKERS

The Green Bay Packers are the most storied franchise in the history of the National Football League, bar none. It's become cliché to say it. But it doesn't matter. It's absolutely true and always will be.

Fans of other NFL teams can make the case for their guys, and rightfully so: that's what being a fan is all about. Every team has had its moments of glory, its great players, and its memorable games.

An Arizona fan could make a case for the "Arizona–Saint Louis–Chicago–Racine Avenue–Morgan Athletic Club" Cardinals. After all, the Cardinals, known in one of their earliest renditions as the Normals, are the oldest team in continuous existence in the league. Unfortunately, no group of supporters loved them enough to keep them. Even today, the team's football fortunes are on shaky ground, though they did become Green Bay's flash-in-the-pan heroes by miraculously defeating the Vikings and propelling the Packers into the 2003 playoffs.

An argument could certainly be made by a Windy City fan on behalf of the Chicago Bears, who are, without a doubt, the second-most storied franchise. This is why the rivalry between the Bears and the Packers has ascended to mythical status. But unlike the Packers, the Bears have always been the chattel of a rich person or a rich family, not the town.

Some fans might still stump for the Dallas Cowboys, who for a time were strangely mislabeled as "America's Team," while everyone knew that this nation's real team was still playing in green and gold uniforms. Other fans will plug the Broncos, the Eagles, the Giants, the Niners, the Raiders, the Steelers, and so on. Even the Patriots, after two Super Bowl victories in three years, will get some votes. The debate will rage on until the bartender shouts, "Last call!"

The bottom line? It just doesn't matter. After all points are made and clear heads and objectivity prevail, everyone must agree that the team that holds the rights to the richest legacy in the history of the game resides in the NFL's small-est member city: Green Bay, Wisconsin. That is not to deny those other franchises their thunder. Nor does it diminish the relative value of a particular Packer opponent on the field of play on any given Sunday. But, in terms of everything that is holy and good, the Packers are something different. No other team has mirrored the frailty of football's early existence, enjoyed the support and adora-tion of its fans through periods of unparalleled success and stretches of dismal performance, or been involved in so many of the richest moments in sports his-tory. The Packers are the story, and that's why rabid Packer fans can be found all over this globe.

Best of all, the Packers were born out of that early phenomenon of the 1890s to 1920s—the town team. The fact that they survived at all is a miracle. Their brethren, other early town teams and other members of the fledgling American Professional Football Association, are now nothing more than tombstones sitting quietly on Pleasant Hill.

Today, as a $295 million-dollar renovation of the shrine that is Lambeau Field carries Packer fans into the next millennium, there's no better time to take a look back at just why the Packers are so special. Despite the new look—which is, by the way, a wonderful old look—the Packers remain just what they've always been, a town team. Sure, it's a hair that can be split, but the essential truth is that this Packer team belongs to the town. And the town knows it has something spe-cial. Only in Green Bay will a guaranteed 50,000 people show up each summer to watch the team battle against . . . itself! The deluxe new stadium, built with a sense of tradition around the hallowed Lambeau Field, will only continue to share the rich Packer history.

But what is that tradition? And just how far back does it reach? And why have this *town* and this *team* always lived for one another? The answer can be found plainly in the team's roots, back in the days when those two words were joined into one phrase, "town team." The essence of the Packers finds its very root in the heyday of the town team, the era when the collective spirit of the boys on the grid and the fans along the sidelines was a match for any crew from any other town that wanted to take them on.

In Green Bay, football has always been a way of life; love our boys, no matter what. During a 29-year drought—spanning most of the 1970s, all of the 1980s, and well into the 1990s—the team oftentimes stunk up the field. But you still couldn't get your hands on season tickets. And today, peering smack-dab into the new millennium, if you put your name on the waiting list for season tickets, you'd only find 40-some thousand people in line ahead of you. The new stadium, with about 11,000 more seats, will no doubt cut into that number, but then the num-ber will grow again. As a legacy, forward-thinking parents put their children's names on the list, knowing that they themselves will never hold season tickets of their own.

But let's take the argument away from the bleeding hearts of Packer fans and add a little "proof" to the equation. An article in the January 21, 2003, *Green Bay Press-Gazette* confirmed what many a Packer fan has felt all along. "In a ranking of every professional sports team in North America," it began, "the Green Bay Packers are No. 1." An *ESPN the Magazine* study, conducted all across the continent, also showed that the Packers, out of 121 professional sports franchises, sat at the top of the list. The team was the only franchise to have landed in the top 10 in each of the study's eight categories.

Football in Green Bay, Wisconsin, however, did not begin in 1919 with the birth of the Green Bay "Packers." Nor did it see the first light of day in 1921 when the team became Green Bay's entry in the American Professional Football Association. In fact, Green Bay saw its first football action nearly a quarter of a century earlier when a ragtag outfit under the guidance of Fred Hulbert played a half dozen games against teams from other towns in 1895.

FIRST QUARTER

1895–1904, "FOOTBALL HAS RECEIVED ITS INTRODUCTION TO GREEN BAY"

Football in Green Bay, Wisconsin, began in 1895 and continues to this day. The organization and survival of the Green Bay Packers is legendary. But the untold fact is that professional football in this little town started because of the efforts of Fred Hulbert, a transplant from Racine via Wayland Academy in Beaver Dam, Wisconsin. From there, it has continued over various swales and berms, including the founding of the Packers, for more than one hundred years. This is not a piece of information that upsets or tarnishes the Packer legacy. It enhances it.

Football has been a constant entertainment in Green Bay since the first "formal" game was played on Saturday, September 21, 1895. That game was played at Washington Park, once located at the east end of Walnut Street. The park included what are today East High School and its entire campus as well as Johannes Park and a residential neighborhood to the south. In the 1890s, Washington Park was a catchall for leisure, recreation, and entertainment. It had a racetrack that regularly featured the fastest horses in the area. It saw baseball games, nature strolls along its many paths, family outings, band concerts, and picnics along the East River. In the Gay Nineties, it represented all the virtues of a public social life. It was a place both to see people and to be seen. Later, Hagemeister Park, the site of early Packer successes, would constitute the northern half of old Washington Park.

It was in the midst of this social mélange that the young and controversial game of football was destined to suddenly crop up one Saturday afternoon. There, in the middle of an open space at the staid Washington Park, quite likely the area just to the west of the race track, a group of two dozen young men suddenly gathered. They were all focused on a very rotund ball. At times, they all stood nearly still, forming what seemed to be two opposing lines. They were sweating and breathing hard. They seemed poised for some kind of action that was just seconds away. Then, one of them would shout some kind of gibberish, like "Dive Down,

John" or "Center Hard Boys" and they would all converge in a flurry of motion. All of a sudden, they were grunting and banging their heads together in a fracas that looked a lot more like a barroom brawl that had spilled into the street than it did any kind of acceptable "sport." There was shouting and the sound of bone on bone. This sort of fracas had only been seen in areas of the East and a small list of sites in the Midwest. Just a few people were brave enough to venture to the fringes of this chaos; others stood watching from the footpaths through the park. It was a watershed moment for the small town of Green Bay.

"Football has received its introduction to Green Bay," declared the *Green Bay Sunday Gazette* the following day, "and henceforth the 'gridiron field' will be the mecca of the amusement-loving public until snow flies." Fred Hulbert's mop of wild hair and John Thomas's speedy heels were both acknowledged as features of the game. And, in sharp contrast to the violence of the actual contact, the plays, which that day consisted mostly of "bucking the ends," were described as "pretty." Football had found a home, despite the misgivings of many.

What does a harness-racing track have to do with football? This one, at old Washington Park, was the site of Green Bay's very first football game on Saturday, September 21, 1895. The contest was most likely played in the open area just west of the track. Today, the area is a part of Johannes Park, just across from East High School. Photo from the Stiller-Lefebvre Collection.

A month earlier, on August 18, another article had appeared in the *Sunday Gazette*. It had been written by a prophet who said, "It is safe to say that once the game is introduced it will be one of the most popular amusements ever seen in Green Bay. It is predicted that the first game of football played in Green Bay will be more largely attended than a ball game, and that each succeeding game will bring out a crowd." If that ancient author were only alive today to pick the next lottery numbers!

While the article was amazing in its enthusiasm and its clairvoyance, it erred in predicting that "at least 18 or 20 games would be played." The Green Bay aggregation managed just six contests with other town teams that year.

The article further suggested that "Fred Hulbert, trainer of the West Side Athletic Association, has the matter in hand, and will captain the team. He is an old member of the Wayland Academy team at Beaver Dam, and has had experience in the game." To date, that Fred Hulbert–Wayland Academy connection has gone unnoticed and unheralded, but no longer.

Later, the article stated that "Mr. Hulbert says that there is no reason why with proper training this city cannot have a winning team." Hulbert's belief went unsupported in contests against Marinette, Stevens Point Normal School, Lawrence University, Oconto, and Fond du Lac in 1895. And during the following year, it experienced additional defeats, twice to Marinette and once each to Oconto and Peshtigo. Over those first two years of play, its victories were few and far between.

The team's first win came in a hotly contested game against Menominee, Michigan, in 1895. Two more were added in 1896, an upset of a superior Rhinelander team and a routing of an anemic De Pere team. A mere three victories in two seasons wouldn't cut it today, but the August prophecy had been realized and football was firmly established in Green Bay.

Taken in 1889, this is one of the earliest photos of a Wisconsin football team. That year, the Cottage Boys were one of two intramural teams at Wayland Academy in Beaver Dam. Eventually, football would make its way from that school to Green Bay, where it would begin a rich tradition. Note the size of the football. Photo obtained from *The Wayland Story*, by Alton Edward Wichman, George Banta Publishing, Menasha, Wisconsin; copyright 1954 by Wayland Academy and used with permission.

Still, the game was hardly new to Wisconsin in 1895. Two games were played on the Ripon College campus as early as 1881, and mention of the sport can be found on the Carroll College campus in 1866. La Crosse historians cite a contest played as early as 1860. The game was gaining much popular ground, among the students at least, at the state's own colleges. In "Athletics in the Wisconsin State University System: 1867–1913," Ronald A. Smith states, "By 1895 each of the six normal schools had a baseball and a football team, with the probable exception of Milwaukee, a school overwhelmingly dominated by women."

To demonstrate the contempt in which the young game was held, Smith cited an article from an 1894 River Falls, Wisconsin, newspaper that spit out, "Football will mean 'arnica', if not anarchy in this peaceful hamlet.'"

Smith also notes that the first "inter-normal football game" took place in 1895 between Whitewater and Platteville, two of the schools in Wisconsin's Normal School System of the time. In that game, Whitewater was soundly defeated, 30–0, but "was entertained in grand style." It was tradition in that day to soundly beat a team on the gridiron and then show them your gentlemanly side over dinner and drinks following the game.

In the rematch the following year, Whitewater, completely forgetting Platteville's post-game hospitality of the previous year, got its revenge by fielding a "team of pugilists." The game ended with Whitewater leading 8–4 when the Whitewater team walked off the field while questioning a referee's decision. To add to the snub of the hospitable Platteville team, the Whitewater squad refused to buy dinner after the game.

LAWRENCE UNIVERSITY—ONE OF THE FIRST

Lawrence University was playing football as early as 1882 and served as a worthy adversary for Green Bay's first town team in 1895. As a result, Lawrence football lore is rife with great stories.

Hold the Potatoes

According to legend, the early, ragtag Lawrentian footballers were hard at practice by 6:00 in the morning with some track calisthenics and a five-mile run. To further their training for the carrion sport of football, the otherwise-civilized Lawrence men ate "mostly raw beef three times a day." This regimen, an early-morning workout followed by several snacks of uncooked flesh, does not seem to have been practiced on all college campuses of the day.

Faculty Runaround

Margueritte Schumann, a long-time Appleton reporter, once explained that the early Lawrence teams "financed" themselves in that they "put the touch on the faculty." The response of Professor Dexter P. Nicholson was allegedly, "Yes, you may put me down for three dollars, and you may collect it from John Blank who borrowed that amount from me when he went out of town with the team three years ago and never repaid it."

A Toast!

In 1904, an essay was written to explain "Why Lawrence Wins in Football." It was accompanied by a wrap-up of the season, thumbnails on each of the starters, and honorable mention for the subs. There was also an "Outlook" for the 1905 season and a sweet essay titled, "Foot Ball from the Coed's Point of View." There was also a "Toast" to the team, probably served up on the Lawrence campus without any heady beverage:

Here's to the football eleven,
Well toasted must they be.

Here's to the faithful "scrubs"
Who helped to win the fame.
Here's to Professor Koehler -
A grand, good coach is he.
Here's to the loyal students
Who love the "grid-iron game."
Here's to the faculty, too,
"Doc Sammy" among the rest.
And here's to our dear old college,
The one we call the best.

You Gotta Love the College Game

Lawrence won at football, according to that essay, for many reasons, including the "good coaching" cited by the team, the "good team work" cited by the coach, the "speed and grit" cited by the "bleacher boy," and the "push and go" cited by the "bleacher girl."

The essay on "Scrubs" used the term *scrub*, as though it were a compliment, a dozen times over four short paragraphs and then went on to name the scrubs who had endured "interminable drudgery and routine" throughout the season. Oh, to be commemorated in such fashion in the college publication!

The girls on campus were hardly ignorant spectators, according to the coed piece. Though they often started out from a point of innocent adoration and hero worship as freshmen, by the time they were seniors they had matured enough by watching the sport to see that the footballer had really gained "in the end a more than double reward, in the form of physical, mental and moral strength, for his training on the old college gridiron has fitted him to meet successfully the bucks and tackles in the larger game of life."

If only professional-football fans of today could come to such realization about their heroes.

"Just Before the Scrimmage, Mother"

In that very spirit of Lawrence University's gridiron warriors, a piece appeared in the *Ariel*, the Lawrence yearbook in the late 1890s. "Just before the Scrimmage, Mother" was written to pick up on the melancholy popularity of George Root's Civil War tune, "Just Before the Battle, Mother," and it captured all the fear and pathos of that famous piece with maidens and professors rushing the field after a brave contest, howling, "You're the bully foot ball boys."

Just before the scrimmage, mother,
    I am thinking most of you.
As upon the gridiron standing,
    With the foot-ballites in view.

Comrades long haired, round me tremble—
    Not of "flunking" ere the game;
But they know that ere it's ended
    They must win or bear the shame.

Farewell Profs, for you may never
    Hear me flunk in class again.
But I know you'll not forget me,

If I'm numbered with the slain.

Hark! I hear the umpire's whistle;
   'Tis the signal for the fray.
Now, oh! co-eds, if you'd help us
   You must make those tin horns bray.

See them massing for our center—
   Here's the chance for glory, boys—
But he drops before the smashers,
   And our side gives vent to joys.

Thus we play the game so foxy;
   Bruised heads and broken shins.
These are not to be considered,
   For it is our crowd that wins.

Maidens wave those flags of linen,
   Profs do shout and howl for joy.
Then they rush to each a grinning,
   "You're the bully foot ball boys."

The University of Wisconsin–Madison took to the game of football even earlier than many of its school counterparts. In *On Wisconsin: Badger Football*, Oliver Kuechle and Jim Mott suggest the simple presence of football at Madison as early as 1883. This is an extremely early mention of the game, but it does follow closely on the heels of the 1876 Massasoit Convention, where Walter Camp wrote the first rules for American football.

Kuechle and Mott write that, "According to *Trochus*, a campus publication in 1883, there were class teams in all sports, each with its own student governing association, and an all-around university field day which was an annual event of the joint associations. The latter included a three-legged race, a football kick, a tug of war, a baseball throw, a potato race, a bicycle race and the usual running and jumping events." They continue, "The *Trochus* in 1883 listed eleven students as members of Wisconsin's first Football Association." Such associations "hired and fired coaches, scheduled games, and took care of all the finances, which more than once meant going into their own pockets or asking Madison businessmen for contributions." The faculty, either by personal choice or the snub of underclassmen, was not involved.

In 1889, Madison played what is commonly recognized as the earliest intercollegiate game of football ever played in the state of Wisconsin. However, Ripon and Lawrence Colleges had met in a roughshod fashion for a game seven years earlier in what really is the first such contest. But that doesn't alter the story of Madison's own inaugural football outing, except to say that it wasn't the very first of its kind in the state.

According to Kuechle and Mott, the Madison crew met up with a group of football enthusiasts in Milwaukee at National Park on the southwest corner of what is now Layton Boulevard and National Avenue. The game was played on the park's cricket field. "It is not hard to imagine," suggest Kuechle and Mott, "the young Milwaukee Blades of 1889 in their surreys or tallyhoes and the students from Madison with their cardinal pennants and ribbons lining the field at the 3 o'clock kickoff of this new-fangled game." The Milwaukee team, playing as the Calumets, won the contest 27–0.

BEFORE THEY WERE THE PACKERS

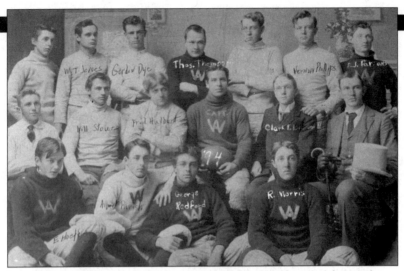

It was at Wayland Academy in Beaver Dam that Fred Hulbert (third from the left, second row, in this 1894 photo) acquired his football skills as well as his love for the game. After graduating in the spring of 1895, Hulbert moved to Green Bay. Photograph obtained from and used with permission of Wayland Academy, Beaver Dam, Wisconsin.

Wayland Academy, Hulbert's alma mater, was another early football participant, at least on an intramural basis. According to *The Wayland Story* by Alton Edward Wichman, "Two teams representing the dormitories, the 'Cottage Boys' and 'College Hall Boys,' played several games although there is no record or schedule of the results." Those early pickup games were also played in 1889. Wichman continues, "In the fall of '91, football at Wayland graduated from an intramural past time to an organized sport."

Fred Hulbert does appear with a regular team in a photo from Wayland dated 1894, which did play against teams from other schools. It was as a member of these early Wayland teams that Hulbert learned the game he brought with him when he moved to Green Bay in the summer of 1895. He also arrived with the first pigskin the town had ever seen.

GENIAL FRED AND HIS RUFFIANS

That summer, Hulbert took up a room at the Broadway House located on the northeast corner of Broadway and Dousman Streets. As a young, single man, this was customary for his time. According to the *Green Bay City Directory* of 1896, Hulbert was employed as a clerk and deliveryman for the Union Laundry located near Walnut Street on Pearl Street. It was just a simple walk a few blocks south for him to get to his job.

But what really caught his fancy sat just a few blocks to the west. There, the grounds alongside Dousman Street School, now Fort Howard Elementary School, presented a canvas upon which one could paint pictures of football action. A vacant lot owned by Ben Garlock was about two blocks farther west. It was Garlock's intention to build a house there. But without one, Hulbert's team could practice. Two years later, Hulbert's guys were still honing their skills there, en route to grabbing Titletown's first-ever football trophy.

Hulbert had moved to Green Bay for a job, but he still wanted to play football and he needed players. On Green Bay's west side, he was surrounded by the modest homes of Irish railroad workers. There, raw-boned, lanky youths with more time than sense were itching for excitement. They gathered in and about the rooms of the West Side Athletic Association, a fairly structured organization sponsored by Green Bay's west side businessmen, who knew that this rambunctious tendency had to be directed. Once Hulbert was hired as trainer for the association, the die was cast.

One can picture the blond, long-haired Hulbert preaching the gospel and the tonic of football to these seething youths. The more adventurous among them took up the gauntlet and joined Hulbert on the practice field at the end of the workday. Others stood in the shadows, curious about this "game" but unwilling to put their safety on the line. In a day when the game involved more force than finesse, Hulbert taught them the basics in short order. Their ability to play as a

BEFORE THEY WERE THE PACKERS

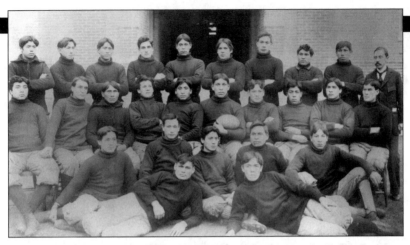

While Fred Hulbert was preparing his dandies and ruffians for some football in Green Bay, three young Oneida men were honing their own football skills at the Carlisle Indian School in Pennsylvania. All of them are seated in the middle row in this 1896 team photograph: (fifth from the left) Tom Skenandore; (seventh and eighth from the left) Jonas Metoxen and Martin Wheelock. All three would soon return to Wisconsin and be heavily recruited by the Green Bay guys. Photo obtained from and used by permission of the Cumberland County Historical Society, Carlisle, Pennsylvania.

team would come later. Their first meaningful and uncontested victory would have to wait until next season.

For some of Hulbert's early recruits, the game was more of an excuse for sanctioned brawling than it was an opportunity for sport. In "Slugging on the Gridiron," an article on Monday, October 28, 1895, the *Green Bay Gazette* declared:

> *The men and boys who play foot-ball and who conceive the game is manly in measure as it is brutal, should learn once for all and speedily that in any game calling for the exercise of physical prowess and skill, sport invariably ends where ruffianism begins.*
>
> *Foot-ball as played in this city and in Madison on Saturday, and as it is being played in most cities most of the time of late, is not only not sportsmanlike but is savage to the point of being disgraceful. Though a noble game, it is liable to be spoiled as a reputable pastime by the ruffians who infest it.*
>
> *The young men who played in the Green Bay game on Saturday and who were gentlemanly in their intentions and play until opposed by the low-lived methods of the slugger, were themselves compelled to become sluggers; they would have been fools at that time and would be fools at any time under like circumstances to refrain from giving as good as they get.*
>
> *All this leads to the conclusion, which the lovers of foot-ball will do well to accept and act on promptly, that any man whose natural coarseness*

and lack of the sportsman instinct prompts him to prefer and to employ the methods of Donnybrook fair, must be "fired out" of the foot-ball team or, as an alternative, foot-ball must degenerate below the point of toleration by decent people.

The boys in the game who love the game for its own sake and who wish to see it perpetuated as a reputable and popular sport, must get rid of the bullies and sluggers.

The game so thoroughly shredded by the *Gazette* on Monday had been played out at Washington Park on Saturday between the Green Bay team and an aggregation from Menominee, Michigan. According to the *Gazette*'s Sunday article, it had been "A Game For Blood." That recap suggested that "to the uninitiated, it looked a good deal like a free fight, but the players state that such was not the case." In the game, Fred Hulbert sustained a broken nose and was knocked unconscious. "Witnesses state that Juttner, who is a tall, powerful fellow, deliberately struck Hulbert. The blow struck him alongside the nose, splintering the small bones of that organ. Dr. Coffeen, who was among the spectators, pressed the bones back into place and Hulbert recovered consciousness in a short time." Juttner was ejected. Later he apologized, vowing that his act had not been intentional. The Green Bay boys would not accept the apology.

With a score of 10–4, this may have been Green Bay's first victory ever, but the game ended in confusion. To no one's surprise, Hulbert fumbled the ball when he was knocked unconscious. A greedy Menominee player snatched up the untended pigskin and raced for a touchdown. Because they felt Juttner's slugging had been deliberate, the Green Bay town team refused to set up to allow the Menominee eleven to kick the goal after the touchdown. This caused referee Salisbury to rule the game in Menominee's favor. But the umpire, Philip Smith, a Green Bay resident, clearly ruled that Hulbert's team had won the game. Salisbury later recanted. But, as the *Gazette* suggested, "the public can take its choice of any of these endings."

A QUICK HISTORY OF FOOTBALL SCORING

1898—touchdowns changed from 4 points to 5 points.
1904—field goals changed from 5 points to 4 points.
1909—field goals changed from 4 points to 3 points.
1912—touchdowns changed from 5 points to 6 points.

Reported scores from individual games could vary greatly. Before leagues brought about the use of uniform rules, scoring was often a matter of a gentlemen's agreement before the contest.

It was perhaps with tongue in cheek that the *Gazette* concluded its Sunday coverage with "Each side played a rough game and threats of 'doing up' opposing players were indulged in on both sides. The members of both teams regretted this act after the game was over and buried the hatchet sufficiently to talk about a return game."

The excitement of its initial season nearly behind it, the team was celebrated in an article in the *Green Bay Advocate* on December 5, 1895. It was headed, "Rah-Rah All Through" and recounted the team's final game of the season, a 14–0 defeat at the hands of a town team from Fond du Lac. Again, Hulbert was injured in the line of fire and had to leave the game. Acknowledging his performance, the *Advocate* said, "When he plays football he plunges into the thickest of the fight, regardless of consequences, and his work is always effective and his injuries about as severe as anyone's." In that day no greater tribute could have been paid. Near its conclusion, the article said, "In short, the Green Bay boys have no reason to feel ashamed of the game they put up. They went up against a heavier and much more experienced team and, though not making a score, showed to good advantage. Green Bay may reasonably hope to do better next season."

1896
ENTER SILVERWOOD

Okay, it's game day and the experts are prognosticating. Inevitably, one of them says, "Today's game will be won in the trenches." Think so? After all, it's in the trenches—those areas on either side of the line of scrimmage where the big brutes of the offense and defense clash and the ebb and flow of every game takes place—that the outcome of every game is decided. It always was. It always will be.

The four- and five-receiver set, the pro-set backfield, the two-tight-end formation, the shotgun, the West Coast offense, the dime-and-nickel packages, zone versus man, prevent, the slant pattern, the blitz . . . they're all frills added to the edges of the basic truth of the game. At the point of attack, where the behemoths of the offensive line meet the leviathans of defense, the game will be won or lost.

The importance of the trenches hasn't changed since the first somewhat-modern game of football was played by accident in 1823. In that contest, some kid named William Webb Ellis picked up a ball during a soccer game and ran with it, refusing to be confined by the day's rules and feeling content to let the thugs hammer it out in the middle of the field. The trenches were just as hot in 1869, when Rutgers edged out Princeton in the first intercollegiate soccer-football game. Indeed, they were probably plenty heated some 2000 years ago when the ancient Romans played a game called "harpastum." This is, after all, only reasonable conjecture, since the black-and-white images of the blocking schemes along the line of scrimmage in those games have not been faxed down from the booth yet.

Enough said. In the 1890s, the game really was "won in the trenches." And the trenches were pretty brutal places not governed by today's rules regarding hands to the face or chop blocks or tripping or punching or completely losing your head for that matter. The warriors in the trenches also didn't wear the armor they do today. "Defis," or challenges to another team, were often issued around the weight of another town team. One team might say, "Menasha eleven challenges any team from this town weighing an average of 145 lbs." to all comers. The emphasis was on brute force, and the tools of the trade were big guys on your side who could push the big guys on the other side out of the way.

The 1896 season began for the Green Bay town team with a surprising victory over what the *Gazette* labeled "a heavier team." "The boys hardly expect to win," an article scarcely promoting the game began. The *Green Bay Advocate*, in a replay of the game later that week, stated that "the average weight of Rhinelander is 187 $\frac{1}{2}$ pounds, while Green Bay is 163." Facing a 25-pound-per-man advantage, the Green Bay team looked for a tough time in the trenches. However, the *Advocate* suggested that finesse may have had some effect in this one. "Every member of the team," it said, "played fast ball."

The game ended with a stunning 6–0 decision in favor of Green Bay. Like small men with a big axe, the Green Bay boys felled the oversized lumberjacks, though not without controversy. Near the end of the game, the Rhinelander boys found themselves without any points of their own, and they determined that they were going to put the smack down on the upstarts from Green Bay. They decided to do that by "slugging so fiercely" that the umpire called the contest over and done and the Green Bay lads escaped to their train with a victory and their lives still in their possession.

RHINELANDER—"AN AGGREGATION OF GENTLEMEN"

When it comes to football, it's nearly always a matter of perspective. Otherwise, how can half the fans watching a particular play cry, "Pass interference!" and the other half say, "He never put a hand on him"? Such was the case with Rhinelander; a view of their team was one of two extremes. Following a contest in that city, the *Marinette Eagle* graciously called the Rhinelander team "an aggregation of gentlemen and the finest lot of visitors who ever came to our city." But it was at about the same time that a Green Bay team had to escape to the train with their lives after they had upset a heavily favored set of brutes from the same place. That game had broken down "in the trenches" when that same aggregation of gentlemen had resorted to slugging the Green Bay guys.

Incidentally, Rhinelander's first town team took to the field in 1895, and today the northern city is the burial place of John W. Heisman.

Following the victory over Rhinelander, the team was joined by Joseph Miller, a star quarterback on the Stevens Point Normal team the previous year. He would coach the team, and Hulbert would willingly take a less-obvious role. What was becoming clear was that Hulbert's raw upstarts were now being augmented by some experienced college men, and Miller wasn't to be the only such addition. The first game under his guidance was a 24–0 loss to Marinette, but rumors from nearby Oneida claimed that several former Carlisle Indian School players were also ready to join the Green Bay eleven and increase the team's skill level. Unfortunately, the rumored players didn't surface in the team's next loss, 34–0, at Oconto.

However, in the following game—an 18–0 loss to Oshkosh on Saturday, October 17, 1896—a former University of Wisconsin–Madison star named T. P. Silverwood was introduced. Silverwood graduated from UW with a law degree and, according to his granddaughter, Judith Silverwood-Sharp, "upon graduating, he rode a bicycle from Madison to Green Bay to explore the possibility of the establishment of a law practice." He subsequently entered into the firm of Ellis and Merrill. Silverwood was on the starting end of a successful law career that would include a stint as Green Bay city attorney in 1904 and several high-profile cases including a Neillsville, Wisconsin, murder. However, football was not far from his mind and, according to Silverwood-Sharp, "may have been part of the draw" to Green Bay. He spent the first part of the 1896 season working for pay and helping get an Oconto aggregation up and running.

UNIVERSITY OF WISCONSIN–MADISON—THE TRADITION BEGINS

Football at UW–Madison. It's still an annual autumn celebration. And no book on town team football would be complete without a short look at that tradition. After all, the "state school" produced early players of note such as Ikey Karel, T. P. Silverwood, Joe Hoeffel, and Frank Shepich, to name just a few. The school was even Curly Lambeau's first choice over Notre Dame!

Athletics received the same scrutiny at Madison as they did everywhere else. Football was an especial scapegoat. However, eventually, a beautifully ornate gymnasium was constructed on the lower part of the campus along Langdon Street, reflecting the school's early leaning toward physical as well as mental education. But it was, according to Oliver Kuechle, on an open field across from this "Little Red Gym" that the earliest outdoor sports were played. In fact, the scene Kuechle paints on this field in the "Gay Nineties" is a rather colorful one with "cardinal-beribboned coeds and their pennant-waving escorts standing along the sidelines."

By all available accounts, 1883 seems to be the earliest detectable mention of football on campus, though records to support the sport's existence are scant. In 1883, the first recorded baseball game was played against Beloit College. As was usually the case, baseball organization and interest set the stage for football as well as other sports, and an intramural network was growing on the campus. Also, a classic piece in the story of football springing up on these college campuses is the likelihood that pickup games had been played somewhere on or near campus well before any "official" game had even been noticed. Those games, thrown together in the twilight of some fall evening, have now disappeared among the whispers of history.

But at that time, Madison did have "official" athletic associations. And so it was that in 1883, *Trochus*, a campus publication, described "class teams in all sports, each with its own student governing association, and an all-around university field day which was an annual event of the joint associations." Among other events, the field day included a "football kick" as well as an assortment of running, jumping and throwing events.

In 1889, the UW–Madison Badgers finally played what Kuechle labels an "intercollegiate" game against the Calumet Club of Milwaukee. By most accounts, the Calumet Club ran in different circles than the usual, gentlemanly athletic club. While some members of the club had attended colleges in the east and learned the game of football there, Kuechle suggests that their main purpose for existence was "dutifully quaffing their beer."

The game between the beer guzzlers and the college boys was played out on Saturday, November 23, 1889, at a 50-acre recreation area on the southwest corner of today's Layton and National Avenues in Milwaukee. Following the game, the Calumets were able to put even more beer to death in celebration, as they had whipped the Badgers 27–0. Probably the most promising thing to come out of the game was the recruitment of Calumet star Alvin Letsch as a pro bono coach for the Badger team. Under his tutelage, the 1889 team played one more contest, a respectable 4–0 loss, against Beloit College.

A picture of the 1889 squad still exists. It's a classic football photo of the day, taken in a studio, the team members assuming varying positions, often with their hands on one another's shoulders. In the center, holding the ball is Mayer, captain and quarterback. The uniforms are neither top shelf nor are they bottom drawer. They don't necessarily match, since it was catch-as-catch-can for each player to come up with their own outfit. In similar fashion, the red "UW" on their moleskin jackets is neither ever-present nor uniform. The gazes of the college lads are either fixed on the photographer or stoically thrust stage left as if they didn't know a picture was being snapped or a gorgeous coed had distracted them with a resounding set of "you-rahs."

The issue of ragtag uniforms was all water under the bridge as the 1894 season began. A war of words between the Wisconsin and Minnesota managers seemed to suggest that a contest between the two of them might have been as tumultuous and interesting as one between their respective schools. L. W. Myers, the Wisconsin manager, was begging for the next contest to be played at Madison, while J. E. O'Brien, his Minnesota counterpart, was saying the Gophers would not go to Madison "until there is something to be gained by doing so." Myers was extending a guarantee of $500 and an option of one-half of the gross receipts. Eventually, O'Brien agreed and the game was set for November 17 in Madison.

The Gophers traveled by rail to Madison, checked in at the Park Hotel under the name, "Minnesota Football Team," and proceeded to have a whale of a pillow fight. They were, they figured, warming up for the next day's contest against the pathetic Badgers. What had they to fear?

The scene was as good as it gets. A puny rope tried to hold back a crowd that couldn't be contained. Temporary bleachers became royal thrones as fans contended over a place to sit. Spectators dangled from every nearby rooftop, open window, and tree worth climbing. Red and white hung everywhere. Maroon and gold hung everywhere else. Gambling was rampant. Odds were huge that the Badgers wouldn't win. According to one report, odds were even 2 to 5 that the Badgers wouldn't be able to score a point. A Madison paper suggested that $5,000 changed hands that day.

By all accounts, the game held everything a contest could in the way of football. The score remained frozen at 0–0 well into the second half. Even that seemed like a victory for the Badgers. At one point, they had even kept the Gophers from scoring from the five-yard line. Then, a hero emerged—John Colonel Karel, a young man from the lakeshore community of Kewaunee, Wisconsin. "Ikey" was his football nickname. Thank God he had a nickname, because he certainly didn't have a lot of bulk. His 5' 10" frame supported a mere 156 pounds. But Karel's 50-yard run around the end was huge. With a kick after the touchdown, the score stood at a whopping 6–0, and time ran out on the Gophers. Wisconsin had broken Minnesota's stranglehold.

That night, Madison was crazier than it would have been had an honest politician been elected. The partying went on until the Minnesota team pulled out of the train station at 9:45 the following morning. Stories of Ikey Karel's play were told and retold. Karel had been so overcome by his success that he sat down and cried. At one point, Karel had actually been tackled on the five-yard line by Minnesota's Van Campen, but the Badgers' combined momentum carried Ikey across the goal line. Karel was so banged up that it took him two months to recover. His exploits that day earned him the grand title of "Red Grange of his day."

The Badger students built themselves one heck of a bonfire that evening and they kept it stoked all night long. They even burned the wooden sidewalk in front of the dean's house. College President Charles Kendall Adams was kept awake most of the night by the sound of his students singing out his window. A Madison paper suggested that every hotel in town had benefited financially from the activity. According to Kuechle, one hotel, the Van Etta, "offered fricasseed gopher on the menu that night and had the Wisconsin team as its guest."

Although a loss, the Oshkosh game deserves some attention—not just because Silverwood had joined the team. That game, like a handful of others in the early years, was held at Webster Park, which was once located on the east side of Webster Avenue across from Woodlawn Cemetery. In the second half of the contest, Oshkosh completed a forward pass and gained several yards. The Green Bay aggregation was livid. The forward pass was not a legal play and would not be legalized until 1906! Despite the vehement protests of the Green Bay eleven, the play was allowed to stand by umpire Sullivan. Was this Sullivan another prophet encouraging a step into the future? Hardly! Either he was unclear on the rules, or he liked the idea of passing the ball and was willing to look the other way on this infraction. It also may have been a "pass" of just a few mere feet. No doubt Sullivan's parentage was brought into question by the Green Bay team for the rest of the contest.

In a game characterized by "mass plays and center smashes," the Green Bay team next lost 4–0 to a tough Marinette team. The last game of the year lay around the corner—a shellacking of a very green De Pere team by the "Bays" 40–0.

At the end of the 1896 season, the *Green Bay Advocate* interviewed Silverwood on "Football Benefits." Identifying him as a "Ball Enthusiast," the interview focused on the brutality of the game and its effect on high school and college students. Silverwood turned the interview toward the rewards of the training and discipline required for football success. When asked, "Is it a brutal game?" Silverwood's response was definite:

BEFORE THEY WERE THE PACKERS

*No! It is no more brutal to the player than the race to the trotting horse.
To be sure there are scratches and bumps and bruises, but these are nothing
to one who has been in the glorious hand-to-hand struggle of a football
game, where all the physical strength, all the brains and all the science of one
team is pitted against all that of another team.*

Accidents on the gridiron could be traced mostly to improper training, conditioning, or discipline, avowed Silverwood.

In an era when men of the cloth were decrying the game regularly from the pulpit, a few supporters of the game saw at least some spark of science in it. This was a point that united Silverwood and Hulbert, neither of whom could be tagged as a ruffian, even on their wildest day. Both men would eventually trim their long locks and become bastions of their families, their careers, and their communities. These two men were held in the highest esteem then and still are by their descendants. Men like this were vital to the game's survival as they ran counter to the sport's reputation. Hulbert, according to his grandniece, Ethel Evrard, was "a strict Baptist and a teetotaler all of his life." Similarly, according to his granddaughter, Silverwood became an avid member of "the establishment" when his football days were over.

So, what was it that could draw these two and many, many men like them to the early game? Undoubtedly it was the fact that they saw in that mass of bodies in the trenches the kinetic pulse of strategy and finesse and a game elevated by their use.

THE CHAMPIONSHIP SEASON!

Does history repeat itself? If not, it sure comes close sometimes. A reflection of the 1897 season showed up perfectly one hundred years later when, going into the 1997 season, the Green Bay Packers had every reason to feel confident. They had just come off their most successful season in recent team history, culminating in a victory over the New England Patriots 35–21 in Super Bowl XXXI. All the pieces seemed to be in place: superior talent, tremendous organization, great coaching, fan support, great press coverage, and strong financial backing. It was all there. That was exactly the story for the Green Bay town team going into the 1897 campaign.

The Green Bay newspapers covered several team meetings in late August and early September, some coinciding with team practice. With west side tailor, Ed Krippner, as team business manager, the team met regularly at the headquarters of the West Side Athletic Association. To accommodate the players with day jobs, arc lights were strung up around the field at Ben Garlock's lot on the corner of Dousman and Oakland for night practice. By now the team had added a "second eleven," which would "meet every evening with the regular eleven for practice." They had every reason to envision success. They were big, they were buff, and they were ready.

Hulbert's presence on the team in 1895 was key to that success, and the addition of Silverwood near the end of the 1896 campaign was also significant. But the enlistment of Tom Skenandore, a bruising fullback from Oneida who had acquired his football skills on teams at Carlisle Indian School in the early 1890s, was the pièce de résistance in 1897. His value was such that he became the only paid player on the team.

Silverwood had come to town, a young attorney on a bicycle, hoping to hook up with one of the law firms in town. Hulbert had started the ball rolling in '95, but Silverwood assumed the position of captain and coach for the '97 outing. He had ideas of how to improve the team off the field, if not on it. A board of directors was formed to ensure community support, and a second team was added to give the regulars real practice. Just as in 1896, Hulbert, deemed "Genial Fred," seemed willing to step back and let another hand guide the flock. In 1896, it had been Joseph Miller, who had now disappeared from the Green Bay football scene. This time it was Silverwood, whose impact would be much more dramatic than Miller's.

Tom Silverwood was a staunch believer in athletics, a gifted organizer, a colorful character with a handlebar mustache, a Republican activist, and a lover of football. Most of all, he had connections. Family documentation states that "In 1897 Silverwood organized, coached and captained the first Green Bay semiprofessional football team. The squad, predecessor to the present Green Bay Packers, played both professional and college teams and was undefeated for two years."

This claim needs to be tempered slightly with the point that Fred Hulbert had started the first town team in Green Bay two years prior. However, it is certainly true that Hulbert handed the reins to Silverwood in 1897, and, with the presence of the first paid player in Green Bay history, Tom Skenandore, Silverwood's squad did constitute the city's first semipro aggregation. The other team members abused their bodies gratis.

The designation *semipro* has come to mean many things to many people, and its appearance in the Silverwood family's archives deserves attention. In some cases, fans would call Hulbert's teams *semipro* because it was a term interchangeable with *town team*. Another take on the phrase supports the idea that all the players were paid some money, usually divvied up from gate receipts per game or per season after expenses, but the amount was never enough to support the man or his family. None of these first squads in the city's history qualified as semipro under this interpretation.

It is safe to say that the family's claim that Silverwood's aggregation was semiprofessional and that, as such, it was the "first" in Green Bay's history is credible because, in another of its interpretations, the term semipro means the presence of both paid and unpaid players on the same team; that was certainly the story of the 1897 Green Bay eleven.

Finally, the claim that the team went undefeated for two years is also true. Out of five games in '97, Silverwood's team suffered only one tie and came out on the bright end of four contests. Their 1898 campaign was brief, but they did not experience a loss.

It was Silverwood's friendship with Kewaunee native Ikey Karel, who'd been tagged as "the Red Grange of the '90s," that brought Karel to Green Bay as a part-time coach and supporter of Green Bay football. It was Karel who, while watching the team practice on Garlock's vacant lot, stated, "Some day Green Bay will be

World Champions." Ikey, obviously another prophet, was seeing well into the city's football future!

The 1897 squad was further bolstered by some of its old hands, including Frank and Jim Flatley, John Pease, John Gray, Charles "Tod" Burns, Harry Hanrahan, Al Van den Berg, Henry VandenBrook, Gerhard Johnson, and Albert Groesbeck. Most of these guys had struggled with Hulbert on the 1895 and 1896 squads, and they were excited about finally being the team to beat. For a team photo later that year, they were joined by their youthful mascot, C. A. "Snick" Gross, who eventually became successful as a Green Bay clothier.

The first game on the team's docket was against perennial nemesis Marinette. In a "stubbornly-contested struggle," Green Bay was on the winning end of a 4–0 result. According to newspaper accounts of the game, "Skenandore, the Oneida fullback, was the star player for Green Bay and the way he plowed through the opposing line set local enthusiasts wild." More important, though, it was a team effort. Silverwood, VandenBrook, and Jim and Frank Flatley all got mentions for their running prowess; Hulbert was acknowledged for his effective tackling.

The second game of the season was against Lawrence University in Appleton. Following a 42–0 whipping of the college crew, the *Green Bay Gazette* said, "Green Bay's team covered itself with glory and has now established its reputation commenced in the Oconto game of last fall." Pease, Skenandore, and Silverwood were cited for their long gains from scrimmage. "Five of the Appleton boys," continued the *Gazette*, "were carried off the field as a result of the hard playing but Green Bay's boys came out of the game unhurt."

Rubber nose guards, moleskin vests, and hurricane pants offered this 1897 Lawrence University team scant protection from rough-and-tumble, line-smashing football. Many times, a college player, returning to his hometown, was the catalyst for the local town team, often serving as its captain and coach. Photograph obtained from and used with permission of Lawrence University, Appleton, Wisconsin.

In early November, Oshkosh bowed out of a scheduled contest ostensibly over money. They had contacted Manager Krippner and proposed a $25 guarantee up front plus expenses. There was another take on the whole situation, however. "The home boys," suggested the *Gazette*, "feel that Oshkosh is afraid of the line and dare not come down for fear of a disastrous defeat."

The third game of the season was another one-sided affair played at Washington Park on Saturday, November 6, against an eleven from Menominee, Michigan. "Not for a minute was [sic] the Menominee boys in the game," reported the *Gazette*. "And whenever the home team wanted to go through the line, they did so." Frank Flatley's center smashes were also noted by the paper.

Game four was played in Marinette on Thursday, November 11. Despite Green Bay's reputation, Marinette held its ground and the match ended in a scoreless tie. In response to that game, a report in the *Marinette Eagle* stated,

> *The Green Bay team played a good strong, clean game. They are a coterie of gentlemen and made a good impression everywhere in Marinette. The gentlemanly manager E. W. Krippner has the true idea of sport and leaves nothing undone in the way of courtesy. The Green Bay team eleven is considered one of the crack teams of the state and Marinette has shown her right to share this reputation."*

Under Hulbert, Silverwood, and Krippner, the team advanced from a crew of street brawlers to a crack unit with a statewide reputation.

The final game against Fond du Lac was played at Washington Park on Thanksgiving Day, 1897. It was played in a snowstorm with an amazing one thousand spectators looking on. "Fond du Lac wasn't in the game one minute," stated *The Green Bay Review*. "The visiting eleven was out-classed, out-played, and outed generally." The final score was 62–0. At a banquet following the game, Fond du Lac "did to the turkey what they couldn't do to our team," chided the *Review*. "They downed it."

In 1919, Curly Lambeau's pass-oriented Packer juggernaut overwhelmed its opponents by a total combined score over 11 games of 565–12, for an average of 57–1 per game. But 23 years earlier, the Green Bay town team had accomplished a similarly remarkable feat; 1897 was part of an era when the emphasis was on defense and preventing the other team from scoring. Touchdowns were worth only four points. Yet, over five games, the Green Bay boys had bested their opponents 142–6, for an average of 28–1 per game.

This 1897 outfit was the very first championship football team in Green Bay history. It declared its status as such at the end of its amazing season, and no challengers issued a defi to say it was otherwise. Curly Lambeau's team won its first National Football League crown in 1929, followed by championships in 1930 and

1931—the first Triple Championship in NFL history. But the 1929 crown was not this town's first. Titletown saw championships in 1903, 1911, 1913, and 1915 as well.

The team photo taken at the end of that year is the first known picture of a Green Bay town team. Going into 1898, the team had reputation, organization, and financial success.

1898
BACK TO EARTH

The newly found success of the '97 season showed in an optimistic report in the August 6, 1898, *Green Bay Gazette*. Ed Krippner, who was unavailable for management duties but still a supporter of Green Bay football, said, "The boys are taking a good deal of interest in organizing a team and I expect to see a football aggregation in Green Bay for next season that not a team in the state, outside of the university, can touch."

Optimism was the rule of the day. The old stalwarts were in place, and there were reports of a practice facility being set up with lights "near the old football grounds." The old grounds in question were those of the Dousman Street School, located just a couple of blocks east of the aggregation's practice field at the southwest corner of Oakland and Dousman. A new manager, W. J. Casey, ran the business end of things. Reflective of their growing fame, a Milwaukee business donated the gift of a football to the boys to be used in their exploits.

CHICAGO—CARDINAL RED

Don't laugh, but here's a little item that seems to be a secret. The Arizona Cardinals are the oldest team in continuous existence in the NFL, and it's actually their rivalry with the Chicago Bears that is the oldest, not that of the Bears and the Packers. The oft-traveled Cardinals sprung from the head of 52nd and Morgan Streets on the southwest side of Chicago. The year was 1898 and the football visionary in this case was Chris O'Brien, a house painter. With his brother, Pat, he founded the Morgan Athletic Club.

For a time, the Cardinals were the "Normals" after they moved to Normal Park at 63rd Street and Racine Avenue. While playing there, they received some hand-me-down jerseys from the University of Chicago. These cast-off jerseys had begun their journey as maroon in color, but they had been washed so many times that, by the time the Normals got them, house painter O'Brien supposedly said, "That's not maroon, it's cardinal red." From Racine Avenue, they moved to Chicago's Comiskey Park, then Saint Louis, and presently Tempe. But even with state-of-the-art jerseys, they remained the Cardinals.

A game was scheduled with their neighbors to the west, the Oneida "Indians," to coincide with the annual Oneida Fair. The Oneida team was a formidable one. Over the next decade or so, Oneida players were often sought out by the Green Bay team to shore up its ranks, or the entire Oneida aggregation was scheduled for spirited competition. The Oneida Fair was held each September and was largely attended by Green Bay's folk and gentry. A football game was on the fair agenda most years, with highly skilled players returning to Oneida from Carlisle, Hampton, and Haskell boarding schools where they had honed their football talents.

But the shine and polish established over the previous three seasons started to fade in 1898 when the team was faced with the reality of keeping a football team in full, powerful action. Scheduling problems cropped up and money issues arose. Keeping players healthy and in the fold started to necessitate the importing of players.

The sophistication and resulting complication of football was beginning to show in a minor scandal. Though it involved the East High School team, the to-do cast a bad light on all of the city's football practitioners. A banner in the October 11 *Green Bay Advocate* read,

ADD OUTSIDE PLAYERS
Local High School Football Team Follows Bad Example
   Not to be outdone by other high schools in the football league, manager Charles Cady and captain Charles Marquardt of the East Side High school team have decided to add players not students of the school to the line-up.

Controversy raged until October 13, when the *Advocate* reported that no outside players would be added. The explanation for considering such an egregious scheme was simple, "Other high school teams are doing this and the boys believed that in this way only could they make a creditable showing."

The players to be added were East High graduates and former team members. This was part and parcel of the growing problem that the fuzzy line of eligibility created in football at the turn of the century. Teams wanted to win, and some sought-after players might play on as many as three different teams: high school, town team, and college team. To illustrate this, the October 11 *Advocate* reported that Green Bay town team stalwart John Gray was being courted by the University of Wisconsin football team, "which suggests it badly needs him." Was Gray to be enrolled as a student or simply added to the school's football roster?

GLADSTONE—DANDIES VERSUS HICKS

Gladstone and Escanaba may be neighbors, but on the football field they have never been neighborly. Their two earliest gridiron contests in 1898 are replete with stories of fording rivers in covered wagons, eating turkey dinners en route, and shenanigans on and off the field. Somehow, it always seemed to be the sophisticated Eskies against the upstart Gladstonians, making the rivalry even spicier.

In the first contest that year, the Gladstone guys had the audacity to show up in slapdash uniforms that George T. Springer in *The Delta Reporter* described as matching "about as well as the country hired girl's adornment on circus day." These were "home made uniforms, consisting of long trousers cut down, with padding in places deemed most useful to the wearer." God forbid and how dare they!

On top of that, the Gladstonians had some very plain play calls. "For signals," remembered George McEwen, one of the early Gladstone footballers, "we used names instead of the numbers that are in use at the present time." Well, it didn't take long for those smartypants from Escanaba to realize that at the cry of "Adams Michigan Lincoln" they should all jam the right side of the line.

The combined scores of those first two games in 1898 were Escanaba 79 and Gladstone 0. But not to worry, Gladstone had its way with the Eskies more than once over the years, starting with a 28–0 victory in 1900.

Another problem for the Green Bay aggregation in 1898 was the vacuum created by the absence of Krippner and Silverwood at the team's helm. Hulbert had remained with the team, but an item in the October 11 *Gazette* reported that his tenure with the eleven also seemed tenuous. When asked about resigning his position as captain, his response to a reporter was, "I have not as yet. I may not, however, play all through the season, but this will depend upon circumstances."

His personal circumstances were beginning to take hold of his time, and his 40-year career in the canning business was looming large. He was also starting a family with his bride, Lucille, in a home a stone's throw from the old practice field. Here was a clear signal that football made demands and that "family" or "business" men usually didn't have the time to get involved in such a violent diversion.

However, football was still very popular inside the Green Bay city limits, at least amongst the brutes who played the game. Local "society" took a feeble kick at the sport in an item that appeared in the *Green Bay Weekly Gazette* on Saturday, October 8. "Green Bay," it scolded, "will have good football games during the winter and the social season promises to be a very lively one but when Green Bay people want to see a good theatrical production they will have to go to Milwaukee or some other town where there is a good opera house." Attempts would later be made to give the hometown football roughs some of the gentility of the opera or theater with the issue of complimentary tickets.

The first game of the '98 campaign was slated for that same Saturday at Washington Park. It would serve as a precursor for the season as a whole; a rising

MONKEYS AT FOOTBALL

The following piece appeared in the *Green Bay Advocate* on October 5, 1898, and was based on an item from the *Brooklyn Times*. The piece no doubt caught the eye of football's critics and was probably cited more than once in an effort to elevate the game's ruffians to a more gentlemanly pastime.

They Likewise Play Cricket, but Not According to Rule

Travelers in South Africa have noted the fact that where monkeys congregate in large numbers they also indulge in games of a certain kind. Two of these games seem to resemble cricket and football . . . The football is of a more advanced type. It is also played with a cocoanut [sic]. The game, if anything, is undoubtedly the "soccer" game and is played with the feet. Of course there is no goal nor any tactics to speak of the object of each animal being to keep the ball to himself as much as possible . . . Still the competition to get the ball makes it resemble a real game of "footer," and the dexterity exhibited by these peculiar amateurs is surprising and wonderful . . . In an evil moment some ambitious monkey may elect to play the Rugby game by snatching up the ball and making off, but the game then develops into war, in which life is sometimes the price . . . No mention is made of a referee, but if there is one about, like a wise and provident monkey, he is probably up a tree.

Oneida team was matched up against a fading Green Bay one. On the previous Wednesday, Manager Casey had visited the reservation to make final arrangements for the game. Oneida stars Tom Skenandore and Taylor Smith had agreed to play for the Green Bay city team following this contest. But with the two Oneida players on the other side of the ball, local papers, including the *Advocate*, saw the contest as a "severe test" for Casey's team.

In a tug-of-war affair with Oneida, the Green Bay boys held on to victory, 20–5. Wilson Metoxen was a standout for the Oneida aggregation with a second-half touchdown run covering the entire field. This, with the extra point, was Oneida's only score. Green Bay had been successful in adding a goal after score to each of their touchdowns.

It was after the Oneida men joined the Green Bay squad that local newspaper reports began calling the city team "Casey's Indians." This was either in response to the addition of the stars from the Oneida reservation or due to the rambunctious play of the team. Fortunately, neither motivation would fly in a game recap today.

In another blow to the stability of football in Green Bay, the site of most football action in the town, Washington Park, was to be divided up into plots for housing. The southern part of the park had already been platted into city lots, but there was hope that the "part lying north of Walnut street could be preserved." This portion was saved and would later become Hagemeister Park and, later still, the site of present-day Green Bay East High School.

The next sign that the Green Bay crew was moving in a more "professional" direction was reported in the Tuesday, October 25 *Advocate*. "Green Bay City Team Secures an Eastern Football Player," it announced. The gentleman was J. Wanna-maker, a substitute quarterback on the Princeton team for the 1897 season. He joined an experienced backfield consisting of Smith and Skenandore. Green Bay had now "imported" its entire backfield.

A local newspaper suggested that a game with Ishpeming, Michigan, was pos-sible, but it never materialized. Casey later lambasted the paper reporting the Ishpeming game, saying the report was false and that he had no knowledge of the supposed game. Then, the on-again-off-again nature of the Green Bay–Ishpeming contest became more interesting than the game itself, taking on a life of its own. The next Saturday morning, November 12, the *Advocate* reported the following:

GREEN BAY WILL PLAY ISHPEMING

The management of the Green Bay football team will immediately answer the bluff made by Manager Randolf of the Ishpeming team and chal-lenge him for a game of football for Thanksgiving day. He will get the team together and will give the "Ishpeming blubbers" the game of their life. The team is not afraid of Ishpeming but it has been impossible for the men to leave their work for two days to play a game of football, but the Ishpeming bluff will not be passed easily. An effort to get Silverwood to play will be made.

Green Bay's town teams were nothing without competition. Games with the 1895 Oconto eleven pictured here were easy to arrange, thanks to the Chicago & North Western railroad. From their first game in 1895 on, the relationship between the two teams was always respectful on and off the field. Players are identified as follows: (seated) Ralph Whitney, Dan Ryan, A. Chloupek, Gilbert Morrow, and Ward Reinhard; (second row) Charles Smith, Harry Hanson, William B. Hall, Louis Cote (captain), V. J. O'Kelliher, Bent Orr, and Peter Davis; (third row) Lynch, Allan Classon, David Classon, Ward Wescott, Leonard (Louis) Steffins, Freeman Gilkey, and Dr. W. G. Oliver (manager). Most of these players turned out to be lawyers in their later days, the rough-and-tumble game preparing them for their future careers. Photograph obtained from and used with permission of the Oconto County Historical Society and Jimmy Hall's book *Believe It or Not*. Oconto, Wisconsin.

This picture, taken the same day as that of the 1895 Oconto city team on page 30, shows four team members staging football action in the photographer's studio. Photographic technology being what it was, action shots were impossible at the time. Here, players identified (from left to right) as Hanson, Smith, and Hall stage interference for Orr, who carries the ball. For real action, the boys could be found at Oconto's Bay View Driving Park, seven blocks north of the downtown on Superior Avenue. Photograph obtained from and used with permission of the Oconto County Historical Society and Jimmy Hall's book, *Believe It or Not*. Oconto, Wisconsin.

After nearly two months of insults, bantering, and diatribe, the Ishpeming game never saw the light of day. In a similar vein, a contest with the Stevens Point team was talked about but never played. The most promising football news was a report of the Oneida team playing an all-star team from Milwaukee.

The next on-field action for Green Bay was at Washington Park with the Oconto "athletics," an all-star team from Marinette, Menominee, and Oconto, on Thanksgiving Day, November 24. It was the team's second and last game of the season.

A headline in the *Advocate* the following day suggested that "Green Bay Played Horse With the Oconto Team Yesterday Afternoon." The paper surmised that Oconto's team was too light. The final score was a lopsided 36–5, with Oconto's single score coming with three minutes left to play and contested by the Green Bay team. In what the *Advocate* called a "fluke," Shorty Schroeder, the Green Bay fullback, lost the pigskin to Oconto's Hall, who tore downfield for 90 yards and an apparent score. The points stood. The touchdown was allowed, despite protests by the Green Bay players that "in making his touchdown Hall of the Ocontos took the ball away from Schroeder after he had called 'down.'"

Crowd support was there, but the squad only managed to compete in two contests that year, hardly enough for football-hungry fans. Consequently, no claim of a regional championship was made.

BEFORE THEY WERE THE PACKERS

Several familiar names rode out the season: Pease, Hanrahan, Burns, Hulbert, Gray, Gronnert, and Frank Flatley. Silverwood's participation that year was undocumented, except for a mention that the team would be seeking his help for the rumored Ishpeming fray.

In a seemingly insignificant item, there was mention of a second game in Green Bay on Thanksgiving Day that year. Just nine blocks away from the Green Bay–Oconto contest at Saint James Park, the "Volunteers" defeated the "Touchdowns," 16–0. But this game wasn't insignificant at all. In fact, the game represented a precursor to football on the "intracity" scale. These were two neighborhood teams doing battle in the shadow of the city team, representing the first mention of teams other than the recognized city team existing in Green Bay. And the audacity of scheduling a contest on the same day as a city team contest and, thus, drawing potential fans and newspaper ink away from the city team cannot go unnoticed.

Intracity play like this, between neighborhood teams, was a phenomenon that continued to ebb and flow in Green Bay for the next 20 years, often shaking the very foundation of the city team. At other times, this intracity action was the only game in town. When players could not take the time to travel for games as members of the city aggregation, they could still play in games involving neighborhoods. They could still knock heads, but keep close to home.

SENSIBA'S FOLLIES

The problems brought about by the impromptu game between the Volunteers and the Touchdowns loomed large in 1899. The inability to find and schedule out-of-town competition and the inability of the men on the team to get away from their commitments had shortened the 1898 season to just two games.

The start of the 1899 season brought some changes in the management of the town team. While Fred Hulbert remained the captain, Casey was out and the new man at the reins was a law student named B. B. "Bert" Sensiba. It wasn't so surprising that this budding barrister would take over the job. Sensiba was employed at the law firm of Fontaine and McGillan, where T. P. Silverwood also was a professional. Some arm-twisting and backslapping had no doubt taken place in the firm's conference room.

Importing players was still the rage. Reports from the *Green Bay Gazette* several days apart mentioned Tom Skenandore and, later, Taylor Smith filling the Green Bay backfield with power once again.

Media coverage started on September 20 with talk of a game against Oneida at the annual Oneida Fair, but this game was canceled. The Green Bay team was experiencing slow going and was unable to get players to practice. Aching for a bone rattling, Oneida opted to play a team from Marinette. Green Bay then shifted its focus to the Lawrence University eleven. This game was slated to materialize on Thanksgiving, and a contract was supposedly in hand. The game never did come to pass.

In the meantime, speculative games were being bandied about with Oshkosh and Stevens Point Normal Schools, Rhinelander, Marinette, and Menasha. The October 10 *Gazette* displayed the headline, "Will Meet Menasha Team at Menasha— Manager Sensiba Anxious to Have Full Line Out Tomorrow."

Unfortunately, three days later, the *Gazette* gave the sporting public bad news. That game, too, was canceled. "The city team has been unable to get their Indians who play on the Oneida team, on account of the game which they have with Marinette tomorrow. The Menasha date will be filled later." Other excuses were offered in the article, including bad weather not allowing adequate practice. The best that Sensiba could manage was to gather his team for practice a few scant nights a week. Hulbert, once again captaining the squad, was cited as saying the team was short of material and that he was "keeping his eyes open."

The fact that the team had to turn to "their Indians" deserves some attention. While several of the Oneida athletes broke the race barrier and played for the Green Bay team, the press still had a tendency to see these Indian players, no matter their football skills, as more an anomaly than fully accepted members of the team. The November 11 *Gazette* said, "In the team can be seen the dusky faces of the Oneida Indians. Metoxen and Skenandore came in yesterday. Smith, the Indian who played such a good game in [sic] the Carlisle team, has also been given a position and materially strengthens the line." The connotation is clear. These players were Indians first and good football players second. However, the Oneida men let their prowess and equality show on the gridiron. The fact that they are mentioned in virtually every newspaper recap of every game in which they played was a credit to their natural skill and training and probably went a long way toward making them full-fledged members of the team.

ONEIDA—"THE DUSKY FACES OF THE ONEIDA INDIANS"

There it sits, the Oneida Nation Gate on the east side of Lambeau Field. Appropriately so! Until recently, Oneida's significant role in early Green Bay football had been overlooked. Now, it's time to celebrate—together.

While Fred Hulbert was assembling his roughshod crew of footballers in Green Bay in 1895, three young Oneida men were being trained in the sport at the Carlisle Indian School in Pennsylvania, which would later turn out one Jim Thorpe. They had been sent there to be trained in the white man's ways. Some books focus on the tragedy of that effort. This one looks at a fortunate by-product: The Oneida guys who went there combined some tremendous natural talent with some state-of-the-art football training under Glenn Scobey "Pop" Warner, and they returned to the area ready to contribute mightily to football success in Titletown, USA.

The first of these, Tom Skenandore, is celebrated elsewhere in these pages. His addition to the 1897 Green Bay city team made them champions. Close on Skenandore's heels was Jonas Metoxen, who thrilled area football fans for years and was so skilled that in 1904 he garnered an offer of $25 per game and a furnished, four-room flat to play for a season in Marinette. Then came a one-season appearance by college phenom Martin Wheelock, who earned second-team honors on the All-American squad in 1901.

The presence or possible presence of these players, and several others such as Taylor Smith and Wilson Charles, on the team was often the source of optimistic football speculation. One of them in the huddle was seen as enough of an edge to turn a struggling team into a champion. Two of them in the backfield were considered a guarantee of success.

However, the Oneida players always seemed to hold primary allegiance to their hometown team, no matter who was paying them to play elsewhere.

Sensiba finally rescheduled the game with Menasha for November 4. The October 20 announcement of this match-to-be stated, "The organization of the eleven is now complete and the team is a strong one . . . The game Saturday can be looked for as an exciting one as Menasha's line is a heavy one."

But the Green Bay boys were in for some tough knocks and lost by a score of 15–0. In a game characterized by Green Bay being "completely outclassed," the *Gazette* offered this excuse for the poor showing: "The team from this city went down short four men, Gray, Burns, Hillis, and Hanrahan not being able to leave the city. These were the strongest men on the team and their loss was felt severely." There was truth in the paper's statement, as the men listed were the heaviest members of the team. A return match with Menasha to be held in Green Bay would be a greater indication of that truth.

The return game was held on Saturday, November 11, and was much anticipated. The *Gazette* reported that both sides were "confident of winning and although the Menasha team is a heavy one, the Green Bay boys have a snap which will undoubtably tell in the final result." The Menasha team was put up at the Felch Hotel on Washington Street, fed a good dinner, and then traveled with the Green Bay team to Hagemeister Park for the big game. Washington Park, the birthplace of Green Bay football, had been reduced to a parcel at the very end of Walnut Street. Eventually, it would be up to Hagemeister Park to maintain Green Bay's football tradition.

The November 18 *Gazette* chronicled the result: In a back-and-forth affair, a 5–5 tie was the final tally. "Never were two teams so evenly matched and both sides played their best," the article explained. One impressive drive credited Shenandore, Hillis, Hulburt, and Marquardt with good runs. Evidently, with all its men in place, the Green Bay team played a much better brand of football.

The newspaper that evening also included an allusion to Manager Sensiba's attempt to plan a night game. Marinette was mentioned as the on-field foe. The plan was to light up Hagemeister Park with 20 arc lights, "which will make it as light as day." Because the day's version of the game consisted entirely of running the ball, even a few crude lights would have sufficed.

An article from the November 16 *Gazette* revealed one reason behind the desire to schedule the night contests. The night games "would draw large crowds and help the financial end of the team." With the growth and change of football in this town, the inevitable connection with money had been made. Other monetary issues for the team included paying Tom Skenandore for his football play. The folly of night football was discarded by consensus a few days later.

Another monkey wrench in the budding football fervor was tossed in when Sensiba found himself toe-to-toe with East High School's footballers over rights to the football grounds on Thanksgiving. This was not the last time that the ragtag organization of a city team deferred to the more-established athletic department of an area high school. In 1905, a city team under the guiding hand of Tod Burns met its waterloo part and parcel due to the hype over an East versus West High School clash.

Sensiba had been throwing out other cities as potential dueling partners. Neither Rhinelander nor Ripon College was able to come to Green Bay for a Thanksgiving showdown, so a final game for the year was scheduled at Manitowoc on November 30. In preparation for that game, the boys were "in good condition," although they had practiced just once on the field at Washington and Doty Streets next to the Green Bay Athletic Club.

The town team ended its season without much hubbub. The report of the November 30 game was either lost or nonexistent in the pages of the *Gazette*. More likely, the game never happened. No mention was given to the next season, appointing captains, or if Sensiba would continue as manager.

However, football was very much alive and well in the city. Intracity play had again cropped up and was being reported. Two teams from the city, the "East Rivers" and the "Cyclones," played a 5–5 "grandma-kisser" that was well attended. Also, the December 4 *Gazette* mentioned the "North Ends" football team scheduling a game with Oneida's second team. In one rendition or another, the East Rivers continued as a vital presence in the intracity football wars for the next two decades, keeping the neighborhood teams alive well into the salad days of the Packers and beyond.

To illustrate the hazy line between teams, eligibility, and football play so prevalent at the time, a game was played between the west-side De Pere city team and an east-side high school squad to a final of 6–0 in favor of the high schoolers. An unnamed west side city team also played the "West Side Clerks" to a 0–0 tie in another football contest.

So in the Green Bay area there were, after only five years of gridiron hijinks, as many as seven squads playing this new and competitive pastime. A most striking change was the new mecca of football in town, Hagemeister Park. It hosted football action over the next 23 years on many levels, including junior high and high school, intracity, and city-to-city. More important, it served as the home for the early Green Bay Packer teams.

It became common for papers to run an "End of Season Injury and Death Story." While the papers were relaying and perhaps sensationalizing the violence of the game, these reports were brandished by the sweaty-palmed, antifootball crusaders from their pulpits. In 1899, the obligatory article appeared in a late-November paper and chronicled the death of John Allen, a right tackle for Christian Brothers College. Allen had been injured in a contest with Saint Louis University on November 11 and subsequently died. Supported by an investigation, several parties sought to put a stop to a game they considered "dangerous," and a Saint Louis coroner's jury also recommended that the game be prohibited.

1900
FLIP THE PAGE

In the fall of 1900, football started up again in the town by the bay, but hardly any fervor surfaced. The enthusiasm of the local press for football had also seemed to fade. A game with Company I of Marinette was scheduled, and speculation over the starting lineup was batted about. Jonas Metoxen, another Carlisle standout, was eagerly anticipated as an addition to the Green Bay backfield. An October 4 article painted a glowing account of his arrival. "Metoxen, the famous Indian football player, came to town last evening for the purpose of getting into practice with the local team for Saturday's game with Marinette." A gentleman by the name of McGillan had taken over as manager and was also attempting to schedule a game with Menasha.

The team left on October 6 at 9:50 a.m. to play a 3:00 p.m. game at the Marinette baseball park. The team was reportedly intact, except for John Pease, who was "unable to get away." A newcomer, Tenner, would play center in Pease's stead. Ward Kelly was expected to take over as a "light, but fast and sure at tackling" end.

The October 8 paper bore the bad news; they were defeated 26–0. The subhead offered excuses for the defeat: "Handicapped in Weight and by Wet Grounds—Plucky Playing Does Not Count." Outplayed, the team was taken to the Hotel Marinette as the guest of the Honorable Isaac Stephenson, rich guy and patron of the athletic arts, and given a banquet. To pump up their squad, negotiations with talents Taylor Smith and Shorty Schroeder were reported as being under way.

The next and very last football report came from an October 12 article titled, "Menasha Game Off." It tolled the death knell of the upcoming game due to a scheduling conflict. A possible Seymour game was mentioned, as was the curious absence of the new manager, McGillan.

Clearly, McGillan, like so many managers before and after, found out that handling a city football team was tricky. At the advent of a brand-spanking-new century, several forces had come to bear hard on Green Bay's football fortunes. Intracity play was becoming more accepted, neighboring communities were struggling to field their own teams, and the entire country seemed braced for and confused on the edge of the next hundred years. The football itself would sit, dusty and waiting to be picked up and played with on another day.

1901

A "LITTLE" GRIDIRON ACTION

The bad taste left in the mouth of football fans at the end of the 1900 season lingered on the palate in 1901. Football continued on its low ebb or was no longer catching the fancy of local reporters. The action seemed to fall mostly into the intracity realm. Reports of football received minor mention amid the society news of the *Gazette* in a column called "The City in Brief." Scant coverage could also be found scattered irregularly within the pages of the upstart *Green Bay Advocate*, but that was it. The name "Midgets" seemed to be the playing moniker for nearly all of these intracity aggregations, reflecting the light stature of the squads and not their playing acumen.

Action for the year started late, on Saturday, October 26, in a small affair between the West Side Midgets and the East River Midgets in tiny Saint John's Park next to Saint John the Evangelist Catholic Church. The score at the contest's conclusion wasn't very big either, with the east-siders sneaking out with a 10–0 victory. The East River Midgets were captained by Jules Parmentier and managed by Franklin Snyder. These same teams clashed again a month later on Saturday, November 23, at the Dousman School grounds alongside Chestnut Street. The results were little different, with East River this time hauling off a 17–0 decision. The paper announced that the two elevens would square off once more, at Cleerman's Field on Dousman Street, on Thanksgiving Day.

A game covered by both Green Bay papers was a cross-town clash between the Green Bay and De Pere city teams on Sunday, October 27, at Washington Park. It was a game that ended without a score, but both papers hailed it as "a classic." Not to be outdone by the *Gazette*, which called the contest the "best game of the season," the *Advocate* tagged it two days later as "one of the best games ever seen in this city." Many people from both towns turned out for the fracas, and the spirit of competition between the two cities led to the hype.

In intracity action at Hagemeister Park, across the street on the same afternoon, the Orions and a west-side aggregation at least put some points on the board. The Orions walked off the victors, 10–0, courtesy of two touchdowns without points after goal.

Speaking to the absence of much more gridiron activity in Green Bay itself, the paper mentioned a game between Company I and Beloit College to be played at Marinette on November 9. Green Bay people, devoid of football events in their city, were said to have traveled to the Queen City to watch alien action.

In 1891, when this photo was taken, football was old hat at Ripon College, where the game had been played as early as June 1881. This bunch of dandies was showing just how superior the college brand of football was to that being played by the town teams at the time. The college players even looked better: contrast the dapper uniforms of this crew to that of the 1902 Stambaugh city team or the 1914 De Pere city team, and you'll get the idea. Photograph obtained from and used with permission of Ripon College, Ripon, Wisconsin.

The lines between high school, college, and town team football remained murky. A new entrant in the area football wars, Saint Norbert College, played the second team from East High School on Saturday, November 23. The East High team, bolstered by a winning tradition, won the contest 11–0. East players who were recognized for their play included Tennis, Peterson, McDougal, and Rose. Saint Norbert did not actually become a full-fledged "college" until 1898. Add to that the fuzzy line that was drawn between high school, college, and town team aggregations of the day. For all intents and purposes, Saint Norbert was a high school team playing other high school elevens until 1898. And, by 1901, just three years later, it had hardly awakened one morning to find itself a serious college contender.

Thanksgiving Day was approaching, marking the usual end of football for the year. The Green Bay Midgets emerged to confront the De Pere Midgets. In a small article, the *Gazette* reported the De Pere team on the short end of a 5–0 final.

BEFORE THEY WERE THE PACKERS

President Theodore Roosevelt began an ongoing relationship with the game of football by attending the 1901 Army-Navy contest on November 30. Following this outing, every ticket huckster for every backwater football aggregation in the country wanted the promise of presidential attendance at his next contest: Wire services reported that 15,000 ticket requests had to be refused for the military contest because rumors of Roosevelt's presence made it a must-see game. Whether he did or didn't fall in love with the bruising sport that day was not reported. His own son took up the pigskin shortly thereafter. But it was an injury to his boy that also put the president at the lead of a charge to tame the sport in 1905.

Obligatory muckraking also marked the season's end. In mid-November, Clyde Williams, captain and quarterback for the long-haired kickers at the University of Iowa, was barred from college athletics forever because he had played professional baseball under an alias, Wiley (which he must not have been), in South Dakota.

1902
THAT "EVIL" GAME

The year 1902 had far more intracity play than city team action, a trend that continued in Green Bay for several years. Reports of the contests were again presented in the small blurbs of the *Gazette*'s "City in Brief" column, where mention of the "Hillside Boys," the "PDQ Boys" (later that year renamed the "Eastern Stars"), the "Orion football team," and the "West Side Midgets" could all be found. These teams bumped heads with each other and with various authority figures. Football was still not appreciated by everyone!

In 1902, the mayor of De Pere, J. A. Kuypers, issued a ban on football in his city on Sundays. In an October 10 article, the *Gazette* reported that

> *a number of complaints were entered by some of the citizens of that city stating that cursing and abusive language is constantly being used on the street by persons who have no respect whatever for the passer-by and in these cases a number of ladies have been insulted. This has taken place generally after games and on account Mr. Kuypers has issued the order which does not allow the playing of football on the Sabbath.*

Luckily, in this day and age, all of the foul language has been taken out of the sport!

Another run-in with the "law," this time in Green Bay, was reported in the Monday, November 8, *Gazette*. This time, an article titled, "MAYOR TAYLER STOPS FOOTBALL" told of a complaint by Rev. W. A. Ganfield that sent the local law representative, Officer Howard, to break up the affair to be played between the West Side Midgets and the Eastern Stars at a field behind West High School.

Apparently, the field, located on the west side of Ashland Avenue at the site of present-day Seymour Park, was too close to the First Presbyterian Church. Ganfield complained "that the hours when the game would be in progress the Sunday school of his church would be in session and the noise would interfere with the hours of study." It is interesting to compare this to today, when some churches have special services to accommodate Packer fans or pastors who offer some prayers of petition for the success of the home team. The intrepid heroes of the Ashland Avenue cancellation, not to be swayed from their desire to play some knock-around, adjourned to another site, only to be stopped by rain after a few moments of play.

Also present in '02 were the requisite accounts of the game's violence. Players getting knocked out or getting broken bones were commonly reported and added fuel to the antifootball fire.

Predictably, the town team was promised to be a great one. A meeting was held at the Felch Hotel on Monday, October 27, at 8:00 p.m., and an ambitious schedule was planned. The big names surfaced again: Metoxen, Hulbert, Pease, Gray, Hanrahan, Gronert, Burns, and Jim and Frank Flatley. Foxey Nelson and Jonnie Greg were also expected to help the squad out. The first game of the season looked to be against Fall River, and the team began to ready itself for the clash.

Speculation for the town team's winning ways continued through October, and the *Gazette* added more names to the aggregation's supposed roster. Green and Fullerton were mentioned as new additions and Harrigan was touted as a skilled player with four years under his belt playing with Rhinelander's eleven. Shawano and La Crosse had joined the alleged schedule, and the first game, against Fall River, was definitely slated for early November. More cities' teams were mentioned as possibilities for the Green Bay aggregation's focus. They included Lawrence University of Appleton, Company I of Marinette, Manitowoc, the Kaukauna Athletics, Fond du Lac, and the Milwaukee Medicals. "Games with these teams," avowed the *Gazette*, "are now assured."

"Stambaugh City Team, 1902." These are the words scrawled across the top of this photo that has somehow survived more than a hundred years. Just 12 men comprised Stambaugh's entry into the football wars that year, and most of their names have been lost forever. But a few of their names, even parts of them, can be recalled by players who followed much later, themselves now a nearly extinct bunch. There's "Jim W-something" (third from left, standing); "Gust West-something" (fifth from left, standing); Tom White (next); Ole Olson (next); and Ed Lundwall (seated far left). Even though they're nearly forgotten, there's no doubt that these Upper Peninsula miners were a tough bunch on and off the field. Photograph obtained from and used with permission of Frank Shepich and Harold Anderson, Stambaugh, Michigan.

But just as in previous years, the bark was way more impressive than the bite. The remainder of October passed quickly and November began to tick merrily along. While the pages of the local papers carried football news, none of it revolved around the fortunes of the rumored city team.

Intracity play, on the other hand, was covered. At Saint James Park on Sunday, October 5, a second contest between the PDQ Boys and the Hillside Boys took place. The Hillside Boys hailed from the Astor Park area near the site of old East High School on the southeast corner of Chicago and Webster Streets. They carried a decided chip on their shoulders, having bowed to the PDQs in their previous contest. That chip proved to be the edge the Hillsides needed. In a game coined by the *Gazette* as a "hot and snappy one all through," the Hillsides took it 10–5.

Two other teams engaged in some serious back-and-forth were Kaukauna and Peshtigo, who had battled it out to a split decision over two games and were looking to decide bragging rights once and for all on neutral ground. Green Bay had been bandied about as such a spot.

On October 20, two local players were injured in a contest between the Orion team and a pickup eleven at Hagemeister. The contest was noted more for the injuries than for the football displayed. In the game, George Lefebvre, playing for the Orions, sustained a broken arm while cruising around the end. He was stopped short and thrown to the ground by a bruising tackler. Attempting to break his fall, Lefebvre broke his arm. James Lehan, a member of the motley crew, was also "obliged to withdraw" and later learned he had broken his collarbone in two places. The game ended 5–0 in favor of the ragtag eleven.

A team of west-siders also cropped up and began to receive some ink. Besides faring well against intracity competition, they traveled to Manitowoc on Saturday, October 18, and delivered a devastating 27–5 defeat. Particular stars for the team were Early and Klaus, who ran the ball at the Manitowocers early and often. The *Gazette* said the local team scored "almost at will during the first half and held Manitowoc for a down every time that team got the ball." The game started late and was abbreviated due to darkness. The first half was regulation length, but the two captains agreed that first, Green Bay was profoundly beating Manitowoc, and second, the second half would last about nine minutes.

The west-siders next put a hybrid aggregation of east-and west-side De Pere school boys in their sights. "The boys tried to get one of the big teams for this date," reported the *Gazette*, "but they were not able to secure a game with any of them. As they did not want to get out of training because of an open date, they secured De Pere for a practice game." Meanwhile, Saint Norbert and East High School renewed their acquaintance with a contest penciled in for October 25. The *Gazette* stated that the college eleven was a "very heavy one," which would "give the East high team a hard rub."

BEFORE THEY WERE THE PACKERS

The *Gazette* also projected a contest for Sunday, November 2, between the West Side Midgets and the Eastern Stars (formerly the PDQ Boys) on the West High grounds on Ashland Avenue. The two teams had met up once before, with the Midgets winning 10–5. The game, as slated, did not occur. Midgets were in short supply, and the Stars stood around the gridiron waiting for competition. The two teams ironed out their signals for a contest one week later, on the 9th, at Hagemeister Park. The results were the same. The west-siders didn't show and the Eastern Stars had to entertain themselves with a pickup aggregation. The final was 5–0 in favor of the more-organized team, the Stars, "although the pick-up team was very strong."

Meanwhile, the city team couldn't seem to get its act together, so some of its past and present members spent their time traveling to contests in other cities. Ed Krippner, John Gray, George Richardson, and Will Grosse attended the Wisconsin-Michigan contest in Chicago on November 1.

1903

HULBERT RETURNS, BRINGS ANOTHER TROPHY

The 1903 season could hardly be as lackluster as those of the previous five years. Everything that could have gone wrong in those years did. The year just previous, 1902, was filled with promise, but true direction never materialized. This was corrected in '03 as Hulbert, a man of vision and true leadership, took the reins. After six years in the burgeoning canning industry, Hulbert was now at the Green Bay Canning Company on the city's east side. His business acumen put him at the helm of the '03 team, and the city's football fortunes took a stark turn for the better.

The *Green Bay Advocate* began coverage of the season's hoopla on October 5. A scrimmage was described, and the high school teams were lined up as further practice for the men. The article also sang the praises of Manager Hulbert.

> *The team has secured Fred. Hulbert as manager and a more satisfactory selection could not have been made. Hulbert was the first to introduce football in this city and also brought the first football here. He was also one of the promoters of the first city football teams and served in the capacity of captain for four years.*

The item was further verification of Fred Hulbert's place as the Father of Football in Green Bay. The article also mentioned that the team would practice at night on the corner of Doty and Washington Streets, where two arc lights were erected. A game was slated for October 11 against the Oshkosh Athletics.

The crusade of 1903 started in earnest with the same kind of buildup given Green Bay football in past years, a keynote article in the October 10 *Gazette*. The article outlined the first opponent, Oshkosh, future opponents, the possible formation of a league, and a lineup of available talent. The average weight of this aggregation was reported at 168 pounds. The lineup was as follows: "Joseph Beth, center; George Harrigan, right guard; Octave Latour, or Joseph Lavelle, left guard; Walter Eckhardt, right tackle; Corcoran, left tackle; Roy Nelson, right end; 'Foxy' Nelson, left end; Wallie Cunningham, captain, quarterback; Herman Saunders, right half-back; Frank Flatley, fullback." This lineup would change somewhat from game to game, but remain essentially the same.

Hulbert again looked for outside players to shore up his squad, a move that Curly Lambeau would also find necessary a couple of decades later. Hulbert said he "intends to have in Green Bay one of the best if not the best team in the league."

The first fracas of the season for the Green Bay boys was against the Athletics, a tough-nosed eleven from Oshkosh. The tilt represented a great start for the Bays. They won a hard-fought tussle, 6–0, due in large part to their quickness. The roughness of the game was clear from the tale of two shoulders: Roy Nelson's, which was "wrenched," and an Oshkosh player's, which was totally dislocated. Saunders was the Green Bay hero with his end runs and the game's only touchdown. Joseph Beth, outsized by a reported 60 pounds, held his own at the center position for Green Bay. In a bit of heads-up coaching, the Green Bay aggregation ran mostly end runs to avoid the 240-pound opponent in the middle.

Two teams were mentioned for the next likely opponents: Company I of Marinette or Battery A of Milwaukee. Evidently, a real "battle" was expected from these soldiers. However, like most pomp and circumstance drummed up in the papers in prior years, neither team was actually available.

Next up was the Kaukauna team, in a contest slated for Hagemeister Park on Sunday, October 18. Two days before the contest, the *Gazette* projected that the game would be hard fought as Kaukauna was reported to be "loading up" for the event. In a bit of loading of its own, Hulbert's team was recruiting a former Haskell Indian College player, Smiley Swamp.

In a clean game, Green Bay was again victorious by a score of 28–0. New players who stood out were Waldron, Byers, and Eckert. Saunders again proved to be the media darling, this time with a 55-yard run. Also noted for their offensive prowess were "Foxy" Nelson, and Frank Flatley. On the defense, Harrigan, Corcoran, and Beth were lauded. For the second consecutive game, Early came off the bench late when an injury to halfback Waldron drew him to the turf. The visiting Bays capitalized on fumbles that accounted for three touchdowns and spelled certain disaster for the slightly smaller Kaukauna crew. The Green Bay team looked sharp and was on a crash course with destiny.

The next football skinny came from the October 22 *Gazette*. The Company I team from Marinette was experiencing player problems and disbanded. Most of the worthy players moved across the border to play for the Peshtigo team. Possible

Back in the heyday of the town teams, railroads provided the essential transportation link between cities. It was from this Chicago & North Western train station that Green Bay city teams traveled to countless towns across Wisconsin and the Upper Peninsula for football action. Today the station is the home to Titletown Brewery, an excellent place to celebrate the town team days—and others that followed. Photo taken by and used with the permission of Rachel Gullickson.

foes for Hulbert's crew were the Fond du Lac Athletics, the Twin City Athletics of Neenah and Menasha, and the Arions of Oshkosh. In a rare bit of correct prognostication and reporting, all of these opponents were actually played later in the year.

The next competition on the itinerary was against the Fond du Lac Athletics. In a game to be held in Green Bay, a former city boy, Ralph Glynn, who had college experience at both Notre Dame and the University of Wisconsin–Madison, was recruited to keep pace with the tough competition. Other reports included the arrival of new uniforms and a fence being erected around the field for "keeping the crowd in place." Here were further signs that football was becoming a permanent fixture in the city by the bay.

The October 26 *Gazette* chronicled the sights and smells of the October 25 contest. The *Gazette* was kind when it reported that Fond du Lac's team "was not disgraced by any means as it had to fight against great odds." The simple fact was that, outweighed and outplayed, the Athletics were trounced 62–0. Green Bay's team was applauded primarily for the tackling of Harrigan and Eckert and the "line plunging" of Flatley, Glynn, and Saunders. The game report finished with a mention that Saunders had a good day "punting." On the surface, this may seem a bit confusing since most 62–0 games offer very little in the punting department by the winning team. Clearly the reporter meant "kicking."

In a show of class and a foreshadowing of the perks that would be accorded to pro football players in the future, the following report was made: "The team management gave the team a box at the theater last evening." Was this an attempt to inject culture into the beasts on the gridiron or a reward for a job well done? Perhaps it was Fred Hulbert's gentle Baptist hand ushering the boys away from the local watering holes. How many of the lads actually set foot in the theater that night was not reported and may be lost to the tides of time.

A large-print ad in the October 31 *Gazette* proclaimed the next challenge. The game was to be played at Hagemeister Park on November 1 against the Twin City Athletics. The billing boasted, "The Twin City Team of Neenah and Menasha is one of the best teams in the State. The Green Bay line has not been crossed thus far this season and the local players are going to do their best to keep up the same pace."

Lineups were given with the addition of Beyer, Leveille, and Peterson for the home team. Long-time warrior Fred Hulbert was also included on the list at fullback, where he would switch off with Frank Flatley.

Another sign that the sport and team organization were clicking along at a great pace was a banner in the same day's *Advocate*, exclaiming "FOOT-BALL! At Hagemeister Park Thanksgiving Day Battery A, of Milwaukee vs. Green Bay." This game was so huge that it began to be hyped four weeks before game time! Obviously Manager Hulbert had a tight grip on the team's schedule, and crowds to date had shown a willingness to turn out with proper notice.

All of the generous words describing the Twin City team's prowess couldn't help them muster enough teamwork to be in the game. Green Bay ran roughshod over the visitors in a 65–0 laugher. In a match called "relatively easy," the locals played to the applause of their loyal fans. Fullback Eckert and left halfback Saunders were chosen as having exceptional performances. In describing Saunders's exploits the paper stated, "The visitors simply could not hold him in most of the plays and his hurdling the line and sprinting around the end with the ball was cheered wildly." The article ended with Hulbert appealing to fans for financial support for travel to upcoming contests; the great money-making machine of the Green Bay Packers was yet many years away.

A combination team from Peshtigo was the next powerhouse to oppose the Green Bay eleven. The Peshtigo crew was actually composed of some players from the great, but recently defunct, Company I team as well as Peshtigo stalwarts. "Tomorrow's game," said the paper, "will be intensely interesting as neither of the

---

END OF THEIR GAME
FOOTBALL UNDER ELECTRIC STREET LAMP CLOSED ABRUPTLY
WHEN THE BALL WAS KICKED INTO THE LIGHT

The sound of breaking glass acted as a most effective curfew bell at the corner of Main and Jackson streets last evening when a number of the boys of the neighborhood had sembled for a game of football under the electric light. During the game the ball was kicked into the light itself and the globe fell in fragments to the street below. The last particle of glass had hardly reached the pavement before the last boy disappeared in the gloom.—From the *Green Bay Gazette*, October 30, 1903

teams has been defeated and whichever way the game goes either team will have its clean line of victories broken with defeat for the first time." Not necessarily so . . .

The *Gazette*'s report from November 9 hailed the affair as the "Most Exciting Game Ever Seen in the City." It featured the strong defensive work of the Green Bay men and the addition of new men Potter and Schneider. The paper vividly recounted the action:

> During the first half of the game the locals ripped up the visitor's line in grand style and skirted their ends in good shape, but in the last half of the game the visitors took a 'brace' and during the rest of the game the ball was almost entirely in the local territory and at times was dangerously near the lines, only to be punted out of danger by Saunders.

Punting, being used as a much more effective defensive weapon, had saved the day and the perfect record of the Green Bay team. The game ended in a 0–0 tie, proving the power of both teams' defense and the relative equality of their skill.

Having survived its toughest competition of the year, the Green Bay team spent extra time at practice to maintain its "perfect" record. The November 21 *Gazette* described the team's practice habits: "Although practice the past week was severe, great care was taken that none of the players would in any way receive the slightest injury and the floor on which the training took place, the team practiced indoors on account of the cold weather, was covered with sawdust or a large mat."

Metoxen, Waldron, Potter, Flynn, Schneider, and "Injun" Lafontaine were all mentioned as outside men playing with the locals. Thus bolstered, the team stood ready for its next squabble with the Arions of Oshkosh.

"Green Bay Is Still Unbeaten" read the headline from the October 23 *Gazette* article depicting the Oshkosh action. To set the record straight immediately, the game was played against the Oshkosh All Stars and not the Arions. The Arions backed out, and the manager of the All Stars "hastily selected the best men of the All Star, Tigers and Defenders of that city and came down to do battle with the challenging team." The paper reported that not all of the Oshkosh team members were willing to play and that some were even "afraid." The game was still action packed, and the Green Bay boys won by a tally of 33–0. The scariest moment for the Bays came when their unscored-upon record almost came to an end. Fortunately, the season-long hero Saunders came to the rescue once again:

> Halfback Graves of the visitors gave the locals a scare when on the opening kick-off he caught the ball and made a 90-yard run toward the line. Sanders [sic], although knocked down three times and otherwise blocked in making the attempt, outsprinted the dodging and hurdling visitor and brought him to earth before he reached the goal line.

BEFORE THEY WERE THE PACKERS

The last game of the season was close at hand for the Green Bay automaton, a "state championship" game versus the Battery A of the Milwaukee team. The game was held in Green Bay. Despite an error by an unknown party that had advertising bills about town stating that the price was 50 cents, Manager Hulbert insisted that he had set the admission price at 25 cents.

The Milwaukee team came to town by special coach via Milwaukee Road. One can imagine the excitement and anticipation that must have been brewing in the city on the few days before that game! It had been five years since the city had seen a full-blown championship, and Milwaukee represented a reach out of the familiar territory for Hulbert's crew.

Green Bay completed the season as the undefeated, unscored-upon champions of Wisconsin. Slippery gridiron real estate fell into the local boys' hands as their "close formations" won the day. The team played so well that the paper from the 27th reported, "Whenever the two teams came together the Milwaukee men were steadily and surely pushed back foot by foot and sometimes many yards at a time."

To add to the glory of the 22–0 victory, Battery A had not been scored upon until that point for the entire season! Newcomer Harmes, Flatley, Corcoran, Eckert, Schneider, Saunders, Nelson, Potter, and Waldron were all adorned as special stars of the day. They were joined by John Gray, a warhorse from the dawn of football in the bay.

In a season that is as impressive as any played in Green Bay, the footballers amassed a record of 6-0-1 and remained unscored upon for the entire season. This feat speaks for itself as a testament to the power and skill of the team. In a city still in its football infancy—it was barely eight years old—the '03 team came of age in a big way. Its record stood as follows:

Oshkosh (6–0)
Kaukauna (28–0)
Fond du Lac (62–0)
Twin City (65–0)
Peshtigo (0–0)
Oshkosh All Stars (33–0)
Milwaukee Battery A (22–0)
Total: Green Bay 216, Opponents 0

The 1903 team, along with the 1897 team, should go into the pages of the incredible championship history that is bandied about in Titletown. At a minimum, it should be in every Packer Backer's arsenal of justification as to why the true "America's Team" is the greatest ever. Winning football has always been a tradition here.

1904
HELLO NSFL, SO LONG FRED

Putting a finger on the pulse of the 1904 season is easy for modern writers. It marks the last year of direct involvement with football for founding father Fred Hulbert. In subsequent years his very name would bolster the spirits of the football faithful, laurel enough to grace the legend. In later years, when the town teams seemed to be lagging in both participation and fan support, his name was tossed about to stoke rumors of his coming back to add his guiding touch, despite the fact that his career in the canning industry had taken him to other corners of the state.

Before the big boys of the town team started up the '04 rampage, the intracity action was in full swing. A baseball team that just didn't get enough action on the diamond formed a football team. The Onward team, as they were known, was basically an east side neighborhood team. They practiced on the corner of Washington and Doty and were ready to bump heads in any fair contest. A game at Saint James Park pitted the Onward team against the Dousman Stars. The Onwards had to borrow a few east side high school boys but came out victorious with a 7–5 win. A return grudge match was scheduled at the Dousman school grounds.

These players and their associates formed the Onward Athletic Club and blueprinted a "modern gymnasium" above Ed Thomas's gun store on Pine Street.

A full-column article in the September 23 Green Bay *Gazette* praised the championship team of the year before. Hulbert, acting manager, still very interested in winning, continued to import players. Some of the strong-shouldered veterans from bygone seasons were reported to be returning, but, for the first time, many of the players were lost to the competition. Charles Waldron, a halfback phenom, went back to his native Marinette to play for the newly rejuvenated Company I team. "Foxy" Nelson and Lewis Corcoran slipped away to Fond du Lac's squad. Also, Frank Flatley and Ralph Glynn were doubtful due to offers from a Colorado state university.

To balance the loss of some of his stars, Hulbert enlisted the most sought-after player in the area, Jonas Metoxen. Metoxen, like Tom Skenandore in 1897, was a bruising back fresh from the Carlisle gridiron wars. Financial support was obviously necessary to obtain his services. Both Hulbert and Metoxen realized the benefits of the Carlisle star playing in this area. Hulbert found himself in a bidding battle for Metoxen's services, including this particularly generous offer from enemy territory: "The management of that eleven [Company I of Marinette] is said to have offered the former Carlisle full-back $25 a game and the use of a four-room flat during the football season."

This was a time when weekly salaries were in the range of $9.25 per week, so they must have held his services and prowess in high esteem indeed. Each game netted Metoxen a salary that the average working Joe could only make in three weeks with his nose hard to the grindstone. For that $25, Metoxen could have bought himself a nice lunch every day for a month or an entire men's dress outfit, or he could have rented a four- to six-room apartment in Manhattan for a month or outfitted his entire football team in style.

Hulbert also expected Herman Saunders of Madison, the star of the '03 season, and Jack Schneider from Menasha to swell his ranks. The final "named" players were Wallie Cunningham, quarterback and proposed captain, a man named Walsh, expected to play end, and Frank Du Chien from Oshkosh at the other end. The *Gazette* article ended, "Manager Hulbert promises that the team will be considerably stronger than last year's championship aggregation." There are just two directions a team can go after a buildup like that.

A small item appeared in another article on the same page: Football veteran Charles "Tod" Burns, a boilermaker, was returning from Minnesota. In 1905, it would be Burns who would take over managing responsibilities from Fred Hulbert, adding another strong presence to the football core building in Green Bay.

So, Green Bay had a reputation to protect, a team on hand, a capable manager, a paper to cover the action, and a public to tap for support. This was the formula for success that football teams across the nation were discovering. All they needed were some games. To this end, farsighted Fred Hulbert facilitated the formation of the Northern State Football League. He acted as president and William Zelms, of Oshkosh, as secretary. The October 6 *Gazette* reported the following teams as members: Green Bay, Fond du Lac, Oshkosh, Twin City athletics of Neenah and Menasha, Appleton, Peshtigo, Marinette, Escanaba, Oneida, and Kaukauna.

ESCANABA—THE "ESKY" KICKERS BEGIN TRADITION

Thanks to Jack Beck, a sports author from Escanaba, several stories of early "Esky" football have been preserved. One such story came from S. M. Matthews who, in his later years, recalled a free-for-all from his youth that looked a little like football. It was played on the dirt street on the south side of the school grounds, perhaps as early as the late 1890s:

> At that time boys would chip in and buy a round, black football, which after sides were chosen would be placed in the middle of the block and kicked off to the other team. After the ball was put in play, it was always kicked on the ground, except occasionally when it could be caught. A game was won when the ball crossed the street line at either end of the block. There was a high board fence and sidewalk on the south end of the street and when the ball fell in between the fence and the walk a battle royal was staged. As it was quite impossible to pick up the ball between the opposing kicks, it became the duty of all to kick shins instead of the ball. Each boy sought to be the hero of the game and the only handicap we suffered was in having no "fair admirers" on the sidelines to applaud us on to victory.

Soon the older guys from Escanaba were at it too, dreaming of some serious football fame. While they may have had a rule book in their hands and a sense of football in their heads, the game itself was actually played on the field—sometimes by other guys who had no bookish inclination. So it was, with a popinjay spirit, that the Escanaba guys traveled en masse to Ford River, "the sawmill town," to take on a crew of "huskies and lumberjacks." Dr. H. W. Long, another old-time footballer, recalled a pretty colorful scene that greeted the Eskimos upon their arrival at the battleground:

> On our arrival we were met with a rousing welcome by the Ford River team, which consisted of Mr. Todd and 10 dummies, for, as we afterward learned, it was not necessary to have more than one man on a team. It was proven that knowledge gained in the school of experience greatly outweighed that obtained from books and that the deluge that befell the visitors was overwhelming. We were returned home quite crestfallen but much wiser, for it was demonstrated that science played as great a role in the game of that time as it does today.

The first game was scheduled for league teams, and the hype began with the Green Bay squad positioned to face the Twin City aggregation. All of the teams had been scouring the countryside for football talent, and every game would be an even match. Also, with the league, close geography would create more interest in rivalries, and larger crowds at a game would net big gate receipts.

But was the league just some fancy clothes on a hobo? Most leagues in any sport at that time fell apart due to a breakdown in the "formula." In short, the formula dictated the need for key people in the appropriate slots in member towns so that the house of cards that was professional sports would not fall down. One good town program could not survive without quality competition.

Leagues had come and gone since the birth of "King Football" in the early 1890s, and they would continue to be given birth amid fireworks and then disappear quietly. The United States Football League, the first rendition of the World League, and the American Football League all were testimony to the ebb and flow of league organization, even in recent times.

A large print ad supported the first game of the season for Hulbert's gang:

FOOT BALL
Rain or Shine
TWIN CITY ATHLETICS OF NEENAH AND MENASHA VS. GREEN BAY
AT Hagemeister Park ON Sunday Afternoon
Game Called at 3 o'clock
ADMISSION, 25 CENTS, BOYS, 10 CENTS
First Game of the Season
DON'T MISS IT

The lead story on October 7 spoke to the readiness of the local eleven. "All the signals to be used in the Menasha game Sunday have been fully mastered. Several trick plays and formations will be tried in the game." The story continued with the anticipation of Jonas Metoxen's arrival in town later that day.

In 1903, the *Green Bay Advocate* acknowledged that eight years earlier Fred Hulbert was "the first to introduce football in this city." It also proclaimed Hulbert as the man who "brought the first football here." Hulbert would be a constant organizer and supporter of Green Bay football until 1904, when his career in the burgeoning canning industry took him to other Wisconsin communities. Ironically, this man, responsible for the birth of football in Green Bay, was born in Chicago. Photograph obtained from and used with permission of Hulbert's great-niece, Ethel A. Evrard, Milwaukee, Wisconsin.

College action was also heating up in the metropolitan area. Saint Norbert and Green Bay Business College were projecting a "mighty tussle" on a Sunday afternoon.

The October 8 paper ran an article exclaiming, "City Team Will Do Battle Tomorrow." The article was run of the mill, with the usual promises for a great game. As in the past, the most highly touted contests often fell flat. Sometimes the game was not played. "Rain or Shine" became "Shine" only, and poor weather forced Hulbert to telegraph Twin City management and cancel the contest.

After sorting through the options at hand, a game was scheduled with the Arions of Oshkosh. The Arions were a team that a year before backed out of a game with Green Bay when it assumed it couldn't win and didn't want to risk its two-year-long unbeaten record. However, the local press reported that the Green Bay squad was not optimistic about its chances in the upcoming "savage game": "Many football men claim that even though the local team has been having nightly practice for some time past and every precaution [has been] taken against defeat, the chances are greatly against winning the first game of the season with such a team as the Arions to go against."

Was this loser's limp, or a clever attempt to make the Oshkosh squad think they had an easy mark? No matter. The Oshkosh manager and league secretary, Zelms, came to town and made arrangements for the team and about 100 rooters from his fair city.

Practice was raised to a fever pitch, culminating in Hulbert forbidding any more "severe scrimmages" due to the toll it was taking on his crew. Frank McMonagle, a West High School product, had assumed the role of right end and Neil Kelly took the left. Jim Flatley, veteran of Green Bay campaigns past, assumed the station of referee for the Sunday clash.

Half-page ads in the *Gazette* on Friday and Saturday, October 14 and 15, took this form:

FOOTBALL
Rain or Shine
AT Hagemeister Park
SUNDAY, OCTOBER 16
ARION ATHLETIC CLUB OSHKOSH VS. GREEN BAY ATHLETICS

Oshkosh has played two games this season, winning both.
DEFEATED
Neenah-Menasha—64 to 0
Oshkosh Colts—40 to 0
Admission—25c
Time of Halves, 30–25 min
GAME CALLED AT 3 O'CLOCK SHARP
WATCH THE LINE-UP.

The final bit of table setting appeared in the Saturday paper. "Famous Indians in the Game Tomorrow, Metoxen and Wheelock to Play with City Foot Ball Eleven," sang the headline. Jonas Metoxen and Martin Wheelock, highly respected football players at Carlisle Indian School, practiced with the team and showed signs of brilliance. The article continued to drum up support, announcing a signal drill for that night at the Washington and Doty practice field.

Financial concerns, ever pressing, prompted this quote: "Manager Hulbert has hopes of a large attendance, as many of his plans for the remainder of the season hinge to an extent on the encouragement shown in the patronage of the opening game." The lineups of that year reflected Hulbert's expertise in gathering football talent. Many old names graced the list alongside new potential. The veterans on hand included Schneider, Gray, Beth, Harrigan, Eckhardt, Walsh, Russell, Cunningham, and Early. They were shoulder to shoulder with new men: McMonigal, Wheelock, Metoxen, and Kelly. It couldn't have hurt the boys to have the familiar faces of Al VandenBerg as timekeeper and Jim Flatley as umpire.

The stage was set for a battle of Herculean proportions in the city by the bay. However, it was still apparent that not everyone in town liked football. Another article in the same issue exclaimed, "Parks Are Not for Games." Mayor Minahan, in an order addressed to Police Chief Hawley, expressed his feelings for the popular but pugilistic pastime:

> *Reliable information reaches me that the parks of this city are frequented, especially on Sunday, by parties who indulge in boisterous behavior and engage in rough games. Our parks are intended for healthful recreation and exercise at all times by all persons, but they are not designed for the ordinary games of football and baseball. Those wishing to participate in such games must seek a suitable place. You will therefore instruct the members of your force to see that such games and behavior are not permitted in the parks to the disturbance of adjoining residents or the exclusion of persons using the parks for proper purposes, especially on the Sabbath.*

How much weight this order carried is unknown, but football did continue to be played in Green Bay, and on the Sabbath! Imagine the quandary that Officer John Pease must have felt, being ordered to break up a game that he himself played and loved. Better yet, it wasn't too far down Green Bay's football road, that some kid named Hawley would, himself, be a prominent area footballer. No, the order did not seem to hamper football in the slightest and Minahan was not elected for another term.

The game against the Arions went well, with the account stating, "the Green Bay football team played rings around the Arions." In a game dominated by the Bays, much more than the 12–5 score was displayed. Jonas Metoxen was the real star. The first half belonged to the home squad, and Green Bay made both of its scores in that half. They played a fast-paced game that quickly slackened due to the poor conditioning of the boys and warm temperatures. The second half took its toll on the under-trained locals, and the only score of that period happened in unusual fashion. The Oshkosh horde managed to penetrate to the Green Bay 25-yard line, and attempted a field goal on third down. The ball missed by a small margin, and was promptly fumbled by Russell of the home team as "it lodged in among the old base ball bleachers." A clever Oshkosh player fell on the ball and was given a touchdown. Out of bounds? Evidently not.

A large audience, fulfilling Hulbert's needs on that end, attended the game. The game produced one serious injury when Spencer of Oshkosh fractured his leg in the middle of the action. Harder practice was promised to make up for the team's poor conditioning and need for frequent rest.

The next game, according to an October 18 *Gazette* account, was against the Neenah-Menasha team. Improvements mentioned were a fence "stretched across the field," though it's safe to assume that the fence was really designed to be stretched "along the sidelines," with new bleachers along both sidelines.

That proposed game was abandoned, so Hulbert set up a duel with Marinette's Company I team. Hulbert, acting as manager of an appreciative Kaukauna squad, went to an earlier Marinette-Kaukauna game as a combination manager and spy. He had high praise for the military men, saying, "I think Marinette has the strongest team in this state with the single exception of the University of Wisconsin eleven." Their team averaged an immense 192 pounds.

A large ad in the October 28 *Gazette* advertised the upcoming Marinette game. It was similar to earlier ads, with the addition of the home lineup and this inflammatory blurb:

> *Co. I has one of the strongest teams in the west and will come here determined to win. The followers of Co. I have $500 to bet that Green Bay will not score. Green Bay will have one of the strongest teams that has been on the field this year and will make a hard fight to win. It's up to you now to see the best game that has ever been played in Green Bay.*

Whoever had a hand in this bit of in-your-face promotion was brilliant. It could have been Fred Hulbert, but, regardless, it challenged the local populace to come out and back their team.

The Saturday afternoon paper contained a cleverly written piece describing the upcoming clash. It spun several clever webs that drew the reader and potential fan to want to see the contest. There was mention of a "horde of Marinette men" ready to put some sizeable bets on their team as well as some backers from northern Michigan's copper region ready to back Company I. A mention of Company I's claim as champions of the state was brought up to counter Green Bay's title of the year before as well as the potential talent that Hulbert had wrangled together for this huge game. The article also noted that Green Bay–Kaukauna interurban cars would be available to bring football fans to the city for the action. Also mentioned was the field itself, which had been a source of pride to the city for years. Hagemeister was described as being in "excellent shape."

Money notwithstanding, the Green Bay boys did their city proud, falling to Company I by a final tally of only 10–0. The loss was mostly chalked up to the Marinette team's "superior brawn and 'beef.'" Although their large stature made the game slow, the paper reported that "The soldiers made practically all their gains by a push-and-pull system of plays between end and tackle. They kept hammering and grinding at Green Bay's left wing and seldom tried the right forwards, in only two instances were end runs attempted and in each case Marinette was thrown back for a loss."

It was a credit to the home team that they held the score to a low one. Green Bay was forced to punt and came out ahead in this strategy, as Marinette usually fumbled or had its own punts blocked.

The running backs on both sides, Metoxen for Green Bay and Waldron for Company I, received the highest praise. Hulbert played the game as a guard against a gentleman named Burns, who outweighed him by 50 pounds. Hulbert held his own in this quarrel.

A promised return match with Company I for the following Sunday was set up to be played in Marinette. Fans from Green Bay were encouraged to travel with the team, and they could get special "club" rates by signing up at McGregor and Prinz's cigar store. Officer John Pease, in his only opportunity to play football without suffering the wrath of his superiors, was recruited to play center for this matchup. Hulbert put a positive spin on the loss to Company I, saying, "while the defeat last Sunday was a bitter medicine to the team and hard to swallow it was good medicine for it cured the team of thinking that defeat to the locals was impossible." He also cited that the team had to invest more time learning "teamwork."

The November 6 game proved to be no better than the earlier attempt. The "bitter medicine" this time was a dose of 22 for Marinette and 0 for Green Bay. Green Bay's death knell was the inability to get key players to compete with the squad on that day. Jonas Metoxen and another Native American named Webster made an impact as usual, but their influence was not enough to make the difference. Marinette's much larger size and team play worked hand in hand to give them the easy victory. "If it ain't broke, don't fix it," seemed to be Marinette's modus operandi.

After the double drubbing at the hands of the soldiers from Marinette, Hulbert's boys prepared for a game with Kaukauna. Kaukauna's manager said to Hulbert, "We will give you fellows the hardest rub you ever experienced." To which Hulbert stated that they were doing extra work to "stand the 'rub.'" The game proved to be a "battle royal."

In a contest shortened in the second half by darkness, the Green Bay bunch won the "fierce charging, old-fashioned football" game by the rather lopsided score of 25–0. The rubbing must have been fierce. The local lads enticed Ralph Glynn to help them out, and, between his and Jonas Metoxen's skills, four touchdowns were made. Glynn's exploits included scampering with a kickoff through the entire Kaukauna squad for a score, only to have it called back to the 25-yard line by a protest that he had stepped out of bounds during the run.

The final score was also attributed to Glynn when he wound his way 30 yards, aided by a screen provided by several hundred fans who had wandered onto the field. He had caught a double pass and was lost in the approaching darkness and mass of people. It rubbed the opposition the wrong way and they protested, but referee Flatley wouldn't have any of it. Whether the protest was over the pass, the human mass, or the darkness isn't clear. The pass wouldn't be made legal globally for two years, but in smaller circles some referees would allow it. The visitors had been offered a chance to quit because of the failing light several minutes before and had refused.

Football at Saint Norbert College had begun in 1904, the year this photograph was taken. For several years prior, the school had been fielding a high school team that played against any high school, college, or town team in northeast Wisconsin that would line up against it. Photo obtained from and used with permission of Saint Norbert College, De Pere, Wisconsin.

The Green Bay squad got healthy again and had an even record at 2 and 2. But the mind boggles at their next choice for an opponent. Green Bay stood toe to toe with Company I once again. This time Green Bay loaded up with some prime ammunition. Making the journey were Ralph Glynn, Frank Flatley, "Rock of Gibraltar" John Pease, and George Harrigan. They promised to help make the difference for the underdog squad. In a seesaw affair, neither team could break the other's 20-yard barrier, and the game ended after 50 minutes of action, deadlocked at 0–0.

The game broke down into a tale of two halves, the first being ruled by the huge Marinette men and the second by the speedy Bays. Money was bantered about, with the initial bets being offered at 2–1 against Green Bay. After the behemoths from Green Bay took the field, bets were even up. On the visiting side, Ralph Glynn put on the most impressive performance. He had several dazzling runs that were stopped only by equally effective defensive actions. The entire Green Bay backfield was commended. Russell, at quarterback, was noted, but several bad passes hampered his effectiveness. Green Bay's line, likened to a stone wall, was equally impressive. Pease at 265 pounds, Harrigan at 235, and Snyder at 185 formed an interior that was challenged only momentarily and then worked around. Marinette reportedly used "goon" tactics including slugging. Hulbert was offered a financial arrangement to bring his eleven back to Marinette for a fourth game on Thanksgiving. He declined and decided to stick with an earlier promise to host Oshkosh on Turkey Day.

The Oshkosh game was heralded in grand fashion. The Wednesday *Gazette* from November 23 told this tale:

> When the referee's whistle sounds the call for the opening of hostilities in the foot ball battle between the Green Bay Athletics and the Oshkosh Athletics at Hagemeister Park at 3 o'clock tomorrow afternoon the signal will be responded to on the part of the locals by the most formidable aggregation of canvas-backed warriors that has represented this city on the gridiron since the days when "Tom" Silverwood, one of the greatest tackles Wisconsin ever turned out; Bert Groesbeck, John Gray, Harry Hanrahan, "Jim" Flatley, "Tod" Burns, Allie Van, John Pease, Fred Hulbert, Frank Flatley and others played on the champion team managed by Ed Krippner.

Hulbert, not one to take chances, kept his squad loaded on information that Oshkosh was bringing a team full of football "celebrities." Among their luminaries was Lawrence University center Holstein and other starters from that university team. The writer of the above article attempted to poke some fun at the Oshkosh manager by reporting that he was "anticipating the result of tomorrow's game with great glee," to which the writer replies, "What a jar is in store for that man!" Anticipation built that quite a beating would commence, with Green Bay on the up side of a 40–0 score. Let the action begin.

Say it ain't so Fred, say it ain't so. A great many excuses were offered for the 5–0 loss Green Bay experienced. One was that the opposition had loaded up with players from the college ranks and only had two from its original squad. Second, the Green Bay boys played a lackluster game with too many fumbles. Third, quarterback Russell "displayed poor generalship in running the team." Fourth, Glynn, the standout back, broke a rib and was replaced by Fullerton, who in turn fumbled, leading to the game's only score. All excuses aside, the Oshkosh team was faster, performed as a team better, and had a more varied game plan. Glynn had an 80-yard run before his injury, which was called back because he had stepped out of bounds. Metoxen was underutilized. They lost; it was time to move on. The pain was too great.

The final game of the season, to be played on November 27, was the fourth attempt to hang a mouse on the record of Marinette. But the first line of the article from the following Monday said it all: "It's no use."

The aggregation had traveled to Menominee, Michigan, to play Company I on the local fairgrounds. It was near freezing, and the only original backfield member for the Bays was signal-caller Russell. The impromptu backfield comprised Fullerton, Kudder of Kaukauna, and Grimes. They simply were not an adequate replacement for Flatley, Glynn, and Metoxen. Borrowing Paul and Holstein from the Oshkosh team shored up the line and they held as well if not better than the other starters. None of the backs exhibited the ability to punt the ball out of trouble, and as such the field-position battle was lost.

Green Bay had stars on the defensive side, including the undersized Wallie Cunningham, who started at left end, and despite the abuse of being "elbowed and kneed," he wouldn't leave the game. He moved back to the safety position and still received his lumps. The bright side of the contest was "the retirement of Gagnon, a Marinette halfback, with a broken nose." The soldiers were known as rough players and according to the newspaper reporter, "the Company I team has never been noted for extreme gentleness and their manner of playing football has not been on the order of ping-pong."

The Green Bay eleven returned home, bloodied with a 12–0 loss. The inconsistency of the new players added to the mix ruined the flow the team had when playing with its best foot forward.

The '04 team finished the season with a 2-4-1 record and a 37-points-for and 54-points-against margin. Most disturbing was that a team that had put up 216 points the previous season could not even manage 40. Another sign of a disappointing season was that in each of its four losses, the team was shut out.

The last order of business was for the city football organization to make arrangements for a fundraiser. It took the form of a public dance and promised to be the "big dance of the season." Whether anyone on the dance floor knew it or not, it was also the last dance for Fred Hulbert in his service to city football.

SECOND QUARTER

1905–1909, "OPERATING UNDER A HOO-DOO"

1905

BURNS GETS BURNED

The growing number of football elevens in Green Bay in 1905 was indicative of at least two developments marking pigskin play all across the United States.

First, the game was spreading in popularity like a house on fire. Sure some of the original spark that had spawned youthful enthusiasm for the sport in the 1890s was now tempered for the game's practitioners by the realities of family, job, and community responsibilities, but there was still plenty of football to be had.

Second, the lines between high school, college, town, and professional aggregations were becoming more and more distinct. Unlike today, the college team was held in the highest regard. It was at the college level that the best training and the best organization could be found. Without a league or a clear legacy, the pro or semipro town team was often relegated to a second tier of public esteem. If the local high school team was smacking them around that particular year, the independent squad's banner might droop even further.

Likewise, the goal of winning games was putting more and more pressure on team managers and coaches to "stack" what were once hometown teams with "crack" players of some reputation who could single-handedly take an average team to a regional championship. These "tramp athletes" were often considered roustabouts by the local football players and fans, but they brought victories to the team, panache to the field of play and the community, and, most important, paying spectators to the game. The local guys were often left to watch and dream from the sidelines in the wake of these gadflies. But, despite the adoration given him on the Sunday gridiron, the vagabond player was seldom going to find himself a per-

64

manent home amid the tidy houses and established morality of the locales where town teams formed.

No doubt about it, the traveling professional athlete was a new and increasing phenomenon. In his excellent book, *Pigskin: The Early Years of Pro Football*, Robert W. Peterson clearly documents these developments in tracing the 1903 season of the Franklin, Pennsylvania, All-Stars. Dubbed the "Greatest Team on Earth" by the *Evening News*, Franklin's team consisted almost entirely of imported players. Of the 15 men on the squad, says Peterson, the "only hometown boys on the Franklin All-Stars, other than manager Dave Printz, were substitutes—guard W. J. McConnell and halfback Chal Brennan." Looking down the line of scrimmage itself seems to have been a pretty enlightening exercise. "The left side of Franklin's line came from the Pittsburgh Stars of 1902," states Peterson, "while the right side were old [Philadelphia] Athletics."

In Green Bay in 1905, the injection of serious money had not tilted the game to that extent, yet. But that year also showed the signs that winning with imported players was better than losing with a purely hometown aggregation. Early in the season, Green Bay acknowledged at a team meeting that it would need a semipro team that year in order to be competitive. Tough teams had sprung up or been strengthened up and down the Fox River Valley while Green Bay had failed to field a consistent team in 1904. In 1905, the aggregation once again struggled to field enough players or haul in enough money at the gates to be successful.

On Tuesday, October 3, the *Gazette* reported that there were "19 experienced players out in uniform" at the first practice session of the year held the previous Sunday afternoon. The article stated that negotiations were under way for a contest with the Appleton Athletics but that the "local boys are still looking about for a manager and the delay in finding a suitable man has been responsible for a hitch in preparations for the playing season."

Fred Hulbert, so long a stalwart of the Green Bay gridiron as star player, captain, coach, and manager, was no longer available, given his involvement in Wisconsin's new and growing canning industry. Since 1895, he had climbed that industry's corporate ladder, beginning with his post at the Larson Company on North Broadway. Hulbert was now residing with his wife, Lucille, and daughter, Virginia, directly across from the practice field that had produced Green Bay's first championship team in 1897.

For a while it looked as if no one would volunteer to guide the team until Charles "Tod" Burns finally stepped forward. Burns himself was in the salad days of a career as a salesman for the Burns Boiler Company on South Pearl Street. Like Hulbert, Burns was a veteran of the city's first team in 1895 and a member of the first championship team of 1897. Immediately, he went to work trying to secure games with the football crews of other towns. By season's end, he had experienced more than a spoonful of the frustration that could come to the manager of a town team eleven.

Despite the as-yet-unknown fortunes of the 1905 city team, Green Bay was rife with football. Intracity football action was found on nearly every available vacant lot and quiet street. The A. J. Lucia Cycle Company was doing good trade in footballs, football uniforms, and football armor, and the Green Bay YMCA, then located on the city's west side at the northwest corner of Walnut and Chestnut Streets, was the hub of football activity for youngsters in the city. Young lads had taken to the sport, as football was now a well-established tradition at the city's East and West High Schools.

Surprisingly, East and West had never met "officially" in head-to-head battle on the gridiron. Thanksgiving Day, 1905, would change that. However, once the Thanksgiving Day contest did roll around, football historians in town would quickly point out that teams from the two schools had met "unofficially" once before. That was the significant occasion of the very first football game in the history of Green Bay, Wisconsin, on Saturday, September 21, 1895. Twenty-two-minute halves had been played, averred the old-timers, and the score had ended in an 8–8 stalemate.

While the two teams that had engaged on the gridiron that day at old Washington Park were not sponsored by either high school, they were, ostensibly, high school teams organized within the athletic systems of the two schools. And one can bet that the friction between the two sides of the river, especially in light of the political changes on the near horizon, found its way to the line of scrimmage that day in 1895. The same two teams met a week later, though they now identified themselves as completely independent of the two schools.

But now it was 1905, and the two schools were positioned to do football battle in earnest. It should be mentioned in passing that, at the time, East High School was located on the southeast corner of Webster and Chicago Streets, the present-day site of First United Church of Christ. West High School was found at 250 South Ashland Street between today's Seymour Park and the First Presbyterian Church. The current schools were not built until 1924 and 1928, respectively.

So, interest in football was soaring in Green Bay, and the wish to play the game, and the demand on football facilities, was growing commensurately. This led, naturally, to the increase in the number of teams, especially neighborhood or "intracity" elevens about town. Unlike membership on the town team, intracity play allowed men to work, tend to their family responsibilities, and still play the game they loved. The more such teams there were, the more the opportunity for football enthusiasts to play. Some of the teams doing battle that year included the Dousman Street Stars, the Onwards, and the East Rivers. De Pere also had a city team that mixed it up in Green Bay's intracity realm. Interest was so strong that the East Rivers even fielded a second eleven.

Besides playing one another at sites like Green Bay's Dousman Street School and tiny Saint James Park, these teams also staged contests at Hagemeister Field, comprising the northern part of the sprawling old Washington Park. The Walnut Street electric car made Hagemeister at once accessible from downtown and yet far enough away to offer a bit of a lark and an excursion to the football fan. "Zeger's Park," basically a cleared and leveled farm field just off the Webster Avenue street-car line behind the present-day Keglers Klub, was also being utilized as a football venue by De Pere and Green Bay teams. A team comprised of Manders boys who lived just kitty-corner from Zeger's field began to make their name known in subsequent years.

Occasionally, these intracity teams also squared off against aggregations from other cities, thus enjoying the best of both worlds: the ability to stay home and tend to business and the opportunity to face elevens from other places. These teams were strictly amateur and did not have to mess with the finances and rigorous scheduling of the official town team. Obviously their victories were less heralded and less celebrated, but the collapse of a scheduled game was also less serious. If a particularly hot contest could generate gate money, the most complicated part of the process was splitting the take among the players once the up-front costs of promotion were met. As far as the players themselves were concerned, they played the same game as the town teams did, and they approached it just as seriously when they took to the gridiron.

Additionally, the neighborhood teams served as an informal "feeder" or "farm" system for the town team that had the heavy chore of facing the best players that nearby towns could muster. In the face of a "defi" from an outside aggregation and the absence of a bona fide town team, these intracity teams would even sometimes merge to form a hybrid "city team."

The *Gazette* reported the "first serious accident of the local football season" at Hagemeister Park on October 9 during a game between the Onwards and the East Rivers when Joseph Nys sustained a severely sprained foot. Following that contest, which ended 0–0, the Onwards stated that they were "considerably outweighed" and challenged "any team in the state with an average weight of 145 pounds" to a contest. For the intracity teams, the season was well under way.

Burns's city team, meanwhile, was struggling with the classic organizational paradigm, repeated year after year in every city, village, or town where "independent" football could be found. Without a league to guarantee some continuity and overall structure, the "five-step shuffle" required for fielding a team would again be repeated.

The Northern States Football League had been formed the year before to take care of these problems in one fell swoop, but it had fallen apart when Fred Hulbert turned his attention toward his family and business pursuits.

THE FIVE-STEP SHUFFLE
FOR FIELDING A TOWN TEAM

1. Meeting to determine player interest.

2. Securing the necessary practice and game facilities.

3. Mustering fan and newspaper support.

4. Obtaining financial support from businesses and citizenry in the form of donations or fund-raisers.

5. Scheduling and rearranging contests with teams from other locales that had managed to successfully do the same.

These steps were not always followed in order and were certainly not always successful.

The meeting to organize the 1905 eleven took place on Thursday evening, October 12. The *Gazette* was nearly giddy when it reported the following day that "what is doubtless the strongest lot of material that has been available for a city football eleven since the time of the old championship aggregation managed by Ed Krippner was represented at the football mass meeting last evening."

Burns had been appointed manager. Will McNerney, football coach at West High, would serve as secretary and assistant manager. Reul Russell, a carryover from Hulbert's '04 squad, would fill the post of treasurer. Further, it was decided to "put a semi-professional team in the field, with not more than three professional players." A practice was slated for that Sunday afternoon, October 15, at Hagemeister Park.

Wilson Charles, another Carlisle standout in football and baseball, was projected as one of the paid players at halfback. The *Gazette* tabbed Charles "the Indian baseball slinger." Other "strong" players listed as possibilities in the Saturday, October 14, *Gazette* included Bert Matthews, Jonas Metoxen, E. A. Schneider, Ed McEachron, "Chap" Schumacher, John L. Alexander, James Hughes, Will McNerney, Reul Russell, Burgoyne, Octave J. LaTour, and George Welsh.

Meanwhile, Burns was hard at it trying to arrange an opening game. Oshkosh, Fond du Lac, and Appleton were likely candidates for an initial contest. The Sunday practice at Hagemeister had been spirited, and the presence of the accomplished Jonas Metoxen sent some enthusiasm up and down the streets of Green Bay. Even better, Charles Waldron, the standout on the tough Marinette Company I teams of the past few years, was labeled "a probability" for the season in Burns's backfield. He was courted both by the city team as one of its paid players at halfback and by East High School as a football coach. Besides, signing Waldron would eliminate a potential threat if the team were again to face Marinette while putting a regional star into its own lineup.

On Tuesday, October 17, Burns had also supposedly secured a 10-year veteran of the city teams, John Pease, at center, which was encouraging. At a reported 275 pounds, Pease was a giant of a man whom the *Gazette* labeled as "invulnerable in the middle of the line." The *Gazette* credited Burns with adding Pease to "the apparent wealth of material he already possessed." Of course, Burns and Pease had been teammates on the city's earliest elevens and their connection ran deep. Bob

Dittmer, who jerked the scales at 198 pounds, further bolstered the line of scrimmage, according to the paper. It cited Ferguson as a person of "considerable" gridiron reputation who would also be reporting for practice. The 1905 version of the Green Bay town team was beginning to look like world champions, at least on paper.

While Burns was busy negotiating a contest with Appleton, the Onwards had somehow, quietly and without seeming difficulty, managed to schedule a contest with an aggregation from that very city. Of course, unlike Burns's crew, the Onwards were not burdened by negotiating terms of the game or securing financial backing so that they could guarantee up-front money to the eleven from Appleton.

This photo, often identified as the 1905 Green Bay City Team, is far more likely a picture of the Onwards, an intracity team, than it is of Tod Burns's aggregation. That seems clear given the presence of Onwards Dave Abrohams, Joe Coleman, and Reul "Red" Russell, and the absence of any players of note from Burns's squad, such as Bert Matthews, Jonas Metoxen, Ed McEachron, John Pease, or Burns himself. It might also be another intracity aggregation, the East Rivers. Given that most of the players in this photo hailed from the east side, it could also be the East Rivers' first team or a combination of Onwards and East Rivers—a hybrid—which had actually ascended to the level of "town team" without being official. Players and others connected with the team include, as numbered, (1) Fred Parmentier, (2) Ed Bader, (3) Bud Stone, (4) Eddie Meulemans, (5) "Red" Russell, (6) Jack Reiter, (7) Joe Coleman, (8) Jack Rothe, (9) Wallie Cunningham, (10) Herman Meyers, (11) Rollie Cunningham, (12) Frank Cartier, (13) George Verheyden, (14) Dave Abrohams, (15) Willie Neister, (16) Jack Heintzkill, and (17) Octave LaTour. Photograph from the Henry Lefebvre Collection of the Neville Public Museum of Brown County, Green Bay, Wisconsin.

Besides facing the East Rivers and the Dousman Street Stars in several unheralded intracity contests, the Onwards had also beaten an aggregation from east-side De Pere in a lackluster match, 8–0. Then, they reissued an area-wide challenge to any team in the state meeting an average weight requirement, this time of 135 pounds. They were getting as much press attention as the city team. On Wednesday afternoon, October 18, the *Gazette* cited Dave Abrohams as one of several new players who were expected "to strengthen their [the Onwards'] line-up considerably." Abrohams's ties to football in Green Bay were just beginning. By 1921, he would be living in Minneapolis, but his cousin Nate Abrams contributed heavily to the success of the early Green Bay Packers. Nate's brother, Isadore "Issy" Abrams, also donned the uniform as a member of the Green Bay teams in the late teens, which would usher in the days of the Packers. Dave's brother Pete also added his name to the rosters of the early town teams.

An item appearing in the *Gazette* on Tuesday afternoon, October 24, suggested that the Green Bay team was toiling to put money into its kitty so it could play some football of its own. It read,

> *DANCE FOR FOOTBALL TEAM*
> *City Squad to Give Benefit Ball on Thursday Evening*
> *The members of the city football squad have decided to give a dancing party as a means of raising a cash nucleus for the team's treasury. Next Thursday evening has been selected as the date and K.P. hall as the place. Heynen's orchestra will furnish the music. Tickets will be offered for sale in advance by some of the members of the team and at several business places about town.*
>
> *The Herrick Clothing company has come to the assistance of Manager "Tod" Burns in the outfitting of the players by offering to donate sweaters for the men on the regular team and the substitutes.*

With Herrick's help, Burns's team had achieved some credibility. But he was also scrambling to schedule actual games to no avail. On Friday, October 20, in an article headed "Burns Hot After a Game," the *Gazette* said he had "kept the wires warm" in an attempt to get an opening game for Sunday, October 29. It reported that he had definitely closed games with Menominee for November 5 and Marinette for Thanksgiving Day. On Monday the 23rd, it reported that he had "closed a contract with the Fond du Lac Athletics for next Sunday."

On Friday the 27th, the paper reported that "gridiron togs" had been received by Burns and that practice was to be held that night and the following night to prepare for the game against Fond du Lac two days hence.

The next day, Hagemeister was the scene of a 2:30 p.m. contest between a second-string team from Lawrence University and the West Highs. Admission cost adults 25 cents and students 15 cents. In promoting the game the day before, the *Green Bay Review* rallied the West High boys and their fans with the closing, "We need you to win."

Putting aside all of Burns's troubles, the season finally did open at Hagemeister Park on Sunday, though not against Fond du Lac. Burns had received a call in the late afternoon on Saturday from the Fond du Lac manager. The Fondy athletes were not coming. In a pinch, he was able to get the Neenah Cardinals. Despite their off-field generosity for pinch-hitting at such late notice, the Neenah team traveled by train to Green Bay only to be rudely treated by Burns's squad, 10–5.

Neenah scored first, and the *Gazette* observed that "at that stage the game looked like theirs. The locals took a decided brace, however, and managed to cross the opposing goal twice after some strenuous battling."

FRANK SHEPICH ADDS A FEW MOVES TO THE FIVE-STEP SHUFFLE FOR TOWN TEAM SUCCESS

Frank Shepich may not have seen the birth of town team football, but he certainly was present when it breathed its last in the mid-1950s. As a player, coach, and manager for the Stambaugh All-Stars in Michigan's Upper Peninsula, Frank knew the town team game from every possible angle. He could dance the five-step shuffle as well as toss in a few subtle moves of his own. He had to in order to assure the All-Stars' survival. He was even part of the town team renaissance after World War II when he agreed to coach the West Iron County Steelers, a bunch of veterans returning from the war.

Frank knew just how fragile the town team's existence was. That's why he appreciated the Green Bay Packers with a passion quite different from that of other fans. He knew firsthand that a team like the All-Stars could be up and running strong one week, and then collapse in a pile two weeks later due to a rainstorm or an injury or a shutdown at the local factory. Yet the Packers had survived!

Frank's tutelage could do much to help Packer fans understand just why Green Bay is lucky to have its professional team today. He could explain just what it took to keep the music behind the five-step shuffle, the formula that it took to make a town team fly. With slight variations from town to town, it looked like this:

1. Recruit talented football players and get them together for a team meeting at the general store or the offices of the weekly newspaper. At that meeting, consider scheduling a series of night practices and choosing a captain, then getting some guy so plied with praise or drink that he would agree to be the coach.

2. Start putting out feelers for which other towns were engaged in the same process. This may have been done as early as the summer baseball season but, if the team meeting had been a success, you could now do it with real vigor.

3. Get some money together to pay for uniforms, balls, and upgrading the local cow pasture. This could be accomplished by getting a local businessman to serve as team manager. Otherwise, your players could take to pounding the pavement themselves. Wives would be called upon for organizing socials and baking pies as needed.

4. Schedule some games once enough money had been put together. Here you could use a good newspaperman. He could toss the "defi" in the direction of a nearby town and stir it with some offensive verbiage, often asking whether the other town had any men in it at all. That kind of talk could usually generate a positive-negative response the following week, right after the paper would be printed.

5. Play the season's first contest against the sissies from the next town over, if possible. If enough people turned out and paid at the gate, and if the home town had also

marked a victory, you could get up a head of steam that might carry you over five or six games. One of those could be a rubber match against the sissies in their town and be hailed as "the best game of the season" even before it was played.

6. Win out, and you would be in a position to move beyond your immediate geographic area. You could then claim the "regional championship" for your team and challenge an undefeated aggregation from 75 miles up the tracks to pay you a little visit for a Thanksgiving Day game.

7. Close out the season with a solid victory and money in the bank. Depending on how much, you might divide it among the players. Otherwise, it could bankroll the start of the following season.

8. Watch any part of the formula falter and your town might not see a team represent it for a decade or more. Make everything work, and the team you save might be the Packers.

Jonas Metoxen had failed to make an appearance, so Burns was pressed to go with "Chap" Schumacher at fullback; the *Gazette* stated that he "succeeded quite well." Reul Russell, penciled in to start at quarterback, was also not in attendance and McNerney was pulled from the end position as a substitute there. Bert Matthews, a veteran baseballer of the state league for Green Bay and Freeport and a star footballer at Cornell College, was "the bright star" of the game, according to the paper. Eddie McEachron, who filled in at the other halfback spot opposite Matthews, was also cited as key to Green Bay's win.

"On the whole," reported the paper, "the showing of the Green Bay team in the initial contest was encouraging to local patrons of football."

That same day, the Onwards had played the De Pere city team to an 8–0 finish. "The game," reported the *Gazette*, "was marked by heavy line charging, but otherwise was featureless."

There was plenty of hoopla in the sports column the following Saturday when the *Gazette* announced, "Old Stars to Meet on the Firing Line. Celebrities Announced for Oshkosh-Green Bay Football Game Tomorrow." The team was looking to increase attendance and pull in some much-needed gate receipts. Given the lackluster season to date, Burns was lucky to have a newspaper still willing to beat the drum.

On the Oshkosh side of the line, the contest promised Herman Saunders, who had starred in both baseball and football games in front of Green Bay audiences; Kinney, a star with the 1904 University of Wisconsin eleven; and Frank Du Chien, a standout for the Oshkoshians. The Sunday before, Oshkosh had battled a tough Company I squad, a team that had given the Green Bay team fits in 1904, to a 0–0 tie.

For the local team, once again dubbed the "Indians" by the *Gazette*, Burns promised Jonas Metoxen and Charles Waldron. Joining them in the backfield would be Matthews, star of the previous game, and McEachron at quarterback. Burns was also beefing up his line with Jack Burns of Marinette and Schneider of Neenah, slated as "cracks" up front. Schneider had played on Green Bay elevens before. Pease, the burly policeman, was also scheduled to put in time at center.

"The football battle between the Green Bay and Oshkosh city elevens at Hagemeister Park tomorrow afternoon," led the *Gazette*, "promises to be an encounter decidedly interesting if all the stars announced by the local management report for duty on the firing line." The paper concluded by relaying that the gridiron itself had been moved closer to the Wisconsin-Illinois baseball grandstand to accommodate a larger crowd as well as "keep the field free from spectators." The wall around the baseball field would help accomplish the crowd control.

For all the hype, the contest ended in relative disaster. While Green Bay won 5–0, a steady downpour kept attendance light as the two elevens clashed on "a heavy field." Burns had "gone to rather heavy expense" to secure his star-studded aggregation, and the treasury of the city team took a major hit. Metoxen had proved his worth, scoring the only touchdown. On that play, Du Chien was knocked silly as he dove to take Metoxen down. He remained semiconscious for the better part of an hour after being hauled off the battlefield. Finally, he was rushed by ambulance to the Hotel Frontenac for the remainder of the afternoon. In a rather strange report, the *Gazette* suggested that "four extra men for whom Burns had guaranteed expenses were not players, but merely spectators."

Whatever the case, spectators who did show did not see a complete game in terms of teams or time. Oshkosh finished the first half with only 10 players following Du Chien's departure, and the contest was called at that point. Burns had scrambled to put together an eleven that would excite the local football populace, but circumstances and the weather had thrown a wet towel on his efforts.

"Straight football was the rule," said the report, "end runs and trick plays being impracticable on the wet field." Enthusiasm for the city team remained pretty soggy the rest of that week. Burns, a purveyor of boilers, had to feel as if controlling the steam on that huge contraption were a lot easier than fielding a semipro town team.

On Saturday, November 11, a small item declared that Burns had been successful in scheduling a contest for the following day between his squad and a "picked aggregation composed of players from Neenah and Appleton." Waldron would not be available for the contest, but Frank McMonagle would take his place in the backfield along with Metoxen and Matthews. Once again, the game never happened.

Monday's *Gazette* suggested that "Manager Charles Burns of the city football eleven believes he is operating under a hoo-doo." The all-star aggregation from the south had failed to show. Burns promised a contest for the following Sunday against Peshtigo, with whom he said he had "closed a contract." But, the next weekend did not see a battle with the Peshtigo eleven either. Rather, a return trip by the Oshkosh city team produced a 16–0 loss for Burns's squad.

Not much was turning out the way Burns said it would. Worse yet, media support was eroding. "Aside from the brilliant playing of Seuss, an Oshkosh guard of great bulk," the *Gazette* declared, "the game was practically devoid of interesting features." The game was "decidedly one-sided," the paper stated, and "the local team, clearly lacking in practice, put up a ragged game."

Burns's backfield had, again, put forth a good showing, with Metoxen joined by "Turner" and "Smith," whose names actually were set in quotes. Exactly what the quotes meant was never explained. One guess would be that the two were "cracks" playing under aliases. The other explanation would be that the reporter was much more interested in hyping Burns's embarrassment than in taking names.

Burns had one more contest left, which was slated for Thanksgiving Day against long-time rival Company I. Company I was the closest thing to an archrival that could be found for the Green Bay city teams, and this game should have been stirring up some interest. Drawing almost as much press as the game, however, was the dance that would follow Thanksgiving night at Turner Hall on the northwest corner of Walnut Street and Monroe Avenue. Burns was hoping for a one-two punch to put some life back into his team and his team's bank account.

Unfortunately, football fans in Green Bay were taking as much interest in the upcoming contest between Lawrence and Marquette universities scheduled for the Saturday before the Green Bay game. Charles Beyer, a former player for East High School in Green Bay, was a halfback for the Lawrentians, and, according to the *Gazette*, "a large delegation of local fans" was headed by train to Appleton for the game.

There was still another wrinkle in the works that upset Burns's plans for a successful conclusion to an "iffy" season. "High Schools Reach Final Agreement. Local Elevens Will Clash for First Time in the History of the City" shouted the headlines that Saturday the 25th. To further conflict with Burns's itinerary, the game was also set for Thanksgiving Day at Hagemeister Park. The paper's explanation was less than accommodating to Burns, making it seem like his contest was a little bit in the way of something really important, the first contest ever between the two schools:

> *The game will be played at Hagemeister Park in the morning. 10:30 o'clock being agreed upon as the hour for beginning active hostilities. The arrangement for a morning contest was made necessary because of the fact that Manager Charles Burns of the city eleven had previously contracted for the use of the park in the afternoon for the game between his aggregation and the Company I of Marinette. The West highs insisted at first on an afternoon battle and this was also desired by the east sides, but Manager*

*Burns was unwilling to relinquish his claim on the grounds and the forenoon
was agreed upon as the next best substitute as to time.*

So there was a football game slated for Thanksgiving Day that was drawing interest, but for most Green Bay football fans it wasn't the upcoming city team contest.

Action between teams within the city limits was also humming along nicely, no matter the fate of the high school or city aggregations. On Sunday, November 25, a hotly contested match between the second team of the East Rivers and the Dousman Stars ended with the East Rivers up 5–0. With their series split at two games apiece, the aggregations were wild to meet again the following Sunday to settle the score for the season. On Tuesday the 28th, the same East River team decided not to wait and claimed "the city championship for teams averaging 128 pounds to the player." They issued a defi to any like team in the county.

That same afternoon, at Hagemeister, the first East Rivers team stood up to a "heavier" Oconto team and came out with an 11–0 victory. Several of the star players for the Onwards had joined up with their cross-town rivals for the game. Reul "Red" Russell, a member of the Onwards and Burns's city team, scored on a rarely successful goal kick from the field. To really confuse things, Russell was actually a west sider. Three weeks prior, the East Rivers had traveled up the railroad line to play the same tough Oconto aggregation to a 5–5 tie, and now, said the *Gazette*, they were "anxious to secure a game with the city team."

In order to refocus the spotlight toward his own contest, Burns told the newspaper on Wednesday that his Thanksgiving Day game the next day would decide "the championship of the northeastern part of the state among city elevens." That might have been snub enough toward the East Rivers. To ensure the success of his eleven, he secured the services of none other than Frank Du Chien, the scrappy Oshkosh player, as well as Leathen, the coach of the Appleton High School eleven. Jonas Metoxen was also promised at fullback.

The dance to follow that night was clearly "a benefit enterprise for the team," suggested the *Gazette*, "which has a depleted treasury as the result of an unsuccessful season." The game with Company I represented Burns's final hope for turning the season around both on and off the field.

Elsewhere in that Wednesday edition, an article asked, "Which team is the best? This is the question which all football Green Bay has been debating earnestly for days." Unfortunately, the paper was referring to the inaugural East–West High School contest, not the city team's declared championship match against Marinette. No matter. Despite what seemed like a lot of disrespect, Burns's game would be played.

The article wrapping up the season after the Company I contest was honest if not flattering. "Disastrous End of Disastrous Season," its headline read. "Box Office

Receipts Suffer Materially Through Centering of Interest in High School Battle." It didn't lay much blame at its own doorstep, however.

The city team had lost to the Marinettes 11–0 in a game that had, said the *Gazette*, "a somewhat farcical nature in some respects." The paper was certain that the high school contest that morning had cut into the later game's attendance. "The patronage was a disappointment to the promoters," it said. And the benefit dance later that day, while "a merry affair," had a turnout that "was only fair and it is not likely that the net proceeds will fill the rather good-sized hole in the eleven's treasury."

The game itself was an embarrassment. Burns was so short on players that he had to delay the contest in anticipation of the arrival of some of his men. Surely they were coming. Then, when it was clear that the needed level of help was not going to show, he himself put on a uniform and borrowed some Company I players.

The scene couldn't have been uglier. "Marinette substitutes," jeered the newspaper, "were drafted into service on the Green Bay side of the firing line to appease the clamor of patrons who had paid for pasteboards at the gate. The contest was short after the Marinette soldiers had scored the second touchdown." And, whether anyone knew it or not, the future of declared city teams representing Green Bay would consequently be tenuous.

MARINETTE AND MENOMINEE—THE OTHER TWIN CITIES

It's time to make a controversial statement. What the heck is the Upper Peninsula of Michigan doing connected to the lower part of the state anyway? In a football sense as well as in nearly every other way, the U. P. and Wisconsin belong to one another. Heck, there are only three Detroit Lions fans in the U. P., and they all live together in a tar-paper shack sans shower facilities.

And, as long as we're at it, calling Minnesota Wisconsin's "sister state" instead of the U. P. is as ridiculous as it gets. Hudson, Wisconsin, exists for one reason and one reason only: So that Wisconsinites stuck in the Minneapolis–Saint Paul area can buy beer on Sundays! That, so they can get drunk and stomach the oppressive Vikings. As far as knocking the Bears goes, let's wait until they have a football team worthy of insult.

Okay, where were we? Oh, yeah . . . the history of football in Marinette, Wisconsin, and Menominee, Michigan. It's a rivalry that is both unifying and divisive, the way all good rivalries are. Every year, these two towns celebrate their partnership in the oldest continuous interstate high school football rivalry in the nation. It was the same way with their town teams. The squads of these "twin cities" had been enemies, and they had been brothers, but they had never been easy to beat. Here are just a few of their stories.

True Colors?

In 1897, Marinette played two games against the lumberjacks from Rhinelander. The sequel was carried out on Thanksgiving Day, with Marinette claiming victory and the score standing at 6–0. The Marinette press called Rhinelander "the holiday turkey for the brawny Marinette kickers." Continuing the extended metaphor, it mused that "with the gridiron as a table and their fleet limbs and strong arms as utensils they picked the bird clean and left nothing but the yawning carcass as a reminder of the feast."

In Marinette, during a snowstorm, the battle had been fierce and furious, yet five hundred fans braved the elements to witness the game. The five-point touchdown happened in the second half as two players dragged another across the goal line. Next, "Jordan then wiped the snow out of his peepers, rubbed his lusty toe and the leather was sent between the goal posts, making the score six to nothing."

In an end note, the paper poked fun at Menominee fans, who attended the game in hopes of a Marinette loss. "They came over to shout for Rhinelander and when they saw that Marinette was victorious quietly stuffed the Rhinelander colors, which they had been wearing in their pockets."

A Hard Wind's a Gonna Blow

In 1901, Marinette set against the Fort Sheridan team out of Chicago. The game proved to be a whitewash for the locals as they came out ahead by the lopsided score of 51–0. "It was like rolling an empty barrel over the gridiron," elucidated the paper account when describing how easy it was for the Marinette team to advance the ball. Some of the starters from Company I retired from the game early in the second half to give substitutes a chance at some action. The rout became so complete that before the final gun sounded one of the Fort Sheridan players was said to exclaim, "Call this thing off. We're up against a cyclone."

The Blind Eye

In 1904, the November 25 *Marinette Eagle* mentioned the Marinette Athletics' dismay over accusations of slugging and roughness in their game with Green Bay. The *Eagle* refuted this: "In all the years when the Marinette eleven have been trouncing everything in the state, they have never been accused of slugging or playing dirty ball." The author of the *Eagle* opinion must not have been around long because rumors of Marinette's slugging were well known and quite widespread. The article went on to state that the slugging may have been an interpretation of Marinette's line-smashing tactics as opposed to Green Bay's more "scientific" approach.

Fall to the Packers

In the 1919 campaign the lads from the twin cities couldn't hope to stand tall against the heavily recruited Green Bay squad. The drawbacks for the losers were many. They were 15 pounds smaller to a man. They weren't as quick with their signals or play calling. The Packers put in subs every three minutes and kept themselves fresh. After the inevitable defeat, the local paper summarized the unhappy results:

CASUALTY LIST
Three black eyes
One Charley Horse
One wrenched knee
Numerous bruises
Two sprained fingers

BEFORE THEY WERE THE PACKERS

Caved ribs
Great Humiliation

That humiliation is a thing long gone. The fact is that the boys on the twin city team were willing to take on the best team in the area and, despite a litany of woes, had a brush with greatness one Sunday afternoon in 1919.

While Burns's efforts were panned by the *Gazette*, the paper celebrated the East-West contest. East had won in a lopsided battle, 21–0. But, despite the fact that the West High team had been "outclassed," the game and the idea of the game had been well-received by the media and the populace. "The 'hill' players," it reported, referring to East's school building which sat on a hill, "had considerable advantage on 'beef,' outweighing the west-siders by an average of nearly nine pounds to a man, but they also excelled in aggressiveness, speed and general team work, both in offensive and defensive playing."

The paper suggested that, going into the fracas, the boards of the two schools felt that "an extreme bitterness of feeling might be engendered between the schools if a match were allowed." But it stated that the game had actually prompted increased warmth of friendly interest between the institutions."

On the other hand, the efforts to field a city team had taken a serious setback. The city team phenomenon, relatively strong in the first 10 years of football in Green Bay, had proven to be a lot of work to maintain and nurture. Burns had found that out firsthand, as had Fred Hulbert, T.P. Silverwood, Ed Krippner, W. J. Casey, and B. B. Sensiba before him. Fielding a top-rate semipro team, while drawing enough at the gate to support it, was a definite Catch-22. It would echo all across the United States and, by the 1920s and beyond, sound the death knell for hundreds of such teams. By the 1950s, with television about to make the world a lot smaller, fielding a successful town team was nearly impossible.

Burns's name would never again be attached to Green Bay football following his "disastrous season" at the helm of the city eleven. For the next 20 years, including the first years of the fledgling Green Bay Packers, the light of true town team football would flicker, fade, rekindle itself, burn brightly, and then die again, depending on how all the factors played out. For the years 1905 to 1917, city teams began, more and more, to emerge from out of the ranks of the intracity teams as they battled each other as well as outside aggregations. It would not be until 1910 before any aggregation of eleven football players would huddle up and call themselves "The Green Bay City Team."

Two items of note from early December 1905 pretty much put a nail in the coffin lid for that gridiron season. The first, appearing in the December 2, *Green Bay Review*, stated that "Dr. J. William White, professor of surgery at the University of Pennsylvania, has presented Theodore Roosevelt's football reform platform." The "gentlemen's agreement" stated that football would institute

First—A simple and uniform eligibility code for all American colleges and universities.

Second—Summary punishment for brutality and foul play.

Third—Umpires to be given widest latitude in enforcing rules against brutality.

Fourth—College presidents to hold to strict accountability umpires who permit foul or brutal play.

Fifth—Permanent removal from the game not only of the brutal player but of the player who is not a bona fide student and amateur.

On the heels of yet another football death, that of G. C. Ficken, a fullback on the junior football team of the Southern Athletic Club of New Orleans, the reforms seemed vital for the future of the sport. Ficken had succumbed to injuries sustained in a November 20 contest. The article concluded by avowing that "it would be a real misfortune to lose so manly and vigorous a game as football, and to avert such a possibility the college authorities in each college should see to it that the game in that college is clean."

The other item struck a sad note for the followers of early Green Bay football. John F. Gray, 28-year-old son of Alderman A. L. Gray, died of typhoid fever contracted while deer hunting in northern Wisconsin. Gray, described by the *Gazette* as "one of the best known and most popular young men in Green Bay," had been a member of the earliest Green Bay football elevens and was a member of the first city championship team.

1906

A TOWN TEAM BY DEFAULT

Far too many accounts of Green Bay football history have used one another as resources to declare that the only year this city did not have a bona fide town team was 1916. The statement is not accurate by any respect. There was a town team in 1916, though it was unable to pull together a high-profile contest against a De Pere team late in the season. But there were several other years when a declared town team simply did not exist. In those years, such a team merely appeared, by default, from the plethora of intracity teams playing one another. Such was the case in 1906.

Football was alive and well in Titletown, USA, in '06 as well as in nearby De Pere; the east side of Green Bay itself had four intracity teams. Following Burns's fiasco in 1905, intracity managers enjoyed their brand of the game much more. They could concentrate on scheduling games and filling rosters and not on paying players, negotiating contracts with other teams, handling gate receipts, promoting the games, and the myriad of other duties associated with a pro or semipro team.

An item from the September 9 *Green Bay Review* headlined "Green Bay May Play Football" relayed that the school board had banned the sport. But the board rescinded its ban with the caveat that students could take to the gridiron if "the game [went] hand in hand with hard work and manly deportment."

To counter the local school board's concerns, the new athletic director at the University of Wisconsin, Dr. C. P. Hutchins, was touting the merits of the gridiron. "Football—the game—is one of the finest, if not absolutely the finest sport for the development of young men to their best powers," he avowed as he assumed his new position. However, in the wake of Roosevelt's football reform measures of 1905, he had his work in promoting the sport cut out for him.

On Saturday, October 6, the *Green Bay Semi-Weekly Gazette* carried good news for the city's sports enthusiasts. Hagemeister Park would remain a "public place." Old Washington Park, which had been the scene of most of the town's earliest football contests, had been further divided up with the extension of Walnut Street toward the East River. While Washington Park had comprised the entire grounds of present-day East High School, Joannes Park, and houses to the south of the park, by 1906 plans were well under way for platting the entire area for city lots. A couple of developments were slowing that effort down. Hagemeister Brewing Company, which owned the northern section, and Mitchell Joannes, who held title to the southern section, were both leaning toward reserving the area for recreational pursuits.

That same day, the *Semi-Weekly Gazette* resurrected football hopes from the ashes of 1905 with an article titled "Plan to Organize Strong City Team." No stronger tonic needed to be introduced than the whisper that the football men of the city had approached Fred Hulbert to manage their fortunes for the season. With Hulbert secured as top man, things would fall back into place nicely. The article continued,

> *Prospects look very bright to the players for a strong aggregation this season, and for that reason they are anxious to get together. Among the players who can be relied upon to don the moleskins are Wallie Cunningham, who captained the city team two years ago, Eddie McEachron, the fast halfback from De Pere, two other De Pere line men, Joss, a man who played for the Kalamazoo team last season, Flynn, a brother of the famous Minnesota player, whose home is in Peshtigo, Schraa, an ex-Oshkosh normal end and others. Metoxen, the Oneida fullback and Waldron, the Company I scrappy halfback from Marinette can be secured for the harder games, it is believed, and no trouble will be encountered in getting a winning aggregation together.*

That sounded great! Unfortunately, the days and weeks ticked down, with the fulfillment of the dream crumbling away.

Rule changes for '06 were meant to open the game up and cut down on rough play. Six men were required on the line of scrimmage, somewhat reducing the massive and brutal "line-charge." A player no longer could call down, but rather, when any part of his body other than the hands or feet touched the ground, the play was over. Four officials were now required. And, in cases where a player was discharged for unnecessary roughness, his team was moved backward half the distance to its goal line.

The forward pass was now legal. But, because of the restrictive rules governing its use, it was hardly encouraged. Most discouraging was the fact that an incomplete pass would turn the ball over to the defense.

BEFORE THEY WERE THE PACKERS

Carroll College—Passing Fancy

A great footnote to Carroll College football history regards an event that occurred during a 1906 practice game against the Billikens of Saint Louis, Missouri. While Knute Rockne gets the lion's share of credit for bringing the forward pass into the modern college football vocabulary, it seems certain that the first modern example of the play was actually witnessed at a preseason Billiken-Carroll contest. The Billiken coach was Eddie Cochems, a graduate of UW–Madison. His name for the aerial play? The projectile pass. And it worked like a charm. For that season, the Billikens made liberal use of the play and, by season's end, had amassed 407 points to their opponents' 11.

Sorensen's Skidoo team became a popular cause in the pages of the *Green Bay Advocate*, in which the Sorensen advertising account was no doubt also something to be respected. Sponsored by the William Sorensen and Company store on the city's south side, the team held an organizational meeting on Tuesday evening, September 11. The *Advocate* reported that the team was looking for "former high school players for football material" and that a number of games had already been scheduled. Besides contests against other intracity teams, the Skidoos would be taking on Kaukauna, the Fond du Lac Centrals, Oshkosh, and De Pere. The lineup featured Charles Lewis, the star quarterback from West High School in the '05 season.

Games continued on the east side at Saint James Park and Whitney Park as well as at the hallowed football grounds of Hagemeister Park. On the west side, contests could usually be found on the grounds of the Dousman Street School and at Union Park, now called Tank Park. Also active on these gridirons in 1906 were the Cherry Street Stars and the South Siders, another west side aggregation.

The Skidoos finally clashed with the East End team at Hagemeister on Sunday, September 30. While the *Advocate* called the contest "one-sided" in favor of Sorensen's team, the score was a clear-cut 0–0 tie at the end of regulation play. Penalties, it seems, had kept the Skidoos from scoring. From the paper's perspective, this had kept the score from reflecting the superiority of the Sorensen team.

By Sunday, October 7, the 1906 campaign was well under way as other Green Bay area teams would now see their opening action of the season. The first would pit the Giants of Green Bay against an aggregation representing De Pere. The Giants were captained by Joseph Connor and managed by Tom Lom. Lom was also a presence in Green Bay football in ensuing years. The *Advocate* suggested on Thursday, October 4, that "it cannot be stated which is the best team as both have very good records so far this season."

The Hillsides were captained by guard Andrew Muldoon, Jr. He proved to be a study in longevity, enduring through the later town teams of 1911, 1913, 1915, 1917, and the Packers in 1919. Muldoon returned to play with the Packers after spending time in the service during World War I. The manager of the Hillsides was Joseph Drom.

The next contest featured the East Rivers against the De Pere city team. The *Advocate* suggested that the Green Bay team would line up against the team from its sister city and "proceed to do things to them." That game, however, was never played when the East Rivers found themselves without an opponent. The Tuesday, October 9, *Advocate* taunted the De Pere aggregation with a question about "cold feet." "Arrangement will be made for a game down there soon," the paper concluded, "and the East Rivers promise that they will be there."

For their part, the East Rivers had made some noise in city football circles in 1905 and were returning nearly the same lineup to the gridiron in 1906. The East Rivers had basically sprung up from the northeast-side neighborhoods of Green Bay to do football battle. They had actually been creating collisions in town since 1899, when they had represented to football fans in the jurisdiction the very first serious football eleven other than a bona fide city team. The *Advocate* cited Homer Rothe, a kid named Stone, and one of the Aylward boys as players of special note. In fact, the *Advocate* stated, the East River aggregation had "cleaned up all the amateur aggregations in the Fox River valley" the previous year.

The *Advocate* added an interesting note. "Fred Hulbert," it stated, "who for the past seasons has had charge of the interests of the city bunch, may be chosen for that position again this year but in case the matter is left open the North Siders will endeavor to defend the title." The nod was going to the East Rivers as the city team of record should Hulbert and his crew fail to take the field. And that's what happened. By default, the East Rivers ascended to the throne as the "city team."

Another contest that same Sunday, October 7, found the East Ends, a.k.a. East Divisions, defeating the Skidoos, 5–0. That game, at Hagemeister, was what the *Gazette* called a "very close and exciting game." While the *Advocate* reported a score of 6–0, the end result was the same. The *Advocate* continued its promotion of the Sorensens by suggesting that "the touchdown the East Ends got was a fluke." The ball had sailed over the head of Kelly, the Skidoos' quarterback, as he attempted to punt, and an east-sider had scooped it up and ran it in for a touchdown. The referee refused to allow the points, but the East Ends walked off declaring the game a victory for themselves. Somewhere along the way, that score was amended to a 0–0 tie for official purposes.

An item in the *Gazette* on Wednesday afternoon, October 10, promised more action from a new quarter when it boldly declared,

NEW ATHLETIC CLUB IS OUT WITH STRONG TEAM
West Side Young Men Organize Football Squad and Are After City Championship.

The West Side Athletics, a newly organized club, held a meeting last night and organized a football team. Jack McNerney was elected captain and Gordon Bent manager of the team. The team is strong and heavy, the average weight being about 150 pounds.

Mr. Bent will have the squad out for practice in a few days and will also send out several challenges to all the city and out of town teams, and all feel confident of winning the city championship this season.

McNerney had been a standout on the West High eleven of 1905, and Bent was involved in the sporting goods business.

Since there would be no "city team" that year, following the disaster that was the 1905 city team, matches between these neighborhood teams and aggregations were becoming increasingly common. On Friday, October 13, the East Ends left on an interurban car for a game against the Kaukauna team, accompanied by many Green Bay rooters. The Kaukauna team was expected to offer up a good match. Likewise, the Sorensen Skidoos had booked an away game with the Oconto city eleven, though that contest never occurred because the Oconto team could not get use of its home field.

By the end of October, things were becoming clearer for some of these teams. The Skidoos and the East Ends were squaring off for a third time to establish some bragging rights. They'd met twice before, once on October 7, in a game with a controverted ending, and again in the middle of the month, playing to a 0–0 tie. Once again, the *Advocate* pumped up the Sorensen boys, citing their hard practice and suggesting that they would play "for all there is." The fact that they hadn't won a game all season seemed secondary. But the paper did admonish its favorite sons with the warning that if the "East Ends are victorious with the two games that ended in a tie score they will be the same as three defeats."

While the *Gazette* might have called the game "close and exciting," it was another 0–0 tie. The two teams met a total of five times that year, and the East Ends won two of the five with the rest ending in a tie. The *Advocate* couldn't have been enthralled with its Cinderella adoptee. Happy with their mixed bag of success, the East Divisions now planned to end their season with a reception and dance on November 27 at Geyers Hall.

The Hillsides, meanwhile, had faced a "heavy" Saint Norbert eleven in what the *Advocate* called "one of the greatest contests of the year" on Sunday, October 28. The Hillsides were known to be a speedy and talented team representing the very proper locale of what is now the Astor Park area, much of which consisted of old money and established families. These guys often put more on the line on the gridiron than just some athletic derring-do. Savageau, a "thick-set" back for Saint Norbert, gave the Hillsides fits all afternoon. Despite the challenge, the Hill boys held on to the college lads for a 0–0 tie.

It was Sunday, November 18, before the Hillsides would extract a little revenge on the entire city of De Pere by defeating that city's Nicolet Stars 18–0. Flint was given serious credit for his line plunges for good gains. The *Advocate* suggested that the Hillsides demonstrated in the contest their "superiority over any team of its weight in the city." A couple of days later, rumors began to fly of a Thanksgiving Day rematch between the two teams.

While this picture is an aerial shot of City Stadium taken in 1931, it shows the rest of the hallowed ground where football was played in the early days in Titletown. At the right, East High School sits on the former site of Hagemeister Field. Above it, one can make out the outline of the baseball diamond at the Wisconsin-Illinois Baseball Park. Farther to the right sat the rest of old Washington Park. The waterway is the East River, from which the neighborhood team got their name. Photograph from the Stiller-Lefebvre Collection.

But the real news was the East Rivers. They'd been celebrated as Green Bay's "city team" ever since it was clear Hulbert was unavailable to rally a squad given his business interests. A benefit dance had been held for them at Geyers Hall on the north side on November 8 to raise some funds to cover traveling expenses. With obvious confidence in his eleven, the East Rivers' manager, William Meister, put them toe-to-toe with a superior team from Peshtigo three times that year. Unfortunately, against Peshtigo, the East Rivers would meet their match.

Traveling to Peshtigo by North Western Railroad, the East Rivers were, in the first game on October 28, "run off their feet in the first four minutes" said the *Gazette*. Peshtigo moved the ball down the field for a touchdown on their opening drive, but after that, the paper declared that the East Rivers were "the aggressors and clearly the better team." Unfortunately, several fumbles cost them the game. In the contest, they found themselves outweighed "by 10 pounds to the man."

Particular stars for the game were one of the Cunningham boys, either Wallie or Rollie, both players but not identified as to who was playing that game, and Eddie Mullemans, star of the Onwards team of 1905. "The former," acknowledged the *Gazette*, "accomplished two long quarterback runs and the former [sic] breaking up interference and circling the Peshtigo ends for long gains."

In reporting a return match set for Sunday, November 11, the *Gazette* wrote, "Tomorrow afternoon on the Hagemeister Park gridiron the Peshtigo team and a picked team from this city, composed of the East River aggregation and several other fast ones, will clash at 2:30 o'clock. It is the biggest match played this season on Sunday and a scrap worth going to see promises to develop when the elevens come together."

For that afternoon, bolstered with some of the best members of other intracity teams they'd faced that year, the East Rivers represented the 1906 Green Bay city team. Had they, by acclamation, actually become that? The *Green Bay Gazette* seemed to be saying so in their coverage of the game the following day. The article also brought Green Bay football enthusiasts up to date on the exploits of the intracity teams.

> *PESHTIGO TRIMMED IN SUNDAY CONTEST*
> *East Rivers Playing Under Title of Green Bay Team Win 10 to 0.*
> *Cunningham and Rothe Stars—Long Run by Former is One of the Features of Game—Hillside Boys Hold Heavy West Side Athletics.*
>
> *Playing under the name of Green Bay yesterday afternoon the East Rivers football team of the early part of the season defeated their Peshtigo rivals of two weeks ago by rolling up 10 points against them at Hagemeister Park. The visitors scored two points on a safety when their kicker sent the oval soaring into the air over the Green Bay goal line on the kick-off after the first touchdown was made. After much wrangling over the question of whether the score counted for Peshtigo the officials gave them the reason of the doubt.*
>
> *Rothe and Cunningham started for Green Bay and were in every play, both on offense and defense. They scored the touchdown, Cunningham's being made after a 45 yard run. Peshtigo attempted to punt on the 50 yard line and the kick was blocked by Rothe. Cunningham grabbed the pigskin and raced down the field, out-sprinting all the rivals who started after him.*
>
> *Rothe gave the large crowd of rooters their first encouragement by picking the ball up on the Peshtigo 5 yard line after a fumble and crossed the goal line. The touchdown came after 10 minutes of play in the first half.*
>
> *Hillsides Keep Up Enviable Record*
> *The Hillside boys, the team of 115 pounders which has not lost a game out of the five played this season, retained their place in the ranks of the undefeated by holding the heavy team of West Side Athletics to a 0 to 0 score*

at Saint James park yesterday. The contest was stubbornly fought from the opening kick-off until time was called at the close of the second half, and the lightweight Hillsides came off the field with all kinds of glory.

In their final meeting of the year, Sunday, November 25, in Peshtigo, the East Rivers confronted what the *Gazette* called a team that was "much too strong and heavy for them." Following the split results of the previous two contests, the game had come to be something of a cause for local football fans. On the day before the game, the *Gazette* had reported that "a large crowd of rooters is planning to go down on the noon train with the team." To their disappointment, Peshtigo won 16–0 probably because they had, according to the paper, "a few professional outsiders and their team averaged about 185 pounds to the local team average weight of which is about 155 pounds."

That game spelled the practical end for intracity play for the year, but a few minor football rumblings revolved around a proposed contest for East High School on Thanksgiving. According to pregame publicity, the East High eleven would face an alumni aggregation, "provided nothing in the line of a game can be closed by Manager Stevens with a high school football team in the state." The alumni game would feature many former high school stars returning home for the holidays as well as others who were making a name for themselves on the intracity teams.

The "dopesters" already have a team made up for the opposition forces and such stars as Beyer and DeBoth of Lawrence and Ripon respectively are on the list. Nolan of Ripon, "Eddie" McCeachron, the long distance runner and star end, "Zack" Taylor, the tall, scrappy center of two years ago, and Brunette, the slashing partner of "Freddie" Schneider two seasons back are down for positions. Besides, the above the possible choice would include Schilling, Kelly, Will Taylor, Elmore and Delaney.

The game, if played, would be held at about 10:00 or 10:30. However, such a game never materialized as East High went up against a highly touted squad from Menominee High School in Michigan. The final score was 16–0 in favor of Green Bay East, with many of the rumored alumni stars serving as referees. The game established East as one of the dominant secondary school squads in the area. The *Gazette* reported that the school was finding it increasingly difficult to schedule games with worthy opponents in the area. "Playing winning football every Saturday has its disadvantages," it suggested.

A smaller football note appeared over the first few days of November that year. Police officer John Pease, a stalwart of the Green Bay city team on and off for the previous 10 years, was seriously injured when he attempted to climb onto a three-ton chemical wagon as it left Hose Company No. 1. He fell and the hind wheel of the wagon crushed his left foot and right thigh. "It is thought," said the *Gazette*, "that it will not be necessary to do any amputation, as the bones were not broken."

The 1906 season was over without the slightest trace of a declared town team and an intracity team, the East Rivers, doing their best to fill the bill.

Any evidence a football historian can find of the existence of a city team in 1907 is not commonly available. As in several other years, the dreamy enthusiasm for such a team going into the year was high but was never realized, at least based on written materials including newspaper accounts from the *Green Bay Gazette*.

The season started off positively enough, with an account in the September 27 edition of the *Gazette* stating that "prospects are bright for a strong city team this fall and the team will be organized soon." The article tapped Wilson Charles, a former Carlisle Indian School athlete, as team captain and suggested that he "has agreed to take charge of the local players." It also suggested, once again, that Fred Hulbert, the man responsible for introducing football to Green Bay in 1895, had been approached by a number of the players "to act as manager of the team."

Of course Hulbert's name had been bandied about in 1906 as well and a town team did not magically appear as a result. By 1907, Hulbert, who had been with the Wm. Larson Canning Company since shortly after his arrival in Green Bay, had achieved tremendous stature in the young canning industry by being named superintendent and manager of the newly organized Green Bay Canning Company the previous May.

His progress in the industry had been steady. He had come to Green Bay as a single man on the verge of his future. From the Broadway House, he had moved to 211 North Oakland, just a football's throw from the practice field of the town teams of the 1890s, where he resided until 1902. In 1903, he was a foreman with the Larson Company and he'd moved his family, including wife, Lucille, and daughter, Virginia, to 806 Dousman Street, again, very near the old practice fields.

Now, in 1907, he was enjoying a young son, Fred McBean Hulbert, the middle name taken in very proper fashion from Lucille's family name. Fred Sr.'s prestigious position with the Green Bay Canning Company and the growth of his family prompted him to move once again, this time to 1535 Morrow Street on Green Bay's east side, not all that far from the old Washington Park. Certainly, Hulbert was a spectator at town team contests on Sunday afternoons at what was now Hagemeister Park or at the Wisconsin-Illinois ball grounds a football's throw to the southeast.

Rumors of Hulbert's involvement with the team must have caused resurgence in football interest in the city. He had been a star player and an able manager and organizer. On the heels of the recent disasters that had haunted the team, his name was a breath of fresh air and a promise of on- and off-field success. In that atmosphere, Charles said he hoped to secure a couple of crack players from Oneida, quite likely Tom Skenandore and Taylor Smith, as well as Ed McEachron, Wallie Cunningham, and Jonas Metoxen, who seemed to be more associated with the city than with the reservation. But Hulbert was sure he "could not give the time to the sport which such a position would demand." He did, however, promise to help the team in any other way he could.

Neenah had actually started off the football season in the middle of September by hurling a defi northward "for the championship of the state" to Green Bay teams in the 160-pound class. If it seemed a little premature to commence battle for a gridiron championship with the baseball season still burgeoning, the Neenah Cardinals' manager, Christensen, was foresighted enough to propose a series of three games, one in Neenah, one in Green Bay, and a deciding game in neutral territory.

On September 14, the *Gazette* bid a fond farewell to native son and football player extraordinaire, Charles Beyer, who headed off to Appleton to resume his studies and his football career at Lawrence University. Because of Beyer's role as captain and star of that university's aggregation, a game for the alleged Green Bay city team against Lawrence seemed a sure thing for Saturday, October 5. Indeed, the *Gazette* reported that the university eleven had already "agreed to play on that date," and it would be the only game that Lawrence would play outside its college regimen.

By 1907 the lines between high school and college and town team football were becoming increasingly distinct. The National Collegiate Athletic Association had been formed in the wake of President Roosevelt's football reform movement of 1905. Student athletes were at all costs to be kept from the rude clutches of the "tramp" athletes to which the town team movement had given rise. No longer would a talented player suit up for a contest with the local high school on Saturday morning, the college that afternoon, and the semipro team the next day. In the case of a Lawrence–Green Bay game, the line would be crossed only because of Beyer's presence on the team and the fact that a good gate could be guaranteed with the hometown connection exploited in pregame advertising. But the game was never played.

In preparation of the (soon-to-be-nonexistent) Lawrence contest, an article in the *Gazette* promised a town team meeting Saturday night at McGregor and Prinz's store "when the situation will be talked over and the organization formed" and pretty much left it at that.

In one breath, Green Bay saw the beginning and end of action for a town team in 1907. A search through the local newspapers for that year uncovers no further mention of any eleven representing the city. Like the year before, the prominent position that would have been filled by an official town team was to be occupied by a successful team from within the city's boundaries and organized mostly to play other intracity teams; the Sorensen Skidoos.

The Skidoos had been involved in Green Bay sports early on, and they were still around in the years just prior to the formation of the Packers. Indeed, Curly Lambeau hooked up with the Skidoos, captained by his old neighborhood buddy, Nate Abrams, for a benefit game when he returned to Green Bay after a brief stint at the University of Wisconsin–Madison in 1917.

The Sorensen Skidoos hadn't faired so well in 1906, and their ascension to the honorable place of "town team" would have struck some Green Bay football aficionados as dubious. They were, after all, a company team more than a neighborhood team like the East Rivers, who had filled the "town team" spot in 1906. But Sorensen was doing what many successful businessmen had done since football had become a community, rather than a college, cause célèbre in the 1890s. He realized that a team was advertising and that a good team was even better advertising.

"Tomorrow afternoon," began a September 28 *Gazette* article, "the first amateur football game of the season will take place when the Sorensen eleven will line up against the East Ends at the league ball grounds." The league ball grounds were the Wisconsin-Illinois ball grounds, surrounded by an imposing wooden fence and located at the very east end of Walnut Street, not that far from Hagemeister Park. "The Sorensen team," it continued, "has a very strong line-up this year the manager securing a number of former high school stars."

The report also suggested that the Sorensens had the Kaukauna city team in its sights for the following Sunday. In a subsequent article, it promoted a game between the Sorensens and the De Pere eleven for October 6. The interurban car, now an accepted mode of transportation from Green Bay to points south made such games a matter of course.

The Sorensen–East Ends matchup was hardly a barn burner. With a final score of 6–4 in favor of the Skidoos, it was a contest mostly characterized by neither team having "the better of the argument." The Sorensens had mostly won on a drop kick for four points in the first half, and fans had been left to wait out the yawner the rest of regulation.

An item from the October 12 *Green Bay Semi-Weekly Gazette* had to snatch the eye of sports haters and lovers alike. "Beware the Game of Ball on Sunday," it screamed, and the Reverend J. B. Davidson of Milwaukee took it from there. According to this illustrious holy man, "nine-tenths of the criminals now confined in the various prisons of the land took their first downward step by attending baseball games on Sunday." The rest of the Baptist ministers at the annual convention in Beer City must have flooded the hall with "amens" of approval at that proclamation.

Want to Feel the Glory?

Visit these Green Bay area sites to see where some early football action took place.

Southwest corner of Oakland and Dousman—practice site in the 1890s.

The east side of Fort Howard Elementary Grounds along Chestnut Street—practice site of earliest teams.

Union Park (now Tank Park)—early intracity game site.

Whitney Park—oldest city park, site of football exploits of the young Curly Lambeau.

The northeast corner of Washington and Doty Streets in downtown Green Bay—practice site in the 1890s.

Webster Avenue Park (now site of Allouez Village Hall)—early game site where the first forward pass (illegal at the time) in the city was thrown and allowed to stand by a hometown ref.

White City—located on the east side of Irwin Street just past Eastman Avenue, site of as many as three contests on a Sunday.

Washington Park, Hagemeister Park, the Wisconsin-Illinois Baseball Grounds, and Old City Stadium—site of most of the great contests of the town team era, especially against teams from other towns.

Seymour Park, "The Cow Pasture"—west side of Ashland Avenue along School Place, once the practice field behind what was then West High School and site of many intracity contests.

Saint James Park—site of intracity contests, including the very first game between two neighborhood teams.

Saint Norbert College—flat expanse between Main Hall and Ray Van Den Heuvel Family Campus Center, early site of many town team and college games.

Bellevue Park—located behind present-day McDonald's at 1609 Main Street, site of Packer games in 1923 and 1924 while City Stadium was being built. It was actually a baseball park.

Packer Practice Field near Indian Packing Company—near parking lot on the southwest corner of Morrow and Henry Streets, practice site for Lambeau and crew.

VFW Park—on De Pere's west side, early practice and game site for De Pere elevens.

Zegers Field—in area behind Kegler's Klub, 3900 block of Webster Avenue, site of many Green Bay, Allouez, and De Pere contests.

While Green Bay continued to struggle to field a city team that fall, chances were that it wasn't just to keep the good lads of Titletown out of prison. Football action was taking place in the city, though with no sign of a town team. On Saturday, October 23, the Green Bay Business College eleven defeated the Saint Norbert College team 6–4 on the Saint Norbert campus. The week before, Saint Norbert lost decisively to the Menasha High School team 17–2. Forward passes had resulted in two of Menasha's touchdowns, and a fumble had offered the third. The college team was composed, said the *Gazette*, "of all new recruits."

A game with Peshtigo was bandied about at football discussions over the next couple of weeks. The Skidoos were slated to travel to the northern city by train on Sunday, October 27, taking a 2 and 0 record with them. The *Semi-Weekly Gazette* was not happy with that simple fact, however, saying, "This is the third game the south side team has played this season and they expect to come home with another scalp dangling from their belts."

Within a month, the Saint Norbert team had improved a lot and, on the heels of a victory over the Peshtigo team, laid claim "to the championship of this part of the state for a prep school." A contest with Saint John's Military Academy of Delafield was proposed for Thanksgiving Day. Saint Norbert actually ended up facing De Pere High School on Turkey Day and getting whipped 28–0.

A Saint Norbert claim to a title of any kind might have caused a few snickers because their record stood at 3 and 3. Nonetheless, such a claim appeared in the pages of the *Semi-Weekly Gazette* on December 4. They could, however, reasonably claim tremendous improvement over the season as Will McNerney, a former football star at West High School and a player destined for greatness on the late city teams, had guided a raw bunch of recruits toward some gridiron success.

Just a couple of weeks later, on Friday, November 8, an undefeated East High School aggregation traveled to Milwaukee, accompanied by what the *Gazette* called "a goodly delegation of rooters from both sides of the river" to face East Division High School. Green Bay East had, according to the article, "perfected to a nicety" the newly legalized forward pass. While they lost that battle by a clear-cut 35–5, one name emerged from the East highlights, Merrill Hoeffel, who "played phenomenal ball." Many of the fans who accompanied the East High eleven were also able to catch a Marquette University–Ripon College contest held in Milwaukee on the same day.

Back at home, the flames of a cross-town rivalry continued to be fanned, with a defi from East High to West High School in the offing. Of additional interest to local football enthusiasts was the upcoming Ripon-Lawrence match, which would involve three former Green Bay high school stars. Beyer, captain of the Lawrence team, was an old member of the East team just after the turn of the century. Also, Louis Klaus and Nick Keyser, former West High standouts, were on the Lawrence and Ripon squads, respectively. Many fans planned to travel by train to see the game.

Wilson Charles had resurfaced as coach of the West High team. At a practice on Tuesday, November 12, the Gazette observed that a "number of new trick plays which are just fresh from the east were tried." "Charles," the paper added, "has a number of other plays which are being used by the Carlisle football team," and he would be drilling the team in the YMCA gymnasium on Chestnut Street. The timing was perfect as a defi was hurled across the river by East High the next day. A clause in the contract that would seal the game stated that the cross-town games would become an annual affair. The game would take place Thanksgiving Day.

Caspian—Iron Heads, Iron Hands, Iron Hearts

When it comes time to talk about football being a brutal game, a couple of stories from Joe Canale, a colorful member of the 1931 Red Helmets of Caspian, Michigan, are appropriate. According to Canale, teammate George Cederna once remarked after a particularly brutal play, "I like this game, you can hit a guy and not be put in jail for it."

Another bit of color, mostly red, from the Red Helmets' 1931 season came at the expense of Geno Compana. Compana was a standout at Michigan Tech, who traveled the 100-plus miles south from Houghton to Caspian for every game. In a contest against Bessemer, a rival U. P. city, Compana was decked by an opposing lineman in the midst of the scrum. He didn't like it. He got up with vengeful intentions. But before he could retaliate, the referee ejected him from the game. He didn't like that either. According to Canale, the language he used in communicating his displeasure to the ref was tinged with blue. The referee wasn't interested in hearing Compana's complaint, so he hauled off and cracked Compana himself. The result was a black eye, a trip to the local doctor, and a story that remains part of Red Helmet lore.

Football news of 1907 ended abruptly with the *Gazette*'s extensive report on the Thanksgiving Day game between the city's two high schools. The final score was 11–0, with East continuing its dominance over the west-siders.

In a grizzly article on November 30, the *Green Bay Review* presented the annual death tally for football. This year had fallen a bit short. "Gridiron Season Comes Within One of Equaling Last Year's Record," the subhead read. Was there some disappointment in that? The report went on to give something akin to a box score, the death and injury results from 1901 through 1907.

In this period, 101 football deaths and over a thousand injuries had been tallied. The report was incomplete, it said, because the 1907 season wasn't over. It must have been crucial to get the news out rather than wait for final results. Injuries included broken legs, arms, noses, jaws, and skulls. Collarbones seemed to take a particular beating, and the number of dislocated shoulders was significant.

Throw in a few torn ligaments and random concussions, and the football critics had more fodder for their attack.

The article ran some commentary that mostly fueled the argument for further jostling of football's rules and equipment. "The revised rules of the game," it said, "have not fulfilled the hopes of their framers. While the deadly mass plays have been eliminated they have been succeeded by evolutions in which the speed and combination plays have proved almost as hazardous to the antagonists." Finally, it related that the mayor of Columbus, Indiana, had banned all forms of the sport following the gridiron death of Earl Ruddell.

The game of football continued to be lambasted during the first decade of the twentieth century, not just because it led young men directly to prison, but because it remained brutal, despite being tweaked from time to time in an effort to promote safety for its practitioners. But, to put things into perspective, it should be noted that, while football was averaging about 14 deaths per season, the country was witnessing about 86 lynchings per year. One might claim that football was corrupting America's youth and keeping them from experiencing the full-blown glory of a public execution.

The question on every Green Bay football enthusiast's lips was simple, and it wasn't whether football was a dangerous sport or whether dead men were well hanged: would 1908 finally see the return of a bona fide town team organized as such and fielded to defend the honor of Green Bay and nothing else?

1908

FOOTBALL AS ADVERTISED

Green Bay did not have an official city team of record in 1908 either. William Sorensen & Company again sponsored the Skidoos, and that aggregation, if press accounts from the day can be believed, was, as in 1907, as close as Titletown, USA, got to sporting a town team that year. That eleven was slated to travel by North Western Railroad to play the perennially tough Peshtigo crew on Sunday, October 4. The Skidoo team, said the *Gazette*, "is in good condition and it is expected they will put up a strong game." The team's manager, Edward L. Meulemans, who lived just two blocks south of Sorensen's company, was also looking for games against other amateur teams in Green Bay as well as neighboring communities.

Players of some significance appeared on the team's roster, including Nichols, center; Collins and Kelly, guards; Koske and Russell, tackles; Scannell and Nelson, ends; Merkel and Meulemans, halves; Martel, full; and Thompson, quarterback.

The contest against Peshtigo wasn't a great way to open the 1908 campaign. While the Sorensen team lost 6–0, it kept the ball in Peshtigo's territory most of the second half.

Other action on the football front was the Green Bay Business College, which played the Kewaunee team to a scoreless tie in the lakeshore town on Saturday, October 24. The game was characterized by an unusually slippery field that, according to the *Gazette*, "did not allow the playing of the forward pass successfully or trick plays."

The following day, Sunday, October 25, a new intracity team, the Nighthawks, battled the Jolly Eleven of Appleton to a 0–0 tie. Field conditions were, again, a factor, and the newspaper report stated that "fast playing was impossible."

Peshtigo wreaked havoc on another amateur Green Bay team, the East Rivers, the following Sunday, November 1. It was the first time the East Rivers, who for all

Nobody Got Rich

In the early town team days, player contracts were nothing but a handshake. Heck, if an agent had shown up to represent a guy, he would have quickly been put to work selling tickets at the gate. Sometimes the biggest job as a manager was keeping the players in the huddle as they shelled out their own hard-earned cash to cover personal expenses. Frank Shepich, player and manager for the Stambaugh All-Stars, recalled some of the "fringe benefits" of playing the town team game:

> Nobody was ever paid. I shouldn't say that. But all the local guys were not paid. Everybody played for nothing. They used to charge a dollar to go and see the ball game. The ball game was back of the school where the airport is now and all they had around there was a single cable [to keep the crowd back]. And everybody who came there paid a buck. The remodeled school was where we used to change and we walked from the school down to the field. At the back end of the school is where the locker rooms were and everybody would walk down to the field on a gravel road.

While Shepich and his teammates were busy warming up for the contest, some of those who were supposed to pay the buck were busy sneaking in. The stories of "sneaking in" are warm, humorous, and somewhat romantic, but each occurrence was also a small nail in the coffin of town team football. Nobody really begrudged the kids who didn't have any money, but what about the tight-fisted adults who were merely looking to "buck" the system?

At halftime, some of these same bootleggers would gather around the team as they circled up to strategize their next moves. They were adoring fans all right. They were also counting their good fortune of seeing the contest for free. What they didn't realize is that their lack of upright activity at the gate would eventually jeopardize the whole thing.

Meanwhile, said Shepich, the home team could occasionally enjoy some of the fruit of their labors. "They used to bring oranges and lemons for halftime for the guys, you know," he said. He told of at least one teammate who "wasn't that good a football player," and, it was rumored, only played for that orange.

intents and purposes had served as Green Bay's city team in 1906, had ventured out of the city in 1908. The final score was predictable, given the usual size advantage for Peshtigo.

The *Gazette* also updated fans on intracity play with a couple of items following the report on the East River contest. The Nighthawk's manager, Al Scofield, a doorkeeper at the Grand Theater, was looking for games against other intracity teams, especially the Sorensen Skidoos. The Skidoos committed that most grievous of football sins on Sunday afternoon when they failed to show up for a game against the Nighthawks.

Another amateur team, the Unions, defeated the Manders on Saturday afternoon by a score of 4–0 as a result of a drop kick booted with just minutes left in the contest. The Manders had sprung up in Allouez just a couple of years before. The Manders family lived adjacent to Zegers Field, a leveled piece of ground on John Zegers's 40-acre parcel and often referred to as the "Allouez grounds" in those days.

On Monday, November 9, the *Gazette* reported that the Nighthawks had been defeated by the East Rivers at the Allouez grounds by the decisive score of 22–0. It seemed apparent that the East Rivers, who had done at least a journeyman's job as an ad hoc town team in 1906, might again carry off the city championship.

While the light was pretty dim for Green Bay football in 1908, action on the gridiron was plenty hot in other locales. Stambaugh, Michigan, put together a team that, at season's end, was hailed as "Champions of Menominee Range"; as such, their visage graced the cover of the Champions cigar box (shown here), sold by Marshall and Curley. Photograph obtained from and used with permission of Frank Shepich and Harold Anderson, Stambaugh, Michigan.

Already in early November the heat was turned up on what had become the annual Thanksgiving Day game between East and West High Schools. The game was scheduled for 3:00, and, for the first time since the start of the series, it was tough to project East as the obvious winner. For the rest of the month, the paper had little coverage on football of any kind. There was no town team, intracity competition had closed, and the looming East-West match, still several weeks away, was about all the football there was.

Finally, Thanksgiving Day arrived. The game between the two schools was so close that the *Gazette* could begin its wrap-up article by citing just one player. "To Frank McGrath," it began, "chiefly through his ability to kick and to run his team on the field, is due the victory for East High School over West High yesterday in the annual Thanksgiving day football contest." The teams had been evenly matched, the game hard fought and the score, 4–0, bore it out.

Green Bay football in 1908 had concluded. It was probably the bleakest year to date for town team football in Titletown, USA.

1909

WHICH WAY TO WHITE CITY?

Thanks in large measure to an enthusiastic reporter from Green Bay's neighboring city to the south, the football news of 1909 was all about De Pere. Once again, Green Bay had plenty of football action at the high school and amateur levels but absolutely no declared town team.

The last year a town team had been truly active was 1905, under the management of Charles "Tod" Burns, and that year was fraught with difficulties. The most recent year the city had seen a team that was successful both on and off the field was 1903, when it won a regional championship. Its 1904 campaign had been a mixed bag with lots of media and popular attention but an anemic record of 2-4-1.

The only football news of 1909 centered on amateur, intracity teams like the Hillside Boys, the East Rivers, and the Nighthawks. While the East Rivers had hung tough in the football wars since 1899 and rose to the level of town team in 1905 and 1906, the Hillsides had been around in one version or another since 1902. The Nighthawks were relative newcomers, first appearing on the Green Bay gridiron scene in 1908.

Even newer to Green Bay's football lineup in 1909 was a team hailing from a playing field on the northeast side of town, popularly known as White City. White City Park, as it was known, was an amazing center of activity for baseball, football, and family outings, including circuses and carnivals. It was located in the Preble area just north of the railroad tracks along Eastman Avenue on what would become Irwin Street when the area was annexed to the city of Green Bay in 1964. White City would, for a stretch of about a decade, offer as many as three football games on a given Sunday. Best of all, it was easy access.

The late Norbert "Nubs" Pigeon, lifelong resident of Green Bay and patriarch of one serious family of Packer fans, recalled going to sporting events at the White City grounds with his uncle and his brother. One of the most striking images

Pigeon recalled from a White City excursion was the wild streetcar ride. The street-car was "open" and ran out to Bay Beach. According to Pigeon, it would stop at the White City track to let football and baseball fans unload. But it was the ride itself that struck Pigeon as the real fun. "There would be a conductor at the front and the back collecting fares," he said, "and the car would stop at railroad crossings. But people would be hanging on like in San Francisco."

Pigeon, born in 1908, and his good friend, Ray Drossart, also deceased, could tell many great stories about growing up in the area as kids. The bay of Green Bay seemed to be a special focal point of their fun. In the summer, of course, there was swimming. In the winter, it was pretty common to find them ice skating from the Reber Street locale all the way out to the bay in the frozen ditches along Irwin Street. There, they met up with the residents of "Muskrat City," an impromptu commune of "little huts on the ice."

Drossart, a young entrepreneur, told the story of a buddy and him making a little money off of wayward men. "There were whorehouses over there," Drossart said, "and guys would come out of there and they didn't want to stick around when they were done. In the winter, my friend and I would be waiting out there with shovels and we'd shovel the guy out and he'd slip us a couple of bits and head out of there. Then we'd throw the snow back into the parking place for the next guy."

Across the street from the ball grounds was Belgian Pete's tavern, otherwise known as the White City Tavern, run by Pete Lagers. Belgian Pete's was the scene of many celebrated victories and drowned sorrows by sports fan and ball player alike. And it was just a short walk across the street back to White City Park to reconnect with the family to catch the careening streetcar back home.

Pigeon and Drossart recalled that the White City area, including the ball grounds, was about six blocks long. Today, the former White City ball grounds are marked off by Irwin Street on the west, Berner Street on the north, Baird Street on the East, and Reber Street on the south.

In a year's time, football interest between the downtown and Bay Beach area had reached such a fevered pitch that White City would field a first and second eleven. Like the East Rivers in 1906, the White City teams quickly assumed, by their own scheduling, persistence, and success, the role of "town team," representing all of Green Bay against the opposition.

The Nighthawks were planning their season opener at the league ball grounds against a fast Kaukauna eleven on Sunday, October 21. The Nighthawk roster had changed little since the team had appeared on the scene a year earlier. Meanwhile, a "double-header" was announced for the same day on the White City grounds. In the first game at 2:00 p.m., the East Rivers would face the west-siders. An hour and a half later, the East Rivers would take to the field again to face the Hillsides.

This "action" photo of the 1909 Stambaugh city team was likely taken on the level ground down the hill from West Iron County High School, now an airport. This was the field on which the Green Bay Packers played the Stambaugh All-Stars in 1919. Photograph obtained from and used with permission of Frank Shepich and Harold Anderson, Stambaugh, Michigan.

Related football news came in late October with an account of a game between Carroll College and the Oshkosh Normal School, in which three Green Bay lads, Emerson R. Grebel, Walter Spooner, and Clarence Peterson, figured prominently for Carroll.

Throughout the year, the *Gazette* carried coverage of noteworthy college contests with a wire service blurb and some photographs. One such feature would have snared the eye of Green Bay football fans who understood the "Carlisle connection" that had figured so prominently in the success of Green Bay's first town teams. At least five Oneida Indians had contributed mightily to the success of those teams: Tom Skenandore, Taylor Smith, Jonas Metoxen, Martin Wheelock, and Wilson Charles.

Above the pictures of the Carlisle and Penn State stars the print read,

SOME PENN. AND CARLISLE GLADIATORS AND
FOOTBALL SCENE
    Philadelphia, Nov. 1—These are the days when every corner lot in all this broad land has its dust begrimed [by] squad[s] of budding football kings rolling one another in tangled heaps to the resounding yells of the coaches and the short, sharp, military-like signals of the captains. Tens of thousands of sturdy youths, filled with the pride of strength, are at the good, husky game, the very dangers of which are responsible for most of its popularity. The broad chested, bowlegged gladiator of the gridiron is king today, and he will continue to reign until the Thanksgiving turkey is a pile of bones.

This was sportswriting at its best! The only loser in these gridiron masterpieces was the turkey.

BEFORE THEY WERE THE PACKERS

On Sunday, October 31, another doubleheader was held at the White City grounds. The first White City eleven defeated the west-siders 5–0. The second White City squad took it on the nose, courtesy of the Hillsides, by the same score.

Though the paper did not report it, it could only be assumed that the day's standard admission of a quarter dollar was being charged at the gate for the weekly "football tournaments" held at the White City grounds. For the youngsters, it was likely the rule of the day: "Sneak in if you can, kid, or hand the man your nickel." Someone had seen the opportunity to bring football players, games, and fans together in one locale. The male members of the family could likely jump off the car at White City to enjoy some rough action, and the ladies, at least in the early autumn, could continue on to Bay Beach for an afternoon of "more appropriate" entertainment.

The following Sunday, November 7, a whopping three games were slated. The second White City team would face the Britton Cooperage employees in the first game in the morning. The D. W. Britton Cooperage Company was located on North Monroe and was primarily managed by the Ellis family. After lunch, the first White City team would play Saint Norbert College, and, an hour and a half later, the East Rivers would line up against the west-siders. In promoting the contests, the *Gazette* said the teams were "all in fine form and some very fast playing is sure to be witnessed by all enthusiasts who attend." The East Rivers, continuing on their

Kaukauna—"Rubbed" the Wrong Way

Kaukauna may well have had the earliest town team to take to the field in northeastern Wisconsin, as early as 1893. That date, two years before Green Bay saw its first football team, suggests that some Kaukauna boy learned the game at one of the area colleges and hauled it home with him.

Bert Fargo, a longtime Kaukauna furniture dealer, recalled that the team had some high school guys but was more a town team since the high school wasn't about to sanction the violent sport—at least, not yet. Besides the students, Fargo remembered, it also had a "few 'ringers' or non-students on the roster." Early games were likely played at Klein Park, located off of Park Street next to the railroad shops, or at Eden Park located just to the west. Not much record of these games exists.

It wasn't long before Kaukauna became a regular participant in the football skirmishes raging up and down the railroad line running from Menominee, Michigan, through Green Bay and down to Fond du Lac.

It was just before a Sunday, November 13, 1904, contest that the Kaukauna team's manager conveyed a curious threat to the Green Bay football players: "We will give you fellows the hardest rub you ever experienced." The rub turned out to be more of a caress as the Kaukaunans ended up losing 25–0. The rubbing ended because of darkness, and both teams were cited for "lackluster play" in a scrap "almost entirely devoid of the finer points of the game." Ah, there's the rub.

path of success, had been victorious in all their contests that season, and it was clear why they were in the featured game.

The Nighthawks continued to play outside of the double- and triple-game format at the White City grounds and lost to a veteran Kaukauna city team on Sunday, November 7, 16–0. Four of their regular players had not made the trip.

In De Pere, what was proposed to be a strong team at the beginning of the season conducted an ongoing squabble with a tough Kaukauna city team throughout that fall. At a meeting on September 26, the De Pere team had selected Joseph Neubauer as captain and Ervin Walsh as manager.

The De Peres lost to the Nighthawks at the Saint Norbert College field located between the Priory and Van Dyke Hall on Sunday, October 3, and braced themselves for a game against Kaukauna. They lost that contest 5–0. That was followed by another loss to Kaukauna, 6–0, at Kaukauna two weeks later. Another two weeks later, a "picked eleven" of west-side De Pere football players took on and defeated the Jolly Rippers of Kaukauna 18–0.

A report in the "De Pere Department" of the *Gazette* on Saturday, November 6, declared that a group of "east side players" were forming for a fight with the Kaukauna team the following day, but such a game never seemed to materialize.

The De Pere team's season seems to have ended with a victory in front of a large crowd on the grounds of Saint Norbert College over one of the White City teams. That same day, the De Pere "Juniors" were headed to Kaukauna to face the Jolly Rippers in a rematch.

Kaukauna also threw its hat into the ring against the East River football team on November 14 while the second White City team battled the Britton Cooperage team to a second tie in as many contests between them.

The last game recorded in the *Gazette* for that season was played on Sunday, November 21, at the White City grounds between the East Rivers and one of the White City elevens. The final score was 11–0 in favor of White City. A game was projected between the White City team and Appleton for Thanksgiving Day, but no record of such a game exists.

Just like that, the football season for 1909 was over. Just like the 1906, 1907, and 1908 seasons before it, the 1909 season saw lots of bodies flying about on the gridiron but no sign of a town team representing the city at the southern tip of the bay. With the growing number of outstanding footballers graduating from the city's two high schools and the number of earlier stars returning from their years at college, perhaps 1910 would be the year.

HALFTIME

AN OLD-FASHIONED, LINE-SMASHING GRIDIRION ARGUMENT (OR, A WORK OF WHIMSY IN THE MANNER OF THE SPORTSWRITING OF THE TIME)

In the days before radio broadcasts, ESPN, and instant updates on the Internet, there was the sportswriter. He (in those days, it was always a "he") often served as the only conduit to what happened at the game. Without videotape or instant replay, these scribes needed a sharp eye for detail and a great memory. With those skills came an uncanny knack of describing the highs and lows of a sports contest. But the influence of sportswriters didn't just begin *and end there. In the town-team days, they wore a couple of different fedoras.*

In the preseason, around mid-September, there was the opportunity for a little hype to help get a team together. The sportswriter became part snake-oil salesman, part agent, and part bandleader. A little drumbeating and a mention of the potential greatness of the boys on the field were standard items of the sports page.

Managers, players, and sportswriters long shared a marriage of convenience and mutual support: no team, no sports story. That idea was played out in the Packer legend with the Hungry Five and sportswriter George Calhoun. It existed in Stambaugh, Menominee, Niagara, and every small town when a crew of able-bodied athletes suddenly became of one mind and declared, "Let's get a team together."

Once a sufficient local "frenzy" was attained and several practices held, it was time to get serious. Letters would circulate, and the sportswriter would add to the excitement. In the gentlest way possible, a team could hang out its shingle with a short letter in the paper: "Team of approximately 130 pounds looking for other teams of similar build. Call Cookie at 2231." If that didn't attract attention, the newspaper would throw down a "defi," a formal—and far more strongly worded—challenge flung at the feet of opposing teams, local or otherwise: "The Midville

Monsters challenge the Eleven from Kidney Pie Junction for fifty dollars, a bag of donuts, and a bottle of rot gut."

These challenges would be accepted or ignored depending on the temperament of the target. If an interested or at least easily riled team was in the crosshairs, a flurry of correspondence would ensue on the pages of the local paper: "The Junction accepts the Midville lads' offer, but has the following changes to the original bet, the stake should be a more manly one hundred dollars, as well as the gate, and a case of the town's best rot gut." Exchanges of such sentiments would either go on for several weeks, turn into a game that Sunday, or disappear without a trace.

Controversy, always an attention grabber, served a double purpose: it sold papers and created conversation. It might take the form of a star player changing teams. Perhaps it involved the importation of players from a distant city. The scuttlebutt could be about the ref's bad call, or help from the sidelines (as in the infamous 1919 Green Bay–Beloit affair refereed by Baldy Zabel). Of course like most rumormongering, the majority of it was false and often as transparent as a ghost.

One of the kings of that sportswriting era was a cigar-chomping hooligan by the name of George Whitney Calhoun. From the pages of the *Green Bay Press-Gazette*, his poison pen could taunt an opposing team into action, and his gentle stroke could cull fans into showing up at a benefit game ("Pass the hat boys, dig deep") He was the mouthpiece that helped launch the Packers in their earliest rendition, not with his on-field antics but with those powerful instruments: ink and paper.

The sportswriting of that era was laden with galvanizing phrases, most of which have been lost in this day and age. Today, the sports pages are full of quarterback ratings, yards per carry, the number of third downs converted in hailstorms during October on the road with "Purple Haze" playing in the background. The writing has become focused on the numbers produced by the performance, not on the actual performance.

In those days, statistics were included only to further the story: "Metwold scooted about the left end for a 20-yard gain." It was about the day, the crowd, the players, the deeds, the feel of the warmly contested affair. "Aggregation," "gridiron argument," "the eleven," "reversal," "old-fashioned-line-smashing gridiron war"— all of these phrases added color and texture to the game. Dazzling plays were few and far between, given the style of play in the era. Most plays ended up as "a bunch of players in a pile on the ground." It was quite likely that a lineman with a particularly bruising style of play would draw more attention than a back who spent all day butting his head against the opposition. At best, a player would be termed a "star" or was said to have "worn the laurels." Unlike today, the quarterback only called the signals and rarely touched the ball. Kicking the ball was the name of the game, literally. Field position became the key to winning the contest. As a result, kicking—both drop-kicking and punting—became a key strategy, and descriptions of the artistry of this or that kicker gave the sportswriter even more reason for poetry. The forward pass was in its infancy, and smash mouth was the game plan.

Readers could count on any plays by the local team to be heroic, while success by the opposition was unusual, borderline legal, or freakish ("A circus play netted the opponents a thirty-yard gain"). The local boys, friends, and families bought papers, so it was a good idea to paint the team in the best colors possible. Instead of the derogatory "A three-yard flop occurred on first down," the local scribe would look on the bright side: "A cross buck succeeded for positive yardage."

Readers who were not at the game could relive it with a glance at the article. They did not have to understand the nuances and mechanics of the game to enjoy the tale: the sportswriter put them there. While it is true that the average game may have had only a handful of truly exciting plays, the writer could always conjure up a few extra colorful plays, as space permitted.

And finally, there were the men of the grid, those players who risked life and limb for the glory of the local citizenry, whether they were fresh-faced youth in a friendly pickup game after school or a cadre of battle-fatigued football veterans returning from a donnybrook up the railroad line. The sportswriter knew that it was the theatrics of these individual players that sold the local rag. "Tank Jones played a whale of a game" was a phrase capable of selling five copies of the daily, while "The boys gave it their all" might sell three.

So here's to the wizards of the sports desk and the way they used to spin their stories. In their honor, the following tale is told. It's a bit of tomfoolery—and entirely fictional—but a thread of reality runs through the whole.

—*Carl Hanson*

Two football behemoths, the established Armbruster Athletic Club managed by Jules Kincaid, right-hand man of Taylor Armbruster himself, and the newcomer Cantorville Professionals were spoiling for a showdown. Kincaid had been hiring men "seasonally" for several years to help out with work at the canning factory and lumberyard, and the football teams rarely lost as a result. "Mass transit" wasn't just how the cans got to your pantry, but also described the players on the gridiron. They played old-time, knuckle-bruising, calamitous football and won often.

The Cantorville team was a contrast, not in size—because let's face it, no one played this brand of ball at 120 pounds—but in style. Cantorville had to pull together to get its team uniformed, on the road, and ready for a fight. The dances, passing the hat, and donations of local businessmen usually got them from game to game financially—there was no "Old Man Armbruster" filling the coffers. The result was that no one called the shots for the Cantorville team. They played a wide-open game; if they had read or heard about a play, it was worked into the game plan. Their passing was crude but usually shocked the average football neophyte. Big lads were necessary, but coordination came at a premium.

Both teams cut a swath through the opposition the whole year. The Armbruster crew had taken it to five area teams in rapid succession over the previous weeks. They had put the clamps on the Seedyville Stars 28–12 and the Northfield Cardinals 12–6. They also went undefeated and unscored-upon at home against the Bonita Bulldogs, the Iron City Tigers, and Cantorville's own archnemesis, the Jones Siding Polar Bears. Meanwhile, the Cantorville eleven had shut out every team they encountered, amassing a collective tally of 142 points to 0 over six games.

The defi from the Armbruster A. C. was as inevitable as the 5:00 whistle. According to the Cantorville Voice,

> *Cantorville Football Team:*
>
> *Your team has experienced a reasonably good season and has completed it with an unblemished record. The Armbruster Athletic Club would invite you to play a game against our championship caliber team. The game would be played at Armbruster Field on Thursday, November 25th at 1:00 p.m. We would consider this game as the Midwest Championship, and would like to also play for a side bet of $500. If the sum is not to your satisfaction we could also just play for the championship honors. We eagerly await your response.*
>
> *Sincerely,*
>
> *Jules Kincaid*
> *Manager Armbruster Athletic Club*

Amid the understandable fervor that arose from this letter, the Cantorville eleven fired off this reply (which was printed in the *McRenn County Traveler*).

> *Armbruster Footballers:*
>
> *The Cantorville faithful will meet your aggregation on your said date, at your said time, for the said Championship. We would like to raise the bet to $1000 and feel our money is completely safe. As you well know, we have not allowed a team any kind of success this season. We demand that one of our own will help to referee the match and that another lad helps to keep time. We also ask that the field be kept free of spectators, as we know of the reputation of games played at Armbruster Field. If you meet our requirements, we will be at the field and ready. Finally we want travel expenses and lodging to be paid out of the gate receipts.*
>
> *The Cantorville Professionals*

Terms given, terms accepted. It was time to play some football. Lineups circulated in each town and posters were created with the men's names emblazoned on them. The lists were as follows:

Cantorville		Armbruster A. C.
Deke Stoffard	right end	"Chute" Browers
Mort Ranford	right tackle	Myron Tucker
Guisseppi Renzeti	right guard	Hamilton Davis
Stan Mahlman	center	Cornelius Watson
Chap Paulson	left guard	Hermann Stebbins
John Paulson	left tackle	Zechariah Holm
Hannimal Filler	left end	Liam "Mick" McInty
Stewart Brown	fullback	"Fat" Lucas
Lincoln Pinauld	left halfback	Ben Wheaton
Mats Kynnenin	right halfback	Hjalmer Konkus
Joseph Stein	quarterback	Sam Alversin

Substitutes
Cantorville: Adrenziak, Penn, Watters
A.A.C.: Jackson, Menke, Torunsin, Palmer, Young, Truffeaux

After a rail journey for the Pride of Cantorville, the Pros arrived in plenty of time to ready themselves for the affair to come. The team and a following of several hundred fans were greeted by Armbruster himself. He led the boys to their hotel and made arrangements for the banquet that was to follow the game. (Taylor Armbruster may have been considered a tyrant in business, but he did know how to take care of a guest.) The lads were shown to their rooms and given some time to rest before the big contest.

About town, some of the rooters were drumming up bets at the town's watering holes and getting as many bets as they could put up money for.

At the ball park the usual pregame rituals were performed, including a bit of loosening up. Pigskins filled the air, propelled by leg or arm muscle, with the best attempts being made to snag them out of the atmosphere. It was apparent that the size advantage was definitely in Armbruster's favor. Surprisingly, the Cantorville squad brought more players to the affair, a solid 16. Armbruster had only 14 beefy men in togs for the game. Of course, to look at the two teams sizewise, it seemed as if Armbruster had more.

Around the park, concessions were sold, mostly coffee and hot cider to warm you and doughnuts and candy bars to fill the empty spaces. The hosts were even kind enough to pass hot coffee gratis to the press squad, a gesture that did not go unnoticed.

ADVENT OF THE NEW HERO.

In the locker rooms of the Cantorville Pros and Armbruster A.C. (as well as in many real football locales), cartoons like these would appear from time to time, taunting the practitioners of baseball with the warning to "get out of the way" before the football season came down upon them. Obtained from the *Green Bay Review*, October 20, 1896.

The table was set, and the football-hungry were about to feast. The whistle blew at 2:00, and the kickoff boomed downfield soon thereafter.

After returning the kickoff to much noise but little forward progress, the Armbruster elite straightened their pads and made ready for war. It was an old-style drive. Armbruster's mammoth backs took turns battering the smaller secondary for 10-yard gains. A long, brutal, smashing campaign culminated in a score for the Armbruster squad. "Fat" Lucas proved his skill in moving the ball downfield with relative ease, courtesy of his immense bulk. After pushing the ball across, they missed the point after. It was going to be a long day for kickers.

The Cantorville drive met with limited success. After fruitless attempts at battering through the line, resulting in the loss of one back, Mats Kynnenin, the Professionals exploited the angles instead. Using end runs and exploiting the pass, the Cantorville sports reached midfield. At that point the drive stalled.

A monstrous punt by Pinauld pinned the Armbruster crew deep in their territory. After three dusty collisions, a booming punt left the ball at the Cantorville 40-yard line.

Cantorville moved the ball with some nifty misdirection plays. Pinauld was again up to task, making tacklers miss and providing expert interference when he did not hold the ball. On one play, he even dodged the leg of an Armbruster spectator that had shot out of the crowd along the sideline. A fumble by substitute Penn cut the drive short. The quarter ended with Armbruster in possession of the ball and on the march. End-of-quarter score: Armbruster 6, Cantorville 0.

The second quarter featured more hard football from the home team. Three minutes into the period they pushed the pigskin over for the second score. After another failed conversion, the score stood 12–0.

The smaller visitors continued to stretch the field. Two unsuccessful drives were experienced by both teams, and then the Cantorville Professionals began to wear their competitors out. The beefy Armbruster lads were tiring, and the cagey Pros took advantage. A fake pass drew the defense away from quarterback Joseph Stein, who scampered 50 yards into the Armbruster red zone. On the next play, Pinauld, the diminutive halfback, got the call. On an end run, he was hit with a particularly crushing blow to the head and staggered drunkenly down the sideline until hit again and declared down. His afternoon of football was over.

Down two backs, the Cantorville team was undaunted. "Pooly" Adrenziak was called into service in the backfield, which was a good decision. With the defense winded and spread out to cover the edges, a smash straight up the middle reaped paydirt. The kicker's luck, however, was bad.

With time dwindling, Armbruster tried to pass with limited success. At midfield they went back to their big boys in the backfield. The battering they were handing out was merciless. Fates did tend to turn. At the 20, during yet another off-tackle smash, Lucas went down in a heap. After the play was declared dead, a circle of players shook their heads, and the rumor went up and down the sidelines that Fat had broken his leg. Jackson was pressed into service, but the drive stalled. The kicker's luck held this time, and three points were added to the tally.

With only time for the kickoff, the Cantorville boys gave the Armbruster lads a scare with a nifty return, but a foot on the chalk line ended the return and the first half. The score stood at 15–6.

During the intermission there was some grumbling about the loss of Lucas. The opposing fans hooted and hollered at each other, and new bets were made or old ones increased. The overwhelming sense was that "the first half was good; the second half will be great."

After a few pep talks, a few sucks from the sponge, and a few pulls from the bottle of courage, the third quarter was ready to begin.

Cantorville couldn't make good with the ball and returned it to the home team after two and a half minutes. Armbruster wasn't particularly creative either, but with the lead they didn't need to be. They continued their sledgehammer tactics and ate precious time off the clock. At the stalling point, their punter unleashed a beauty, and Cantorville had its back against the wall yet again. Three plays later the ball was punted, weakly. Hopes were fading for the Cantorville crew.

The Armbruster Athletic Club was feeling very secure at this point. A nine-point lead, possession of the ball inside enemy territory, and time fading in the third quarter all led to their sense of invulnerability. Their guard was down. On the first play of the drive, they predictably ran a smash off tackle right. The Cantorville defense sold out and all went that way. Armbruster Ben Wheaton never stood a chance. He lost the ball midway into his run and was separated from it by a wave of visitors. Cantorville greedily seized both the ball and the momentum.

A great balance of plays then came from Cantorville: misdirection, passes, and multiple handoffs. The quarter ended, but the Armbruster faithful were a bit nervous.

At the start of the final period, the playbook was ripped wide open and anything that the football sages from Cantorville knew was thrown on the field. The result was a rapid march down the length of the field. The capping play was one with backs Brown and Penn crossing the goal on both the left and the right, both untouched. Only upon closer examination did the referee see who had the ball. Without the extra point, the score now stood 15–12.

The Armbruster A. C. had only one job on its mind: protect the ball and its lead. Predictability was ensured, but they started to work outside a bit more. The drive seemed to last an eternity. The slow march of the Athletic Club couldn't have worked more to their advantage. They gained the 10 yards, it took them three plays, and they took time off the clock. Cantorville was in a fury on the defensive. They threw themselves headlong at the ball carriers in an attempt to get them to lose their grip. Time was fleeting.

With the game in hand and the clock down to mere minutes, the incredible occurred. Although no one later would admit to ordering it, the Armbruster quarterback attempted a pass. His poor skills and rusty arm resulted in what can best be described as a "wobbly" pass. The pigskin was snatched out of the air by Stoffard of the Cantorville Pros, and time was immediately called. After the yelling had stopped and the timekeeper consulted, the shout of "Two minutes and ten seconds remaining!" rang out. It was time for a Cantorville miracle.

Having thrown caution to the wind to get their previous score, the Cantorville eleven had little left. A run and a pass gained a first down, but on third and long, and with halfback Adrenziak limping badly, the huddle took longer than normal. A wobbly Adrenziak took his position in the backfield, looking very unsteady. The ball was snapped and the quarterback spun to hand the ball to a back, but he smashed into the damaged halfback. Both players went down in a heap, with Adrenziak screaming, "It's broken, you rotten . . ." and in obvious pain. With the defense frozen, quarterback Stein popped up and ran like the devil himself was on his tail. He crossed the goal line as the fans mumbled in disbelief. One of the officials scratched his head and signaled a touchdown. Chaos ensued.

It quickly became apparent that the Cantorville back was not hurt, and the whole play was a ruse. Arguments echoed up and down the field. Fans started fistfights, and the police were called into action. In an ironic twist, Adrenziak was kicked in the leg and left the game due to his injury. The hometown referees were puzzled, but, painted into a corner, they couldn't in good faith reverse the score, especially in front of this many fans. After a delay, obviously to check with Taylor Armbruster, the play was allowed to stand. The hometown fans howled. The extra point still failed, and the score was 18–15 in favor of Cantorville.

The timekeeper was again consulted and shouted, "Thirty seconds remaining!"

The kickoff was quickly smothered, and Armbruster's boys lined up in desperation. Despite the obvious time shortage, the home eleven was given four plays to make good. Each was smothered by Cantorville. By now, handfuls of spectators had already made their way onto the playing field, creating an obstacle course or a smokescreen should another play be launched. The timekeeper, with an uneasy look on his face, glanced at his shiny timepiece and nodded to his neighbor. You could almost hear the tick of the second hand, which became an audible thud as that of a coffin lid being closed over the perfect season of the Armbruster Eleven. The gun was sounded. Moans and groans escaped from some of the home fans as they reached for money they never thought they would lose.

The place emptied out quickly, and it's quite likely that a few bets weren't honored, but that was to be expected. The thousand dollars was delivered by Jules Kincaid with scarcely a word spoken. True to his word, the feast was held at the hotel, but it was not well attended by the locals. The food was of the best quality and no expense was spared.

Armbruster, being a man of his word, paid his debt to the team and asked Cantorville to stay for the Thanksgiving banquet. However, he didn't show his face anywhere near the hotel, probably admonishing his team members or hiding from angry locals who had lost their beer money for several months.

SECOND HALF
THE DECADE THAT PRODUCED THE TEAM

It was 1910. Football had been played in the city on the bay ever since the weeks of practice leading up to the very first game on Saturday, September 21, 1895. But its light had flickered some in the years between 1905 and 1909. The realities of fielding a town team had taken some of the shine off of "one of the most popular amusements ever seen in Green Bay."

But the years between 1910 and 1918 would prove to be something different. There was no shortage of football of either the town team or neighborhood variety. Better yet, the decade would see the resurgence of strong town teams that would bring home championship banners. These teams would eventually evolve into the most-heralded of all town teams, a juggernaut called the Packers. This would also be the decade when a school boy, Earl Louis Lambeau, better known as "Curly," would begin to distinguish himself on the football fields of Green Bay's near east side. By 1919, the city team would have corporate sponsorship in the form of the Indian Packing Company, and the rest, as they say, is history.

Indeed, the only thing that distinguished the year 1919 from any of the previous 24 seasons was the loose assignment of the tag "Packers" and the $500 contribution to the team for uniforms by Frank Peck, one of the managers of the Indian Packing Company. Curly Lambeau was not new to the team in 1919, nor were many of his teammates—Nate Abrams, Riggie Dwyer, Andy Muldoon, Jim Coffeen, Gus Rosenow, and many others. Lambeau had even taken a short leave from his freshmen football squad at UW–Madison to join his buddies for a game on Green Bay's 1917 city team.

While the Packer organization itself acknowledges 1919 as its inaugural year and celebrated its 75th anniversary in 1993, controversy still exists over when the team actually began. The Packers' first season in the American Professional Football Association (now the NFL) was 1921, when they were sponsored by the Acme

Packing Company. Plenty of Packer apparel these days bears the year 1921 as the team's birth date. Ironically, the team was also booted out of the league that same year for using ineligible college players under false names and reinstated at a league meeting on the heels of a $2,500 loan by Green Bay businessmen.

At that point, Curly Lambeau was the owner of the "Green Bay Football Club." In a letter dated September 17, 1922, to Art Schmael, who had left the team and was being courted by Lambeau to return, Curly referred to his team as "formerly Packers." He did not much like the Packer name anyway, and he was glad to get rid of it. But to confuse matters even more, the letterhead he used clearly states "Wisconsin Professional Champions since 1917." So, there it was, an entirely different date for the founding of the team.

What, then, is the real date? Is it 1917, 1919, or 1921? One of the purposes of this book is to help clarify and/or confuse the whole question by offering a radical suggestion: the founding date of the "Packer" team could actually be traced back to the fall of 1895. The era covered in this half of the book is little heralded in Packer history, but it gives great insight into the general convergence of events that form the Packer universe we know and love today.

THIRD QUARTER
1910–1918, THE TOWN TEAM RETURNS

1910
THE RENAISSANCE

On Monday, September 19, 1910, the *Green Bay Gazette* ran a front-page item about baseball that was an amazing precursor to the ultimate survival of football in this town. The article factored prominently into whether this small northeastern Wisconsin town would have a team beyond 1923, the year of the first Green Bay Packer stock sale; whether there would be one beyond 1935, the year of the second stock sale; and, amazingly enough, whether there would be a Green Bay Packer team today.

Sure, the item was about baseball. But baseball had nearly always paved the way for football. It was the older brother, not quite as rowdy, but skilled in his own right. And its earnest efforts, while probably less charismatic than those of its kid brother, were absolutely requisite for junior's survival and success. The article read,

START EARLY ON BASEBALL PLAN
Fund to Retain W.I. League Franchise Being Subscribed to Now
Seek to Have 200 Fans Give Sum of $25 Each
Proposition Now in the Hands of Interested Ones and a Determined Effort
Will Be Made to Have Guarantee Ready When League Directors Meet.

The first steps were made today in an effort to retain the franchise held by the Green Bay Baseball association in the Wisconsin-Illinois league of Professional Baseball clubs during the 1911 season.

An early start in this connection is being made in order that some assurance may be had before the first meeting of the directors of the league is held that a sufficient amount of money be guaranteed to carry the club

through the season. The matter of raising the guarantee was taken hold of by President Frank E. Murphy of the club, Frank R. Weeks, Edward Barth, John F. Martin and other fans, and these gentlemen, aided by others, will work on a proposition they conceived during the next few weeks.

The proposition they are working on is to have 200 individuals agree to give $25 apiece toward the support of baseball. The subscription paper which has been arranged makes no signer liable for the amount unless 200 subscribers are secured.

That the baseball proposition can be carried through is the opinion of those who have charge of it. In view of the several conventions to be held here next summer they believe that baseball can be made self-sustaining, further that they city cannot afford to lose the franchise. When a city once loses a baseball franchise, it is difficult to again secure a franchise, they say, and the city does not want to drop out of the baseball world.

A similar idea had been floated near the end of the 1907 baseball season, when the 2,000 tickets were to be sold at one dollar each "to raise a sufficient sum to pay all debts and retain [the baseball] franchise." The scheme was for fans and players to sell the tickets "good for Saturday or Sunday's game with Oshkosh, with grand stand coupon attached" to individuals of "moderate circumstances . . . who are willing to do a little to help out the association."

Stock sales to save the Packers would rely on similar verbiage and a little person-to-person arm-twisting to achieve the same kind of franchise certainty. For sure, sales of everything from old turf to $200 shares of stock as recently as the 1990s to keep the team solvent and "in Green Bay," were no different. When the team again approached the populace in 2000, this time for a major face-lift for Lambeau Field, the pleas and reasons for support had a familiar ring.

Packer fans have always loved their team. Better yet, they've supported the team with hard currency in times of need. This certificate comes from the very first stock sale conducted to save the team in 1923. Thank God for people like Ernest Stiller, who bought five shares of Green Bay's future. Photograph from the Henry Lefebvre Collection of the Neville Public Museum of Brown County, Green Bay, Wisconsin.

The Wisconsin-Illinois Baseball League was a good idea. Clearly, leagues in all sports were good ideas. Hulbert had the foresight in 1904 to seek the strength the Northern State Football League would provide. The key to it all seemed to be a set schedule. Opponents could usually be found, but if they couldn't be penciled in in a timely manner, the games would fall by the wayside as could the entire season. Leagues in varied sports were successful at least in the short term. In 1904 there was even mention of a bowling league being set up along the Green Bay–Fond du Lac interurban line. Hulbert's '04 football league followed the same transportation lines. Of course, leagues also brought with them some fallout, including a loss of home team autonomy. But autonomy could also take you right to the football cemetery.

An item in the *Gazette* from September 23 suggested that rule changes for the 1910 season would make the task of coaching "hard work." Once again, the "powers that be" were trying to make the game less brutal, at least in appearance. Motion toward the line of scrimmage was allowed by only one man, forward passes were now permissible anywhere across the line, and sidelined players could return to the contest at any time except in the last quarter. Tackling and blocking, however, had been seriously gentled. "Interlocking interference" was illegal as were diving tackles. Body checking would-be receivers was now forbidden as was crawling on the ground with the ball after being tackled. Unfortunately, forward passes of more than 20 yards had also been banned. The massaging of the game continued.

As far as Green Bay football went, it was 1910 and there hadn't been a true city team of record since Tod Burns had given his all to field an aggregation five years earlier. But intracity teams continued to flourish. The city had grown from a population of 18,684 in 1900 to 25,286. With a 33 percent growth in its civilian count, the question was no longer whether Green Bay could field a team and support it, but, rather, would its attention remain on just one team that represented Green Bay? This new development—an increase in the number of intracity teams—could have proved just as damaging to the survival of football as the lack of a declared city team.

White City, a football stronghold since 1909, was the first Green Bay locale to form a team in 1910. The Saturday, October 15, *Gazette* announced that the White City eleven would line up against an aggregation from Green Bay's west side for a contest the following day. The White City grounds had become a mecca for Green Bay football. "It is expected," said the *Gazette*, "that a large number of enthusiasts will be on hand to witness the tussle, this being the opening game at these grounds. The game will be called at 2:30 o'clock sharp."

White City lost the contest but was hardly about to fold its tent for the season. By the following week, the *Gazette* reported that the eleven had been considerably strengthened "with several heavy and fast players." Cyril Bunker had been elected captain, and Hans Sibert was taking over the duties of manager. "Both," said the paper, "have had considerable experience in these positions and will do all in their power to make a showing with the team." Their next contest, on the 23rd, put that acumen to the test as they were, reported the paper, slated for a tussle with "an eleven representing Green Bay." An eleven representing Green Bay? What was that supposed to mean? Yes, Virginia, there really is a town team.

"A fast game of football," led the *Gazette*'s report, "was played before a large crowd of spectators on the White City grounds Sunday when the White Citys and the Green Bays met for their first game this season." The game had been marked by "fast work" and "much enthusiasm aroused among the witnesses." The game ended in a tie. The White City team played the rest of their games in their new, stylish, white-and-purple jerseys.

De Pere's football news was also promising. Its city football team had slated its second game of the season for that same day, Sunday, October 23, against Green Bay's Nighthawks. The De Peres had nipped a scrappy team from Green Bay's east side by the score of 12–11 in their first contest. But their second game never took place because the Nighthawks failed to show.

On the following Sunday, the 30th, Green Bay played a doubleheader, which had become the *repas ordinaire* for Sunday afternoons on Bay Beach Road. The first game kickoff was set for 2:30 p.m., when the White City eleven would line up against the East Ends, a Green Bay aggregation. The *Gazette* penciled the teams in as "very evenly matched, the players on each eleven averaging 147 pounds."

The second game would be pushing darkness by the time its final whistle sounded. That contest had put "the north side boys," as the *Gazette* tabbed the White City team, against another Green Bay intracity aggregation, the Comets, who averaged about 145 pounds a man but was known for playing "a fast game."

In the first game, the White Citys won over the East Ends 11–0. The second contest never got off the ground because the Comets failed to make an appearance.

The sports pages of local newspapers like the *Gazette* had put their ears to the ground and heard a hue and cry among football fans in northeastern Wisconsin for news about football at all levels: high school, town team, and college. When high school stars graduated from East or West high schools and moved on to stardom at universities across the nation, local enthusiasts took note, kicked their fortunes around over coffee and cigars, and demanded updates on their exploits.

Merrill "Joe" Hoeffel fit the bill perfectly. Hoeffel had graduated from East in 1908 and was tearing it up and lettering every season as a left end on the University of Wisconsin–Madison eleven. It was noteworthy. "Not for over a decade has Green Bay had a representative on the Wisconsin university eleven," reported the *Gazette*. Other local boys had swelled the ranks of the gridiron elite at institutes of higher learning around the nation, but Hoeffel was a part of the city's football lingo for another decade to come.

Local football news faded from the newspaper for over a week and didn't resurface until an announcement appeared, proclaiming, "Double Header for Sunday Football Bill." Those games were set for Sunday, November 13, again at the White City grounds. Two aggregations from Appleton were set to travel by train to Green Bay for the contests. The first game would see the Green Bay and Appleton city teams clash; the second matchup would pit the Jolly Eleven of Appleton against the White City team.

The Appletons wished they had never made the trip, but Green Bay fans could feel pride in both their town team and the White City boys. The actual contests had been flip-flopped from the schedule, suggesting that the Green Bay city team was being billed as the pièce de résistance. The White City aggregation nipped the Jolly Eleven 2–0, after what the *Gazette* called "a hard siege." In the second game, the Green Bay city team took it to the Appleton Cubs, 6–1. The weather was football perfect, and a large crowd enjoyed the excursion.

That week, several related items caught the eye of football fans reading the *Gazette*. First, in a shocking turn of events in the war against football violence was the issuing of a warrant in a football death:

FOOTBALL PLAYER IS CHARGED WITH DEATH
Tommy McCoy Says He Will Return to Wheeling, W.Va. and Stand Charges.
(By United Press)
Canton, O., Nov. 14 - Tommy McCoy, the football player, charged with the death of Rudolph Munk, while playing at Wheeling, West Virginia, Saturday, today protested his innocence, and said he will return and stand all charges.

WARRANT IS ISSUED
Wheeling, W.Va., Nov. 14 - A warrant formally charging Thomas McCoy, right end of the Betheny college football team, with murder in connection with the death of Capt. Rudolph Munk of the West Virginia university team, was issued here on Sunday by Magistrate R. G. Hobbs. The action followed partial completion of the inquest by Coroner W. W. Rogers. Munk sustained injuries in the game between the two teams here on Saturday from which he died within five hours without regaining consciousness.

The story was further ammunition for those dead set against the game, and the issuing of a warrant only supported their contention that this was a violent game appealing primarily to thugs.

The second football item to appear that week spoke from the other end of the football spectrum. "Senator Provides for Football Boys' Comfort," the headline in the *Gazette* declared. The report went on to outline the lengths to which U.S. Senator Stephenson of Marinette had gone to pamper the members of the Marinette high school team during their stay in Appleton on Saturday, November 19.

Marinette's high school eleven was there to face Oshkosh for the state scholastic football championship on the Lawrence college athletic field. "Reservations of the best rooms and special meals have been made here at the leading hotel," reported the paper, "and the Appleton band has been engaged to 'make a noise like Marinette.'" Stephenson had instructed the management of the Marinette high school team to "spare no expense in making the boys comfortable."

A third item appearing on November 12 and updated a week later must have set some prim tongues to clucking and heads to shaking. Jim Coffeen, who would be a near-legend on Green Bay city teams just prior to the advent of the Packers, was bagged for playing at Beloit College under false pretenses. According to the *Gazette*, Coffeen had presented himself to college officials as a graduate of East High School. In truth, he hadn't graduated.

If Beloit had sported only a run-of-the-mill aggregation for the 1910 pigskin campaign, it wouldn't have been so earthshaking. Unfortunately, they were laying claim to the state championship, and, worse yet, Coffeen had been responsible for a lion's share of their victories. In some back and forth between the college and the high school, neither side was willing to shoulder the blame for the error. Beloit leveled a charge of "delayed answers to inquiries," and East fired back with the accusation that college officials knew "over one month before the matter became public."

The bottom line was that Beloit was about to surrender its claim to the state championship. Coffeen, however, went on to some pretty good-sized notoriety as a member of Green Bay town teams in the late teens and as an announcer for early Packer contests.

In 1910, town team play had finally returned to Titletown, and it would continue rolling until it produced the Packers nine seasons later. This photo from that year shows several players noted for their contributions to town team football, Green Bay-style, including Homer Rothe, Myron Scofield, and Joseph O'Connor. Photograph obtained from and used with permission of the Green Bay Packer Hall of Fame.

College and high school football continued to get notice in the newspapers. Many Green Bay football fans were headed by train to Waukesha to watch Ripon College take on Carroll College. In a small web of interest, "Issy" Smith, a former Ripon star, had been helping out with the backfield of Coach Stiem's Green Bay high school team, which had sparked some curiosity in the city in Ripon's football lot.

RIPON COLLEGE—"LET US HAVE A CONTEST"

Football in 1881? No way! But it's true—if you believe the student publications at Ripon College. The first is the June 1881 *Ripon College News-Letter Commencement Issue.* After describing the colorful scene of the field-sports day and the winners in the mile run, the running-jump, the mile walk, the potato-race, the sledge-throw, the half-mile run, the tug-of-war, the "Siamese-twin race" and the 100-yard dash, the publication offers the following slight, but crucial, statement: "In the game of foot-ball, Merrell's side won."

Later that day, following the field-sports events, the *News-Letter* reported:

> An excellent supper was gotten up by Dauben and thoroughly enjoyed by the boys, especially the lucky sides in tug-of-war and foot-ball, who had theirs gratis, or rather at the expense of the losing sides.

The second mention, also from the campus *News-Letter,* is of an October game, played between the Economia Club and the Spartans. Actually, it was an abbreviated affair, punctuated with the bursting of the proposed game ball, after which the boys walked home, spirits a bit deflated. The *News-Letter* ran two separate references to the event:

FOOT-BALL.
Let us have the contest
We think that the Economians propose fair play
We hope that the juggling has not been for the purpose of evading the contest .
. . The athletic excitement for the past few days has been a foot-ball contest between the Economians and the Spartans - or rather it is a proposed contest. On Monday, the two bands met and contended with desperate efforts for a short time for the honors and the oysters staked; but the excitement culminated in the bursting of the ball. It is expected that the contest will be renewed, but at the present writing it is not known when.

From there on, Ripon football was a sure thing and one surely to get recorded. Both Ripon and Lawrence recognize the significance of an intercollegiate game played between the two schools in 1882, and a traveling trophy, the Doehling-Heselton Memorial, is awarded each autumn to the winner of their contest. The matchup between the two schools has proceeded to this day, with some molehills and some significant bumps in the road. Molehills? Well, they'd include every contested call in every game ever played between the two. Significant bumps? They'd include things like Ripon refusing to meet the Lawrence eleven for a 1908 scrap because the grapevine had the Appletons jacking up their squad with a non-student Oneida Indian player.

The 1882 contest was slated for Saturday, November 18, in Appleton. Ripon won 2–1.

The season was winding down and heading into the traditional closing contests featured on Thanksgiving Day. In the two weeks prior, Saint Norbert College had lost a couple of times to West High School and was hoping to hand a Turkey Day reversal to Manitowoc. But rain ruined the rhubarb for a number of Thanksgiving Day contests, including the Saint Norbert–Manitowoc contest.

The annual East–West High School game did take place, however. Who would have had the moxie to cancel it, even in the rain? Attendance was down because of the downpour, but a drop kick by Earl Leaper put West on top for the final count. West was working hard to get a longtime monkey off its back, and it amassed 279 yards to East's measly 54 in the process.

The last noticeable football news of local interest appeared in an item, "Two Football Games to be Played Sunday" on November 26. Again, a doubleheader was slated at the White City grounds. In the first contest, White City took on the Green Bay city team. The second battle pit the Comets against the East Ends. "This will be the last game to be played on the White City grounds this year and, it is expected, that there will be a large number present."

There it is—a second mention of a 1910 Green Bay city team in print. The year *did* see a team playing under the Green Bay city team moniker. But with a lot of football around, they didn't get the kind of ink they would have drawn in the early days. They did have their photo taken, however, and one copy of it resides at the Green Bay Packer Hall of Fame.

The boys on the 1910 squad were no slouches. As with the lads in many of the previous years of town team football, they represented a snapshot of talent as well as ties to Green Bay's gridiron past and future. The aggregation stood 13 strong, 11 regulars and two subs. Myron Scofield was a standout, but so were Homer Rothe, George Madden, and Joseph O'Connor. The team was capable and rounded out with Charles Younkle, Bill DeKeyser, Harold Rawley, Frank Tatosky, Art Pinchard, Jack Buresh, James Dobry, Sr., Ernest VanErmen, and Herman Barrett.

So after five long years, Green Bay fans were now able to discuss the pitfalls and the promises of a "city team." No, they weren't "champions." The clamor around the simple declaration of being a champion had focused sharply and a team had better be ready to back it up with a serious game. The presence of many more teams in many more towns meant a champion had to really ascend to the throne with victories rather than unchallenged words.

But the fact that there was, finally, once again, a true city team had to make local football fans smile. Its arrival on the scene was a harbinger for the decade, a decade that would see a resurgence of designated city teams and, as an ultimate result, give Green Bay its Packers.

"NEWS OF THE SPORTING WORLD"

Not much had changed when football started up in earnest in 1911. Unlike previous years, the *Gazette* had acknowledged the significance of sports reporting by finally setting off a section called "News of the Sporting World." The high art of sports reporting had become more sophisticated as well.

"News from the Sporting World" was a regular feature in the *Green Bay Gazette* in 1911, and it gave Green Bay football enthusiasts a glimpse into sports of all kinds at all levels. Usually the end of the baseball season dovetailed into the beginning of pigskin season in October. It's apparent when surveying the pages of the *Gazette*, the primary news source in Green Bay at the time, that football was gaining in popularity all across the United States. While the controversy over its violence still raged whenever a report of serious injury or death echoed through the press, the game had lasted long enough to become a staple in the popular psyche.

On Friday, October 6, an item suggested that the 1911 season, on a national scale, promised "to be one of the most successful in the history of the game. The new rules reduced the number of accidents to a minimum last year and the rules as now modified promise to eliminate a great deal of the danger of players being hurt."

Though the rules had changed little since 1910, attention had been given to further encouragement of the forward pass, "and," reported the press, "there is much speculation as to whether in its new dressing it will be a success."

"According to the new rule," the report said, "a forward pass is illegal when the player receiving it fails to hold on to the ball." An "uncompleted forward pass" was defined as "one that hits the ground before being touched by any player on either side." In either case, the ball was returned to the original line of scrimmage, and the next play was launched.

The game was once again evolving, and, on Monday, October 16, the *Gazette* carried an article vowing that "Football Needs a Fast Back Field." The forward pass was said to be the "big factor," and "the major college teams are making efforts to develop fast, active back fields with a strong line to protect the backs in the execution of intricate plays."

"Most of the mentors," the report continued, "are throwing into the discard the big, lumbersome backs who used to be in such demand when the ultimate makeup of a team was considered. In fact, the same thing is true of the line." The article included a picture of a svelte and speedy player, "Captain Howe of Yale, Ideal Backfield man under the new rules."

Yet another article headed "Football Danger is on Decrease" appeared in the paper on Wednesday, October 25, and it marked a sea change in attitudes toward football as well as the strategies employed:

Old Time Players Believe Injuries Less Liable Than Before.
Remembers Newell's Story
Former Harvard and Cornell Coach Taught Tackling by Heroic Measures—
Changes in Play Make Different Game.

> *Old time football players maintain that the game has shown a marked decrease in unavoidable roughness since their day, and they believe, too, that the actual work of learning the game has ceased to be drudgery. Ten or fifteen years ago the coaches paid little attention to the trainer, keeping their men at work when they were thoroughly fagged. The coaches used to say that they could teach a tired team better than a fresh one and that the men ran less risk of injury when they were practically exhausted. All that has been changed, and some of the best conditioned teams are those that have had short periods of work. So many different types of men get into the game nowadays that the team is constantly freshened in practice and the men do not become mentally or physically as tired as they used to.*

> *The interest of the linemen, who have to do the heavy work, is kept up nowadays by the simple process of teaching them generalship as well as the backs. The up to date coach expects his forwards to be letter perfect in the plan of campaign, to know just what play ought to be made in a certain part of the field, as well as the quarterback who is running the team. Every man on the team has a chance to study the generalship diagram, which is supplementary to the blackboard talks, and the guard on one of the big teams can tell you every detail of the grand tactics. The team, every member of which measures up to the quarterback in all around knowledge of the game is the ideal eleven.*

> *Another thing that has improved the game is the abandonment of the heavy, hard and dangerous "armor" and the leather tackling bag with the heavy stuffing.*

Obviously, a game that had been noted for its mass plays rather than its finesse was becoming more sophisticated. Really, it was the only way for the game to go. Given the reports of the game being banned in various cities and railed against in Sunday sermons, the sport would never survive by gravitating toward its cruder nature.

Still, 1911 saw a report of a death on the gridiron in nearby Manitowoc when Thomas Higgins, a 16-year-old high school junior, died a day after sustaining injuries in a game between two "scrub teams" on Tuesday, November 7. After a kick in the head that fractured his skull, he "was rendered unconscious," reported the *Associated Press*, "but recovered sufficiently to walk home."

WAUSAU—DATELINE, 1911.
FOOTBALL BAN PROPOSED, DOESN'T WORK!

While debate raged on football's violent side, action against it was taken in some towns. Wausau's football story wasn't very different from that of other towns. High school guys and older men learned to play the game in the 1890s and mixed it up as best they could despite the constraints of rules, families, and social expectations of gentlemanly behavior. Swearing and rough play were an occasional by-product of the game but surely not the only aspect of the game the guys enjoyed. Right? In 1911, however, the city council reviewed a resolution to ban the game completely from the city's parks. Alderman Richard Schmidt had had enough. He was offended and characterized the game as "dangerous." Football, however, survived the ban and continued at the local high school as well as in the town. In fact, Wausau had football well into the last days of the town team era with its Muskies.

The Muskies faced the Chicago Ravens in their sixth game of the season, and so far the weather for their home games had been terrible. Attendance was way down, and the Chicago game was supposed to resurrect the team's treasury. The turnout wasn't great, but it wasn't bad. The Muskies were on the field, it was kickoff time, but the Ravens had not yet arrived. Well after the appointed time, the fans began to trickle, and then pour, out of the stadium, demanding a refund, of course. Only the Muskies were left to ponder the absence of their opponent. The Ravens did eventually arrive at the field about two hours late. Their bus had broken down en route. They could play now, but the fans were long gone and there was no way to get them back. It was the last game ever scheduled for the Muskies; town team football disappeared from Wausau with the last football fan that drove away that day.

In Green Bay, a 13-year-old Curly Lambeau was known to play the now-widely popular game with a mock-up football. According to early Packer historian, Arch Ward, "It wasn't of the inflated type which Curly these days [1946] follows with the eyes of a hawk. It was truly a homemade job, born of a discarded salt sack, and stuffed with Green Bay's falling leaves and a modicum of pebbles and sand." Soon enough, Curly would be able to lay claim to any official pigskin he set his eyes on, and no one, including his coaches, would utter one syllable of reproach as he walked off the football field with a decent ball under his arm.

When they could, he and his neighborhood squad scooted off to Whitney Park or to the grounds of Whitney School on the corner of Pine Street and Webster

Avenue. Often enough, they were happy to move a block north of the Lambeau home to Saint Claire Street, an unpaved road along the East River. Wherever it happened, it was football, it was fun, and it got the blood racing through the veins. And, while Lambeau didn't mind the running and the tackling, the art nouveau of the forward pass seemed in particular to tickle his fancy. Neighbors later recalled Curly's penchant for passing that crude ball into the air even as a kid.

Not every football man in the country loved the pass, however. A November 20 story appearing in the *Gazette* quoted Mike Murphy, the "veteran trainer" of the University of Pennsylvania, as suggesting that the pass was a mere fad that violated the "elementary principles of football." Murphy was clear in his understanding that fans wanted to see the ball moved downfield "by a series of well-executed plays cleverly designed and operated." He called the forward pass a "basketball feature" and concluded by saying it was "certainly not good for football." If Murphy could have witnessed just one of Brett Favre's game-winning tosses, it's almost certain he would have volunteered to eat his own words along with a regulation-size pigskin.

De Pere was also hotly involved in the game, and its city team was organized the first week of October with George Crabb as captain and Earl Walsh as manager.

For the first time in a long time, Green Bay had seen solid town team play in back-to-back years. The group in this 1911 photograph was a declared town team, not a neighborhood or intracity aggregation that had been forced to defend the city's football honor by default. Pictured are: (front row, left to right) Elmer Behrendt, Zick Feldhausen, Ernie La Tour, John Dockry; (middle row) Ferris Nelson, Frank Tatasky, Myron Schofeld, Ernie Van Ermen, H. Sullivan, Hank Geyer; (back row) Andy Muldoon, Omer Rothe, Claude Kelly, Homer La Tour, Bill Speck. Photograph obtained from and used with permission of the Green Bay Packers Hall of Fame.

Crabb and Walsh had joined forces to field a De Pere aggregation for several years, recognizing that one man couldn't do it alone. The best teams featured split duties between a football man and an organizer. A call was issued for all interested De Pere footballers to meet at the high school grounds near the school on the northwest corner of College and 4th streets at 10:00 a.m. on Sunday, October 8. "Several games have already been scheduled," relayed the *Gazette*'s De Pere correspondent, "and a good team is looked for."

Despite pickup games everywhere, the roundhouse of football as well as baseball activity in Green Bay remained the White City grounds on the city's northeast side.

On that same Sunday the 8th, the White City crew was aching to take on the Green Bay Jolly Eleven in a 2:30 contest at their home grounds. While the teams were evenly matched, the White Citys, playing in their purple-and-white uniforms, won.

On Tuesday afternoon, October 17, the *Gazette* ran a defi from the Wellingtons, an Oshkosh eleven who were looking for a game against a Green Bay squad averaging 150 pounds. Herman Hollup was the team's manager.

Going into the weekend football action of Friday, October 20, the *Gazette* took a long look at the contests slated for the east- and west-side high school elevens. West High would be facing a Kaukauna squad that the paper said was "strong and plays fast ball." The East Highs were traveling over rail to Oconto. The east-siders were banged up and were sending a team of substitutes up to do their best. "Oconto is a heavy and good aggregation," Coach Beyer stated, "and I don't expect to do much against the team." Most noticeable among the ranks of Beyer's squad were the names of a couple of future Packer players: Fritz Gavin and Wally Ladrow.

Sunday, October 22, held promise of a 3:00 contest on the White City grounds between that team and the Oshkosh city team. "A good game is looked for," guaranteed the *Gazette*, "as the teams are about evenly matched in weight and science." No longer was the pregame hype concerned solely with the size of the two colliding giants, now "science" had been brought into the mix, a good 15 years after Tom Silverwood had spoken of its essence in the game.

The account of the game was glowing for the White City crew. They had gone up against a "fast" Oshkosh conglomeration that hadn't lost a contest in four years. Del Thompson, a locomotive fireman from Green Bay's west side, drop-kicked twice for White City. The final score was 17–5.

The next Sunday, October 29, the White City team, which was still undefeated, tore up an eleven from Allouez, 29–0. While the *Gazette* reported that the Allouez team "played a stiff game," they were outweighed by the White Citys. Highlights of the game included a 45-yard drop kick by Dutch Kemnitz and four touchdowns by a speedy right halfback named Martin. White City had faced the Green Bay city team in an earlier contest and come away victorious. Their next contest would be at Oshkosh against the same aggregation they had defeated on the 22nd. "The

White City team has not been defeated this season and has been playing some of the best teams including the city team," reported the newspaper.

Also on the 29th, the Hillsides traveled to Kaukauna for a contest against the Kaukauna city bunch. The Hillsides had been a perennial participant of intracity football since at least 1902, and their success was indicative of the ingredients for successful football with scope and sequence. They had dedicated management, team spirit, and a football priority. In Kaukauna, they battled an aggregation that had been around in one way or another since at least 1893 to a 0–0 tie. While Kaukauna had failed to make an appearance for a scheduled contest on the White City grounds on Sunday, October 15, they remained a well-established team. The Hillsides' relative success prompted them to lay a claim toward winning the "championship of Green Bay," and they tossed up a defi to any Green Bay football crews ready to meet their match.

Elsewhere on the football scene, the University of Wisconsin eleven was also promising to show some football stuff that fall. "Wisconsin is looming large upon the western football horizon," reported the national press, "and early season prospects are that the Madison university is to be better represented on the gridiron this fall that [sic] for several years back in history."

The first discernable mention of a 1911 Green Bay city team appeared in the pages of the *Gazette* on Monday, October 23, after an 8–11 victory over the Jolly Eleven of Appleton. According to the paper, Burash, who was likely John Buresh of Elm Street, had scored a touchdown, and Myron Scofield, of South Monroe Street, had made a drop kick from the 45-yard line.

Also grabbing some of the headlines in "News from the Sporting World" was a young Carlisle Indian School athlete. According to the article, he is

> *a fine basketball player, a baseball pitcher of great talent and has played a creditable game at halfback on the football team. He can fill any of the positions on these three teams, and in addition he excels at lacrosse and tennis. He plays handball, hockey and indoor baseball with equal skill and finished third in the annual cross country meet last spring. He has put the sixteen pound shot forty-three feet, broad jump[ed] twenty-two feet ten inches, run a hundred yards in 10 seconds flat and cleared six feet in the high jump. He has run the high hurdles in 15 4/5 seconds and the low hurdles in 28 seconds. In one track meet last spring Thorpe won five events and was second in another.*

Jim Thorpe was, of course, destined for even greater athletic feats. But in 1911, his name was just beginning to hit the sports world.

The science of the game was also continuing to develop, and it was influencing play at the least likely of scientific fronts, the center position. "Years ago under the old rules," reported the press, "the middle man on the line was generally a place for the fattest boy in the college, but the new code has given that doctrine a black eye."

The center was now responsible for snapping the ball to any player in the backfield, all of whom were standing upright. He had to be agile enough to pass the ball backward accurately at any angle. It was all shotgun formation! The article bemoaned the absence of good center men in major colleges that year.

On the defensive side of the ball, the report said that "Nowadays it is the fashion to play a 'loose' center. That means that the center need not necessarily play right on the line every minute in defense and that it is not incumbent upon him to stand his ground and resist the attacking center. He can slip to one side and get after the man with the ball if he is alert enough to follow it through while it is being passed."

As had always been the case from football's early beginnings in the eastern states, colleges continued to spearhead the game's evolution, this time toward the "scientific." While it took a while, sometimes a long while, for the finesse to find its way to all levels of the game in all corners of the country, there was no turning back. And, at least on one side street in Green Bay, a young, curly haired kid was taking serious note of the "open game."

Football season in Green Bay was winding down. The last account was a game featuring the Hillsides. On Sunday, November 5, they sojourned south to take on the Neenah city team. Ernie Van Ermen ran 40 yards, and Joe O'Connor drop-kicked the pigskin from 55 yards out for the only points in the contest. The final score was 3–0.

A black-and-white photo of what has long been identified as the 1911 city team exists. That image represents what is only the fourth known photograph of an aggregation representing Green Bay. It is more likely the third, since a picture from 1905 probably represents the intracity team, the Onwards, and not Tod Burns's 1905 city team.

Most notable among the 1911 players pictured are four men. Andy Muldoon had been a presence on city teams since 1906, and he continued to be so until he played for the fledgling Green Bay Packers in 1919. His playing days spanned the era between the city teams and the Green Bay Packers. As a result, his is a name that every fan of football in Green Bay should know. Even more so than Curly Lambeau, Muldoon is a connection between the early days and what was to come as football moved into the relatively sophisticated era of the National Football League.

Myron Scofield, the young athlete holding the ball near the center of the picture, was particularly noted for his drop-kicking acumen in a game against the Appleton Jolly Eleven. Scofield had also starred on the 1910 city team. Additionally, the picture shows Homer and Ernie LaTour, brothers who lived on Green Bay's far east side. The picture identifies the team as "Green Bay Champions, 1911."

The guys were pretty good footballers, no doubt. They were the precursors to a decade of fairly decent gridiron success for Green Bay, culminating in the Green

Bay Packers. Where they got the mettle to lay claim to being champions, however, wasn't borne out by newspaper accounts of their overwhelming football exploits. But, as had so long been the case, if you claimed to be champions, had some reason to say so, and no one showed up to challenge your claim, you were champions.

1912
THE GAME TAKES TO THE AIR

"Ishpeming Football Team Issues Challenge" shouted the headline in the "News of the Sporting World" section of the *Green Bay Gazette* on Friday, October 4. Via the editor of the *Gazette*, Manager Joseph Leffler Jr. of the Ishpeming city team issued a challenge indirectly to an extremely successful White City team from 1911 "for a game to be played at Green Bay, some time during the month of November, the early part."

Leffler was confident in his squad's ability to trim the White City sails, stating, "We have had a strong team here for four years and are out to win the championship of Northern Michigan. Our average weight is about 155. Hoping you insert this challenge in your popular newspaper, at an early date." The two teams would never meet, but the issuing of a defi by Ishpeming elevated White City to a position of some standing, if not to the position of ad hoc city team.

For their part, the White City lads had started off their 1912 season in good order, nipping the Allouez team 6–5. The Allouez aggregation was obviously improving, given the sapping they had taken at the hands of the White City thugs in 1911.

But would the 1912 version of the sport be a kinder and gentler variety? No! According to Tommy Clark, a sports columnist who authored "Spicy Sporting Chat,"

> This year's variety of football rules has been accused of being everything from a return to the old eat 'em alive mass play rules to being a slight modification, which will have little effect on the style of play. Actually a survey of the new football laws leads to the belief that the game that will develop under them will be a close cousin to that played in 1909—an invitation to the tackles to stand up and be killed.
>
> Last year's rules favored the defense to such an extent that scoring was almost impossible and fluky in the extreme. It appears that in their effort to

strengthen the offense the rule makers have gone to the other boundary and that scoring this year is likely to be enormous and that any defense developed will be helpless against a heavy, fairly fast back field, working to gain ten yards in four downs. The mass play died when pulling and pushing a man through the line was abolished. But the tackle now will have to stand the shock of his opposing forward and then of a heavy man bent on making two or three yards. He will not in all probability get much help from the secondary defense. To weaken the defensive back line unduly will be simply an invitation to the offense to work the now unrestricted forward pass to its heart's content.

Today, we call it the West Coast offense, among other things. But in 1912, the exact balance between the running and passing games had become, for the first time, a matter of open and hot conjecture. It still is, and the debate will never change. But the controversy wasn't possible until the forward pass was elevated to the level of an extremely effective football strategy with the necessary rule changes.

The rule changes that Clark was referring to were the broadest changes that the game had experienced since 1876. Touchdowns were now worth half a dozen points. The field had been shortened by 30 feet to 100 yards. The offensive team now had four plays to move the ball 10 yards as opposed to the previous three plays and 10 yards. The ball was slimmer to accommodate the forward toss. Clark's concern was that teams would now be able to bull the ball with less yardage demanded of every play.

The rule changes caused the national press to make even more forecasts about their impact. "College football will encroach more upon professional baseball this season than for a good many years," declared one item appearing in the *Green Bay Gazette* on Saturday, October 12, 1912. The article surmised that the bevy of changes had forced a number of universities to call for candidates to be ready to work by the middle of September. "Any institution which waits until the last week of September to unravel the mysteries of the game is bound to suffer early season reverses," it promised.

The rule changes, however, had the opposite effect of their desired outcome. The article continued by stating that "The most important conclusion which football men have drawn from the new rules is that they give the big teams a decided advantage over their smaller opponents which they have not had since the introduction of the forward pass." It cited three college contests played in 1911 involving Princeton, Harvard, and Yale, which it speculated would have had different outcomes if just one of the rules of 1912, the change to four plays per series, had been in place the previous year.

Back in Green Bay, some distance from football's cutting edge, the rule changes had less of an impact. Teams usually went with what they knew, the run.

An end run was razzle-dazzle, and a play with a forward pass was likely to be referred to in the local press as "a circus play."

The Hillsides traveled to Kaukauna on October 16, where they experienced a good smacking of 45–10. If nothing else, the change in a touchdown's point value was giving the statisticians more to keep track of. The "features of the game," reported the *Gazette*, "were an 85-yard run by Bergin for a touchdown, also a drop kick from the 30-yard line by the same player, and the tackling of Ridgley of the Hillsides." A return game was set for 14 days later.

In the interim, the Hillsides were scheduled to toe up against the White Citys at the White City grounds on Sunday, October 27. "These two teams," reported the newspaper, "have been playing a good article of ball this fall and a stubborn contest is looked for tomorrow." The game wasn't played.

In one game that was played out that Sunday, the Green Bay city eleven traveled to Kaukauna to avenge the defeat of their fellow city men, the Hillsides. The final score was 14–6 in favor of the Bays. Two names of note emerged from the contest. Alois "Ally" Romson was credited with both of the team's touchdowns, while Jim Coffeen was heralded with carrying the ball "for long gains" and "some effective punting." Romson also starred on the 1913 squad. Coffeen became, along with Andy Muldoon, one of the players of stature during the days just before the birth of the Packers and was also involved in the years of the team's infancy.

The game that did take place at White City Park that same day was between the White City team and an eleven from Algoma. White City lost the contest 12–6 and faced an aggregation from another lakeside city, Kewaunee, the following week.

The East Rivers, an intracity eleven formed in 1899, were also still around and got some ink on November 6 in a report covering their victory over a team called the Maple Leafs. The contest, played at the "city park on Main Street," presumably Whitney Park, ended in a 12–6 final verdict and featured "the good work of William Lardeau, Rasco Whitney and L. Cannard."

Next, the East Rivers faced the Allouez team at the White City grounds for a 2:30 contest. The *Gazette* proclaimed the success of the East Rivers, stating that the "team hopes to make a record this year as they played ever[y] Sunday without being defeated by any team since their reorganization." Unfortunately there is no record of this game.

A small article in the November 12 paper mentioned the Green Bay city team playing to a scoreless tie with Oshkosh. The report stated that Jimmie Coffeen and Ally Romson "played star ball for the Green Bay team," and ended by mentioning that the same two teams would meet the following Sunday and that "the championship of the northern part of Wisconsin will be at stake."

Whether Green Bay fans understood all the "inside workings" of football or not, the Green Bay city team was positioned for what the *Gazette* labeled a "Championship Battle" with the Oshkosh city team at Hagemeister Park on Sunday, November 24, at 2:30 p.m. "if the grounds allow it." The two teams had met in Oshkosh earlier that season and pitched themselves into a tie. The game would decide the "championship of northern Wisconsin," reported the newspaper. How important that game was was vastly overstated. The game was neither played nor reported, and no explanation was forthcoming.

Green Bay football enthusiasts were delighted by an item that appeared in the *Gazette* the following Monday. It was headed, "Recall Carlisle Play":

HARVARD MEN WILL REMEMBER HIDDEN BALL
TRICK BY INDIANS

> *Perhaps the greatest trick play ever worked in football history occurred at Harvard some years ago. The Crimson was playing the Carlisle Indians, well known as trick warriors anyway.*
>
> *It was growing dark, and the various shifty formations of the redskins were followed with the greatest difficulty. Suddenly the Carlisle backs directed a play at left end, dashing together in a well knit interference. The whole Harvard squad, in a determined effort, smashed up the formation, but the various tacklers didn't know which Indian to down, for the ball wasn't in sight.*
>
> *A moment later a wild yell directed Harvard's attention to its own goal line. There, sitting on the ball right behind the posts, was a Carlisle player. He had taken the oval from the quarter, concealed it under his ample sweater and during the mixup in midfield quietly stole around the other end and went down without a Harvard tackle to oppose him.*
>
> *There isn't a Harvard graduate who has forgotten this play.*

Unfortunately, the article was tremendous in reporting the drama and deficient in relaying the actual facts of the famous play. The year was 1903 and Carlisle had never beaten the Harvard squad, despite their scrappy efforts. Harvard always seemed to have the Indian players' number. Carlisle didn't beat them this time either, but the "hidden ball" play would become the stuff of football legend.

Perhaps that tough little Carlisle squad was well ahead of its time in taking what appeared to be a pretty basic concept to another level. Even by 1912, only a few fans, suggested the national press, were savvy enough to understood the "inside workings" of the game.

"Contrary to baseball, where everything can be seen, the inside workings of football are nearly always concealed, even to the students of the game, and only apparent to the coaches." An article to that effect, appearing in the *Gazette* on

November 13, suggested that a spectator would need to see "the blackboard talk" of the sport in order to realize that on every play every player had some specific duty that must be met in order to facilitate a desired outcome and that, by each man fulfilling his own responsibility to his best ability, a synergy would result that would guarantee the aggregation ultimate success.

Some people probably thought all that was overblown poppycock. Thank God our clichés today have remained simple. "The game will be won in the trenches." "It's a game of inches." And, "You call that holding?"

In order to educate football spectators on all of those inside workings so intricate in the game in 1912, the *Gazette* ran regular features on how the massive rule changes that year had altered the game as it had been known.

One suggested that "good toe artists," that is, dropkickers, placement kickers, and punters, were now a valuable commodity. "The six points allotted for the touchdown and one more for the goal from touchdown made it impossible for opponents by booting two field goals to tie a team which rushed the ball across the line and kicked the goal from touchdown," it said.

Another reported on the Minnesota "wing-shift," suggesting that no play "is more often used by players and is less understood by spectators." Tom Shevlin, former captain of the Yale team, had introduced it to the Eli as early as 1910, the report continued. But it was Dr. Harry Williams who really masterminded the complicated maneuver, which, today, is illegal. The play usually consisted of moving the tackles behind center, where they would then move together to one side or the other, putting more men on the line of scrimmage to the side a team was running to. It would catch the defense unprepared or in the process of adjusting as the ball was snapped. To today's fan, however, it isn't considered much as far as "inside workings." Of special note to Green Bay fans was the end of the college career of Joe Hoeffel, a Green Bay lad who captained the University of Wisconsin eleven and closed out a tremendous four-year stint there. Hoeffel had made the varsity aggregation as a freshman and played in every single contest over his tenure as a Madison student. He was named to the all-western team as a junior and, as a senior, was named that team's captain.

Two items of note closed out the 1912 football season, which had seen a massive alteration of the sport. The first suggested that not much had changed, despite the complete overhaul. "Twelve killed and forty-one seriously injured was the toll of football during the season of 1912," an article stated. All of the dead, it reported, "were between the ages of 14 and 20 years. Body blows caused five deaths, concussion of the brain four and other causes the remaining three. Four of the dead were high school players."

The second item questioned the sportsmanship that the forward pass had introduced into the game under a circumstance where the "passer when he sees he

THE FOOTBALL GOES ON A DIET

With the increasing use of the forward pass, the pigskin went through a series of changes to make it more aerodynamic.

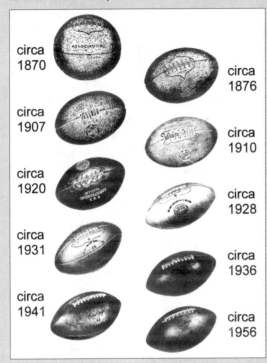

circa 1870

circa 1876

circa 1907

circa 1910

circa 1920

circa 1928

circa 1931

circa 1936

circa 1941

circa 1956

1870—since the "prolate spheroid" is primarily used for running, it is best at its most rotund self.

1876—a smaller, more oblong ball is more easily cradled in the runner's arm.

1907—one year after the forward pass is legalized, the darn thing is still tough to throw!

1910—does a smaller ball encourage passing or does passing encourage a smaller ball?

1920–1936—as the old "projectile pass" makes its way into more and more playbooks, it begins to look more and more like today's football.

is being crowded or his receivers are covered merely flings the ball two or three yards in front of him." The article went on to suggest that whether "such a defensive measure is in keeping with the spirit of the rules is the point being raised."

Another maneuver questioned by this particular author was "deliberately hurling the ball out of bounds thirty or forty yards beyond the scrimmage line." Following that practice, the other side got possession of the ball at the point of its departure from the playing field, but the pass actually was being substituted for a punt. The issue was whether the rule makers who had prompted the increased use of the play at the beginning of the season had "intended that a forward pass should be so employed."

1913

MAKE ROOM ON THE MANTEL

Football action in the Green Bay area was more widespread in 1913 than ever before. In addition to a bona fide city team, all kinds of intracity teams made their presence known on the various open stretches of turf that would serve as appropriate gridirons.

On Saturday, October 4, the *Gazette* whetted the appetites of Green Bay football rooters with the head, "City Football Teams Will Battle Tomorrow." Company G, an independent military team, was slated to fight it out with an aggregation of former high school stars representing the Green Bay city team at the League Ball Grounds.

"The guards," reported the paper, "are former high school, navy and college players." The lineup for Company G was the following: ends, Noble and Gilling; tackles, Evaard and Nicholson; guards, Van and Catoor; center, Jahn; halfbacks, Nicholson and Boyce; quarterback, Raiche; fullback, Carl Jacobs; substitutes, Brogan, Gilling, and Ralph. Talent was being drawn from both sides of the river.

Jim Coffeen scored the first touchdown about two minutes into the game, and after that the floodgates stood open. The final score, 31–3, belied the *Gazette*'s summation that the game was well contested. The city eleven displayed the considerable prowess of Jerry McGrath, Earl Skogg, Joe Umberham, George Madden, Buck Anderson, Andy Muldoon, Andy Lom, Warren Spoffard, Clarence "Shorty" Dashnier, Hawley, Joe Brozak, Harry O'Neil, and Ally Romson. Muldoon and Romson had paid their dues on previous city aggregations; most of the other players, like Dashnier, figured prominently into the future of football in Green Bay, helping to usher in the Packers.

Notice came on Thursday of the following week that the Tiger football team of Racine would like to meet any team in Green Bay or cities in the vicinity with members averaging 135 to 138 pounds in weight. Carl Miller was the Tiger manager and entertained any defis thrown toward the team.

BEFORE THEY WERE THE PACKERS

RACINE—WELCOME TO THE NFL

Four cities from Wisconsin had teams in the pro ranks at one point or another. Today, it's just one. But Racine can stand right proud of its membership in the NFL, and who's to say that, had things gone a little differently, football fans from Titletown wouldn't be traveling south to Milwaukee, Racine, or Kenosha for their Sunday fare.

One beautiful autumn day in 1919, a Racine crew rode the rails to Green Bay for a football game. It was about as bloody a game as could be. By game's end, Racine had used up every one of its substitutes and Green Bay had hauled two of its own players off the battlefield. Lambeau's crew racked up 76 points, mostly through the air. Racine's lone touchdown also came on a series of passes. The abuse left a bad taste in Racine's mouth, but they avenged it often enough during the 1920s.

In 1922, they joined the elite and became members of the prepubescent National Football League. By all football standards of the day, Racine had arrived, and they did not disappoint. Any football fan living in Racine can point to the 1922 season as a moment in the sun. The Racine team then was sponsored by the American Legion Post and playing under an appropriate moniker. They enjoyed mixed success, including in their contests with the Packers, until 1924, the last year they enjoyed legion sponsorship. The 1925 season proceeded without them.

In 1926 Racine returned a team to the NFL lineup, this time as the Tornadoes. The team's new sponsors, the American Business Council, had money enough to field a team but only enough football talent to muster an anemic 1 and 4 record. The one game this aggregation played against the Packers was a 35–0 humiliation. That was signal enough that, at least as an organization, Racine was out of it. The NFL never again saw an entry from Racine. But it didn't see entries from a lot of other cities either. Racine was once a member of the NFL, and that's enough for any football fan sitting at any bar in that city.

Speculation still raged as to whether the extreme rule revisions of 1912 had streamlined the game or dragged it back to its earlier and cruder days 15 and 20 years prior. Under a photo showing a mass of bodies, the American Press Association ran the following caption:

> The accompanying illustration was snapped during the Yale game last week. It is a scene typical of scores occurring in games under the redrawn football rules, which, according to the gridiron solons, have made football a really open game, doing away with the old time "brutal mass plays."
>
> We fail to see any difference between the scrimmage scene shown above and the scenes in a scrimmage following an old guard's back play or a revolving wedge or a tackle back lunge through the line.
>
> The rule makers, it would seem, have abolished several of the once popular plays that were highly useful to gain a result that has not been attained at all. As a matter of fact, Harvard and several other colleges had more men injured this year in the first two weeks of practice than ever occurred before in the same period of time.

Regardless of the raging debate, the League Ball Grounds in Green Bay witnessed a Sunday, October 12, match between the Green Bay and Appleton city teams at 2:30 p.m. The Appletons were said to be a "strong aggregation," yet Green Bay won by the convincing margin of 22–3. While the Appletons scored first with a field goal, the Green Bays put the ball to the ground across the goal three times while failing to convert two of its kicks after touchdowns. An added field goal rounded out the score. On the heels of that game, the Hillsides defeated Company G 13–0.

Next up for the city eleven was the official Kaukauna crew. The city boys were still undefeated, with games against tough and well-established aggregations from Marinette and Oshkosh still in the offing.

The following Sunday saw a contest between two intracity teams, one each representing the east side and the west side. The two aggregations battled to a 19–0 outcome at the "west side grounds" with the west-siders ending up on top. Sterner was cited for good work at quarterback for the west-siders. Badore and Reed were also noted for "good work."

On a national scale, reports said the globetrotting Carlisle team was traveling to Spokane, Washington, for a game on Christmas Day. The press was billing this as the first-ever battle between East and West on the gridiron. The Carlisle team was believed to represent the class of the eastern style of play, while Washington was a fair representative of western football. The contest would allow, said the press, for an "intelligent comparison" of the two venues.

In other news, the American Press Association reported the reintroduction of the line-hurdling play, with the tongue-in-cheek comment that "gridiron lawmakers claim to have eliminated the bone breaking features of the gridiron sport."

Picking up on a tradition begun at White City in 1909, another double-header was billed for Sunday, November 2, this time at Hagemeister Park. The first match-up pitted the Kaukauna and Green Bay city teams, while the second put the Company G eleven against the Allouez crew.

"Kaukauna," the *Gazette* stated, "is reputed to have a strong team and will give the city boys a hard fight, but with such a galaxy of former high school and college stars, as Coffen [sic], Morgan and Rompson [sic], the local supporters of the team are confident of victory." The Green Bay and Kaukauna tilt ended in a 7–7 stalemate. Both teams were evenly matched, but the locals Coffeen, Romson and Morgan, the aforementioned stars, were up to their billing.

In the second game, Allouez was trounced by the Company G squad 13–0. Allouez was said to have "put up a stiff fight," but their opponents were "superior in weight and teamwork."

On the following Sunday, the Oshkosh city team was supposed to come to Hagemeister for a game. Again, the *Gazette* reported the opponents as a "strong team" and, in hyping the game, quoted the local players as expecting that "the game tomorrow will be one of the hardest of the season." However, there was a big storm the Saturday before that dropped large amounts of snow and caused temperatures to plummet to about 28 degrees. The paper predicted colder temperatures on Sunday. The cold weather and sloppy snow on the field led to a cancellation of the football festivities the next day.

The long-term evolution of football reared its ugly head in an article in early November announcing the demise of an old gridiron tradition. The piece caught the attention of long-time football fans and players with the headline, "Long-Haired Fraternity," declaring that it

> *Ceases to Exist on Gridiron and Football Headgear is Given as Reason for Disappearance.*
>
> *It's no longer the "long-haired fraternity" on the gridiron. The chrysanthemum head has ceased to be the pride of the football lad and the cartoonist who draws him that way nowadays is out of date.*
>
> *Football headgear is the answer. The football hero of olden days used to claim his heavy locks were a cushion to save his skull when he landed hard. Football helmets are now almost universally worn by college and high school footballists. Long hair and perspiration form a combination that makes helmets almost unendurable.*
>
> *Either the helmets or the hair had to go and the gridiron lads had their locks shorn.*

Shorter hairstyles weren't the only signs that football was continuing to evolve in 1913. An item appearing in the Tuesday, November 25, edition of the *Gazette* proposed an interesting question that, from today's perspective, seems humorous. "Why not number the players on all football elevens?" it queried.

The article, relying on some reporting by the *Detroit Free Press*, relayed the story of the Heralds, the Detroit independent team champions. The Heralds wore numbers on their jerseys, much to the delight of the fans that turned out at Mack Park to watch them play. The fans could tell who was doing what.

The Heralds appeared in their maroon jerseys with large white circles on the backs, and in the center of the circle was the player's number in red. A "key chart" was then posted in sight of all spectators. The report also stated that the same system was used by the Carlisle Indian team.

The NFL didn't make numbering the jersey mandatory until 1937, when the rule, quoted from *Total Football*, stated, "All players must wear minimum 6-inch Arabic numerals on front and minimum 8-inch Arabic numerals on back jerseys, whose color must be in sharp contrast with color of jerseys."

With or without long hair the De Pere city eleven handed the Company G team an old-fashioned gridiron whaling, 26–0, on the Saint Norbert College field.

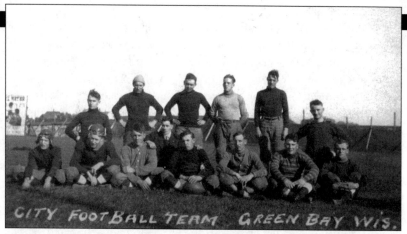

In every year after 1910, the evolution of the Green Bay Packers took another step forward. The 1913 championship team pictured here featured one early Packer, Andy Muldoon (seated, second from right), as well as the stalwarts of the city's best town team years. This aggregation included: (seated, left to right) Jerry McGrath, Earl Skogg, Joe Umberham, George Madden, Buck Anderson, Muldoon, and Andy Lom; (kneeling) Warren Spoffard, Shorty Dashnier, and Hawley; (standing) Joe Brozak, Harry O'Neil, Ally Romson, and Jim Coffeen. This crew would continue to represent Titletown in 1914 and 1915, joining forces with more of the men who would make up the first Packer teams. Photograph obtained from and used with permission of Orville Anderson, Green Bay, Wisconsin.

A large crowd witnessed the "very fast and interesting" contest, and the De Peres moved the sights of their collective gun toward Green Bay's Hillside team for a match the following Sunday.

Then, from out of the blue, a game was announced on Tuesday, November 18, to be contested the following Sunday between the Green Bay city aggregation and the new Saint Patrick's Athletic Club Team. The scrap would be over the "city championship" and would take place the next day at the League Ball Grounds. One had to wonder how the Saint Patrick team ascended to such an honor immediately upon its organization. This was especially true, given that the Hillsides had been hard at it with a reasonable degree of success, despite their waterloo against De Pere. Certainly the Hillsides were asking themselves the same question. No matter, the Green Bay–Saint Patrick contest was on.

The city team lineup was basically unchanged, with Umberham at center; Muldoon and Skogg at guards; Petchka, Lom, and Abrams at tackles; Dashnier and O'Neil at the ends; Coffeen at quarterback; Martin and Duchateau at the halves; and Romson at fullback. The list reads like a who's who of the late town team and early Packer rosters.

Saint Patrick's brought Lally at center; Hawley, Lannoye, and Hogan at guards; Gary and Early at tackles; Crevecoure, Tenton, Clemens, and Rispold alternating at the ends; G. Dwyer at quarterback; Clark and Brehme at the halves;

and F. Dwyer at fullback.

"The city team," reported the *Gazette*, "has put in the past week in practicing and as the men had no game last Sunday they are in the pink of condition for tomorrow's battle. Saint Patricks team is composed of former high school stars, and spent some time in practice."

A large crowd turned out for the contest, which actually took place at Hagemeister Park. As expected, the Saint Patrick's boys put up a dandy of a fight and held the crack city unit to two touchdowns. "The game," gushed the *Gazette*, "was marked by smashing plays on both sides, open football being used little."

The Saint Patrick's eleven scored first in the opening quarter with a field goal, and supporters of the west-side outfit were heard to say, "told ya so" up and down the sidelines. But with a minute left in the same period, the city team "sent a man over for the first touchdown."

The city aggregation put up their second touchdown just a sliver into the second quarter. But that was it for scoring. "After that score," wrote the *Gazette* reporter, "the ball see-sawed the length of the field until the game ended." Working out of the backfield, Jim Coffeen and Ally Romson were hailed as the stars of the city eleven.

GLADSTONE—CHEER OR JEER?

Women have always stayed out of the heat of battle created during a football game. Right? Au contraire. Even in the prim and proper days as the nineteenth century turned into the twentieth, it seems that the "better half" could become the "bitter half," stirring up emotions in their boys on the field that would never be confused with love.

Such was the case when a Gladstone town team faced a weak-kneed aggregation from Manistique, their favorite football whipping boy. The game was a 15–0 snore marked with plenty of line bucks for the Gladstone lads. While the play on the field might have been pedestrian, a crowd of Manistique coeds brought some of the college atmosphere into the mix and began what the Gladstone players called "a rather uncomplimentary jingle in rhyme."

Later that season, it was time for Gladstone's debutantes to repay the favor. At the return game in Gladstone, Manistique's players were greeted with the following chant from Gladstone's fairer sex: "Big and clumsy, slow and weak. Bughouse, bughouse, Manistique!"

"Considering the fact that it was their initial appearance the Saint Patrick's players gave a good account of themselves and it was due to lack of practice alone that their stubborn fighting was less productive," concluded the paper.

By November 24, it seemed as if the city eleven's best game of the season had already been played. Green Bay football fanatics now turned their collective attention to the East and West High School contest, a town affair since 1905. That same day, the *Gazette* announced that the two schools had agreed on the officials for the contest, Harry Sylvester, a player of some renown from Lawrence University, and

OSHKOSH NORMAL SCHOOL—
"UNIFORMS SO SOFT AND FINE"? COME ON!

In its earliest days, the Oshkosh Normal School was a teacher training ground, and football was way off in its future. The bloodiest competition of the day seemed to be had by the debate team. "Take no prisoners!" was their cry as they traveled from Oshkosh to Ripon and Appleton, sending tremors of fear into opponents with their speaking skills. Oratory was sufficient for many, but there were always the recalcitrant few who were not satisfied by the pound of flesh extracted verbally; they wanted action bordering on fisticuffs. These roustabouts, men and women, probably made the best teachers; football was just the thing for them, though the girls would have to enjoy the sport from the sidelines.

In his book, *Here to Serve: The First Hundred Years of the University of Wisconsin–Oshkosh*, Dr. Edward Noyes reports that "Athletics were popular at Oshkosh before 1898." Noyes also writes that "Football began encouragingly enough on the Oshkosh campus in 1894." While football types weren't usually great speechmakers or wordsmiths, Noyes did find the work of a campus poet who could articulate the dash of the young men on the school's first team and the game that caught their fancy:

The Football Game
At last the men were ranged in line
In uniforms so soft and fine,
Eye to eye, hip to hip, knee to knee,
As bright and keen as they could be.
. . . .
The battle o'er, the fighting done,
We've but pity for Appleton.
Twenty-four to nothing was the score;
The honors from the field we bore.

E. A. Clemens from the Oshkosh Normal School. The football exhibition was to take place "at the park leased by the Green Bay baseball club at Hagemeister Park, and the kickoff is scheduled for 2 o'clock."

The *Gazette* went on to address a rumor that was cruising through the city suggesting that the East squad would put forward a pretty pathetic display on game day. "The players are light but have improved their play as the season advanced, and the student body is confident that the team will give the West High players a battle they will remember," promised the newspaper. They did, but only because the unbalanced score of 38–0 would serve as a major dish of embarrassment for East for some time to come. While the paper pointed to a "costly" fumble on the first play by East, that one misstep didn't nearly explain the shellacking that West delivered. It was the sixth-straight win for the boys from the west side of the river, but they enjoyed bragging rights for a few more years to come.

Not everyone in the area was at the East-West matchup. A smaller, lopsided Thanksgiving Day skirmish took place between the De Pere city team and the

Allouez eleven. In front of a good-sized crowd, the De Pere team bludgeoned their northern neighbors 21–0. In the game, Denisty, an Allouez player, sustained a fractured collarbone.

Then, from out of nowhere, real sparks started to fly. "Hillsides Claim Title of Gridiron Champions," fired a headline in the *Gazette* on Friday, November 28. It was a small item, really, but it did its job:

> *The Hillsides football team, through its manager, Ray Conley, has issued a challenge to the City football team for a game to be played next Sunday for the city championship. The Hillsides claim they possess the championship through victories in past seasons and through their record of four victories this fall. They claim they are entitled to recognition as the champions. The scores made by the Hillsides this year are as follows: H.S. 20, White City 7; H.S. 13, Company G. 0; H.S. 7, De Pere City team 6; H.S. 34, East Rivers 0.*

It didn't take long for the city eleven to pick up the gauntlet. Would they hand it back to the Hillsides, or would their season end with a limp wrist? The next day the *Gazette* stirred the mix with "City Team Accepts Defi of Hillsides":

> *TEAMS WILL MEET ON THE GRIDIRON AT LEAGUE BASEBALL PARK TOMORROW AFTERNOON TO SETTLE CITY TITLE.*
>
> *The challenge, which was issued by the Hillside football team through the Gazette yesterday, was accepted last night by Manager Dashnier on behalf of the City team, and the game will take place tomorrow afternoon at the league baseball park. The ball will be kicked off at 2:30 o'clock. The game is expected to be the best played by professional players here this fall.*

The stage was set for an action thriller: the scrappy Hillsides versus the crack city aggregation. David versus Goliath. And the four-act play was not a disappointment either.

The Hillsides "rang a surprise," reported the *Gazette*, "when they made the first touchdown. The city team had been penalized 50 yards and on the next play the ball was fumbled and recovered by the Hillsides on the 20 yard line." After a couple of line plunges, Bader swept around the end and scored for the Hillsides. On the ensuing kickoff, the city team scored a response touchdown primarily on the shoulders of a 40-yard pass play to Morgan. The city eleven missed on the point after, and, going into the second half, the upstart Hillsides held a one-point advantage.

Then, Goliath swung his massive arm and David fell back. In the third quarter, the city squad "rushed the Hillsides off their feet and secured another touchdown." Then, in the fourth quarter, the city team's stars displayed their "superior playing." Coffeen and Romson once again emerged as crack players through a "series of line plunges," moving the ball to the Hillside's 10-yard line. Then, Wally Ladrow "was sent over for the final touchdown." The game clock ticked down with the city team in charge, 19–7.

"Manager Dashnier," reported the paper in its last paragraph, "claims for his team the championship of the Fox River Valley having met and defeated Appleton, Oshkosh and Kaukauna and local teams. The City team closed its season with this game."

The final football note of the year was a small one, but it rang a familiar bell for true fans of the sport in Green Bay. Francis Flatley was named captain for the East High aggregation in 1914 amid much speculation about the team's ability to step up after a dismal 1913 campaign. Flatley came from a football family. His father and his uncle had played on the earliest town teams and on Titletown's first championship eleven in 1897.

1914

FOOTBALL ON EVERY CORNER

Town team football, Green Bay style, got an earlier-than-usual start in 1914 with an announcement in the *Gazette* on Saturday, September 12. The baseball season was still in full swing, but some anxious footballers couldn't wait for the last inning to end. The article heralded a reorganization meeting of the city team at Baur's Buffet that night. The team had "made a good record" in 1913, the paper averred, and Manager Carl Dashnier wanted to get the fellows back in line. He was looking into the season with some degree of optimism, the paper reported, because "a majority of the veterans have signified their interest in returning."

What this meant was that Green Bay football fans were once again able to get behind the gridiron glory of a team willing to put the reputation of the entire town on its shoulders, though the team was now known as the Baur city team. After completely disappearing following the disastrous season of 1905, city teams had been resurrected and prospered since 1910. In fact, the 1913 Green Bay eleven had claimed the "championship of the Fox Valley" and went unchallenged in their declaration.

Baur was none other than saloon owner Eugene Baur. Like other entrepreneurs, he understood the advertising power of a few diamonds in the rough with the slight polish of some gridiron elbow grease put to them. They were doing battle under his banner, and all they required, besides some mostly matching jerseys and a modicum of other football equipment, was the immediate gratification of a few, quite a few, or too many to remember, beers after the game.

The fact that football had taken serious hold in Titletown by 1914 was evident in the genuine lack of respect that the intracity teams displayed toward the city team. Defis thrown at the city team by these upstarts came fast and furious, and being the declared city team proved to be an even more complicated endeavor. Obviously, Baur city team manager, Dashnier, would handle the scheduling and contracting with teams from other towns. But he would also have to deal with the challenges of neighborhood teams that did not have to put the reputation of the entire city on the line each time they took to the field of play.

High school football had also begun in earnest by September 12, and the *Gazette* sports reporter cited "strenuous" workouts on both sides of the river after school on Friday, September 11.

The east-sider lads had gone toe-to-toe with an alumni aggregation composed of Issy Abrams, Al Petcka, Warren Gleason, Lee Forsythe, Abe Rosenthal, Harry O'Neil, and Vance Van Laanen, which was supplemented with players from the East High second team. "Among the alumni," reported the *Gazette*, "were five former captains of the local high school teams of former years." Several were also standouts on the teams playing semipro in the city that year.

On the west side, enough high school boys had turned out for football that three full teams were formed. "The first and second squads are fairly evenly matched," declared the paper, "and from the manner in which the second string boys held their own with the regulars, [Coach] White, should experience no difficulty in finding competent subs." White was assisted by fellow teacher, Harold Collette, who was making quite a name for himself as both a player on the semipro circuit and as a coach.

The traditional East-West Thanksgiving Day classic was already shaping up nicely, but, in the meantime, a doubleheader, featuring both squads, was set at the Wisconsin-Illinois ball field for Saturday the 26th. East would square off against the Kewaunee varsity eleven, and West would meet up with the Saint Norbert College men.

With town teams relying on the income of bake sales and dances to field a team, uniforms were basically a catch-as-catch-can proposition, usually cast off by the local college. Here, what was a very good De Pere city team makes an unusual fashion statement, but it does so with a ton of tenacity. This 1914 picture was quite likely taken at Saint Norbert College, the scene of many early games involving Green Bay and De Pere. Photograph obtained from and used with permission of Louie Leiberg, De Pere, Wisconsin.

"Athletics at Saint Norbert's" had augured a banner in the September 12 *Gazette*, and it hailed the beginning of the college eleven's football campaign for the year with a matchup set for the following Monday afternoon. The college eleven would open its season against a scrappy prep crew and was being given "only an outside chance of taking the West High men into camp."

Besides the opportunity to witness the exploits of the Baur city squad and the school teams, 1914 Green Bay football fans were also able to support the exploits of a bevy of intracity teams such as the Moose, the Hillsides, the South Sides, the Riversides, the Saint Patrick's Athletic Association, and the Lucky Eleven. These crews were joined by a resurrected "Skidoo" team that had lost its Sorensen sponsorship but picked up an added "d" in the bargain. They would do their football battle forever after as the "Southside Skiddoos."

Plain and simple, the town now boasted a population of about 27,000, and, with that number, it was getting easier to recruit football players as well as fans. The increase in neighborhood teams meant that a little tension could be felt as the "boys from down the street" took their best to "the guys from a few blocks over." Street conversation between friends and passers-by could now be peppered with references to the teams' exploits as well as some expletives.

White City also continued to sponsor a team and to host football at its grounds on Bay Beach Road. The White City baseball team that year had done well, and they posed for a photo at the end of their season. Labeled as the "post office boys" by local papers, a handful of these guys delivered mail for a living. When a chill began to spread through in the air, some of them gladly slid into football togs.

An aggregation representing the Green Bay Motor Boat Club had even thrown its rather delicate headgear into the ring with an organizational meeting on Monday, September 21, in the club's rooms. According to the *Gazette,* the group discussed two items of real importance over ice cream and cantaloupe: a "wild duck bouillon" social to be held on Saturday night and the formation of a "new football team which the club will put on the field this fall."

The motorboat boys had risen from the neighborhoods of Green Bay's near west side, and they boasted a number of former West High stars in their huddle. And, despite their penchant for gourmet delicacies, they were unabashedly looking at the city team as their first opponent for the following Sunday. They had also decided to purchase a new Victrola from the Groix store and appointed a committee to "secure the instrument." Without football to work out their issues of masculinity, these dilettantes may have been relegated to the social register and escaped the notice of the brutes who favored football as their bill of fare.

In an encounter with the varsity squad of their alma mater that Wednesday, the motorboat boys gapped their spark plugs and tuned their engines. The scrimmage produced only a 12–12 result at West High's practice field on Ashland

Avenue. Some top-notch forward passing by West's Charles Mathys put the high schoolers up in the opening two periods. Harold Collette, who had been offering an assistant coach's guidance from West High's sidelines, then took position at left half with the Motor Boat Club. With his addition, the alumni churned down the field for two scores before the end of the game.

As a warm-up for a contest against the city team, the battle with the West High squad had served its purpose. Unfortunately, the city team snuck off the following Sunday to battle with the Saint Patrick's Athletic Association, another westside aggregation that had come out of nowhere to throw a defi to the city team in 1913. Thus, the city boys narrowly escaped the wrath that sherbet, fruit, and fine music can induce.

The Hillsides were also busy. As a neighborhood team, they were celebrated enough to be mentioned when Arch Ward wrote the first comprehensive Packer history, *The Green Bay Packers*, in 1946. Though Ward said the Hillsides were "largely ex-West High athletes," the team was actually composed of many players from the "hill" neighborhoods around East High School and Green Bay's Astor Park area. They didn't play for cash, so Ward said it was pretty much *pour le sport* with them. Their initial lineup for the season included Joe Lally at center, Clyde Basche and Jack Taylor at guards, Walter Busch and Bill Schaut at tackles, Mannebach and Green at ends, Alvin Martin and Bader at halves, Roy Conley at full, and Gleason at quarterback.

On Tuesday, September 22, it was announced that the team's manager, Warren Gleason, an east-side electrician, had scheduled a game with the southside team for the following Sunday "to be played on the grounds of the latter." The kickoff was set for 2:00. According to the *Gazette*, the Hillsides were anticipating a "strenuous season" and were inquiring for games against the Menasha and Oshkosh city teams.

By season's end, the Hillsides would reissue their defi to the city team. That glove would be snatched up by the Baur city team, and the results would be markedly different than they had been in 1913. Ultimately, the Hillsides would gain stature nearly equal to that of the city team, and they would thumb their noses at the cross-town competition with a certain amount of arrogance.

The south-side team was also ready to list a lineup that would toe up with the Hillsides, and it did so in the next day's *Gazette*. Spranger would start at fullback, Anderson at left half, Russell at right half, Wooders at right end, Reed at left end, Rushlean at right tackle, Spranger at left tackle, Taylor at left guard, Putzke at right guard, Nelson at center, and Dwyer at quarterback. Also ready to jump into the fray were Deshast, S. Anderson, C. Anderson, Olson, and Grant.

The South Sides were also from west side of the river, living primarily south of Walnut Street. They hailed from around State Street, where the Spranger crew all resided, and from Broadway, Ashland, and Chestnut Streets. They had been around for several years, merging in and out of the Skiddoo lineup as well as those of other west-side teams, and they had met with a modicum of success in the intracity wars. Their home field, for 1914 at least, was West High School's practice grounds which were commonly referred to as the "Cow Yard" because the surrounding houses had, for years, utilized the open area as pasture. The South Sides were, said the *Gazette*, "desirous of meeting all the good local football teams" and expected to "be as strong as they have been in former seasons."

Amid the scrambling for early season games and promotion of the superior skills of each of the individual teams, football across the United States had reached a plateau of recognition unpredictable in its earliest days of infamy. The game was still labeled as "violent," no doubt. By November 23, when the bulk of the 1914 season was over, the death toll would stand at 12. Two of the dead were college players, none of the dozen victims were over 24 years of age, and "tackling was responsible for the greatest number of fatalities."

But fans were becoming savvy. Their expectations were increasing as was their knowledge of the game. The sidelines were no longer dotted with myopic men and swooning coeds lost in adoration of the long-haired kickers of a quarter century earlier. Fans shelled out good money at the gate and happily moved up and down the sidelines with their noses as close to the action as was practicable. But they expected good play, and they wanted accountability on the part of the individual players.

Numbering all players on the field, a development usually credited to the Detroit Heralds as early as 1913, was growing in popularity. The sweeping rule changes of 1912 had primarily opened up and encouraged the forward pass. Teams were now starting to adopt it as a winning strategy. The emphasis on the mass play in which a pile of men twisted and squirmed for just inches was long a thing of the past. And, as players distinguished themselves on the gridiron with long passes, beautiful catches, and evasive treks down the field, the fans wanted to know who they were. "I like the game," the *Gazette* quoted one college coed, "but honestly, I don't know who is carrying the ball half the time."

W. G. Penfield, coach of the Princeton Tigers, was pushing for universal numbering of all players and the idea was catching on. "It is our plan to number our players this fall," he said. "The only objection to numbering is that it enables scouts from other teams to follow the work of the individuals better. This, in my mind, is rather a childish and unsportsmanlike objection."

"Local sentiment," summarized the *Gazette*, was "in favor of numbering every football man." That amelioration would probably address a small part of the issue of crowds pressing their way onto the actual fields of play. This concern was addressed a number of times, not only in this season, but in many others before and subsequent. Most recently, the issue had been advanced following the high school doubleheader. The *Gazette* described the effect of the crowd's intrusion as well as it could: "Mathys had attempted to punt and the kick had been blocked. The quarterback picked up the oval and with a badly broken defensive field and but a short distance from the goal, he had more than an even chance of planting the pigskin behind the line."

The crowd, however, had gathered around the two teams in a circle just little more than 100 feet in diameter, and when Mathys unexpectedly broke free and started for the goal, he collided with several spectators on the inner edge of the circle and was held until tackled by one of the opposing men.

Because the game was played at the Wisconsin-Illinois baseball field and because the baseball park owners had disallowed play on the infield, the grandstand bleachers weren't an adequate option for fans who wanted to see the action close-up. The *Gazette* took a little literary license in explaining crowd psychology, but what the heck. "People are like sheep," it purported. "One of them steps forward over the side lines for a closer view and the others take unto themselves the same privilege."

The game itself was also getting more exacting and was demanding more from its practitioners. East High School Coach Carroll Nelson was said to be utilizing "considerable 'Minnesota stuff,'" meaning different sets and shifts in the backfield, in his game plans. "If the boys can put their whole thought into the execution of the play rather than struggling with mental arithmetic trying to figure out what the formation is to be," Nelson was quoted in the *Gazette*, "I believe the results will show in their work."

Nelson used "typical Williams formations," said the newspaper, "dispensing with a quarter and training the backs to do their receiving direct from the center. The square backfield formation with the innumerable variations possible, will be the forte of the team." This was the genesis of the single-wing offense, not to mention the shotgun formation. Of lesser note, the East High players had received their shoulder pads and used them for the first time in their scrimmage on Monday, September 21.

Through universal numbering, scouting, continual massaging of the game through rule changes, and "mental arithmetic," the game was indeed getting more and more sophisticated. While those developments were being kicked around in the local press, the L. C. Snavely company "near the big elm" at 410 Main Street was doing good business in footballs:

> *Complete line of Reach balls $1.00 to $5.00*
> *All fresh, clean stock and guaranteed to wear.*
> *For the little fellows I have a dandy football—a genuine Reach ball, backed*
> *by the Reach Guaranty—slightly under regulation size. Special $1.00.*

Extra bladders to fit any football, guaranteed one year—$.50, $.65 and $.80. Shin guards, $.50 to $1.00.

So, by late September, gridiron action, not just talk, in Titletown was truly heating up. Four straight years of strong city teams hadn't hurt the situation either. The bout between the "reorganized" city team and the crew from the Saint Patrick's Athletic Association was set for Sunday, September 27, at Hagemeister Park. It marked the first contest of the year for both elevens. The *Gazette* also reported that the city team was facing upcoming games with town teams from Kaukauna and Peshtigo. The Saint Patricks had issued a challenge to the city team in 1913 but had come up short primarily, reported the *Gazette*, because of a lack of practice. They were now enjoying their second year of organization and could promise a more polished product.

In preparation for the Saint Patrick contest, the city team had scooped up the services of Collette at halfback, even though his primary allegiance was to the west side. Collette had starred at Michigan, and getting him in the fold was a good move for the city team. His presence would, said the *Gazette*, "add a world of strength to the ball carrying squad on that eleven."

"Collette," continued the paper, "demonstrated beyond a doubt that he is 'there' when he put on a suit in the recent game of the Green Bay Motor Boat club team against West High." Unfortunately, no account of this game is readily found in the pages of the city's newspapers but, if it was played, it is certain that the Baur City eleven would have come out on the winning end of things.

Allouez was also preparing a football crew and had the Hillsides in mind for the following Sunday. The Allouez lineup was as follows: ends, Roy Ducharme and Ernest Wilmet; tackles, M. Johnson and Richard Brighton; guards, "Baldy" and Julius Wilmet; center, John Solomon; quarterback, "Red" Anderson; fullback, Ed Christensen; halves, David Prenonsur and Cyril McKeough.

Sunday, October 4, offered up a number of contests for Green Bay area football watchers. A "misunderstanding" between the Baur Citys and the De Pere city team had caused their game to disappear, but everywhere around town, contests were actually set to see the light of day. The South Sides matched up with the De Pere city team, the Hillsides battled the Allouez eleven, and the Riversides faced up to the Skiddoos at the West High practice grounds.

The De Peres had gotten themselves organized in late September and had been practicing at the De Pere High School grounds regularly under the direction of Captain Clayton Ruel. Ruel, a sharp-looking young man with the much the same visage of the young Joe DiMaggio, was a classic example of a guy who couldn't get his fill of football. While he captained the De Pere townies, he was also a standout on the Saint Norbert college team.

In similar fashion, the Riversides had pulled themselves together on Tuesday,

September 29, and elected E. C. Jensen as manager and Herbert De Groot as captain. The Riversides were taking an average weight of 150 pounds into the skirmish with the Skiddoos and wielded a challenge to "any team in the Fox River valley."

Still three more teams had emerged from the dust of neighborhood ball fields to strike some profile in the intracity matrix: the Lucky Eleven, the Northsides, and the Doo Wah Jack club.

The Lucky Eleven also hailed from Green Bay's near west side, the hotbed of Fred Hulbert's first Green Bay team nearly 20 years earlier. On Sunday, October 4, they played more like Attila's Huns, sweeping across the river, where they whipped the East Sides 7–0 and then headed for home. And they did travel light. At an average weight of 119 pounds, they invited contact from any team of the same swagger.

The Luckys' lineup was William McCloskey, left guard; A. McWey, right half; Ed Sternard, quarterback and manager; Frank Sternard, right guard; Edward Bedore, right end; James De Cota, left halfback and captain; John Brogan, fullback; F. Robinson, left tackle; Francis Sullivan, left end; Robert Icks, center; and James Burns, right tackle. The team was a mixed bag of backgrounds and pursuits, primarily with connections to the near west side. Several were tied to family businesses, others practiced a trade, and still others were students.

In their game, the Hillsides nipped the Allouez team 7–0 at Zeger's Field just off Webster Avenue. Conley made the points for the Hillsides in the second quarter with a 12-yard run off tackle. Alvin Martin also starred for the Hillsides as did Henry J. "Tubby" Bero. Bero, like many players from these intracity teams in the mid-1910s, served on the earliest Packer aggregations. For Allouez, Kid Stack brought down his share of Hillsides runners and then some. Wilmet, Cowles, and Ridgley kept the contest in hand as officials, and Madden and McKeough served as timekeepers.

A 7–0 result also came from the Skiddoo–Riverside contest. The Skiddoos brought far more confidence out of the close contest than one might have expected, declaring that they were in line for the city title and willing to play any team in the valley. Their lineup was—O'Brien at fullback; Art Hansen at right halfback and captain; William Larson at left halfback; Buck Anderson, Servais, and Smith at ends; Melos Hamachek and John Bangert at tackles; McMaster and Dynamite at guards; Ferris Nelson at center; and Edward Kolbrak taking the snaps and serving as manager.

Finally, in what could only be labeled the tongue-twister tumble of the day, the Doo Wah Jack football club of De Pere clashed with the Kaukauna Ristau Brothers' bunch at the Saint Norbert field near Main Hall. The game ended in a 6–6 tie, with John Kearnan tossing a touchdown lob for the Doo Wahs. The two squads hooked up in a rematch the following Sunday, this time in Kaukauna.

BEFORE THEY WERE THE PACKERS

In football news from the ensuing week, Manager Dashnier announced a game against the Oconto city team for Sunday, the 11th. The squabble was set for 2:30 at the Wisconsin-Illinois ball grounds, and Dashnier projected that his boys would "show the visitors something in the way of football." Appleton, Menominee, and Oshkosh were also bandied about as possible opponents, "providing the support of local rooters warrants such a step." Dashnier had sustained an injury to his right eye but was still ready to take his place at end against the Oconto lads.

Other contests for the upcoming Sunday were either falling into place or falling apart. The Riversides, coming off their loss to the Skiddoos, were set to meet the Hillsides at the White City grounds the same day. The Lucky Eleven were no longer interested in tangling with the west-side football team because the west-siders were just too darn heavy. The Luckys took on a smaller team, the East Sides, who, said the Gazette, expected to "offer a bunch of resistance."

The Skiddoos, now touting the "Skiddoo 23" label, issued a challenge to teams in the Fox River Valley who weighed in at about 155 pounds. The Skiddoos had games scheduled against Allouez for Sunday, October 18, and the Hillsides for Sunday, October 25. Again, challenges were officially issued through Captain Hansen or Manager Kolbrak.

The Lucky Eleven proved to have more than good fortune on their side as they humbled the East Sides 42–0. "The East-siders played well," attested the *Gazette*, "but by continued fumbling of the ball, lost any chance they might have had for victory." The paper must have considered fumbling a pretty minor football offense.

The city team was even more brutal, treating its Oconto visitors like unwanted, red-headed stepchildren. "A poor crowd," reported the paper, "witnessed the overwhelming defeat administered to the Oconto team by the local Baur City team at the W-I. Park on Sunday when the home boys trimmed the visitors by an 81 to 0 score."

Clearly the Baurs had secured the talents of the some of the intracity squads for this contest, and the results were plenty staggering. The locals, said the *Gazette*, "were never in a position where punting was necessary and waived chances at 6 or 7 goals from touchdown so the ball might be put in play sooner."

The stars for the Baur city team were enough to fill the entire night sky. Jim Coffeen, his Beloit College skeleton hung well away in his closet, was cited for good ball carrying, as were Jerry McGrath and Ally Romson. Dashnier hadn't played, serving as one of the timekeepers instead. Collette had also stayed out, his talents probably proving to be superfluous. The rest of the lineup included Andy Muldoon, Earl Skogg, George Madden, Joe Umberham, Hawley, Andy Lom, Harry O'Neil, and Joe Brozack. Without fear of overstatement, this was clearly one of the most formidable aggregations of football players to ever answer the muster on a Green Bay football field, and one can only feel an appropriate amount of empathy for the Oconto crew.

On the heels of the Baur City massacre, Green Bay football fans had plenty to laugh about already, so the tongue-in-cheek item in the *Gazette* on Saturday, October 17, may have just come from a giddy spot in someone's sense of humor. The "East High Football Men Get Nine Pants" headline chuckled,

> As a result of the publicity given the pantless East High athletes by the *Gazette* when announcement was made on Thursday that there were more football candidates than trousers at the Hill institution, Xavier Parmentier Sons' sporting goods store has donated nine pairs of the moleskin coverings to the school. They were received yesterday afternoon.

On Saturday, October 24, the Saint Norbert eleven came out on the long end of a 20–0 battle with the second team of Lawrence University of Appleton. A large crowd had turned out to witness the exploits of Saint Norbert stars Johnson, Dart, and, of course, Clayton Ruel, who had each hit pay dirt once. Next up for the Saint Norbert eleven was the Stevens Point Normal team. The "abnormal" team, as usual, stayed home.

A doubleheader was slated for the next day, and it had to turn the heads of Titletown gridiron aficionados. The first contest would put the Baur City squad up against an Appleton city team that was more qualified than the Oconto eleven. The second game pitted the Hillsides against the De Pere city team.

This time, an already-incredible Baur City aggregation was bolstered by the addition of Issy Abrams, who, said the *Gazette*, "was the strong man for the locals on plunges through the line." Coffeen was again a major contributor and gave what the paper termed "an exhibition of gameness by returning to the conflict in the final period" after being injured. Buck Anderson came over from the South Sides for the contest. Other than that, the lineup remained pretty constant. A good crowd turned out, and the final score stood at a solid 18–6. Fries, a standout left halfback for the Appletonians, pitched in their only points.

In the second game, the Hillsides honored the stately pride of their well-to-do section of town by whipping up on the De Pere city team 27–0. "The Hillsides of Green Bay did things to the De Pere City team," the *Gazette*'s account began. The paper cited the De Pere team for "a fine game of football," but it was pretty clearly a one-sided affair. Morgan, playing at the right halfback slot, "tore off a circus run in the second period when he grabbed the ball on a punt at his own 30 yard line and ran through the opposing team for a touchdown." Mannebach, the paper said, also put in a noteworthy performance at right end, while Cubby Johnson, a halfback, had accounted for most of De Pere's real estate.

The Skiddoo 23 game for that same Sunday had fallen by the wayside when the opponents, a newly resurrected East River team, had failed to show up. There was probably good reason for the disappearing act. The Skiddoos and the South Sides had joined forces for the East River contest and for the remainder of the season. As a result, they presented what *Gazette* reporter called "one of the strongest amateur football teams in the city." They continued to play as Skiddoo 23. But the Hillsides were out there waiting for this hybrid aggregation, and, whenever it might occur, the *Gazette* forecast a "rattling good game."

The city team was now zeroing in on Marinette as its next foe in a match set for the following Sunday, October 25. While the Baur lads could be encouraged by their showing against Appleton, Marinette, going as far back as 1894, had never been pushovers. "Last year," the *Gazette* said, "the Marinette City team was a hoodoo for anything else of its class in the state and they profess their intention of doing things to the Baur boys." But Manager Dashnier had a chip on his own shoulder. "We'll ruin them," he predicted.

Going into the 2:30 contest at the Wisconsin-Illinois park, the Marinette team waved championship flags of northern Wisconsin and Michigan from 1912 and 1913. "Someone is going to be beaten," declared the local press, "and the locals are confident that they will not be the fall guys." "Fall" they would not, but a small misstep was definitely in their future.

"The Baur City team met their first defeat in two years on Sunday at the W-I park on Sunday when the Marinette City team nosed out a lucky win from the locals by a 6 to 0 margin," reported the *Gazette*. Brozack, Lom, and Madden had all been absent for this outing, and it clearly left some holes in Dashnier's lineup. The solitary score came on a run by Marinette's Erdman set up by an offside called against the Baur boys. Disappointment seemed pretty thick when the *Gazette* suggested that Dashnier was "not sure if he [would] bring Oshkosh here on November 1, although negotiations have been entered into regarding the game."

The undefeated Lucky Eleven also took it on the beak from a tough Goose Town team by a tally of 12–6. It was the Lucky Eleven's first loss of the season and against some goose hunters from the southwest side of Green Bay. According to the *Gazette*, the ball had spent most of the afternoon in the middle of the field in a "closely contested" game. James De Cota and J. Sullivan had stood out for the Lucky Eleven, while Manders and Mathews had starred for the Goose Towns. A 76-yard carry by James Burns represented the only break for the Luckys.

Another new player in the intracity squabbles was reported as victorious in the Monday, October 26, *Gazette*. The Nitchee Cheemans had turned up against a Saint Norbert aggregation, and after the 25–0 drubbing, the Saint Norbert boys found themselves asking, "What's a Nitchee Cheeman?" While they may have had a hard time answering that one, they could, no doubt answer the questions, "How did John Brogan score two touchdowns?" and "How did Riley, Peterson, and Dwyer each score one?" and "Why did we let Mathews add a goal after touchdown?"

The Nitchee Cheemans had also arisen from the west side of town and featured two players, Dwyer and Wes Leaper, who would serve good time with the first versions of the Green Bay Packers. The entire roster of the Nitchee Cheeman crew included Karl Perkins and Peterson at ends, Hugh Brogan and R. Riley at tackles, Wes Leaper and B. Fontaine at guards, Icks at center, Dwyer at quarterback, Mathews and George Riley at halfbacks, and John Brogan at fullback.

A rubber match was likely for Saturday, November 7, and there was talk of a game between the Cheemans and the West High team. This is where things would get sticky, since the Nitchee Cheemans had a least one West High player on their roster, and there was at least one brother-to-brother matchup in the proposal. It may have been all friendly banter anyway as the press never reported such a game.

Sunday the 25th also saw a bludgeoning of the Allouez team by some amended version of the South Sides. The score, 41–0, was pretty good evidence that "the South side boys ran away with the Allouez team through superior handling of the ball and a greater knowledge of the game."

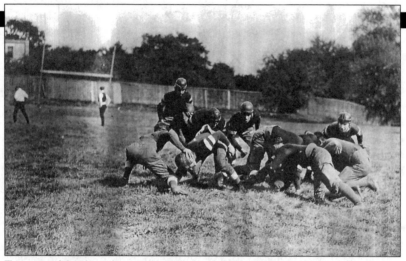

The names of the players here, and even the teams, for that matter, are lost to history. This photo, obtained from the archives of Saint Norbert College, was probably taken on the grounds southeast of Main Hall, most likely between 1915 and 1920. Note that there isn't a full compliment of 22 players, suggesting this is some kind of practice scrimmage or an intramural contest. Photograph obtained from and used with permission of Saint Norbert College, De Pere, Wisconsin.

A couple of smaller football items caught the eye of Green Bay football acolytes the following week. Harold Collette was off to the Tharp School in Louisville, Kentucky, to take a position as a Latin and German instructor, head of the athletic department, and coach of the school's five major sports, including football. Also, Curly Lambeau, a sophomore right halfback on the East High School team, had earned himself a sweater from Professor Don Birdsall for scoring the first touchdown in East's game against the Appleton Papermakers. Somewhere down the road,

Curly would be awarded an entire shrine seating some 60,000-plus screaming fanatics to acknowledge his football prowess. One can only wonder whatever happened to that sweater.

Football action for Sunday, November 1, was subdued by the standards set the week before. The Hillsides handed White City a 17–0 defeat at the league ball grounds by playing a "violent defensive game."

The Lucky Eleven were undaunted following their first tar and feathering by the Goose Town gang and rebounded to double up on the North Ends, 28–14. At the half, the North Ends were holding the lead, 14–7. But in the second act, the Lucky Eleven "rushed the North Ends off their feet." Blaney, McWey, Gallagher, and Sternard were all given the nod for good games for the Luckys, and Vandenbrook was credited for a sweet catch for one of the North Sides' scores.

The Lucky Eleven were now gunning for the East Side team on their home grounds the following Sunday, November 8. The lineups were announced on Tuesday, the 3rd. For the Lucky Eleven it was F. Sullivan at center, Frank C. Sternard at left guard, L. McCloskey at right guard, Praeger at left tackle, Jack Burns at right tackle, C. Miller at left end, R. Leicht at right end, Ed Sternard at right half, Ed Vieau at left half, Arthur Gallagher at full, and F. McWey at quarterback. For the East Sides, it was G. Basten at center, F. Gavin at left guard, Shelby Ridgley at right guard, E. Merritt at left tackle, Samuel Cohen at right tackle, E. Joshlin at left end, B. Madden at right end, Clyde Fiedler at right half, Nate Abrams at left half, Clement Simonet at full, and N. Spelling at quarterback.

On Thursday of that week, an announcement was made that the Hillsides would "line-up" against the Skiddoo 23 the following Sunday at the Wisconsin-Illinois Baseball League ball grounds. The Hillsides would have Bero at center, Lande at right guard, Basche at left guard, Green at right tackle, Bergen at left tackle, Gleason at right end, Mannebach at right end, Morgan at right half, Ladrow at right half, and Mader at quarterback.

Next to the item posting the Hillside lineup appeared a bit of yellow journalism that would have bemused Mark Twain:

MARINETTE SCRIBE IS UP ON HIS EAR
Bombards Local Sport Editor With a Flock of Choice Vituperation
The sporting department of the Gazette is covered with confusion because of the awful things said about it by the Marinette Eagle-Star. The shiftless editor of this department has been accused of charging the Marinette team with trying to "get" Lambeau in the East High-Marinette game here Saturday.

Among other things he is ungracious, uses poor judgement, is afflicted with failing eyesight and "should take something for his grouch." Outside of being rather a grammatical mess, the story is good in that it is comprehen-

sive. It reviews the physical and mental limitations of the dastard quite completely.

Ejaculation.

Sirup of Figs! Also pooie, pooie!

When a man is down and another leaps upon his head that is assault and battery. In football it is called "getting him." Likewise, when a man is looking upward and he receives a kick in the stomach the event is an unfailing indication of his unpopularity. This knee action similar to the German "goose step" is a delicate hint upon the part of the would-be recipient of a forward pass that he does not wish to be molested until the pass is complete.

Much as it may peeve the Marinette scribe who splashed ink all over our previously pure reputation, we must admit Marinette's remarkable proficiency in this art.

No! They didn't try to get Lambeau. They nearly ruined him.

As Twain himself once said, "Get your facts first young man and, then, distort them as you please."

The Friday, November 6, edition of the *Gazette*, besides carrying another swipe at the "sport shark" of the *Eagle-Star*, ran a letter from the Skiddoo 23 captain, Art Hansen, declaring the upcoming contest with the Hillsides off:

After trying to secure a game with the Hillside football team for the last six weeks and being unable to secure it through any other source than gambling, the Skiddo[o] 23 organization have [sic] decided to play the White City football team Sunday at the W.-I. park.

If the Skiddoos defeat the White City boys they will challenge the winners of the Hillside-City game. The Skiddoos are backed by South side business men.

This little bit of vituperation was no surprise. During much of the season, the Hillsides and the south-side Skiddoos had carried on a contest off the field that was every bit as hot as any battle they would wage on it. While it may have begun with the Hillsides' aloofness in scheduling a match with the Skiddoo 23 team, it was seriously exacerbated by the Hillsides' netting a match against the Baur city team at the league baseball grounds for Sunday, November 15. The Skiddoos figured they were as "in line" as the Hillsides for such an honor.

From here on out, the war and each of its individual battles ran somewhere between hot and hotter than hell. The day after Hansen's letter appeared in the pages of the *Gazette*, Roy Gleason, the Hillside manager, reportedly took "exception to the statement of the Skiddoo football team which charges his aggregation with demanding a side bet on the game which was scheduled between the two elevens for Sunday."

BEFORE THEY WERE THE PACKERS

Gleason suggested that the Skiddoos had backed out of their scheduled contest over the money issue and that he didn't want to play them now, with the Baur City contest in the offing, for fear of injury to some of his stalwarts. Gleason continued, "They then dared me to play for $5 and I raised the ante to $25. They agreed but later found they could not secure the money and so the game was called off."

By this time, the Skiddoos' lineup was pretty much a who's who of citywide gridiron standouts and included Oscar Nelson at center, Melos Hamachek and Otto Putski at guards, Art Hansen and Joseph Spranger at tackles, Woodard and Carroll Anderson at ends, Francis Brehme at left half, Rocheleau at right half, Reul Russell at fullback, and Nels Anderson at quarterback. The squad was further bolstered by A. Olson, B. Grant, J. Anderson, and Bill Spranger as subs.

And one had to wonder whether this contest wasn't shaping up into the classic paradigms of establishment and upstarts, east- and west-siders, old money and roustabouts, businessmen and laborers. Besides, if the two could iron out the details and get a game scheduled, they would be able to work out their differences just fine on the field.

The Skiddoos were set to take on the White City eleven on Sunday, November 8; this was one game that would indeed be played out, much to White City's chagrin. The final score was a whopping 26–5, and the Skiddoos remained undefeated for the 1914 campaign. Standouts were Rocheleau, Soren Anderson, Nels Anderson, J. Anderson, Russell, and Brehme. They were still waiting for the Hillsides to commit to a contest and were feeling a bit edgy about the snub that these Astor Park boys had given them in their effort to toe up with the Baur Citys.

In other action, the Lucky Eleven and the East Side team, neither of which had been lost in the heat of the Skiddoo-Hillside controversy, did battle on the home field of the east-siders. The Lucky Eleven claimed to have been seriously outweighed by their opponents and to have taken only four of their regular players into the melee. The final score was an unbalanced 42–0. The Luckys also claimed that those behemoth east-siders were dragging their feet over crossing the Fox River for a skirmish on their turf.

With Thanksgiving approaching, teams were either focused on closing out in style or figuring out the best way to cut their losses and baste the holiday bird. The November 10 *Gazette* relayed some rumblings from De Pere that some "former West side De Pere city team football players" were putting their heads together in anticipation of a challenge to "the East side De Pere city team" for a game on Thanksgiving Day. Tommy Heesacker was said to be managing the west-side crew.

But the big news, of course, was the approaching Hillside–Baur city scrap. They both boasted prior success and a brace of football talent. The Hillsides hadn't yet been scored upon. Their record for the year was listed in the *Gazette* on the 11th: October 4, Allouez, 7–0; October 11, South Sides, 14–0; October 18, Riversides,

42–0; October 25, De Pere, 26–0; November 1, White City, 17–0. Meanwhile, the Baurs had shouldered the larger onus of a city team and done pretty well.

The big showdown was drawing near.

In the week prior to that riot, many interesting developments took place. The Peshtigo city team, a perennial powerhouse, had come out of the woodwork to play a return game against the De Pere city team on Thanksgiving Day. The two had squared off to a tie on October 11 in the northern town, and Manager Earl Walsh promised to put his boys through "some hard practice" in preparation. The game would be played on the De Pere High School grounds with a reception following. The De Pere lads would be selling advance tickets in the hopes of raising the funds to pay for the Peshtigo boys' train ride. All indicators were pointing to a shindig of major proportions.

As it turned out, the Peshtigo–De Pere contest did not happen, and Oconto filled in at the last minute in what the De Pere reporter for the *Gazette* called "a big game." Two of Peshtigo's players were unable to play because they had a "small" problem, like the smallpox, and two others had been injured. So the De Pere eleven proceeded to do to the Oconto team what they had planned to do to the Peshtigo team. Church, Dart, and Rupiper were all stars for De Pere in front of what the reporter called the "largest crowd that ever attended a football game in this city." They must have been delighted, too, with their hometown boys on the better end of a 19–0 outcome.

Art Hansen of the Skiddoos was still repudiating the upcoming Hillside-Baur city contest, but he had at least scored a small victory. Hansen had added a certain curious twist to his challenge to the Hillsides by saying that the Skiddoo 23 boys would face the Hillside team anywhere, anytime, anyhow, "providing the Hillsides are not defeated before that time." Clearly, his aside was meant to indirectly challenge the Baurs as well.

Manager Dashnier of the Baur city team did take note. Dashnier said they would honor Hansen's defi with a game if they came out on top of the Hillsides in their upcoming contest. The domino effect was working this time, and Gleason, the Hillsides manager, was intending the same. So it was the Skiddoos' fate to wait. The *Gazette* ran their record as well. They were undefeated with a tally of 21–0 against Allouez, 41–0 against the Riversides, 26–5 against White City, and 7–0 against a Riverside-Allouez conglomeration.

In the face of its upcoming contest with the Hillsides, the Baur city aggregation loaded up with Red O'Neil of Eau Claire at quarterback. One Kenneth Colburn also traveled toward Green Bay to line up with the Baurs. So, like any great chemical reaction, the mix was seething and about to foam out of the container.

Meanwhile, the Saint Norbert schedule had been closed out, and college officials were declaring the season a "good" one. The college squad had won four and lost two, totaling 97 points to their opponents' 36. They had defeated Menominee High School, champions of Upper Michigan who had gone undefeated for four seasons, in their final game of the year.

So, all that remained was the residue that was the Hillside-Baur city contest. All the small distractions had been cleared up one way or the other, except, of course, for the sideline-skulking Skiddoos.

The Hillside-Baur fray turned out to be a squabble of tremendous proportions for nearly the entire contest. Most of the time, the ball was batted back and forth on the city team's side of the field, but no one had been able to cross the goal line. Then, with two minutes left to play, Jim Coffeen punted the ball into Hillside territory, and Morgan, the Hillside halfback, scooped up the pigskin and raced 60 yards for a score. Wally Ladrow followed the touchdown with an extra point, and the game ended 7–0 in favor of the Hillsides.

The Baur Citys claimed foul, asserting that "interference of the crowd contributed directly to the lone score made by their opponents" because "Morgan was protected from tacklers by circling the crowd." The *Gazette* reporter agreed that the spectators had indeed "persisted in invading the field." No matter. The Hillsides left the contest, claiming the "city and Fox River Valley championship by virtue of their victory."

Bottom line, all footnotes aside, the city team was the loser.

An item appearing on the same page as the *Gazette*'s reporting of the contest declared that "Fans Should Not be Blamed for Crushing up to the Sidelines." That article referred to a high school contest that had taken place at the league grounds on Saturday, not the Baur City–Hillside contest the following day.

But, in a reversal of its viewpoint from earlier that season, the paper did sympathize with the fans. The "rooters cannot be blamed for their action in the Saturday game when they over-rode the authorities and crushed the sidelines," it stated. "The spectators pay their admission with the expectation of seeing something, not guessing at what is happening." Without tiered bleachers, late arrivals had little choice but to squash in and try to get close to the action.

Getting fans to a game, collecting their fare at the gate, and delivering a game that would entertain them would remain a challenge for "the authorities." It always had been. And local lore in every town that fielded a team was rife with stories about young boys (and, maybe, full-grown men) sneaking in when someone wasn't looking or crawling under the fence along the outhouse wall. During really big contests, there were even stories of crawling through some part of the outhouse itself.

During the difficult days of the Great Depression, the *Iron River Reporter* berated football fans on a weekly basis, declaring that fans that slipped in without paying their share were contributing to the extinction of football in their community. That legendary derring-do, "sneaking in," would continue to be a part of

IRON RIVER—THE BULLDOG

One player who came from the Iron River area in the Upper Peninsula but played on Stambaugh's squad was Vic Turosky. Arguably the best player in the area in the late teens and early twenties, his talents were so sought after that the Iron Mountain team wooed him away from the All-Stars in 1924. Nicknamed "The Bulldog," Turosky was not a particularly large man. He stood at 5' 10" and weighed 185 pounds. As a fullback and defensive end, Turosky took a great deal of punishment. And, when it came to physical stature, he made this general comment: "A good big man is always better than a good small man." Of course there's another old saw out there that speaks to Turosky's ferocity and that goes: "It's not the size of the dog in the fight, it's the size of the fight in the dog."

Upon his return to the Iron River area, Turosky played for the Stambaugh All-Stars. Now, a seasoned professional, he had the opportunity to play against Bill Marshall, the first black man to play Big Ten football, a star for the Duluth Kelleys. During a huddle, the Stambaugh center, Frank "Slim" Freghetto, said, "Hell, Vic, we'll run right over him with the ball," referring to Marshall. The Bulldog took the ball and, with some juking, eluded Marshall and picked up a first down. Marshall then drew a bead with his finger on the Bulldog's prodigious nose and proclaimed, "Don't try that again, kid!"

In the next huddle, Freghetto said, "The hell with him, Vic, we'll do it all over again." This time as Vic made his move, he was sorely surprised. Marshall grabbed him by an ankle, hoisted him into the air and dropped him on his head. At this point Turosky reflected, "That's when I knew what real power was."

Despite that rude treatment, Turosky remained active in sports in the U. P. for years to come, serving as a long-time recreational director in Iron River.

Green Bay Packer legend until recent days, and it would be hard to find a person in his forties who didn't know someone who had snuck into a Packer contest at City Stadium. Purists might even argue over whether the elimination of such a possibility, in some small way, has taken the game out of the realm of the fans.

It didn't take Art Hansen, manager of the Skiddoos, more than two days to issue a challenge to the Hillsides for the city championship, with the following notice in the November 25 *Gazette*:

> The Skiddoos again challenge the Hillside football team for a game not to be played later than Dec. 12. We are willing to play at any place or under any condition, (not gambling). If this challenge is not accepted the South Side Skiddoos claim the city championship as we have as much claim to it as the Hillsides have.
>
> The Skiddoos have had five points scored against them to 7 to the Hillsides and have defeated any team that has met the Hillsides by larger scores.
>
> Please answer this challenge through the paper as we wish to let the public know how we arrange our games.

BEFORE THEY WERE THE PACKERS

Would the Hillsides, who had challenged the city team to a contest to determine the city championship in 1913 and lost, accept such a challenge from another team after finally reaching their quest in 1914? They had little to gain from such a battle, and a lot to lose.

Manager Warren Gleason of the Hillsides fired back on November 28, claiming that the Skiddoos had no right to claim the city championship or to question the supremacy of his eleven. His aggregation had defeated the Baur city team, 7–0. They had also trimmed the Skiddoos in a "practice game" early in the season 14–7. Besides, claimed Gleason, the Skiddoos had lost to a De Pere team, 22–0, which the Hillsides had whipped 26–0. Furthermore, the Skiddoos had set, and then canceled, a game with the Hillsides for November 8 because the south-side team "could not raise the $25 side bet."

As a final kick in the seat, Gleason said his team would like the Skiddoos to "get a reputation next as we beat teams from all parts of the city."

But the issue wasn't over yet! On December 1, Art Hansen shot back. "Manager Hansen of the Skiddoo football team," chuckled the *Gazette* sports editor, "again deposeth and maketh the answer to the taunts of the Hillside team." In full, Hansen stated,

> Mr. Gleason says that the Hillsides have defeated the South Side team which now goes under the name of the South Side Skiddos [sic].
>
> The team of South Siders which gave them such a scare were nothing but a few of our will-be football players. I will name the men composing the Skiddos [sic], the asterisk to show who played with the South siders in the game referred to.
>
> J. Peters, center; B. Devroy, right guard; B. Anderson, right tackle; Pate Oleson, right end; A. Muldoon, left guard; A. Hansen, left tackle; N. Anderson*, left end; B. Hetherington, left half; F. Brehme, right half; R. Russel[l]*, fullback; D. Thompson, quarter; J. Durjer, sub.
>
> The Skiddos' [sic] record which stands to this day is that they have never been defeated by an East side team nor canceled a game for fear of defeat. The closest game of their season was with the East Ends with a 4 to 0 victory. Again this season we defeated Riverside 42 to 0, Allouez 21 to 0, White City, 26 to 5, East River, 7 to 0 and Riverside 7 to 0 in a practice game.
>
> I hope Mr. Gleason will come to before Dec. 1 and answer our challenge because we never tried to claim the city championship without having the greatest right to it. We are still giving the Hillsides until Dec. 1, to put in their answer to our challenge and if not accepted then will claim the title of Green Bay.

It was already December 1, and the chances of getting a game in before the weather prohibited it were unlikely. The attention of state sports fans was already turning toward basketball, particularly the brand played at the University of Wisconsin–Madison, where the varsity teams had captured the conference title three years running. It seemed for sure that any Hillside-Skiddoo contest to settle the dispute was a lost cause, would never be played, and that those involved would be left to a winter of discontent to debate the issue with the 1915 season in the offing.

The final and, to many, more important football action of the season had not been lost in the midst of the brouhaha. Thanksgiving Day games had been set for Thursday, November 26, whether the Hillsides and Skiddoos fielded teams or not. Besides a De Pere–Oconto scramble, the annual East-West contest was being touted with two evenly matched and talented squads.

Completely ignoring the Hillside-Skiddoo tussle, the *Gazette* declared that the high school contest would "decide the championship of the city of Green Bay." The paper ran a major spread featuring the two lineups the night before the squabble. The two teams were displayed in two separate photographic spectrums across the top and bottom of the same page.

A scan of the starting lineups for the two teams reads like a constellation of gridiron stars for Green Bay town team football and for the first years of the Green Bay Packers. Names that should ring a bell for any true Packer fan included Nichols, Gallagher, Leaper, McLean, Mathys, and Dwyer for the west-siders and Lambeau, Wittig, and Flatley for the east-siders. This was a young who's who of Green Bay football, past, present, and future. Two of these guys would become Green Bay Packer coaches, five of them would be key performers on the early Packer squads, and the others would represent ties to Green Bay football from 1895 all the way to 1918, the last year before the Packers appeared as the ultimate town team.

The total lineups were impressive in their own right. Rounding out the West High lineup, which was shown in approximate formation near the top of the page were Platten, L. Gallagher, B. Duncan, and team captain Warwick. The East High aggregation, displayed across the bottom of the page, was bolstered by Lomas, Martin, Moeller, Binish, Van Laanen, Theisen, Counard, and Jenske.

Green Bay football in 1914 cannot be closed out without mentioning one of these young footballers, who was getting such serious local attention. Curly Lambeau, of course, would become synonymous with the Green Bay Packers for the first 30-plus years of the team's existence. A mere 10th-grader, Lambeau had been hailed once during the gridiron season as a rising football star in Green Bay as well as an early proponent of pitching the pigskin downfield. "Lambeau is a sophomore," began the *Gazette*, "and has two years of high school football ahead of him. He weighs 175 and is an expert in the sending department of the forward pass game."

The *Gazette* would also recognize him following the Turkey Day game, again pointing out that he still had two years of high school exploits ahead of him. "He gave a wonderful exhibition of gameness in the Thursday game," it said. Lambeau, of course, had turned football heads a couple of years earlier when, as a member of an 8th-grade crew from Whitney Grade School, he had helped his team to an 18–0 outcome over a freshman squad from East.

So, the stage was set for another East-West showdown—a virtual gunfight, if you will. The starting time had been moved up 15 minutes to 2:15, and an "extra force of police" had been secured "to preserve order and keep the crowd from trampling to the side lines." They were probably needed. After four quarters of what the newspaper called "A Fierce Battle," West emerged victorious for the sixth-straight year in a row, this time holders of a 12–0 blanking.

It would take Curly and his east-side crew a little while yet, but they would turn the tide of West High School dominance before he graduated. Nonetheless, Curly's high school career as a media darling had already, in just its second year, reached a plateau never before enjoyed by a single football player in the city's history. It would continue like that, over rough and smooth, for another three dozen years or so.

On the heels of an exciting 1914 season in general, it came as a major shock when, following the East-West Thanksgiving Day contest, President Frank Murphy of the Green Bay baseball entry in the Wisconsin-Illinois league, announced that there would be "no more football games on the league grounds" and that any independent football teams would "have to look elsewhere for a gridiron."

Murphy was angry about the condition his field was in following all of the football games played on it that season. He wasn't speculating about 1915 yet, but it was clear that the field was off-limits for any more contests in 1914. "It will cost about $75 to put the field back into the condition it was in before the football season began," he said. "And I do not wish to risk any further damage."

The winter of Murphy's discontent gave him some time to cool his heels, and the 1915 football season proceeded much as the previous 20 seasons of Green Bay football had, with games still being played near the place where Walnut Street made its move toward the East River. That might be at Hagemeister Park proper. It might be in any other open space large enough to mark out a gridiron. And, by God, it might be right there on the space reserved for baseball where Mr. Murphy said, "No!"

A fun item made its way into the *Gazette* on December 3, 1914. Tongue well in cheek, it predicted lots of fat to chew for armchair quarterbacks anticipating football in 1915:

HOT STOVE LEAGUE OPENS THE SEASON
Full Schedule Being Arranged For the Vociferous Order of Gabfesters

With the close of the football, baseball and deer season comes the formal opening of the Hot Stove league. The league is expected to enjoy an even more prosperous season this winter than last not only in the United States but through contiguous portions of Canada. An ample supply of food is available for the heel toasters to mumble on.

As a charter member of the Vociferous Order of Gabfesters and associate member of the society for the protection of Convivial Conversationalists, we hereby come to bat with the following list of the most desirable and consequently unimportant subjects to be settled at 82, stoveside.

Will Madison have a team next year? Will Racine have a team next year? Will Oshkosh have a team next year? Will anyone have a team next year? Will the Feds go to the wall before Aug. 1, 1915? Who will manage the Hopeless Yanks? Will the Braves be able to repeat? Will Ty Cobb be able to curb his hatred toward butchers? How much longer will Christy Mathewson last? Where does Charles Watchful Murphy come in? Was he ever out? Will Edward Engles ever find that chest protector? Will Peewee Vaughan play with the Bays in 1915? Should Clemens have declared the ball dead when it beaned him in the East-West game? Should Harold Mathews get a place on the all city team? Is Lambeau dead? Who started the canard? How much chance have the officers for the Elks' club championship? Etc, etcetera, ad infinitum and so on until the grass grows green in the spring, tra la.

It was at best an afterthought and a lot closer to a joke when, on Saturday, December 5, the *Gazette* announced, "Hillsides to Meet Skiddoos on Sunday in White City Park." According to the paper, the managers of the two teams had "got together last night and cleared up their difficulties regarding the proposed game which has been hanging fire for a month." Bader, the Hillsides' quarterback, attested that both managers had put up their $25 side bet and that the game was set for White City Park at 2:30 on the next day, Sunday, December 6. The team that won the contest would obviously lay undisputed claim to the Green Bay City Title. "The game is the result," said the newspaper, "of a hot flock of challenges which have been flitting hither and to yon for some time past." That comment could have appeared alongside the dictionary definition of *understatement*.

Call it bad reporting, lousy reporting, or a trip into the twilight zone on some really bad stuff, the defis from the Skiddoos were now being issued by team captain Arthur *Olson*, not Hansen, and things were getting embarrassingly complicated, if not bizarre. The game set for Sunday, December 6, had not become reality. But Arthur Olson wasn't done:

Sporting Editor, Gazette: A. Olson, captain of the South side Skiddoos, claims they have won the city title. About four weeks ago the Hillside Athletic *association's football team challenged the South side Skiddoos to decide the city title. Captain Gleason wanted to form a $50 pot, winner to take all. The Skiddoos raised the necessary $25 while the Hillsides collected but $6.*

The Skiddoos then offered to play the game for nothing, but the Hillsides didn't want to play:

For the benefit of the South side merchants we will say that even though we failed to get a chance to show [,] we were there with the goods. We wish to thank the contributors to our $25 fund most sincerely for their support.
Yours truly,
"Arthur Olson."

Hopefully, that was it: A riddle wrapped in a mystery inside an enigma inside a whole lot of weirdness. Who, exactly, was to know? Arthur Olson? Art Hansen? The fact was, football, 1914-style, had come to a twisted end and an argument over money wasn't the only symptom. What a football fan in Titletown couldn't carp about was a lack of spark, on or off the field.

Despite the sarcasm, the questioning, the angst, and the laughter, town team football was alive and well—and about to enter a new era. The stars that had made their name in 1914, earlier, and later, would eventually form the nucleus of something very big. They just didn't know it.

A tackle or a pass or a kick or a run on the field were specific acts performed to great acclaim on the Green Bay gridiron. They were the split seconds that, together, made up a lifetime. Fred Hulbert and a cadre of his buddies had given them birth. Tod Burns had tried to nurture them in their young years. Various people had adopted them and tried to raise them to adulthood. Now, they were 19 years old and about to step out on their own. What they were leading to was anybody's guess. It was a collection of disparate moments, some good, some bad, some completely obscure, adding up to an identity. What they were leading to, unbeknownst to the players themselves, was the very birth of the most storied franchise in football history, the Green Bay Packers. The next five years would shape the talents, the organization, and the promotion of the greatest town team of them all.

Finally, two minor football notes closed out the 1914 season. "As an answer to the recent charges that football players are paying too much attention to their game and too little [to] recruiting," began an Associated Press news release from London, "it is announced that plans have been completed for sending to the front 1,100 men composed entirely of football players, both amateurs and professionals." Global strife, in the form of World War I, was beginning to make some demands of its own on football men.

Also, Howard "Cub" Buck had been named captain of the 1915 Wisconsin Badger football eleven. In 1920, Buck would join some of the stars of the 1914 East-West high school game on the Packer crew, the last year for the Packers as town team.

1915

THROWING OUT THE SPONGE

After a year of citywide action and constant defis hurled to and fro, why would 1915 start any differently? The popularity of football was apparent, and heroes were starting to surface nationwide. Little boys were picking up the pigskin and giving it a workout. It was the fall of 1915 and football was in full swing.

Was the game still rough? Yep! Despite rule changes that would modernize the game to an extent, people still got hurt playing the bone-crunching game. Green Bay East star and, later, legend Earl "Curly" Lambeau suffered a broken bone in his right leg during a "light" scrimmage at Whitney Park. Also, 12-year-old Arthur Delauruelle became seriously hurt when, after watching football practice, he was tripped by a friend demonstrating a trick play and hit the rough edge of a sidewalk with his temple.

Other changes in football would take on less-violent forms. One article lamented the loss of a valued sideline friend, the football sponge. Because it was considered unsanitary, the use of a sponge dipped into a bucket of water and given to the athlete was discontinued:

> An athlete is all in from a kick in the slats. As he lays on the ground the sponge is shoved into his mouth. He takes a pull, wets his mouth, gets up and runs countless yards for the winning touchdown!
>
> What a crying shame that this practice had to be stopped when the rejuvenating powers the sponge possessed could do what modern science could not.

With militarism brooding in Europe, the inevitable comparison between war and the football gridiron was brought up in an article titled "Football Players Will Use Invisible Uniforms Like German Soldiers." Coach Murphy, having read that the German use of greenish-gray uniforms made them hard to pick up on a natural background, had decided that the traditional purple colors used by Northwestern

University were too conspicuous. He decided that greenish-gray was the color to work with and ordered uniforms in that shade. History shows that at some point this was abandoned and Northwestern returned to its much more optically pleasing purple and white hues.

Another bit of visual tomfoolery was perpetrated by "Pop" Warner of Carlisle Indian College fame. In the spirit of his now legendary "hidden ball play," Pop had footballs painted on his team's uniforms to confuse the "enemy" as to which player actually had the football. There was no indication whether this had any affect whatsoever.

In an attempt to silence the squabbles that would develop every year over who was the champion of the city, state, region, universe, galaxy, or neighborhood, an article from the September 17 *Gazette* suggested the organization of a league. This was attempted in 1904 and failed miserably, despite efforts by founding father Fred Hulbert. The solution was spelled out in one relatively concise paragraph. Once the league was formed, the article suggested, "Elimination games could then be played, and at the end of the season the surviving teams could fight for the title. In order to equalize the combat the teams might be divided into a number of classes, say for 100 pound or under squads; those of 125; then the 150 pounders, and finally all those above that mark."

This obviously made far too much sense for anyone to take it seriously and the idea died without a whimper. The simple fact was that, in a system that was already impromptu, any extra organization was way too much to ask.

So the various teams went about their business of gathering players, trying to get games, and drilling. In Green Bay a crew of players was brought together by the Supply Company of the Second Infantry. The team was to be comprised of local talent and members of the company. The added bonus was having uniformed, nonplaying company members patrolling the playing grounds to keep nonsense to a minimum.

The backfield that was projected to set the standard was made up of newcomers Morris and O'Malley, fresh from western college football experience, as well as veterans Jim Coffeen and Ally Romson. Linemen with potential included Massey, Ernie LaTour, Warren Spofford, and Smith. Ends were expected to be Abe Cohen, Bill Wittig, and Sullivan. The rest of the organization was made up of East High coach Carroll Nelson as team official and West High coach Harold Collette as player-coach.

Other players who figured prominently in Green Bay football history, either as players on this successful aggregation or on previous and later Green Bay town teams, included Andy Muldoon, Earl Skogg, Al Petcka, Isadore "Issy" Abrams, Dick Murphy, and Jim Coffeen. The military squad proposed skirmishing with other military-sponsored teams and promoting "scientific, up-to-date, clean football."

BEFORE THEY WERE THE PACKERS

A SMATTERING OF TEAM NAMES

The Colorful
Evansville Crimson Giants
Frankfort Yellow Jackets
Hartford Blues
Kenosha Maroons
Minneapolis Red Jackets
Orange Tornadoes
 (Orange Athletic Club of New Jersey)
Neenah Cardinals
Chicago Cardinals
Caspian Red Helmets

The Curious
Bessemer Speed Boys
Columbus Panhandles
Providence Steam Rollers
Tonawanda Kardex
L. A. Dons
Kingsford Flivvers
New London Bulldogs
Oshkosh Arions
Locket Stars
Motor Boat Club
Dayton Oakwoods
Cincinnati Celts
Dayton Triangles

The Duquesnes
Oorang Indians

The Vocational
Clintonville Truckers
Green Bay Packers
Detroit Heralds
Muncie Flyers
Stambaugh Miners (All-Stars)
Saint Louis Gunners
Minneapolis Marines
Buffalo Rangers

The Pedestrian
Oshkosh Athletic Club
Racine Legion
Crystal Falls Legions
Akron Pros

The Namesakes
Decatur Staleys
Sorensen Skidoos, Skiddoos
Louisville Brecks
Duluth Kelleys
Rochester Jeffersons
Staten Island Stapletons
New York Brickley Giants

An article from the September 29 *Gazette* mentioned that an Appleton team, the City Tailor Shop football team, was seeking games with strong teams averaging 155 pounds.

From the De Pere "News in Brief" section on the same date, their Badger club hurled a defi to other teams of the 130-pound weight class.

On the 30th, the paper mentioned that the Hillside Junior team, which had recently defeated the South Siders, 18–13, was looking for teams in the 125- to 135-pound range. The leadership of that team consisted of Captain Bob Madden and Manager Art DeBroux. They were looking for a game that Sunday. They found it with the De Pere Badgers.

The Hillsides, in prior years, had dominated the football landscape. In 1915, extra bodies allowed the formation of a "junior" squad to take on local, smaller, and less-threatening elevens. Many of their sturdier players had also gravitated toward the military team, leaving in their wake a lighter brand of footballer.

A game between the Hillside Juniors and the De Pere Badgers provided some of the sought-after gridiron excitement. The Juniors won the contest, 30–6, relying heavily on their speed. The game snapshot from the *Gazette* on October 5 mentioned that the Hillsides wanted games, but with a "fast team, weighing about 125 pounds."

Requesting games in newspaper articles rather than trying to drum up games based upon old contacts became a common practice. It had been used for years, as in the case of a salvo fired off by an Ishpeming team aiming to take on a Green Bay aggregation. For the most part, it seemed to be fairly successful. It also allowed another team to respond in kind and start a war of words that was the "official" defi. The newspaper management could not have minded these "typeset-insults." For a change, they weren't the ones stirring the pot.

The Supply Company team of Green Bay turned up the heat on its season with the announcement of a game with Company M of Oconto. The Green Bay bruisers tipped the scales at a well-fed 190-pound average. The uniformed sideline patrols served to eliminate any unpleasantness, thus, on paper at least, attracting the gentler sex to view the activity.

Another article putting candle to the flame of the Supply Company clash mentioned that with Green Bay's "beef" and "experience" they would "stow Oconto away as the first victim."

In a display of sheer dominance the Green Bay squad trounced Oconto's Company M by a final reckoning of 63–0. Company M was described as "stepped on and then rolled over." The Green Bay boys were described, after only one game, as being "a safe bet for the Fox River Valley championship" and "should stand a good chance for a state title." Of course, based on the proven skills of some of the team's players, there was also history behind that claim. O'Reilly, Vaughan, Dick Murphy, Coffeen, and Romson were all mentioned as players of note. For Oconto, Burke was given notice as a great runner, and Payne was given the "tough guy" award for continuing to play with a broken rib. Never was the game in question, and the Green Bay boys relaxed in the second portion, scoring only four tallies.

Another advertisement for a local team involved the South Side Stars, an eleven comprised mostly of gents who had knocked heads together in the 1914 campaign and were ready for more of the same. Several had put in time on the scrimmage line as members of the Skiddoo squads. The lineup was F. Brazner, left end; F. X. Coniff, left tackle; H. Coniff, left guard; J. Lallomont, center; A. Anderson, right guard; G. Getzlaff, right tackle; H. Anderson, right end; E. Bedore, quarterback; E. Vieau, right half; C. Anderson, fullback; Allen Proctor, left half and manager; extra men W. Cayer, J. Getzlaff, R. Praeger, and W. Hetterington. They announced their wish to play teams of 130 to 145 pounds in average size.

In local college action, Lawrence College was trounced by the University of Michigan by a score of 39–0. Colleges had not yet entered into their divisional format, but Michigan was still a much-larger university with an established athletic program, making the score understandable but the game legitimate.

Yet another team of pigskin chasers named the Locket Stars showed up in the October 9 *Gazette*. The Locket Stars probably drew their name from the lockets their sweethearts carried close to their hearts, and they presumed that their pictures, not those of a favorite pet or some roustabout, could be found inside. They averaged 140 pounds and were ready to face the White City team at White City Park. The Locket Stars lineup was as follows: Evarets, right tackle; Denisty, right end; P. Denisty, right half; Dingbat, left tackle; Massopust, left guard; Lingbach, left end; Mann, left half; Burnett, fullback; Seidert, quarterback; possible subs included a third Denisty, Vincent, Thompson, and Brice.

Local action was never hotter than during the fall of 1915. A west De Pere team put the South Side Stars to shame with a 12–0 blanking. The victorious De Pere lineup was center, Jensen; right guard, Van Gemert; right tackle, Van De Walle; right end, McIntyre; left guard, Mathison; left tackle, Desmond; left end, La Fond; left halfback, Leo Van De Walle; right halfback, Collen; fullback, Guerin; quarterback, Steinfeldt.

KEEPING IT ALL TOGETHER

When it came to the whole menagerie, including the financial end of things, a team manager had to think he was bearing a lot more responsibility than just that of a man in charge of on-field organization and direction. Reflecting on his turn at the helm of the Stambaugh All-Stars while he was still a player, Frank Shepich said years later, "I was kind of the coach and the business manager and the whole 'shitaree' sometimes."

Whole shitaree or not, Shepich recalled some awfully good times for the All-Stars in the 1930s, even though, in telling the stories, he seemed to indicate that there was a distance for him as player–coach–business manager that kept him from the center of the action. One fond memory for Shepich was the fashion in which his footballers liked to enter an opposing town for a game:

George Cederna played the concertina on the bus. When we'd come into the town that we were gonna play at, the Fageol had a hood on it about as long as a Model T Ford and George would sit up on that and play. And these guys were kind of mature already. And there was a little bit of drinking went after the game on the way back.

Like I say, you know, these guys worked at the mine all during the week and when you travel two hundred and some miles to play a football game the same day, that was kind of tiring. But we had fun. That was one of the fun times for the guys. They'd drink a little bit and George with his concertina. I remember coming back from Sault Ste. Marie and those guys in back, they broke a window out of that old Fageol. And the damn thing sucked in the exhaust and they got sicker than dogs.

Today's football coaches have tough jobs. What Frank wouldn't have given for their problems.

The omnipresent Hillside Juniors had put the De Pere Badger team down in an earlier game. The losing Badger lineup included fullback and captain, Charles LeRoy; left half, Charles Paterson; right halfback, L. LeRoy; quarterback, Ted Wellens; center, J. Radamacher; right guard, H. Danen; right tackle and manager, Francis Clabots; right end, Arthur Burckle; left guard, J. Hermsen; left tackle, I. Burckle; left end, C. Riley; subs C. Klaus, L. Golden, and Adelbert Dohn. The west De Pere squad advertised for games in the 130- to 140-pound range.

The Supply Company team, in its second competition of the year, faced an unusual task, a championship game. They were to take on the "Queen City aggregation" from Marinette in a game to "settle the titular honors for northern Wisconsin." Captain Smith's supply team was bolstered by the addition of some new talent, Herb Nichols and Regney "Riggie" Dwyer. The expectation of a win by the local boys was high, and class was expected all around. Already the boys were claiming the "military championship of the state" and were expected to play well enough to support their claim.

The Marinette game was much more of a challenge than was expected. The local boys, playing at the familiar home of football in Green Bay, Hagemeister Park, won the closely contested matchup, 8–6. Isadore "Issy" Abrams made the first score when he caught a Marinette player behind his goal line for two quick points by safety. After some back-and-forth arguments, the Marinette team managed to sneak over a score and led 6–2. It seemed to be enough. A long drive by the home team died as time expired in the first half, with the team at the three-yard line. Any more scoring would have to wait until the second half. The Green Bay terrors pulled the game out in the fourth quarter when Don Vaughn slipped over for the last score. Vaughn, Schulz, Nichols, and Abrams were all cited as having a good game, the former two for running prowess and the latter for defensive effort.

In intracity action, a new team, the Neidl Colts, had also picked the bones of past Skiddoo aggregations, and was set to take on the Locket Stars. Fast play was expected as both teams were equally matched in terms of weight. In other small-circuit action, the South Side Stars planned to take on the Badger club. Again, bantamweight and quick play were expected to be the rules of the day.

The Neidl Colts defeated the Locket Stars and set their sights on the much more experienced Hillside team. The Hillsides were billed as one of the strongest teams in the city and were even credited with the 1914 city title. Their next challenge happened to be with the upstart Neidl Colts. The Colts' lineup for the game was as follows: Bob Woodward, left end; P. Olson, right end; N. Anderson, quarterback; Christensen, right guard; Presten, left guard; Peters, center; Springer, right tackle; H. Anderson, left tackle; Canard, right half; Pinchard, left half; J. Springer, fullback; Kemnitz, guard; Jesselz, guard. The game was to be played at the White City Park.

A large crowd watched the two local teams play to a 7–7 draw. The Hillsides had laurels for Ladrow, possessor of their score, and likewise the Colts hoisted N. Anderson for his 70-yard run and score.

The next game for Green Bay was against Appleton, but the team seemed worried. Manager Ray Nicholson predicted a tough time due to the loss of a few of his men. Center Skogg, Murphy, Vaughan, and O'Reilly would all be missing from action. A call for new blood and a rally to beat the "Paper City players" was given, with the caveat that the team "must put everything into the battle." A side bet of $50 was thrown into the ring, with the possibility of other side bets. All served as inspiration.

The Appleton vs. Supply Company contest was, at best, a one-sided affair. A newspaper headline jokingly exclaimed that "Kick it off, boys" was the phrase most coined during the matchup. Another scathing comment was "As a football game the contest was abominable, but as farce it was laughable." Also, "The soldiers should schedule real opponents for coming clashes, and give the fans more games like the one with Marinette." When the bleeding stopped for the visitors at the W-I League Park, the final tally was 118–0. That's not a typo folks, it's real. The affair was so one-sided that the paper listed the players who scored by the number of touchdowns they notched: Townsend 2, Wittig 4, Murray 2, Vaughan 1, Abrohams 1, Nichols 6.

APPLETON—118 TO 0?!

Under Lawrence University's shadow, Appleton town teams had a tough time staying alive, let alone scoring points. "Donnybrook" didn't even begin to describe their 1915 contest against one of the crack teams in the state, the Supply Company of Green Bay. Of course, the Supply Company was already developing into the Packers of 1919 with some early Packer players already on the roster. Besides that, the strength of material in the men who didn't make the Packer team suggests just how tough the Packer team was. What matters is that, despite a 118-0 whooping, town team football in Appleton continued for another 20-some years. By the 1930s, Appleton would be fielding a pretty decent team, however, the Appleton Reds.

After the walloping of Appleton, the hue and cry went out for Green Bay's best to start the march to a state title. The next logical step was to take on Oshkosh, a team with a similar undefeated record. The proposed cycle was that the winner of the Green Bay and Oshkosh meeting would play Milwaukee for the state championship. To get Oshkosh to agree to come to the city, management had to promise a large chunk of cash, and, because of this, they appealed to the teeming masses to come out in record numbers to ensure a large gate take.

To ready themselves, the Supply Company team went through their signal drills, head-knocking, and pigskin-chasing at the team practice facility by the

Cherry Street armory. A later report also stated that during the Green Bay–Oshkosh clash, Milwaukee and Racine would play an elimination match to ensure that a true championship would occur.

DE PERE—THE FOOTBALL WAR OF 1915

"Football Contest Ends in a Row," the *Press-Gazette* headline screamed. "Special War Correspondent Describes Hostilities as seen from the Trenches."

In the second quarter, a 1915 contest between the town teams of east and west De Pere shifted from football to warfare and not just in a rhetorical sense. The action even spilled over onto the sidelines, and women were as guilty of barbarism as were the players. The game was just supposed to settle who had the better football team, not which side of the river could beat the living crap out of the other.

"De Pere football fans 'made Rome howl' yesterday," wrote the reporter. "It was the most exciting day ever witnessed in this city. The young people of both sides of the river went wild with enthusiasm, and woke up the city to its furthermost confines." Overstatement? Hardly! In a nutshell, it started like this: The ref gave a west-side player the boot, profanity was a big part of the exchange, the ref was called "crooked" and the player refused to leave. His buddies didn't help when they told him not to leave. The police chief was called but "accidentally" got trapped in a crowd of west-side fans. Finally, the mayor arrived with a compromise: the player could hang around, just not play. Ah, a politician.

Next thing, the girls from the east side were marching around the field with a large banner and the west-side girls "[charged] the enemy and soon had the big banner trailing in the dust." Then, a nasty exchange took place between two ladies and ended with something like "For a cent, I'd slap all the powder off your face." Two other females had gotten into a hair-pulling match.

On the field, the football guys kicked the ground and swore back and forth but refrained from anything further. The ref declared the contest "ended in a forfeiture to the West side team by a score of 1 to 0" because the east-siders had refused to play after the mayor's compromise.

Eventually, the field cleared. But parades up and down the streets on both the east and west sides of the Fox River lasted until 6:00 that evening. At that point, the crowds finally stopped shouting insults to the other side and headed home for a polite turkey dinner with family. Four hours of whooping it up had created some serious appetites.

The taunting and talk of "you'll get yours" filled much of the next work week, and it was only the eventual onslaught of winter that put the argument on the back burner to be resumed the following season.

Meanwhile, the Hillside Junior football team continued its swath of destruction through the intracity circle. They beat the Drive Calk team, 44–0, and were still ready to meet all challengers in the 140-pound range. The apprentice 'hill' squad was made up of the following go-getters: C. Simonet, right guard; Manders, right tackle; A. Fleming, right end; A. Manders, left guard; J. De Cota, left tackle; C. Fiedler, left end; W. McGrath, center; S. Bergen, right halfback; B. Bero, left halfback; H. Bero, fullback; R. Madden, quarterback; J. Reckhoff and F. Sullivan as substitutes. Many of these names had been listed with other squads, and the Manders boys had even sported a team of their own.

Another variation of local footballers, the South Side Colts, put up a decisive win against what was called "the strong Pollock team" by a final of 35–0. In one fell swoop, the paper exclaimed that they were now in the running for the 135-pound championship of the city.

The Hillsides had taken a blow to their lineup when Walter Ladrow was declared out of action, having broken his collarbone in the Neidl Colts fracas. Another long-time Hillside player, John Mannebach, was ill with blood poisoning, making the Juniors scramble for adequate replacements. Their next foe was to be the Locket Stars at White City Park.

The hype over the Oshkosh game continued. No less than five articles went into detail on the role each player would have, how the training would affect performance, and how big the gate would be. Ads appeared on at least two occasions including the teaser, "State championship game." The home team's lineup now looked like this:

Center	Skogg or Momearts
Right Guard	LaTour or Donchers
Left Guard	Willis, Spafford [sic], or Carter
Left Tackle	Muldoon
Right Tackle	Murray
Right End	Nichols or Murphy
Left End	Wittig or Cohen
Left Half	Abraham
Right Half	Townsend
Fullback	Romson
Quarterback	Mulligan

The game was scheduled for 2:15 at the league ball grounds, part of Hagemeister Park. For the first half of the highly touted affair, no one could start up the scoreboard. After the break, the Green Bay soldiers did all the scoring they would need in the third quarter. First, Townsend scored a touchdown after marching downfield and the team converted its goal. Then, Oshkosh was careless with the pigskin and was caught behind their goal line for a safety. Oshkosh caught their luck with about four minutes remaining in the game when a 40-yard scamper netted them their first and only score. End score 9–7, with Green Bay looking forward to the title shot at Milwaukee. Bragging rights, not to mention a sizeable amount of side-bet money, were on the line.

To tune up for the title game, Green Bay agreed to a return match with Oshkosh to take place in that city. Not much hoopla was expected. Green Bay was certain of a win and was very much looking forward to the big chance.

Hopes and dreams aside, the return match proved to be a hard-fought, straightforward game. Few razzle-dazzle plays were working, so hard line-smashing was the recipe of the day. Both teams proved to be strong defensively, and the game ended at a deadlocked 0–0 finale. All indicators pointed to a Green Bay versus Milwaukee showdown, which ended up falling by the wayside, corrupted by too many logistical problems. Having closed out their season by winning their appointed contests, the 1915 crew could puff out their chests and claim one more championship for Titletown. By the time winter was breathing down everyone's neck, no one had crawled out of the darkness to challenge the claim, so it stood.

In the years before the nation's involvement in World War I, militarism was on the rise, and many town teams actually arose from or were sponsored by local military units. This was the case in 1915, when the Green Bay town team played under the "Supply Company" banner and hauled in one more championship. The salad days of the Packers were approaching and the skill level of the team was growing. Pictured here are: (sitting, left to right) Andy Muldoon, Ernie LaTour, Earl Skogg, Al Petchka, Warren Spoffard, and Joe Donkers; (kneeling) Abe Cohen, Issy Abrams, and Mommaerts; (standing) Captain Smith, Dick Murphy, Ally Romson, Don Vaughn, Harold Collette, Jim Coffeen, Bill Wittig, Lieutenant Carole Nelson, and Lieutenant Ray Nicholson. Photograph from the Henry Lefebvre Collection of the Neville Public Museum of Brown County, Green Bay, Wisconsin.

Back in the "minors," the Locket Stars–Hillsides game ended cloaked in controversy. The Hillsides claimed a 0–0 tie at the end of action. The manager of the Locket Stars, Denisty, saw things differently. He claimed that a squabble ended action, both teams walked off the 'iron, and that his team had a 6–0 lead at that point, so his team deserved the victory. A replay was scheduled with a substantial side bet as the prize.

The November 15 *Gazette* next reported that the Hillsides whipped up on the Neidls by a score of 25–0. Fast aerial attacks spelled disaster for the unsuspecting

OCONTO—FUTURE LAWYERS FIND
ROUGHHOUSE FOOTBALL TO THEIR LIKING

Back in 1895, a dapper-looking crew of footballers gathered under the Oconto banner and did the city proud. Their home games were played at the Bay View Driving Park, seven blocks north of the downtown area on Superior Avenue. Today those grounds are part of the Bond Community Center. That fall, a newspaper announcement presented the following enticement to local sports fans:

PLAYING FOOTBALL
EVERYBODY SHOULD THOROUGHLY LEARN THE GAME
The Oconto Team Daily Practicing Preparatory to Meeting the Foe—Vigorous Exercise Applauded by the Faculty of the Leading Colleges.

The 1895 team distinguished itself both on and off the field. It seemed as if there weren't a slouch in the entire group; the most common future career of the men was that of barrister. Following one game that fall, the Oconto County Reporter cheered the team's exploits:

Chloupek played a great game as center, never letting a man through, and holding a player that weighed ten pounds more than he with greatest ease.

Ryan and Morrow held their positions perfectly and could always be found where they were wanted.

Whitney and Hall made great holes in Rhinelander's line and well deserve the positions they fill.

Smith and Foster held their ends well, making some pretty tackles and great rushes. Smith made the second touchdown and Foster the longest run of the game.

O'Keliher played an elegant game as quarter-back, making several tackles, and passed the ball with great ease.

Wescott is a great trainer and a good ground-gainer, and his tackles are a game by themselves.

Cota goes through the center like a shot and is always called upon when ground is wanted.

Orr, with his "Trilby bangs," plays a great game a half-back, and his equal is not easily found.

The team's cheer was a spirited "Wah Hoo Wah! Zip Boom Bah! Oconto, Oconto, Rah, Rah, Rah!" The team's fans used that cheer as a way of taunting archrival Marinette and celebrating football brotherhood with teams from Green Bay.

Unfortunately, the last year for town team football was 1921, the very year the Green Bay boys saw their way into the ranks of the American Professional Football Association. The cause of death, according to the *Reporter-Enterprise*, was a lack of fan support and nothing else. "Due to the fact that a large number of fans take the back fence route into the game instead of paying at the gate," it chastised the locals in the "obituary," "the management has run behind in finances and the players, working on the theory that if the followers of the gridiron want football they should be willing to pay for it, have canceled all future arrangements for games and turn their attention to other sports." That was a sad day, and the authors request a frothy glass of that long-lost nectar, Oconto Beer, as a means of toasting the Oconto Crew.

Neidl team. Dart and Rochleau were the scoring phenomena credited. The Hillsides came out of the fray confident enough to mention taking a swing at Company M of Oconto.

The next unexpected challenge for the Hillsides came from the upstart Motor Boat club. Claimed as the last game in the city championship elimination series, it had all the implications the state championship game had. The west-side Motor Boat team was fast, pass-oriented, and, surprisingly enough, favored in the contest. The newspaper article also stated that the winner would only be opposed by the Supply Company team for the city championship.

Building tension ensued when the game was said to be for the "City Title." Teams came out of the woodwork staking claim to the title shot. The Locket Stars wanted their chance at the winners of the Motor Boat–Hillsides tilt. The boat club listed this roster:

Center	L. Platten
Guards	E. Platten and Lannoye
Tackles	Fred Leicht and Frank Platten
Ends	Nichols and Crevcour
Quarterback	Mathys
Halfbacks	Perkins and Matthews
Fullback	Early

The "sailors" proved their worth in a 13–6 decision over the Hillsides. The Motor Boat club benefited from a blocked punt and snappy forward passes to account for their scoring. The Hillsides' Schneider maneuvered a pirated fumble for a 55-yard score. The Hillsides seemed to be a more disciplined team, but that did not present itself in the score. The only downside to the hot football action was the crowd ruining plays by creeping onto the field.

After the salve was applied, the Hillsides adjusted their lineup and took on the Badgers of De Pere whom they had beaten earlier that year. The lineup they carried into that affair was center, Gleason; left guard, Hogan; left tackle, De Cota; left end, Fiddler; right guard, Schneider; right tackle, Basche; right end, Madden; quarterback, Bader; left halfback, A. Bero; fullback, H. Bero; and right halfback, Berger.

In a small clip from the *Gazette*, the Walnut Street Stars beat the Catholic Boys club 35–21 at Whitney Park. Sherwood Toohey and James Crowley stood out for the Catholic group, and Orville Detjen, Ares Detjen, Clarence Lobenstein, and Arnold Servotte were the heroes of the Walnut gang. Crowley later gained immense fame as one of the "Four Horsemen" of Notre Dame.

With the win, the Motor Boat Club drew the attention due all champions and the constant challenge for their title. A team from Ishpeming, Michigan, sought to knock heads, as did a group of East High alumni. Both were aching to take a shot at the champs and get themselves a piece of the glory. Whether or not either one of these would come to pass was a mystery, but other games were mentioned. Also, the Hillsides were spoiling for the De Pere Badgers.

The year finally saw its last tilt, and the best was saved for last. The South Side Stars got their dander up and challenged the Hillside Junior team for the City Lightweight Title. Manager Allan Proctor brought on the defi with a letter, published on December 9, to the *Press-Gazette* sports editor:

> *Sporting Editor:*
>
> *There has been considerable discussion amongst followers of sport as to just where the honors lie in the lightweight football division supporters of the Hillside, Jr. and South Side Stars claiming the distinction of being 'It.'*
>
> *We of the South side are naturally interested in a method of determining the exact status of our teams. Now, we contend, that having passed through a season undefeated and with one tie, the proper thing would be a game with the team that tied us.*
>
> *Of course, now that the regular season is over, it would be easy for either side to furnish 'ringers'. But relying on the same teams that represented us all season, we expect the same of other teams who might accept this challenge.*
>
> *This letter, though addressed to you, is directed at any and all of the Hillside Juniors. The following is the lineup of our team: Right end, C. Dwyer, captain elect; left end, H. Brazner; right tackle, H. Andrews; right guard, H. Mathews; left guard, C. Dumal; quarterback, H. Rud, captain; left tackle, E. Bedora; right half, E. Vieaux; left half, A. Procter, manager; quarter, C. Anderson; center, Dickey.*
>
> *A. Proctor*

The reply from the Hillside Juniors came two days later by way of the December 11 *Press-Gazette*:

> *Sporting Editor:*
>
> *The 'Hillside Juniors' will accept the challenge of the South Side Stars, issued in the* Press-Gazette. *The Juniors defeated the Stars in the initial game of the season by a score of 18 to 13. The Juniors have been undefeated this season and will play the Stars Sunday, Dec. 12, on the East high campus. The lineup for the Juniors: Right end, Bob Madden; left end, C. Fiedler; right tackle, J. De Cota; left tackle, Clem Simonet; right guard, V. Pelegrin; left guard, W. Gleason; center, W. McGrath; right half, S. Bergen; left half, G. Bero; fullback, H. Bero.*
>
> *A. Bero, Manager*

The newspaper editor seemed delighted to apply the press for the game and stated that "this seems to indicate that a merry little backyard football scrap will be staged in this city soon. Both teams are good, and the contest resulting should be a corker."

Weather was probably the factor that cancelled this contest, however, leaving the potential players to speculate on its outcome. No matter. These two letters signaled the dropped curtain on the 1915 Green Bay football season, and the 1916 campaign stood in the wings waiting.

However, the 1915 season cannot be put to rest without mentioning the annual East–West High School game on Thanksgiving Day, as had been a tradition for a decade. Just as for six years prior, West emerged from the contest with city championship honors, this time by the slim margin of 6–0. But the tide was beginning to turn in East's favor, thanks to junior Curly Lambeau as well as other maturing east-side players. The game, said the *Gazette*, was marked by "savage" playing from both sides, signaling just how important a victory in this contest had become on both sides of the river. After all, it would be another 365 days before a loss could be avenged either way.

A further sign that football was becoming a true American pastime was an article from the December 13 *Press-Gazette* claiming, "Combination Game Is Invented at Cornell." The game was called "Gridiron," and it was played on a regular football field by eleven men and shared similarities with football and basketball. A rugby ball was used, players could only run with the ball for five yards, passing was encouraged, and tackling below the waist was forbidden. The game was invented by Professor C. V. P. Young, and the speculation was that "the game may be developed to take the place of soccer in collegiate sport at Cornell." Football seemed to be in no immediate danger from its bastardized cousin.

1916

SETTING THE RECORD STRAIGHT

This is the year of controversy, at least if you believe the histories of Packer football published to date! It has been widely reported by other sources that Green Bay didn't have a city football team in 1916. That statement can be interpreted several ways. First, no team played football in Green Bay, Wisconsin, that year. Second, no team calling itself the Green Bay town team played that year. The truth lies somewhere in between. A team was organized, though there is no record of it having played a game. Toward season's end, it struggled mightily to toe up against a class De Pere eleven. That contest went the way of ashes, but it wasn't for the lack of a city football team.

Besides, football was alive and well in town and was being played in several other venues. The Jolly Eleven football team announced its lineup in the September 27 *Press-Gazette* and advertised for teams of the 145-pound demeanor. The names on the roster included S. Anderson, J. Spranger, Willmet, DuCharme, D. Anderson, Brazner, Proctor, Dwyer, Johnson, B. Spranger, R. Anderson, Getzloff, Bedy, Vieu, and Christenson.

Intracity play continued at fever pitch with battles being waged among the South Side Stars, the Hillside Juniors, the Hillside Seniors, and the White Citys. They had all been around for a few years, they all put everything they had into beating up on one another, and, in 1916, they all took their turn losing to a rising De Pere city team.

Area schools had also organized teams for the 1916 season, with Saint Patrick's, Saint John's, and Howe schools battling back and forth for supremacy on the mowed pasture. The same article announcing the school results suggested that the Messenger Boys of the Western Union Telegraph company were throwing their helmets into the ring. They were looking for games with any team "averaging not more than 120 pounds." Prospective opponents were asked to "call 4321 and ask for Olive."

On the high school front, 12th-grader Curly Lambeau was a star for his East High School gridders. He had recovered from his fractured leg and was ready to delight fan and foe alike with his formidable talent. Reports of Captain Lambeau's prowess became common in the paper. In a 40–0 drubbing of Sturgeon Bay, he led his fellow Hilltoppers with his brilliant running. Curly accounted for at least four touchdowns that day, while teammates Raymond Lambeau, his brother, and Bell balanced the rushing attack. Later in the season Curly would lead the Hilltoppers to their first victory over West High in eight years.

Football coverage in the pages of all of Green Bay's papers was spotty at best during September and October. That wasn't so unusual. But football was being played all over the place. It just wasn't being covered with any consistency. Curly's exploits at East seemed to be the extent of it, while older players such as Jim Coffeen, Bill Wittig, and Ally Romson seemed to have slipped off the face of the Earth. Because of such a dearth of gridiron news, football historians who have looked through the usual site of such reporting, the autumn sports pages, came up empty-handed and decided that a city team just didn't exist. Wrong.

Toward the end of September, a city team was formed of some of the best talent obtainable. Fund-raising for the hybrid aggregation was discussed in the form of a pas de deux for the football beaus and their ladies and a date of October 8 was given for their first on-field tug-of-war. That contest didn't materialize and wasn't reported in the pages of the *Press-Gazette*.

A week later, perhaps out of the ashes of the fund-raiser, two teams from the bay, big brother Hillside Seniors and little brother Hillside Juniors, took the field. The Juniors were handled by a spirited De Pere city team to the tune of 20–0.

The Seniors fared better in a contest on Sunday, October 15, against a fast Kaukauna team in the southern city. The team, which returned with a 19–0 victory, was hailed as "Green Bay footballers," and its lineup included Nate Abrams, Bero and Riley, Bader, Bergen and Wheeler, Pete Abrohams, Spranger, Andy Muldoon, Wirtz, and Cordee. They had "played exceptionally good ball," said the game report, "and had the fast Kaukauna team guessing most of the time."

As usual, when little brother gets roughed up, it's time for big brother to step in. The Seniors accepted a challenge from the De Pere bullies, and a game was slated for Sunday, October 22, at the high school gridiron. Unable to avenge the Juniors' loss, the Hillside Seniors fell 6–0. The lone score in the second quarter of a sloppy-field affair came via a pass to Steinfeldt of the De Pere men.

Both Hillside teams had been humbled by a De Pere city crew that was on a great string. The De Pere team was rained out of a tussle with Little Chute the next week but handed the White City team a drubbing 31–0. Now, this rolling De Pere aggregation set sights on the Allouez team but, once again, weather played havoc with De Pere's gridiron dreams, and a second game had to be postponed.

The team kept Manager Earl Walsh hopping, and soon De Pere had a game set with Kaukauna for November 26. The reputation of the De Pere city team was now growing in leaps and bounds as Kaukauna was ousted from an "exciting" game 6–0. Earl knew what had to be done to set his team's reputation in stone.

In late November of 1916, as most things about town were slowing down for another wintry season in northeastern Wisconsin, a challenge was brewing up between neighbors. The Green Bay city team issued a challenge to the De Pere city champions "for the gate receipts, a side bet, or a bag of peanuts." A letter was sent to De Pere's manager, Earl Walsh:

> *Dear Sir—We would like to meet the De Pere City Football team Sunday. In a game in this city. We feel so confident of defeating them, that we will play them for the gate receipts a side bet or a bag of peanuts. We have a strong team, and one that will well merit the title of City team of Green Bay. If De Pere wants to take this challenge let them send in a reply to you. But perhaps they don't want to play us here.*
>
> *Manager Green Bay City Team*

While this wasn't as explosive as an interview with a modern-day middle linebacker after missing a tackle on a play that lost the game, the message is clear: "Play us or risk losing your reputation as area champs."

It took six short days for the answer to hit the Tuesday, November 28, evening edition. What follows was what the *Press-Gazette* termed a "warm" reply. "Warm" is a bit gentle, but readers can judge for themselves:

> *Dear Sir:*
>
> *In answer to the challenge of the Green Bay City team to play the De Pere City team for a bag of peanuts or gate receipts or a side bet, the De Pere team accepts the challenge and will play the Green Bay team on Green Bay grounds or any other grounds on Sunday, Dec. 10, 1916 for a bag of peanuts and gate receipts and a fifty dollar ($50) side bet or anything else the Green Bay team wants to play for.*
>
> *It will be remembered, De Pere has played five Green Bay teams this season namely: S. S. Stars, 0 De Pere, 6; Hillsides Jr, 0 De Pere 20; Hillside Sr, 0 De Pere, 6; White City, 0, De Pere, 40. Total of points made by De Pere, 72; Green Bay, 0.*
>
> *That the football season is over Thanksgiving day and De Pere is simply playing over the season to give Green Bay another chance to earn a reputation. In looking over the scores of the aforesaid teams. It looks as if the Green Bay teams have been playing "Bag O' Peanut" games all through.*

This is the first that has been heard of a Green Bay City team this season. Speak quick boys, the season is almost over.
    Yours Truly,
    Manager of the De Pere City Football Team.

While one might question the manager's ability to count to five, the tone was unmistakable and, with a challenge like that, probably more than "warm." A monumental game could only hope to follow. But before the tumult between the Green Bay and De Pere teams could come to bear, the Hillside Juniors lined up one more time.

In what can best be described as "a gory time," the Juniors beat up on another Green Bay standard, the South Side Stars, by a final of 44–0. The article reflected the game in a brutal light: "Doctors were more in order than referees and timekeepers at the game played for the city lightweight title." The reckless affair featured the following casualties:

H. Bero, Hillsides, broken nose
N. Vieux, Hillsides, broken rib
Unknown, Hillsides, broken nose
D. Anderson, Stars, sprained wrist
Unknown, Stars, wrenched ankle

The scoring for the Hillsides included touchdowns each for Merritt and H. Bero, as well as one each for P. Bergin, A. Fleming, and De Cota. The Hillsides, battered as they were, could claim the city's lightweight championship in good conscience.

Bill Wittig, the Green Bay manager, set up the Green Bay–De Pere game for December 10 at the league baseball grounds at the site of old Washington Park. He gathered up the best talent he could find, and, with the amount of money that was said to be on the line, the game was "likely to be a fight all the way through." One can imagine the cross-town brawls that ensued. Side bets reached untold heights; family feuds erupted over the imminent clash.

Unfortunately, Saturday's paper closed the door on the challenge, the money, and the potential that the Green Bay vs. De Pere game promised. It was a double-edged sword. From the De Pere angle, Manager Walsh cried "foul" because Green Bay wanted to renege by not getting out proper advertising and wanting the De Pere team to pay all the expenses out of their potential winnings. From the Green Bay angle, Manager Wittig stated that the De Pere team wouldn't travel north unless there was a big crowd, guaranteeing a large gate receipt. Green Bay's attitude was that the game was all that mattered, not the gate, crowd, or guarantee. In the December 11 *Press-Gazette*, sportswriter A. H. Israel replayed the two grievances but claimed that De Pere ultimately canceled the game. The truth may never be known, but the fact is that the game was not played, and the controversy over the lack of a town team in 1916 was born.

The facts have been stated on earlier pages. The historical record needs to be set straight. Was there a town team in Green Bay in 1916? Yes. Bill Wittig organized the team, it was called the Green Bay town team by the paper, and it had practiced and was ready to play a game. With Wittig in charge, the team would have drawn its talent from several intracity squads, namely the South Side Stars and Motor Boat Club from the city's west side and the Hillside Junior and Senior teams and White City team from its east side. From this talent pool, as well as the ranks of the 1915 Supply Company team, one could have put good money on Green Bay's ability to field a giant.

The argument that the team in question did not play anyone holds no water. In years after 1905, several seasons passed without one team standing out as the "town team." The simple fact is that football caught on in Green Bay by the hand of Fred Hulbert in 1895 and was played every season in Green Bay ever since. End of controversy, end of discussion.

A contest that did materialize was, of course, the traditional bloodbath better known as the East-West Thanksgiving Day Game. East had held the earliest bragging rights, defeating West in 1905, 1907, and 1908. It would have likely done the same in 1906, but no game was played. In 1909, however, with a slight 5–0 score, West stole East's thunder, and they kept it for eight long years.

In 1916, however, thanks in large part to senior Captain Curly Lambeau, East got the monkey off its back, squeaking by West with a 7–6 final. While Lambeau couldn't have played the game alone, the Friday, December 1, edition of the *Press-Gazette* suggested that his work may have "dimmed the playing of the other men on the two teams." Lambeau was credited for "great ground gaining, heavy booting and hectic defense." He was, said the report, "in every play." The newspaper did mention other players who contributed, but they appeared as bit parts in Lambeau's one-man show.

The following Monday, the paper followed up with an in-depth look at the value of Lambeau's contributions in the Turkey Day contest. It relayed that he had accounted for 165 of East's 200 yards in the game. But, even more significantly, he had out-gained West's entire unit. This Thanksgiving Day display was Curly's last game of a celebrated high school stint, and he headed off to college with a whole locker full of accolades. With Lambeau's departure, the pendulum would swing back across the river, and West would resume its usual routings in 1917, beating the east-siders 34–0.

1917

A CHARITY GAME FOR CURLY AND HIS CRONIES

The football climate changed greatly in 1917. The addition of George Whitney Calhoun to the *Press-Gazette* sports staff guaranteed faithful and punchy coverage of football action, especially pertaining to one local football talent. The September 29 paper lamented the loss of Curly Lambeau to college, but stated that

> the majority of football critics consider the Green Bay boy one of the best gridiron prospects that has ever been turned out of a high school. Lambeau sure was nearly a whole football eleven by himself when he cut up capers with East high up in this neck of the woods and there is little doubt but that he will more than make good with the Badgers.

With such high praise it was not hard to believe that later Lambeau and Calhoun would become great friends.

Yes, contrary to popular belief, young Lambeau was enrolled at the University of Wisconsin–Madison before ever donning a Notre Dame jersey. A rule of the day, reflective of the tightening standards on collegiate play, stated that as a freshman Lambeau could not play on the varsity team. So Curly took his classes and waited for varsity action while he showed his wares as a member of the freshman squad.

Back in Green Bay, the first town team action, deemed semipro by the November 7 *Press-Gazette*, included the Marinette Badgers against the hometown Green Bay All-Star team. Jimmy Coffeen, longtime Green Bay football enthusiast, was the driving force behind the locals, and the game was to be held at the league baseball grounds. The visitors were talents from the high schools of Marinette and Menominee and had won every game so far this year. As the first game of the year for the Green Bay boys, it promised to be an uphill affair. The "semipro" moniker came in part from the fact that all proceeds from the game were being donated to the Red Cross.

BEFORE THEY WERE THE PACKERS

Green Bay was home to plenty of good footballers between 1910 and 1919, when the local crew got sponsorship from the Indian Packing Company and blazed across the pages of history. This is a never-before-published photograph of one of the stalwarts of those town team days, Andrew Carroll Anderson. He and his brother Buck had much to do with the success of the Green Bay town teams leading up the early Packer elevens. For this day, Anderson was decked out in his football finest. Photograph obtained from and used with permission of Orville Anderson (Andrew Carroll Anderson's son), Green Bay, Wisconsin.

Calhoun, ever the quintessential sportswriter and pundit, drummed up support for the contest in his unique style (the following Calhounian quote should be spoken as if you were chomping on a cigar and wearing a battered fedora slightly askew):

> Lines between the East and West side will be forgotten here, on Sunday when the Green Bay All Stars lineup against the Marinette Badgers. Stars from both sides of the river will lineup against the visitors and this includes many schoolers who have fought it out like tigers in former years on Thanksgiving Day. Manager Coffeen has got the best men in the city to face the Northerners and the Marinette team is going to buck up against the real thing in the football line when they come here on Sunday to play for the benefit of the Red Cross.

Is there any doubt why Curly wanted this guy to help do press for his Packers?

Calhoun's November 10 report gave major information about the game to come. Lineups were provided, and a large crowd was anticipated. Ticket presales were even offered at local cigar shops. Imported men were the plan once again for Green Bay, as they borrowed Sylvester and Spaulding from Appleton and Saint Thomas from Racine.

The following were listed as probable lineups. Remember that this was a benefit game, and the eligibility lines between high school, college, and professional football were still not so clearly drawn that college freshman Curly Lambeau couldn't participate:

Green Bay	position	Marinette
"Cowboy" Wheeler	Left End	Anderson
Spaulding	Left Tackle	Hallen
Andy Muldoon	Left Guard	Ostrenga
Earl Skogg	Center	Bergrem
Retza	Right Guard	Fenisyn
Joseph Saint Thomas	Right Tackle	John Dory
Nate Abrams	Right End	Bilek
Sylvester	Left Halfback	Gander
Allie Romson	Fullback	Newman
Curly Lambeau	Right Halfback	Behnke
Jim Coffeen	Quarterback	Stanley Dory

"Green Bay Trims Marinette Stars by a Large Score" shouted the headline from the charity game. In a 27–0 "warmly contested game" the boys from the bay took it out on the Queen City lads and handed them their first defeat of the season. All the more unusual was the charitable nature of the game. All participants participated for nothing, including the referees. Calhoun even noted that the press

In the fall of 1917, when this photo was taken, Curly Lambeau returned to Green Bay from UW-Madison, where freshmen football had been canceled due to a lack of numbers, to play in an "All-Star Charity Game." Pictured with Lambeau on the city team are: (left to right) unidentified, Earl Skogg, Lambeau, Ernie LaTour, Jim Coffeen, Joe Umberham, Frank Binish, Art Schmael, Andy Muldoon, Isadore "Issy" Abrams, and Nate Abrams. In the Stiller-Lefebvre photograph collection, this photo is labeled "Start of the Packers," offering up an interesting twist on Packer history to date. Photograph from the Henry Lefebvre Collection of the Neville Public Museum of Brown County, Green Bay, Wisconsin.

"came across clean at the ticket window," something that the press rarely did, and "the gate tender nearly had a severe attack of heart failure."

In the spirit of charity, the game was clean and free from unnecessary slugging but hard played. Lambeau was the big star for the home team, accounting for two touchdowns, with Nate Abrams and Jim Coffeen making their mark also. Sylvester and Saint Thomas also came up big for the home boys and made their presence felt keenly. For the visitors, fullback Bergren and the Knudson boys did their best to keep Green Bay guessing.

The game conditions suffered toward the end as the crowd swarmed onto the field after plays in the fourth quarter, and the two policemen did their darndest to keep order. It often took several minutes to clear the field. This had always been a problem, and the stories about the impact of the crowd on a game could fill a book of their own. Celebrated Packer fan, Nubs Pigeon, recalled one such anecdote when he relayed the events of this or another particular game at Hagemeister Field. At one point, Nate Abrams tore down the sidelines for a pass hurled by Lambeau. A young boy, Norbert "Nubs" Pigeon, had strayed into the line of action, and the pass smacked him in the back. Abrams cruised over to Pigeon, grabbed up the pigskin, and told the boy, "Better get off the field son, you're gonna get hurt."

Clearing the field alone proved to be an uphill battle, as the paper reported that more than 1,200 spectators ponied up hard cash to see the game.

Other doings in 1917 included an argument over who was the best high school team in the state. Included in this bit of bickering were the undefeated teams from Marshfield, Marinette, Waukesha, and Watertown. The championship was proposed to be played in Green Bay, but there were several versions of who should play the game and why. One organizational proposal was a bracketed affair in which each team would have a chance, and the best aggregation would eventually emerge victorious. The final game was played in Green Bay between Marinette and Watertown. "Climatic conditions put an awful crimp in the attendance figures but those who braved the wintry blasts were well repaid for their nipped ears and frozen digits by a corking good exhibition of pigskin chasing." The Marinette boys won via the pass. The final was a resounding 27–0.

Also hot was the topic of "soldier football," in which "inter-camp pigskin chasing" was making "a big hit with the football fans as they like to see the soldiers in action on the chalk marked field." The connection between football and warfare as a game of conquering territory and gaining objectives so paralleled the struggle going on in Europe. "Drive seems to be our soldiers' middle name and when they get across the pond Kaiser Bill's defensive line is apt to be badly smashed at every point along the war front."

The dangerous nature of football was still on the minds of many naysayers, but an article balanced out the reality of the situation. It explained that fatalities generally occurred on teams in high school or semipros, where training was not up to snuff. This sentiment had been expressed by many of the early game's supporters, including Green Bay barrister T. P. Silverwood as early as 1896. Also mentioned was that more men had died in hunting accidents in 1917 than in the three previous years at the not-so-merciful hands of the football gods.

Football was alive and well, and nearing a pivotal point in Green Bay's history.

1918

WAITING IN THE WINGS

The year 1918 was relatively balanced, if active, for football in Green Bay. Pigskin chasers were abundant and coverage was plentiful and poetic, but, for the most part, it was business as usual. The golden age was nearing, and forces were gathering to ensure football success in town for years to come. It would not be easy, but 1918 would prove to be a keystone year.

The home team was a success, but there was little chitchat about a state title. Some of the big names of Green Bay football history were still around: Lambeau, Flatley, and Gallagher were taking a turn slugging in the ranks, ready for the rough stuff. But they stepped aside midseason to make room for some new heroes. Men who would answer the call and join the bruise brigade included Gus Rosenow, Art Schmael, Lyle "Cowboy" Wheeler, and the Zoll brothers. The Abrams boys were still there in full force, making their presence known and playing tough ball.

This year marked the end of innocence for football in the port town; football would grow up in 1919, and people would take notice. This is the last year that the best team in town would be a "city team." After 1918, it would be the Packers, and, with a few bumps along the way, it would be the Packers that would control city football destiny. The adolescence came to an end in 1918, but at times the game still seemed like a gangly teenager on his first date. Let's chaperone.

Worry over the site of football games in town came up in early August. Like Washington Park before it, the fate of Hagemeister was in the hands of developers. They saw the east end of Walnut Street, with its close proximity to the conveniences of the downtown area, as prime real estate. The southern part of old Washington Park had already been divvied up for houses, and now it looked as if Hagemeister might go the same way.

Was Hagemeister Park, the site of games as early as 1899, about to be destroyed? No new football site had been offered up. A hue and cry was sent out to solve the problem. Evidently the cries were responded to because the home games in 1918 were all played at Hagemeister Park, with the gridiron moved only slightly to the north or east toward the river.

A team calling themselves the Skiddoos started off the gridiron action on September 15 in De Pere with a crew from that town. These weren't the same old Skiddoos that hailed from the southwest side of town. Only a few members of that team, in the form of the Andersons, remained.

Played on the East De Pere High School grounds, the game was termed "a fistic encounter and a verbal battle." On the gridiron, eight Green Bay lads along with Chicago import, Art Schmael, took on a full eleven from De Pere and handed them a 13–0 defeat. The Skiddoos consisted of "Cowboy" Wheeler, "Curly" Lambeau, Schmitz, Pete Abrams, Nate Abrams, Schmael, Matthews, Anderson, and Schneider. Lambeau and Schmael were the stars of this affair and were described as "hurl[ing] themselves through the opposition front line, as though it were made of paper."

Once more, the action off the gridiron proved to be as volatile and interesting as that occurring on it. At some point during the contest, an orderly from De Pere commanded a Green Bay fan to step to the rear of the crowd and was met by a refusal and, eventually, fisticuffs. De Pere police managed to stop the fracas, but a sportswriter likened the area around the fight to a battle on the Western front. For a time, the attention of the spectators was about evenly split between the actual game and the shenanigans in the crowd.

Soon after that contest, Lambeau headed off to Notre Dame to join up with Knute Rockne's aggregation. His stay with the Irish would be short lived. An ensuing tangle with tonsillitis and a resulting departure from Notre Dame would put all the pieces in place for his date with destiny and the "founding" of the Green Bay Packers. Of course, Curly wasn't inventing something new; he was merely taking an idea once conceived of in Fred Hulbert's brain and shaping it into a modern variation.

A team called the Whales, which had risen from the ashes of the Skiddoos, was next to receive attention from the football prognosticators. They would be defending the town's honor on September 22 against the 1917 state champions, Marinette. Referred to as "Lumberjacks," Marinette's name of record was actually the Badgers. They were expected to bring a large cadre of rooters to make noise for their boys as well as a huddle full of crack players. A potential roster was listed in the newspaper account, but it only vaguely resembled the actual list of participants. That fact alone suggested that imported players were being brought in by Marinette, even at the very last minute.

The game was an old-fashioned drubbing that was becoming a habit in town. Green Bay once again stood on top of a 42–0 shutout. The game was so one-sided that only once did the visitors penetrate the 10-yard line of the Bays. For the Whales, two men made the highest grades. Nate Abrams broke into the limelight from his end position with some fantastic pass receptions netting him three goals. His speed and agility made him a formidable opponent. On the other side of the talented squad, Schmael used his beef and brawn to batter opponents for his three scores. Schneider made his mark with an interception and a broken-field master-piece of a run for a 50-yard score. The most appropriate description of the game was that "Green Bay had it over them like a tent."

To keep fans off the playing surface, Ninth Infantry Wisconsin State Guards under Captain Freward circulated in the crowd. An added bonus was two dozen of Green Bay's prettiest ladies on hand to sell tickets. It was noted that few spectators escaped without paying their "bit."

As Hagemeister Park gave way to the construction of East High School, Green Bay football, Packer-style, moved to temporary quarters at a baseball field on Main Street known as Bellevue Park. Confusingly, Hagemeister Brewery was close to Bellevue Park and appeared in the background of many of the early photographs of the day. This photo is of a game between the Packers and the Saint Louis All-Stars, October 7, 1923. Photograph from the Stiller-Lefebvre Collection.

After losing much of the team's football talent to college, the town eleven made another attempt to bolster their ranks: an article ran, asking for volunteers for the team to contact the *Press-Gazette*.

A team called the Appleton Crescents hurled a defi to Green Bay's football men. A game for gate receipts was proposed and hyped in the *Press-Gazette*. Manager Hart from the Appleton "Paper Mill" team mentioned adding talent from the Lawrence College squad. The Appleton squad had defeated Little Chute, Kaukauna, Oshkosh, and Fond du Lac earlier in the season and expected Green Bay to be no different. In Green Bay, Coach Art Schmael and Captain Abrams were dubious as to the quality of their "green" squad. A drill practice was set up at the armory on the corner of Cherry and Jefferson Streets, with a plea that all players show up in a timely manner.

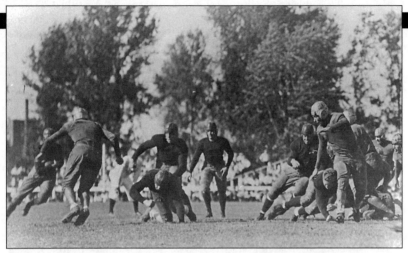

This is one of several photos taken at a game between the Packers and the Saint Louis All-Stars, October 7, 1923. They are some of the earliest action shots of Green Bay football available. Photograph from the Henry Lefebvre Collection of the Neville Public Museum of Brown County, Green Bay, Wisconsin.

All fears Coach Schmael had of the ability of his team must have been put to rest quickly as his "green" team put Appleton's eleven to shame 72–0. The dominance was complete in that the opponents never once crossed the Green Bay 40-yard line. "Before one of the biggest crowds that ever attended a Sabbath day conflict in this city," the Green Bay aggregation bullied their way through the enemy with little problem. The game was kept clean, and the field was clear from spectators. For the locals, Nate Abrams continued his class act of receiving, and the entire backfield shared the ball-carrying load. Appleton's Dooin, Murphy, and Faville were cited for their hard effort on the field. Bruises were their only reward.

The usual challenges were beginning to crop up for Green Bay. Convincing wins over good teams usually went one of two ways: opponents anxious to make a name were coming out of the woodwork or their phone lines had all gone dead. Fortunately, the Whales' success wasn't having the latter effect. That had happened to Green Bay teams in earlier years and it would again in 1919 and 1920 when the Packers had contests falling apart left and right. At least at the beginning of the season, Little Chute, Oshkosh, Oconto, and Menominee were all looking for a scrap—a chance to take it to the new powerhouse.

The never-fail writings of "Cal" Calhoun kept pace with the activities of the team. Practices were held, new players were called into action, and old players were harangued into attending drill sessions.

The next hot ticket was rival Kaukauna. Coach Schmael's city team drilled continually and seemed in shape. McCarthy, manager of the Kaukauna aggregation, had a strong lineup that had handed Clintonville a 70–0 defeat. The picture was painted, potential lineups were handed out, and all was ready for the cacophony on a Sunday at Hagemeister Park.

Green Bay, on the surface, seemed to have had very little trouble picking on the Kaukauna team in its fourth straight win, 64–0. Calhoun, not one to mince words or run low on them, saw things differently. "Green Bay failed to show the expected class. Coach Schmael's team went like a house-fire in the first half but their work was rugged in the closing quarters." Not an easy man to please.

After Green Bay tallied 40 points in the first half of play, Kaukauna's spirit was bruised but not broken. They played hardball but could never manage a threat. In the third quarter, Dwyer snagged a touchdown on a 30-yard play described as a "fake pass formation." The fourth quarter saw three scores in quick succession for Green Bay.

Hagemeister was peaceful on that October 20. On-field, the referees kept all nonsense contained, penalizing the home team several times for offsides. Off-field, the state militia kept all other hijinks under wraps. At four and zero, rumblings went up for the local lads to play a champion—to show their worth.

One historical revisionist has mistakenly labeled this crew as the 1918 Packers. But the name was used only after 1919, thanks to the team's sponsorship by Curly Lambeau's employer, the Indian—and, then, Acme—Packing Company. This collection of photos is actually a composite, no doubt assembled in retrospect, clipped from the Packer team photos of 1919, 1920, and 1921, as well as from at least one other source. But it hardly matters. These guys were on the verge of greatness because 1918 is the last year that town team football would be played by the "Green Bay City Team." Photograph from the Henry Lefebvre Collection of the Neville Public Museum of Brown County, Green Bay, Wisconsin.

More mention of games on tap piqued the public interest. The boys were winning big and attracted the attention due to them. Calhoun kept the keys warm. The next game was against football phenom Menominee and promised all the challenge due to the squad from the bay. As had become the norm for most later-season games, both squads were undefeated, and both potential champions.

The first half featured Green Bay overwhelming the team from up north by 25 points. Sauber of Green Bay provided most of the muscle behind his weighty center Osterman. Nate Abrams was the mastermind at quarterback, calling the plays that signaled pay dirt four times in the first split.

The Doyle boys knocked the Green Bay line about like tenpins en route to Menominee's first score. The locals didn't seem to enjoy that bruising very much and held the northerners scoreless the rest of the half.

Halftime put some lead in the Green Bay team's shorts as they battled up and down the field but managed no scoring threats. Working the forward pass to serious advantage, the Menominee lads knocked their way down to the 15-yard line before being contained by the Green Bay toughs. Coffeen, this year playing for the Menominee team, drop-kicked for three points, and the lead was trimmed, slightly. Seesaw action commenced, but it wasn't until late in the fourth that Menominee battered, bumped, and bruised their way across the goal line for another score. Time expired soon thereafter, and the final score rang out at 25–17 in favor of Green Bay.

It was by far the toughest challenge Green Bay had faced that year and for some time in recent history. The sense of complete dominance was shaved away, and Green Bay had to know that more practice was necessary.

The end of the article spoke of the late start for the game and the completion being done under "semi-darkness." It also mentioned that five Menominee players were late and missed the train back home. They had to find alternate transportation, and, shabby as it may seem, "they were forced to make the trip by auto and a Ford at that." Poor lads.

Like all great battles, this one screamed for a rematch. It was delivered. This time the stakes were $100 and all the bragging rights one team could enjoy. The game was set for November 24, and the acceptance letter to Menominee's defi was sent to be printed in the *Press-Gazette* as follows:

> *Dear Sir:*
>
> *The Green Bay City Football team accepts the challenge issued by the Marinette-Menominee eleven for a football game in this city on Nov. 24 for a side bet of a $100.*
>
> *A Copy of this letter has been mailed to Manager Doyle of the Marinette-Menominee eleven and we hope to close negotiations immediately.*

BEFORE THEY WERE THE PACKERS

The Green Bay team is willing to play any football team in Wisconsin or Michigan and the acceptance of this challenge shows that we are not in the habit of backing water.

Green Bay City Team

Tough words call for a tough game. That was expected and that was what was delivered.

Perhaps it was hubris that brought Green Bay to play a second time with Menominee. They were the only team to score on the Bays, and more than once! The "Northerners" had loaded their team for the trip to Hagemeister with the best talent they could find, working even harder this time to secure it than they had for the first scrimmage. There was even mention of adding a "pair of Jackies from Norfolk training station," one, in particular, named Knutson.

This game was to be characterized by brute force and, as described by Calhoun, "the smashing type." Mistakes on the Green Bay side were a decisive factor in the game. The Marinette/Menominee boys played vicious defense, with Hansen and Sam Powers in the spotlight. So impressed were the Green Bay lads with Powers's powers that they enlisted him for their 1919 campaign, their first as the Green Bay Packers. The M and M offense never really posed much of a threat, failing to penetrate the 30-yard line during the entire game.

The first quarter was full of sound and fury but signified nothing. Worthy defensive stands were contributed but little else. Lady luck was homebound on November 24: on four drives, the Green Bay team made their way inside the opponents' 10, only to fumble the ball away. Schmael, Nate Abrams, and Gus Rosenow made their best efforts but weren't able to keep a tight grip on the pigskin as it and time slipped away. Cal tapped the "old hoo-doo" as the cause for all the dropped balls, but they may just have been fumbles. All that remained at the end of the game was an underused scorekeeper and an expired clock. The final score? A disappointing 0–0 tie.

Like any draw in a heavyweight title match, the masses as well as the players were soon clamoring for yet another rematch. The usual conditions were argued over. The northern lads, under the guidance of Manager Doyle, wanted the Green Bay boys on their home turf. The Bays wanted another at Hagemeister. An article from the Wednesday, November 27, *Press-Gazette* didn't seem very sure of anything. It simply stated Marinette/Menominee's refusal to play in Green Bay again and that Doyle had made a good offer to play the game up there.

All must have fallen apart at the seams as there is no further mention of football that year. Once again, Thanksgiving Day slammed the lid shut on football action for the season.

It had been another impressive year for Green Bay town football. The motley assortment enjoyed a 5-0-1 record, shutting out its opponent on five occasions. The point differential of 216 for to 17 against was equally impressive. While it's true that the boys did stay fairly close to home, not many came knocking on the Bays' door to challenge them as in previous seasons. The tide was about to turn. Success had been building for a long time in the town to become known as "Titletown," and nothing could stem the sweeping power that Lambeau would bring back to Green Bay and its future football history.

On a "lighter" note, 1918 had seen the addition of heavyweight wrestler, Carl Zoll, to the team's lineup. Throughout the season, football news had been spiced with a sprinkling of Zoll's wrestling exploits. Zoll was known as the Green Bay heavyweight champion and was one of the guys Green Bay pigskin fans "in the know" liked to point out in gridiron action. He was usually the one latched onto the opposing ball carrier. On Monday evening, November 25, at Turner Hall, he found himself in the firm grasp of "The Strangler" Hill from Davenport, Iowa. Some bets had been couched. Attendance at the match had been affected by an influenza epidemic in the city, but Zoll prevailed over the Strangler, taking the first fall in 29:59 and the second in 12:46. The Strangler had choked, and Carl Zoll continued to post an undefeated record.

FOURTH QUARTER
1919–1921 AND BEYOND, HAIL THE PACKERS

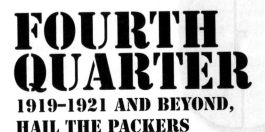

1919
LAMBEAU AND CALHOUN CREATE A LEGEND

The year of destiny for Green Bay football was, without a doubt, 1919. All pieces of the football machine were carefully oiled and in place. With a sharp pen, George Whitney Calhoun held the public in thrall with his reports of the organization of the team to come. Curly Lambeau was molding the on-field antics, gathering the best available talent. The public was holding up their end; the town was ravenous for football. All in-town football events were well-attended and interest was high.

To put it simply, Green Bay had the most dominant team in the area on the gridiron, and their end-of-the-year tallies bore that out. The formula for success? Pass-oriented offense, stone-wall defense, and a deep bench full of equally talented substitutes. The defense wasn't new, but the other two concepts were. The ability to reach into the splinter squad and not lose a step on the field was a luxury that most teams couldn't afford. A team normally had 14 to 15 men, and substitutions were only made when a player was carried off the field. Lambeau's boys didn't wait for that. The addition of the pass, used in a consistent and successful way, made the running game seem better by spreading out the defense. While that may seem common sense to today's learned fan, in those days it was original and damn near unbeatable.

The newspaper coverage whipped up a frenzy starting in late August, much earlier than in previous years. The August 27 *Press-Gazette* called for "Footballers on the Indian Packing Corporation squad" to meet in the editorial rooms of the *Press-Gazette* on Friday, August 29, at 7:45. It is safe to assume that Curly personally approached each member of the squad to verify their membership for the upcoming campaign. The article mentioned outfitting the players "in college style" and further mentioned potential foes in the conglomerations from Milwaukee, Waukesha, La Crosse, Madison, Marinette, Menominee, Oconto, Oshkosh, and Appleton. Some of these towns would actually meet the Green Bay team and leave the encounter with bruised bodies and egos.

Calhoun kept the fires lit with no less than 13 articles from August 23 through September 13. These were all written before the first game was even played! The stories covered topics including the first team meeting, the first practice, and potential gridiron opposition. Captain Curly Lambeau was busy with the organization, and Bill Ryan was being put to task as coach. Ryan's duties as coach of Green Bay's West High School in previous years had made him an acquaintance of Curly's. Lambeau himself had done a little coaching across the river, and his exploits as a prep footballer made him a topic in the coach's office at both local high schools.

Maybe today's garb is a little less formal than that of these railbirds. Just drive down Green Bay's Oneida Street any day in late summer, and you'll see this year's version of an old tradition: fans gathered like birds on a wire to watch their Packers and speculate on things to come. Note the wire fence and wooden posts, meant to keep the fans off the field during games. The dapper gentleman in the dark fedora leaning on the post is Buck Anderson, himself a football standout during Titletown's town team days. Photograph from the Stiller-Lefebvre Collection.

LA CROSSE—SELLING TONIC

According to La Crosse historians Albert H. Sanford and H. J. Hirsheimer, the game of "football" was played as early as 1860. What version of "football" was played that day is question enough, and considering that it predated the Massasoit Convention, it's safe to say that it was more like a game of rugby-soccer than it was today's football. Nonetheless, Sanford and Hirsheimer cite a newspaper account of a "football" game being played by "the entire crowd" following a baseball game "on the Square." The Square "or Public Square," as it appears on the Bliss and Spear Map of 1859, was "the half block now Cameron Park, probably treeless."

In August 1919, George Whitney Calhoun, in his usual fashion, was firing up the Packers and their fans by suggesting that the "Packer management is mapping out a schedule which will include games with the best professional gridiron elevens in Wisconsin." Calhoun listed La Crosse as one of those. Of course, it was his habit to name every team he could think of as a possible opponent, stirring up interest in his Packers from every corner of the state.

A couple of weeks later he fell upon an item from the *La Crosse Leader-Times* that indicated to him, at least, that "defeating Green Bay at football would be La Crosse's greatest pleasure." The item read,

> Over in Green Bay, where they eat once in a while in the autumn between football games and football controversies merely to keep the spark of life within the body, they have organized a city-football team of former college stars. The team is seeking games and is anxious to land a contest with some La Crosse aggregation. This is the dope, fellows: "If you feel inclined, there is plenty of material here for a winning football team and defeating Green Bay at anything would be a pleasure."

Calhoun wasn't about to let the dust settle with that:

> According to the aforesaid article, the spirit in La Crosse seems to be walloping Green Bay. Here's the opportunity. It raps but once, so grab it with open hands, La Crosse.
> We do not think the La Crosse team would have an easy task defeating the Indian Packing Corporation aggregation but will give the former a chance to prove their mettle. There are open dates on the schedule.

Before any account of the games of the 1919 season can begin, there is the little matter of a glass of beer and the team meeting to be touched upon. Both of these have been covered in other Packer histories and they've become the stuff of legend and conjecture. What stands without question is that Calhoun and Lambeau got together late in the summer of 1919 to discuss putting a bigger and better version of a town team on the field that fall.

That meeting may have been over a glass of beer, several glasses of beer, a gourmet meal, or a fire hydrant. It doesn't matter. In *The Packer Legend*, John Torinus says it happened at a Green Bay bar. That's as good a place as any. During that meeting they put together a scheme that started with a call to arms for some of the best players of the town team era immediately preceding 1919. The meeting was set for Monday, August 11, in the *Press-Gazette* editorial rooms. Calhoun used his article announcing the meeting to put out an APB for particular players whom he singled out by name.

So the stars were in alignment; Curly was assigned to field duty and Calhoun had the press humming. Did they know they were about to launch a legend? Sometimes from humble beginnings . . . Articles describing the lid-lifter with Menominee, scheduled for September 14, set the League Ball Field as the site for the collision. Preparing for the battle with the North End Athletic Club of Menominee were as many as 24 men scrimmaging at the Indian Packing facility, a lot located between the current Henry and Morrow Streets. Expectations were high in the city, and the boys did not want to disappoint.

The Saturday, September 13, paper gave a great preview of the game. The visitors were expected to arrive on the Chicago & North Western at 11:00 a.m., catch lunch downtown, and get to the ballpark by 3:00 p.m. Lineups were provided, and all arrangements had been considered. A last blurb mentioned Coach Ryan's 7:30 blackboard talk to be held at the Continuation School building. These boys seriously wanted to win and used every bit of their football know-how to do just that.

In no way did Green Bay disappoint on Sunday. A record crowd was on hand and they witnessed a total team victory. Under the subheading "Team of All-Stars" was the following bulletin: "There were no individual stars in the game, each man doing his part and in good shape. This is what made the team play possible yesterday. The men all played together in mid-season form and proved a big surprise to the huge crowd that had gathered to witness the fray."

It was all Green Bay as Menominee never mounted any offensive threat. The Green Bay defense was masterly and played the game on the Menominee side of the field the whole time. On offense, the Bays passed and smashed through with little difficulty. Truth be told, Curly Lambeau's accurate passing could be considered the star attraction in an otherwise total team effort. Keeping up with the new strategy, the Bays used 20 different players and each showed their worth. The tally stood at 53–0 at the final whistle with Green Bay notching a first dominating win to the ballyhoos of their loyal fans.

Coach Ryan was not so easily impressed and called for practice to be held the next day at 6:45.

After this easy victory the Packers could have rested comfortably, assuming their superiority was obvious to everyone, but this did not happen. The paper on the 16th confirmed the "Indian Packers football squad" practice the next day, with Marinette next in the ring. Evidently, Marinette's team must not have been in close communication with their northern neighbors, Menominee, or they might not have been so eager to enter the fray. More men were tagged to join the already fearsome crew. Wallie Ladrow, Jen Gallagher, Milton Wilson, and Herb Nichols were all ready for hijinks.

BEFORE THEY WERE THE PACKERS

Calhoun had high praise for the players in the September 17 paper: "The Packers showed that they were football players of first water against Menominee Sunday. The entire squad played like seasoned veterans and every man Coach Ryan sent into the game was a credit to the game and the team."

Another boxed-in passage from the same page gave some sage advice appropriate to even today's modern football warrior:

DON'T BE GUILTY OF FUMBLING BALL

Many a football game has been won or lost through a fumble at a critical moment of play. Never be guilty of making one of those costly blunders. Don't pick up a ball in the open field if there is anyone near you. Fall around the ball when you see it on the ground. Never stick the ball out ahead of you when tackled — someone may steal it. And above all practice handling
    New balls.
    Old balls.

The earliest New London town team was called the Merchants, but they eventually became the Bulldogs, named for young Gordon Meiklejohn's pet, pictured front and center here. The Bulldogs played their home games at Raussman Athletic Field, a.k.a. City Athletic Field. They became a part of football history in 1919 when they played the Packers after an Appleton crew backed out at the last minute. The Bulldogs took it on the nose, 54–0, but they fared better than some aggregations. Photograph obtained from and used by permission of New London Museum, New London, Wisconsin.

Wet balls.
Dry balls.

The final hype for the Marinette game was printed in the Saturday, September 20, *Press-Gazette*. Some of the bonanza promised a fenced-off playing area at Hagemeister Park, extra car service to and from the park, 14-minute periods, and a "hard fought fracas." The game was deemed a "semipro" affair, with Bill Doyle's Marinette All-Stars fully "leaded" to ensure a victory.

The All-Stars proved to be anything but and were coined as "hopelessly outclassed." The forward pass, courtesy of Curly Lambeau, Jim Coffeen, and the rest of the backfield confounded the "lumberjacks," and the score skyrocketed. Green Bay's defense continued to be as worthy as ever, allowing only one first down and stingily prohibiting the Marinette boys from getting closer than 43 yards from the goal line. Despite Marinette's larger men, they fell to defeat, 61–0, mostly due to their inability to defend the forward pass. The legend was building.

Next to face the juggernaut was the Crescent City Footballers from Appleton. The game was a hastily scheduled one after the Sheboygan Falls motor team begged off at the eleventh hour. Manager E. J. Hilliman from Appleton promised a "husky line-up" that had done some tuning up against the Lawrence College squad.

After Tuesday's announcement of the Crescent City clash, Captain Lambeau called for a Friday afternoon practice at 3:30 at the company gridiron. The cagey captain felt the need to get ready, and he expected his men to show. They were even mentioned by name and told to "be on hand without fail."

In the second cancellation of the week, Appleton slipped away, allowing New London to save the day as well as the chance for a game that week. The New London Athletic Club team boasted six men from their Edison basketball squad, which had been runners-up at the Amateur Athletic Union basketball tournaments that spring. "This is enough to guarantee a corking good game of football on Sunday" promised an article. The opposition also bragged a line that averaged 170 pounds, a hefty amount for that time. The game was slated for a 3:00 start at Hagemeister.

The opposition proved unworthy once again in what was mistakenly hailed a as "Hard Fought Battle." The tale of the game was favorable to the New London team, saying that they showed "plenty of fight." The simple fact was that the Edisons were outplayed by a superior team. The Packers moved the ball with relative ease, racking up 54 points and allowing none. Conditioning was the decisive factor as the New London boys "were strong at the beginning of the periods, but their strength gradually waned as the time progressed." No one was singled out for the Indian Packing team; rather, they were likened to "a well-oiled machine." The Packers had once again shattered the opposition.

Smaller scale, intracity football was going on in town despite the fact that the Packers were drawing most of the media attention. The September 30 *Press-Gazette* mentioned the Lawtontown football team of West De Pere had cleaned up on the South Siders of Green Bay 66–6. In retaliation, the South Siders promised to "bring a heavier line-up to De Pere next Sunday" for a rematch.

The Packers were next ready to lock horns with a team comprising war vets from Sheboygan called the "Company C" team. The military team, together in 1916, were runners-up for state honors, and had gone into the service in the same company. They kept practicing while stationed in Waco, Texas, in 1917 and while serving in France in 1918. A tough row to hoe was expected.

Coach Ryan, ever mindful of keeping his talent pool strong, let leak that he had talked with one of Carlisle's star athletes, not to mention a former teammate of Jim Thorpe, a man named Gus Lookaround. A later paper edition informed that Lookaround had "left the city and will not be seen in action."

Val Schneider in his "Looking 'Em Over" column in the *Press-Gazette* painted the Indian Packers as a dominant force in local football. He laughed at the first three opponents and mentioned a running back from the upcoming foe who tipped the scales at two hundred pounds. He opined, "We, at least hope there is one man who can give the Packers a little opposition."

Later in his column, Schneider became clairvoyant with the following prophetic words:

> Football will soon hold the reign in the realm of sport all through the United States. The pigskin sport came back this year stronger than ever, augmented by the return of many stars from Uncle Sam's service. Mostly every city and hamlet on the map is represented with a football team. High schools give promise of having crack football elevens this autumn, back to pre-war days.

The stage for the fourth game of the 1919 season was once again Hagemeister Park, and those tough Company C soldiers, with a three-year history together, were the cross-line opponents. This game should have been the toughest one of the young season. It wasn't.

In the biggest blowout of the year, the Packers humbled their Company C foes 87–0. The larger, more nattily attired eleven from Sheboygan looked fearsome but provided little to no opposition to the locals. Again the Packer defense was insurmountable and the visitors posed no threat whatsoever. The forward pass, again courtesy of Lambeau, wowed fans. "Lambeau was shooting 'em all the way from 20 to 40 yards," Calhoun raved, "with the other back fielders and ends making sensational catches."

The Packers still had not met a bona fide challenge.

In an attempt to get a "game" opponent, Green Bay next looked to Racine, southern Wisconsin champs of the prior year. The October 8 *Press-Gazette* pre-

Every town with a successful team for any stretch of time had a guy at the local newspaper who would celebrate the team's antics and bewail their stumbles. In Green Bay, that role was filled admirably by newspaperman George Whitney "Cal" Calhoun. Talk about silver-tongued? This guy could make sparks fly between Green Bay and any other football locale he set his sights on. One of his tactics was to dangle the bait at the end of the summer and see what teams—prompted much more by barroom bluster than brains—would bite and then get whaled on by Calhoun's Packers. Photograph from the Stiller-Lefebvre Collection.

sented a scouting report on the Racine aggregation. The article showed high praise for the opponents when it mentioned that the Racine squad was undefeated in 1918 and called the contest "one of the best games of the season because the visitors come here with a guaranteed reputation as footballers." The skinny on size was that the entire team averaged 165 pounds.

The Packers, never ones to sit back and let things happen, scheduled a "blackboard talk" at the Continuation School building for that night and a scrimmage practice for the 10th at the Indian Packing practice field.

The newspaper did an excellent job of pumping up the opponents that the Packers were to meet each week, but the teams just paled in comparison to the hype on the field. Racine became like the rest of the opposition in 1919 when it fell to an embarrassing 76–6 mark. The game was a rough-and-tumble affair, with Racine using up all of its reserves and Green Bay adding Sammy Powers and Tubby Bero to its injury squad.

For the first time in two years, the Green Bay team was scored on. It took quite a bit of effort for the goal to come to pass. Ironically, the forward pass set up the scoring drive and got Racine to the two-yard line. After holding for three downs, fullback Somers punched the ball over the line and the scoreless era ended. Much to Green Bay football fans' delight, the forward pass still seemed to be the king. When the dust settled, the Bays had knocked off a Racine championship team that had not been beaten in two years and had further shown that they were a team that could not be defeated.

BEFORE THEY WERE THE PACKERS

Modern rules guru Walter Camp was spreading around his knowledge of the game in 1919 via a series of articles run in wire service papers. The articles, which mirrored earlier writings by Michigan football star Johnny Maulbetsch, were a primer on football positions. The advice seems campy by today's standards but was clear-cut for the popular offensive and defensive schemes of the day. One nugget of wisdom pertaining to the guard position was

> A guard must take care of his own little section, charge up and give his man a shove—a hard one, but then keeping his feet. Immediately after the charge he should stand spread with his arms and hands ready and looking for what is coming. In driving his man, the guard should shove him back and diagonally so that he fills up one opening while his feet fill the other.

Some shared print borrowed from the *Racine Journal News* ran in the October 15 *Press-Gazette*. The Racine paper excused their team's showing in the earlier 76–6 beating at the hands of Green Bay. "The Green Bay team is made up of a bunch of former college stars who are imported by that city for the express purpose of playing football." A more true statement about the boys of 1919 was never made. Many

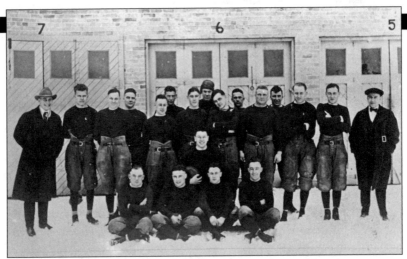

Here they are, the 1919 Green Bay City Team (now the "Packers"), standing near the loading doors for the Acme Packing Company. It's cold and there's snow on the ground. Likely, the boys have gathered together one last time, at season's end, for the team photo. Most of them are sporting smiles, and rightfully so. After all, they've outscored their opponents 565–12 and lost just one game, that one a serious question mark. Two years later, hardly any of this crew would be on the Packer team that would join the professional ranks: (sitting, from left to right) Nate Abrams, Fritz Gavin, Ray McLean, and Tubby Bero; (kneeling, in the center) Curly Lambeau; (standing, from left to right), Nichols, Sam Powers, Jim Coffeen, Martin Zoll, Martin, Charlie Sauber, Herm Martell, Wes Leaper, Wally Ladrow, Jim Desjardin, Carl Zoll, Andy Muldoon, Gus Rosenow, Al Petchka, and George W. Calhoun. Photograph courtesy of the Henry Lefebvre Collection of the Neville Public Museum of Brown County, Green Bay, Wisconsin.

of Lambeau's players were former college stars, that much is true. But they were also, at least at this point, mostly hometown boys who had returned for a little football. They were a purposefully made construct of football, certainly not the first ever, but the first in this area and destined for greater things.

The next game to be played had been on the back burner for 20 years, a clash with the crew from Ishpeming in Michigan's Upper Peninsula. Several times over years gone by, the hearty band from up north had passed a defi to Green Bay squads to increase their own reputation, and such a game was finally coming to fruition.

For this affair, the Packers would head up to Ishpeming via the Chicago & North Western's special Pullman car, the "Packer Special." The car was festooned with banners from Packer boosters. The team and rooters left the station at 12:45 early Sunday morning, October 19, and were expected to roll into Ishpeming around 7:15 a.m. After the game the team was expected to depart the northern town about 6:00 p.m. and get back to Green Bay by midnight. The newspaper dossier conjured up the usual banter about this game going "a long way towards deciding professional gridiron honors of the middle west."

Gambling, an ever-important part of the sideline activity in this and any era, was heated. Green Bay money was rumored as being matched in large sums at 5 to 3 odds for the northerners.

All of the stereotyped images of a game in the early days of football came to life in bright colors for the trip to Ishpeming. Both teams were very sure of themselves and could scarcely imagine a loss. The team and two dozen diehards made the trek north in their decorated iron carriage. As they pulled into the station, the Ishpeming fans took a look at the players and began cries of "Whatta bunch of kids!" and "How are you boys gonna beat our men?" Yet the rumored betting was scarce and odds were set at 10 to 8 for the Ishpeming locals. The raucous, mixed crew meandered to the field, situated some two miles out of the town proper. As the crowd gathered, about 1,200 locals circled the Union Park grounds with their band whooping it up. At game time, the sidelines swelled to about 3,500 bodies, yet the Packer boosters could be heard occasionally over the general din of the crowd.

The reputations were established: the Packers had been scored upon only once in the last two years and were without a single loss. The Ishpeming team had not lost a game on its home gridiron in five years. The collisions would be heard all the way in town.

The Green Bay players were an average of five pounds per man lighter but had a much more advanced game plan than their foes. The Packer offense was fast and punchy with the utilization of the forward pass; their defense was impenetrable. Both offense and defense were buoyed by their ability to offer substitutes without loss of skill. The hometown referee did his usual amount of "Defensive Work," calling holding and offsides when the Packers were on a roll. It was quickly apparent

ISHPEMING—FOOTBALL BATTLE CONTINUED IN THE PRESS

Up in the U. P., Ishpeming had tossed defis Green Bay's way since 1898, but it wasn't until October 19, 1919, that the two cities finally met on the football field. That's the day the Twin City Legion Team—made up of players from Ishpeming and Negaunee—faced the Green Bay Packers. Afterward, some of the locals wished the whole thing hadn't happened.

The fans, who had often helped their team by stepping onto the playing field and interfering with the opposition, didn't turn out to be much of a problem in the Packer contest. Instead, they spent much of the day trying to hide their wallets. Bets from the game were said to have cost the U. P. residents upwards of $800. As much as $2,400 more could have left town, wrote the *Press-Gazette*, but "the Michiganders wanted 10 to 8 odds."

The whipping cast a pall over the area. Not only had the locals lost some serious cash, but the football reputation of their boys had been burned to ashes. Then the battle found itself continued by members of the fourth estate. First, Green Bay sportswriter, George Whitney Calhoun, gave the twin cities a scathing tongue-lashing, questioning their manhood and their ability at the game. Then, the editor of the *Ishpeming Iron Ore* shot back. "It is understood that the Ishpeming management will negotiate with the Packers for a pinochle or ping pong contest to take place some time this winter."

that the referee couldn't do all the work without a major incident, and the best he could hope for was to hold the score in the respectable range.

The game was rough. All of Green Bay's substitutes were pressed into action and got some bruises for their trouble. The paper stated that "the water boy and doctor were right in their glory." Nevertheless, the formula remained unchanged and the Packers remained undefeated. The final was 33–0. Most of the band had packed up their instruments in the first quarter, so one can imagine that the hike back to the

OSHKOSH—FOOTBALL SINCE 1893

Organized football was being played in Oshkosh by 1893 when, according to an article in the *Oshkosh Daily Northwestern* of Friday, June 26, 1953, "Oshkosh High School's first football team took the field." That article also suggests that some sandlot ball was being played as early as 1887, though no official records exist of such contests. Because few high schools had football programs at the time, and those that did were not organized into any kind of sports conference, the *Northwestern* suggested that the high school eleven was "forced to accept playing dates with college elevens."

Oshkosh town teams were active early on and represented the most common opponent for Green Bay teams up to and including the Packers. The Oshkosh team played under any number of names including the Athletics, Arions, Colts, and All-Stars. Early games were found at South Park at South Park Avenue and Ohio Street as well as at Menominee (North) Park. When the Eastern Wisconsin Electric Company or EWECO Park opened on Lake Winnebago in June of 1903, football also could be found at the Ball Park there.

In 1919, Oshkosh was one of the local teams that toed up against Curly Lambeau's steamroller, the Packers. In retrospect, the 85–0 shellacking endured by the Oshkoshians doesn't look quite so bad. It wasn't the worst a team was beaten by the Packers that season, nor was it the only game in which the opponent was unable to score.

The football light may have dimmed in Oshkosh after that, but it came back in a big way via the Oshkosh Comets between 1949 and 1954. The Comets did pretty well in their first few years and hauled in the league title in 1949 and 1950, winning their first 10 games over that two-year stretch. They played their games at the Jackson Street Field against aggregations from Little Chute, Iron Mountain, Manitowoc, Sheboygan, Sturgeon Bay, and Two Rivers. The Comets' five years left behind a lot of colorful recollections for team players and owners alike. Harry Gorwitz, a co-owner, recalled that, after games, the owners would feed the players and the players often brought their girlfriends to the feast. "Boy they knew how to eat," he remarked. He had to have been referring to the players, right?

station was a quiet one. Betting netted the Green Bay rooters a mere $800, but a good time was had at Michigan's expense. Local fans were spirited but not rude to their visitors and never crushed onto the field, despite being four deep around the action.

The Ishpeming referee, despite efforts to help his boys out on the field, was lavish with praise for the Packer team. "Best team that has ever played in Ishpeming," he said. "The best thing about the Green Bay team is the fact that your extra men can be sent into the game without weakening the line-up."

Lambeau and his men had survived their most fistic encounter of the year, certainly bruised but intact and most important still undefeated. Their reputation now included the central part of Upper Michigan, and the team sat back and waited for the challenges to come in.

In the wake of Green Bay's latest destruction, more teams were eager to run for cover rather than face the formidable team. The Falls Motor Corporation team of Sheboygan Falls had signed papers for a Sunday, October 26, game but pleaded for a cancellation claiming three of their men had gone down with broken legs. The team planners were now reaching beyond the Fox Valley to find opponents who could make it to the gridiron.

Oshkosh stepped up to the challenge, and the Professionals loaded up an all-star crew to storm Hagemeister Park. To prepare, Lambeau had practices scheduled for Thursday at Hagemeister's Roller Rink and Friday at the Indian Packing practice field.

Other areas of the country were also maturing in professional football. On the horizon was a professional football league, and powerful elevens across the landscape were taking notice of each other. A vision of a nation of professional football fans was coming to fruition; college football was fine but regulated, and the country wanted the next step.

BEFORE THEY WERE THE PACKERS

Oshkosh's aggregation, at the bequest of Manager Weid, would invade Hagemeister on the 26th. Expecting a crew of 170-pounders as opposition, Lambeau's team wasn't fazed in the slightest. They were a beefy club, averaging 190 pounds, and, despite a few lingering injuries to Al Petcka and Jim Coffeen, the team was in great shape. Coach Ryan was adept at shuffling his lineup to fill in gaps and he had a quality surplus to choose from.

The Oshkosh game was not hyped as a championship struggle or a fierce contention, and justly so. The game was a farce, even with Green Bay short four starters. The results were another flogging and castigation of the visitors by the degrading score of 85–0. The game plan was solid and was followed to a tee: pass the ball downfield and play solid defense. Fifty-eight points were run up in the second half, which lasted only 28 minutes.

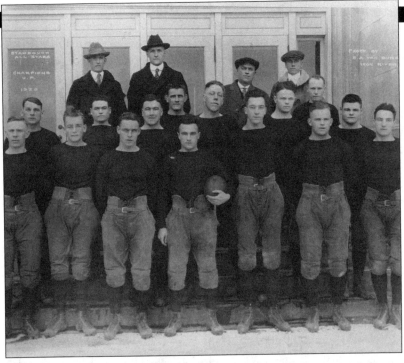

In the 1919–1920 season, when the Green Bay Packers overwhelmed their opponents in 11 games by an average of 57 points to 1, this scrappy crew of miners from Stambaugh, Michigan, stood their ground on what is now West Iron County Airport in a 17–0 loss. But times were getting tough for the town teams. While the Packers were in the process of joining the professional ranks, the Stambaugh All-Stars, one of the class teams of the U. P., would continue to struggle as a town team through the 1930s, reappearing in the 1950s as the Iron County Steelers. But for one brief moment, this crew fully deserved to be on same field of play as the Packers. Photograph obtained from and used with permission of Frank Shepich and Harold Anderson, Stambaugh, Michigan.

The next football faction with enough confidence to face the chastisement of the Packer pride was the Maple Leaf Athletic Club of Milwaukee. The Cream City team promised to be of worthy opposition and expected to "take Green Bay into camp."

There just wasn't any hope for the opposition at Hagemeister Park. The home field advantage was total. And the Packers were damn good.

Once again no subterfuge was necessary; the Packers threw the ball and played defense like a wall. The team was exactly that—a total and effective team. Six different players scored, showing that offensive weapons were plentiful and that the opposition couldn't possibly key on one man. The reckoning came to 53–0. Good-bye Milwaukee.

As the sphere of influence expanded, more opponents arrived from across state lines. Now a Chicago bunch called the Chilar Athletic Club was ready to step to the fore and enter the spiderweb that Hagemeister had become. A hefty 175 pounds on average, the club, under Manager Berg, was comprised of excollegians. The youngest fans at that game would be disappointed to know that Green Bay management intended to herd the kids away from the east end of the field near the billboard to provide more space for taller spectators. One can assume it was financially motivated.

Another large crowd witnessed the Packers' latest victory. This time, the emphasis went away from the passing game, and line smashes became the fodder of victory. Injuries skyrocketed that day, but both teams had spares and could continue the rough-going until the end. The toughest team on that field was Green Bay. The final stood at 46–0, with the opposition proving negligible.

A MOMENT IN THE SUN FOR STAMBAUGH

Because he was only seven, Frank Shepich had only a vague recollection of the buzz in town when the Packers showed up to play the Stambaugh All-Stars. He remembered "definitely big excitement." There weren't that many automobiles in town, so he recalled that people walked up the hill to the game. "There were a couple of restaurants downtown and lots of saloons all the time, you know. So there was activity, no doubt." At the game, "there [would] be a guy with a can or a hat going around and you're standing on the ground level and here's a cable, you know. And the team is playing."

Because the game was played on a Sunday, Shepich remembered that the entire town had turned out, saying that

the only people who worked [at the mines] on Sunday were pump men. You see they had to pump these mines in order to keep them dry and so the pump men and the guy that put them down in the hole, the hoist men, were the only people that generally

BEFORE THEY WERE THE PACKERS

worked [on Sunday] excepting if there was repair work to be done, you know, they'd have a crew out but they weren't mining. Sunday was the day off.

After the game, Stambaugh was still vibrating with excitement. Sure their boys had lost, but the All-Stars had given the Packers everything they could handle that day and wrestled them to a 17–0 victory, the closest contest for the Green Bay team to that point in the season. The best of the U. P. had met the best of northeast Wisconsin.

One autumn day, just 18 football seasons later, the Packers would be playing their NFL opponent of the week and the All-Stars would be a fond memory. But that one day, in 1919, they stood toe to toe on the gridiron and fought a battle that would be forever etched in the annals of football history.

Upcoming foe Stambaugh had sent nine members of its squad to scout the game and "get an eyeful." The Stambaugh All-Stars were another powerhouse from the northwestern part of the Upper Peninsula and were commonly thought of as the Champions of the Copper Range. The game drew heavy interest.

The Stambaugh team had its share of myth and reputation behind it and was backed by loyal fans. They were reportedly undefeated that season and were huge. The All-Stars were also reported to be "loading up" with talent from the Chicago area. Lambeau and Ryan were ready to take their unblemished record to the northern woods to face a gang of rough-and-tumble miners. After the Ishpeming game, they decided that a group of rooters would be a good thing and made arrangements for some of the locals to accompany them. Added incentive was the betting that would go on and the opportunity to take some extra money home.

The usual practices were scheduled, and fans signed up in large numbers to head north. Green Bay had every player healthy and ready for the game. All indications pointed to a whale of an event. The train pulled out at 12:50 a.m. early on Sunday, November 16, bound for Stambaugh, Michigan.

The game proved to be a stellar affair. The mining community proved to be excellent hosts; special trolleys were provided to and from the field, betting was lively, and steps were made to keep the game free from any type of shenanigans. The Green Bay community brought 300 fans armed with megaphones to holler for their boys. Some 3,500 roisters witnessed the event. Good fun was in the making.

The game was everything it was set up to be, hard played and free from unsportsmanlike activity. Stambaugh simply could not put up any kind of offense against the Packer defense. The miners never cracked the stone wall erected at the 40-yard line and, thus, could put no points on the scoreboard. Green Bay's offense was treated more rudely than they were accustomed to. The forward pass was as successful as ever, but the run was stopped with little forward progress. End runs were successful for Green Bay, but between the tackles was no-man's-land. A great battle ended with the miserly score of 17–0 in favor of the Bays.

The locals had ponied up about $3,000 in bets but paid without complaint. For the most part, the locals said things like "the better footballers won." Without a doubt the game was hard fought, and there were a few injuries due to tough play. The All-Stars gave the Packers everything they could but hadn't learned how to deal with the newer passing game. Respect was earned all around.

The most notable outcome of this game was the abuse of Green Bay's backfield, according to some historians. Three of the Packer's backs were knocked out of the game on consecutive plays with "broken legs." Although all of these backs were in action the next week against Beloit, dulling the three plays–three broken legs legend, Curly Lambeau was sufficiently impressed to comment that "those miners were tough." Some circles have reported that the three plays–three broken legs legend comes from the Ishpeming game of the same year. Most accounts say Stambaugh, so let's go with that. The fact is, no matter which game it was, all three players were back in action a scant seven days later, belying the level of their injuries or crediting the mystifying healing powers of Green Bay's drinking water—or beer.

In choosing the next opponent, Beloit, the management of the Packers made a major mistake. While the Fairbanks-Morse Company sponsored "Fairies" was certainly a worthy opponent, going down to Beloit to play the game proved to be a tactical error.

The game played at Morse field in Beloit took place on November 23 and is recounted in infamy. A major factor in the game proved to be the shifty referee Baldy Zabel. On three different occasions he made spurious calls after the Packers had crossed the goal line, thus negating their scores. One Beloit touchdown was earned, and it proved to be enough when combined with Zabel's "skill." Many accounts of the game exist, and the vast majority feels it was highway robbery. "Beloit won the game before the teams stepped on the gridiron" reads a quote from one such account. Other factors that prevented the Packers from getting back into the game included the fans blocking the field on drives in the second half. The game can only be classified as a travesty of poor sportsmanship and deserves its place in the "Hall of Shame." A team that may well have beaten the Packers on its own merits is now relegated to the back shelf of a joke of a game.

To put "the game" behind them, a contest with De Pere was quickly scheduled, and the hype came flowing quickly. The southern neighbor's team was to be loaded up with all-star talent and provide "a great little football fight." To prevent repeats of fan interference, police support was enlisted. The game was to be held in the familiar confines of Hagemeister Park come good weather or bad. Snow would need to be scraped off of the field, but that didn't seem to threaten the game's existence.

While the De Pere game was being prepared, a return to Beloit was in the works as well. A special train was planned, with spots on it reserved at a price of $10.72 for

CARROLL COLLEGE—SOME THINGS NEVER CHANGE

The Beloit fiasco was just one more case of "crooked ref!" Check out the story of the 1915 De Pere battle for another. By 1898, football was a foregone conclusion at Carroll College, and its teams began to focus exclusively on other college teams. That year, the Carroll eleven seemed to have found itself in a rather heartless contest against Sacred Heart College of Watertown, labeled "the problem game of the season." While the game ended in a tie, Carroll's newspaper, the Echo, branded the referee from Watertown "the most unfair and unscrupulous fellow." It went on to suggest that he was "really a part of the team, for he never saw any wrong acts by the Sacred Heart boys, and once tried to make Carroll forfeit the ball because the center's hair was offside." Was the guy's last name Zabel? Anyway, thank God complaints about refs are a thing of the past. Right?

the round trip. The game, to be played on November 30 regardless of weather, met its match courtesy of an ice storm that deposited six inches of ice on the field and surrounding area, making a game impossible. Winter had arrived, and no more games would happen that year. Green Bay would have to wait until the next season to avenge its "loss" to Beloit.

The 1919 season was remarkable. The Packers managed 565 points to their opponents' 12 and managed to legitimately win 10 out of 11 games. This indicated that the team was a phenomenon and posed a threat for the future. Curly Lambeau had returned to Green Bay to stay and planned to keep football at a competitive, nationwide level. The game plan also rose to the next level: use the pass and keep quality substitutes at the ready and use them to keep your troops fresh. The Packers had also played teams all over the Midwest, stretching their recognition and potential opponents.

There are several well-documented facts about the 1919 season; the major players each got a split of the take for the season, a whopping $16.75. Lambeau was given $500 to buy materials for his team by boss Frank Peck of the Indian Packing Company. George Whitney Calhoun served as manager for the team and wrote glowing reports of team exploits. The team had been dubbed semiprofessionals. Curly quit playing college ball to take a job for $250 a month and to be with his sweetheart, Marguerite Van Kessel. Bill Ryan coached and supplied strategy to the team.

All of this has been well-documented, but the fact of the matter was that the team, comprised mostly of men from the Green Bay area, made the team successful. Their sweat and gristle put the points on the scoreboard and kept opponents at bay. The team's composition would change slowly in 1920, but by 1921 the "town" would leave the town team. Men could still not earn their bread and skittles solely from the game. It was a stellar diversion but just that, a diversion. The year 1919 was the start of something big for Green Bay football but also a death knell for locals playing for the Green Bay football team. The game itself was getting too important for roster spots to be used up on locals, when talent could be imported.

1920

END OF AN ERA

THE 1920 SEASON STARTED with the Green Bay team riding high on the accomplishments of the previous year. Getting the men together wouldn't be tough; a winning reputation has a way of making that job easier. The August 4 *Green Bay Press-Gazette* gave testament to the new direction that town team football was taking. The article was titled "PRO FOOTBALL TO BOOM THIS YEAR IN STATE CITIES." The essay went on to mention the following areas as hotbeds of professional football activity: Green Bay, Menominee, Fond du Lac, Oshkosh, Milwaukee, Racine, Kenosha, Beloit, Janesville, Eau Claire, and Superior. More towns were ready to make the jump to professional football and gather the notoriety and money provided there.

This year, Elbridge "Neil" Murphy took on the role of team manager for the Packers and immediately assembled talent from the area. A few new names came to practices along with the core of warriors from the exploits of 1919. Jack Dalton, a gentleman from Janesville, was rounded up to coach the team, and practices were held continually to tune the men up. Curly Lambeau, while he still remained a Packer player, was also tapped to coach at his alma mater East High.

The activities of old enemies were reported in the local paper. Stambaugh was rumored to have started practice early that year in hopes of a rematch with Green Bay. Great efforts were made to get the northern champs down to Green Bay for a battle. Other foes that were given paper space included the twin cities team of Marinette/Menominee, the Escanaba eleven under Bill Doyle's guiding hand, De Pere under manager E. J. Van Vonderen, and the Ishpeming football club. The overall sentiment in most of these football towns was that they looked forward to a chance to gain revenge on the Packer team for past defeats.

An article appearing on August 25 showed Green Bay's "love" for referee Baldy Zabel, the instrument of defeat from the Green Bay versus Beloit game. Zabel, a pitcher for his town baseball team, had lost a game to a team from Janesville called the Sampson Tractors. The Janesville crowd evidently gave him a hard time during his time on the mound, something that didn't sound at all disappointing to the author of the blurb.

Management took the difficult task of scheduling games seriously and began to set dates aside for games. But just as in seasons gone by, actually seeing a scheduled game played could prove a miracle in and of itself. Hagemeister Park continued to be the site for football, this time both for practice and games. Manager Murphy got things moving when he sponsored an effort to get the Hagemeister field surrounded by a fence. He stated that it would take volunteer effort and about $1,400 to make the project happen.

They were playing a pretty good brand of football in Illinois, too. Indeed, the man seated front and center in this picture, George Halas, was the mirror image of Curly Lambeau. These Decatur Staleys had faced many of the same trials and tribulations as most other town teams, but in 1920 they relocated to Chicago and were taken under the wing of the Chicago Cubs baseball organization—and became the Bears. In 1921, many of these players would take to the field against the boys from Green Bay for the first time. The fire lit that day has never burned out. Photograph obtained from and used with permission of Jim Jameson, Red Granite, Wisconsin.

The first fracas was scheduled with the Chicago Boosters on September 26. The Packers were well-practiced and had every reason to expect good things. The game proved to be a well-balanced affair, with both teams showing offensive prowess but getting sloppy with the ball when it counted. Lambeau and Abrams were up to old tricks with the forward pass but couldn't put a touchdown drive together. The fourth quarter saw all of the scoring, with the Chicago men booting a three-point place kick for the only score to that point. With time waning, the men from the bay snuck their way downfield, and Curly saved the day with a

31-yard dropkick to tie up the mess. The game ended in a 3–3 tie and Green Bay was happy to escape without a loss.

A notable part of the game was the arguments over the referee's calls that happened on the field. Evidently the vociferations became so heated that twice policemen had to come onto the playing surface to calm things down. A short, boxed article exhorted players to learn the rules of the game and not resort to fisticuffs. "Players who can't control their tempers should not be allowed to remain in the game. The fans pay to see football and not fights." The article also mentioned that both teams were guilty of "gooning" it up.

The Green Bay roster for the initial game of the season was the following: Dutch Dwyer at left end, Milt Wilson at left tackle, Martin Zoll at left guard, Charlie Sauber at center, Carl Zoll at right guard, Sammy Powers at right tackle, Nate Abrams at right end, George Medley at quarterback, Buff Wagner at left halfback, Curly Lambeau at right halfback, and Wally Ladrow at fullback. The only new talent that appeared on the field was Buff Wagner, a Carroll College athlete and Marinette High school standout, along with quarterback Medley. After saving the game thanks to his talented foot, Curly Lambeau was elected captain of the squad, a position for which he was a natural.

Next on the agenda was a Kaukauna squad, sponsored by the American Legion, and coached by Howard "Cub" Buck. The only major switch that Green Bay planned to make was the addition of Fritz Gavin at the center position.

The other city teams were getting little coverage in the paper. Interest in these amateur teams seemed to have dried up at least from the newspapers' standpoint.

An article from the October 4 *Press-Gazette* discussed the social aspects of football in Green Bay. The article, "Green Bay Goes Crazy Over Football With Many Kinds of Insanity on Exhibition," had been penned tongue firmly in cheek. Bylined "The Girl Reporter," the missive discussed the type of people who watch football games as well as their reactions to the game itself. "Mrs. Society clutches her fur stole closer about her and murmurs indignantly, 'Oh, the brute! Did you see the mean thing? He just ought to be put out of the game,' while her husband heartily applauds." The author also astutely compared the two different types of crowd present at Saturday high school games and Sunday professional games. The Saturday crowd was described as "sarcastic badinage as to the respective merits of the teams flew thick and fast, each one [side of the crowd] trying to severely squelch the opposing element." Whereas the Sunday crowd "was purely out to see a good football game."

The Kaukauna game ended in a rout favoring the Green Bay eleven. The final stood at 56–0 and showed once again that the Packers were up to snuff. The team altered its personnel a bit, playing coach Jack Dalton at fullback for three touchdowns. Smith took over at left guard, and Gus Rosenow covered the left halfback position. The forward pass was the gem that won the day once again.

Stambaugh, the Copper Range champions, was to be the next challenger. All due practice was held, and fans kept on razor's edge. The Sunday contest was a soggy event: The field was covered in water, and the 800 fans who showed up to see the action were rewarded with a damp body for their troubles. A quarter drop-kick by Curly Lambeau provided the only scoring as Stambaugh couldn't generate any offense, and Green Bay couldn't crack Stambaugh's defense. The mud bath was free from cheap shots, but injuries were numerous. How Lambeau managed to get off a dropkick in "ankle deep mud" remains unknown. The fans, in particular the 300 Stambaugh faithful in town for the game, kept high spirits but sacrificed umbrellas to the wind. The only unfortunate event happened when one of the bleachers collapsed, spilling some 40 people to the ground.

If not for Curly Lambeau's on-field skills and off-field dedication to keeping the team alive, the Packers would not exist today. Although that's a bit of an exaggeration, there is no doubt that Lambeau wanted his team to reach loftier heights than the rest of the town teams he and his fellow Packers were laying to waste. Over the next 30 years or so, that spirit would be his undoing, and he would find himself on the outside looking in. But if anyone is responsible for rekindling the football fire that Fred Hulbert lit back in 1895, it was Lambeau. Photograph from the Stiller-Lefebvre Collection.

Poor gate and muddy fans aside, it was time for the team to move on and meet its next dance partner, Marinette. The game was a rough one, and both teams used up all available talent to maintain full strength. The forward pass was stymied for the first time, and the Packers line had to rely on opening gaping holes in the defense to allow the backfield to get sizeable gains. Fee Klaus took over as center, and anyone able bodied was called into service. Marinette player Dave Knutson showed his disdain for personal pain when, after dislocating his jaw, he had it popped back into place by the doctors available and went back into the fray. The report read 25–0 in favor of the Bays—yet another shutout for the powerful football men.

The next to step into the ring was De Pere. The southern neighbors had just handed a humiliation to the Menasha Cardinals in a 114–0 blowout. Coach Carey's De Pere Professionals expected to put up a great showing against the Packers. The manager for the De Pere team, Van Vonderen, denied a rumor that he was "loading" his team for the upcoming contest. "Aside from the Indians from Oneida, who have played with us all season," Van Vonderen stated, "there will be no outsiders in our line-up."

De Pere fans went from feast to famine when their Professionals met the Packers at Hagemeister on October 24. A capacity crowd of 3,500 rabid football fans gathered to watch the action. Trees circling the field were pressed into service as spots of observation as was the roof of the roller rink. The Green Bay lot put up a balanced attack and moved on the Professionals with little trouble. Wes Leaper joined the crew at left tackle. Coach Dalton single-handedly accounted for six touchdowns, with Lambeau, Dwyer, and Wagner each garnering one. Green Bay's defense was its usual best, and De Pere didn't post a solitary point. The final score stood at 62–0, and De Pere's boisterous fans were quiet on their way south.

A long-awaited matchup loomed on the horizon for Green Bay's men. The Beloit Fairies were coming to Hagemeister, and everyone in the bay was looking forward to sweet revenge. To add to the hoopla was the acquisition of the Green Bay and Western band, a 30-piece outfit that was going to supply music for the festivities. Confident in their team, the Beloit backers were holding onto the short end of 10 to 8 bets and likely getting many of them filled. The Fairies' lineup was very similar to the crew that filled the ranks in 1919. In an article titled "Let's Show 'Em How," one of the sportswriters exhorts the Green Bay faithful to show true sportsmanship when the Fairies come to town. The previous year's

FOOTBALL WEATHER?

Just what is football weather? Ikey Karel, a standout on some of the earliest UW–Madison teams, had this to say when weather threatened an 1895 Thanksgiving Day contest between a Fond du Lac team he had coached and a Green Bay team he was coaching:

That's the beauty of football. It can be played in any kind of weather; rain or snow, clear or cloudy, mud or slush, none of them interfere with the game. People are just beginning to discover this fact, and a year or two ago in this state many people would stay away from a game if the weather was bad, thinking of course it would not be played. They have just about found out this year that such is not the case.

The game was played and, despite Karel's tutelage, Fond du Lac beat Green Bay 14–0.

fiasco was to be forgotten, and exploits on the lined pasture were to stand of their own judgment.

The event proved to be a show of defensive strength; rain kept any offensive efforts to the simplistic. Both teams allowed little in the way of gains for the opposition. Lambeau was injured and did not play, except for an attempt at a field goal that was blocked. The luck of the Irish was with the Hagemeister home team when, during the third quarter, the Packers punted to a backup for Beloit who lost the pigskin at the hand of a bruising tackle by Riggie Dwyer. As the ball bounced into the end zone it was promptly covered by Buff Wagner. Wagner had entered the lineup as a replacement for the dinged-up Curly Lambeau. Dalton kicked the point after, and the defense made that score just enough. Fifty fans from Beloit were sent packing in a poor state of mind. A few clusters of De Pere fans were on hand to give rhubarbs to the Packers and wish the Fairies well, but the final score was 7–0, Packers.

Meanwhile that Sunday, the Menominee city team handed another solid beating to the De Pere Professionals by a reckoning of 47–7.

Who would be next on the Packer victim list? Milwaukee's Maple Leaf Athletic Club had put together an "aggregation of college players" under the moniker All-Stars. The All-Stars were motivated by the promise of a big money game with the Chicago (a.k.a. Racine Street) Staleys or Chicago Tigers if they could defeat the Green Bay eleven. Green Bay, of course, was ready for the challenge and had healed up all of its members in preparation for the fracas.

The Milwaukee team was made up of some of the Maple Leaf players Green Bay had faced the year before. They were still smarting from their 53–0 defeat. Lambeau was again expected to be out of the lineup, but his jersey-clad comrades didn't seem concerned.

The game, played on Sunday, November 7, appeared to be of little threat to Green Bay; the score stood 9–0 at the end. But, the Cream City lads had showed some nifty running and tough defense. Green Bay's defense was up to snuff and turned aside threats inside the "danger zone." The most-cited hero was the big lineman Wilson. His kicking kept the All-Stars pinned back most of the game, as he averaged 45 yards per kick. The Packers managed a touchdown in the second quarter by Wagner and a dropkick of 36 yards by Lambeau, who had dragged himself into the fray in the fourth. Most of the game was characterized by a seesaw battle of field position won by Green Bay and its fortunate punting.

That year, the men of the Green Bay aggregation were winning but not putting up the points they had in 1919. Part of the blame could fall on the fact that their most explosive player and team captain was hurt. The rest of the explanation fell to the fact that other teams were catching on to the newer game. They could now defend the pass; it was no longer the surprise weapon.

BEFORE THEY WERE THE PACKERS

During the following week, Manager Murphy announced that he had received a wire from none other than Jim Thorpe. Thorpe was interested in signing the Packers to play his Canton Tiger team in Canton, Ohio, on November 28. Unfortunately the Packers had already inked a commitment to the Lapham Athletic Club of Milwaukee on that date. Murphy had countered with the possibility of December 8 as a date for his Packers to face Thorpe's eleven. Unfortunately, such a contest never saw the light of day.

The next game scheduled was actually a return engagement with the Beloit Fairies. Under what sort of altered consciousness the Green Bay management decided that a rematch with the Beloit team was a good idea can only be speculated upon. Obviously such a contest would produce a good return at the gate and this was now professional ball. But the Fairies had every motivation on their side. They had recently suffered a narrow defeat to the Packers, and this time they had them at home on a field that might still echo with bad vibes for the Green Bay team. The financial guarantee had to be the motivating factor driving the third meeting in two years.

An interesting side note was that the game was only part of the trip this time. The Packers team and some of the die-hard rooters were heading down to Madison for a Saturday collegiate game. Madison was playing Illinois and the Green Bay players and fans alike wanted to see the action. The plan was to leave early Saturday morning, catch the college game, and then rest up for Sunday's action. The hubbub was that great interest was being paid to the Beloit/Green Bay game and that Janesville fans were said to be reserving 200 seats to root for the Packers. The Janesville delegation was primarily due to their hatred for the rival Beloit collective and compounded by the infamous Fairy sleaziness against the Packers the year before. Additionally, Jack Dalton was a Janesville native.

Estimates put the expected attendance at 7,000 for the Beloit game. Five hundred Green Bay fans were expected either by train or by automobile to accompany their team into the confines of Morse Field.

The event was to be a great exhibition of football. The two teams adopted very different styles. Green Bay stuck with its passing attack but Beloit went with old-fashioned straight football, dives and smashes at the center of the field. While the Packers' passing game was successful at midfield, whenever they came within the shadow of the goal posts, the Beloit scrum stopped them dead. Calhoun recalled that "forwards," his term for passes, were "smeared up" on six different occasions that should have resulted in touchdowns. Green Bay was in for a long afternoon.

Beloit squared its shoulders and rammed the ball down the field between the tackles. On two separate drives, the Fairies pounded their way downfield for a score with the extra point after. Green Bay posted the first score of the game when Curly finessed a booming 45-yard dropkick. The Pack just wasn't up to tricks.

Also, the crowd wasn't anywhere near the predicted size. Cal stated that "there were nearly as many Green Bay and Janesville rooters at the game as there were followers of Manager McCarthy's team." He also jibed, "Evidently the weather was a bit too cold for the Beloiters."

Green Bay had little excuse for losing that game. All of the Packers' normal starters were at the game and officiating was fair. Again they had fallen victim to a team that knew how to defend the pass properly. The final score, 14–3 in favor of the Fairies, couldn't be called a trouncing, but it was certainly quantitatively amplified by the history between the two teams. A rubber match to be played in the safe confines of Hagemeister Park on Thanksgiving was proposed. The proviso was that, since each team had won one game, the third would be for the "Pro" gridiron title of the state. The public waited patiently.

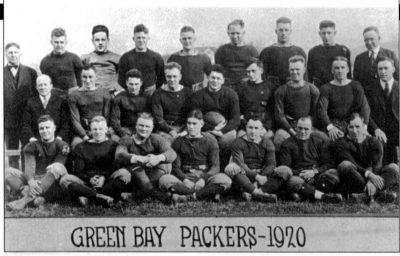

In 1920, the last year the Packers played town team ball, their roster was a combination of the best football talent Green Bay could offer along with imported players who could help take them to another level. But they were still considered the "City Team." (Seated, left to right) Martin Zoll, Wes Leaper, Carl Zoll, Herm Martell, Ray McLean, Nate Abrams, and Medley; (kneeling) H. Tebo, Al Petchka, Fritz Gavin, "Cowboy" Wheeler, Curly Lambeau, Wally Ladrow, Buff Wagner, Dalton, and Frank Jonet; (standing) J. Delloye, Sam Powers, Dwyer, Fee Klaus, Nichols, Gus Rosenow, Milt Wilson, Charlie Sauber, and Neil Murphy. Photograph from the Henry Lefebvre Collection of the Neville Public Museum of Brown County, Green Bay, Wisconsin.

The Menominee team was next on the list. They were billed as having "a firm hold on the professional football championship of the upper peninsula in Michigan" and "have been walloping 'em all with due regularity." The Packers had a bit of loser's limp and went to their injury list as a possible excuse for an upcoming defeat. Lambeau had a broken nose and sore ribs, Wheeler a sore foot, Rosenow busted ribs,

Medley a dinged-up knee, Dalton a bad ankle, and Klauss a bum leg. The optimistic writer, despite the six starters with injures of a most grievous manner, regaled, "the rest of the squad is blessed with a lot of pep and some of the vacant holes may be plugged up in good shape."

A bit of schedule juggling occurred next when Green Bay and Beloit tried to back out of their previously slated games in order to meet at Hagemeister on Turkey Day. Sadly neither team could, and hope of a third, decisive game was put to rest.

NEW LONDON—A BETTER BARGAIN

A great piece of New London football lore—from somewhere in the 1920s or 30s—came from Adolph Klatt via the February 8, 1979, *Press-Star*:

Supposedly Mac Donner saw a farmer from Lebanon running back and forth on the sidelines, screaming and yelling. He asked the man how come he was so excited when Mac knew he did not understand football. The man replied "I pay fifty cents to watch two fellows fight in the ring, and here I can see twenty two men fight for the same price."

The next game, a war with Menominee, wasn't a bloodbath, it was a mud bath. The game on Sunday, the 21st of November, was played in a downpour that turned the field into a quagmire within three drives. Fans were scarce early on, but those in the stands disdained fellow fans with umbrellas. Cries of "Put down that umbrella!" were heard with regularity. The start of the first quarter was little more than the trading of punts; neither team could establish ground or aerial attacks. A great punt return of 45 yards by Teicher put the Michigan champs in striking distance. A "roughing the passer" call against Green Bay netted another 15, and a score soon developed. At the end of that quarter, the score stood 7–0, and Green Bay looked to be on their downhill slide.

The second quarter saw Green Bay reassert their focus and score 13 unanswered points. The attack made the team start to look like the 1919 team, and they grew in confidence. Another score was tacked on in the third when Lambeau flipped a pass into Cowboy Wheeler's outstretched arms. The fourth quarter was unremarkable and the only real scoring threat was a missed field goal by Lambeau.

Green Bay had placed a decisive victory into its win column and shook off the demons of the Beloit loss. Buff Wagner, a Marinette man, had a great game against his home city's rival Menominee. It could be said that his two touchdowns in the second quarter swayed the tide toward victory. How glad Wagner was to help dismantle Menominee was displayed in a short article in the *Press-Gazette* on November 26. "RIOT ENDS GAME" was the lead. In a game between Wagner's hometown team, Marinette, and traditional rivals, Menominee, the game was called at the end of the first half when Marinette fans stormed the field to dismember the referee, a man from Niagara. The game ended in a forfeit in favor of Menominee and was scored 7–6.

The Green Bay squad had but three days' rest before they faced always-tough Stambaugh on Thanksgiving Day. The mining community from Stambaugh brought a sizeable fan pack to cheer on their rough-and-tumble team. The defense of Stambaugh was likened to "a bunch of wild cats," and, on seven opportunities, the miners stopped the Packers on downs inside their five-yard line. The game boiled down to an unusual factor—punting.

A game of field position ensued when neither team could shatter the other's stone-wall defense. The Green Bay men had the advantage at this point. Lambeau's punts on average were 20 yards longer than his Stambaugh counterpart "Tallow" Youngren's. Both of Green Bay's touchdown drives happened when Youngren, with his feet entrenched in his own end zone, punted poorly. Working the shorter field, Green Bay pounded the pigskin past the massive opposition once in the second and once in the fourth quarters. Once again the Stambaugh offense failed to make any sort of showing against the bay team. The two teams had met for the last time and an era was ending.

The last game of the Packers' season was played on November 28 with the Milwaukee-based Lapham Athletic Club. Another club deemed to be "contenders for state football honors," they put up a game fight but were outclassed by the Green Bay bruisers. The Packers were said to have played their most disjointed game of the year. Teamwork was flung out to dry and individuals made their presence known. The only real difference in personnel for the Green Bay men was the addition of "Cub" Buck at right guard. His huge presence made it impossible for the Laphams to get by on that side and running behind him was an easy feat. He even caught a few passes that required a half-dozen of the Milwaukee lads to bring him to the turf. Lineman Carl Zoll even carried the pumpkin for a first down!

The Lapham A.C. fans, some 300 strong, were first-class rooters. They brought specially labeled noisemakers and made their unified effort felt. But their cheering couldn't help their boys conjure up any points, and, once again, a contested affair at Hagemeister ended in a shutout. Scoring for the Packers were Lambeau, Wagner, and Rosenow, and the atmosphere of the game was more of a pickup event than a serious game. The final was 26–0 and the season was over for the Green Bay Packers.

The 1920 season was another huge success, the reputation for excellence was growing, and, despite the problems with scheduling, Green Bay could get as many games as it wanted. The midseason rumor that Jim Thorpe wanted to meet up with the Packers on the hallowed rectangle only furthered their reputation. The team managed to pitch eight shutouts and only allowed 24 points in 11 games. While their numbers weren't as gaudy as the 1919 team, they still found 227 points lying about and compiled a 9-1-1 record. Yet, huge changes were in store for the Packers team in terms of players, philosophy, and locale.

IRON MOUNTAIN—REMEMBERING THE TOWN TEAM DAYS

Muzz Pucci, a great character from Iron Mountain, Michigan, was happy to share some memories of the city in its town team days as well as his trips to Green Bay to watch the Packers in the 1920s. He was a bit wistful when he remembered, "It was something like, we used to have a baseball team every Sunday and that. Those things, they're gone. I don't know why, you've got the Green Bay Packers takes care of everything." When asked about the biggest change he'd seen over the years, Pucci said, "You gotta use your head to play now." And back in the earlier days you didn't have to use your head? "No just a lot of bull and bulk."

Muzz recalled stopping at the Sportsmen's Bar in Lena on the way to Green Bay, on the way home from Green Bay, or both. There, his memory became a little fuzzy. After the games, Muzz said they enjoyed the diversions that a party town like Green Bay could offer. When asked if they spent the night in town, Muzz replied "No, no, no, no, we came back, although we wouldn't get home until pretty God darn late the next day after Sunday. Because we'd stop at whorehouses or whatever there was. We were young, what the hell." Whether Muzz ever met Johnny "Blood" McNally in his spins about town, he couldn't recall.

When asked how much they charged for games in Iron Mountain, Muzz couldn't exactly remember because he had never actually paid. "Well, we used to sneak in," he snickered. "There was a toilet there and we made a hole and come in that way."

The 1920 season was over for the Packers, but an accident to one of the team's own brought about an extra game. Evidently, Riggie Dwyer, in a very unfortunate turn of events, had an accident with a train. In the aftermath, Dwyer lost both an arm and a leg but survived and was hospitalized and in quite dire straits. His friends and relatives in the football community took it upon themselves to help old Riggie out by scheduling a benefit game. The presales of tickets flew, and 3,000 or more tickets were bought and paid for by the Tuesday before the game.

The two teams to tilt were the Bellevue Ice Cream lads captained and coached by Curly Lambeau and the Northern Paper Mill men headed by Jack Dalton. Both men had coached one of the Green Bay high school teams and had some friendly fire in their bellies over their team's exploits in that intracity contest. Of course they were also brethren in the Packer fold, Dalton serving as a player and coach of the squad and Lambeau as its captain.

The game was set up to be a huge success. No one was allowed to enter the grounds gratis; everyone involved put in their money, from players to referees to police protection. All work that day was also donated so that all funds involved would go directly to the fund for Dwyer. Some 4,000 people showed up and witnessed some class pigskin antics. The lineups for the two teams read like a who's who of football greats in town. All the stops were pulled out to acquire the best and brightest. One can imagine that a few heated debates were overheard in discussion of who would play for what team. When Cub Buck was added to the Northern Paper Mill squad, Lambeau chased after and got Jimmie Crowley. The lineups were posted long before game time and looked very close in talent and brawn.

The game was everything it was billed to be, with the exception of Buck and Crowley. Neither one materialized on the playing field. But it didn't seem to dampen the festivities one bit. Buck had played a game with the Canton Bulldogs on that Saturday and couldn't make it back in time; Crowley didn't want to risk his amateur status with several years left of college ball. Conditions couldn't have been better for the December 5 game. The sun was shining brightly and the field was a fast track. The Northern Paper team borrowed the green sweaters of Saint Norbert for the game and the Bellevues used East High's red and white coverings. A band provided a serenade for the Mill team as their warriors took the field. The crowd was worked into a fever pitch and ready for action.

The actual play-by-play of the game was inconsequential. It was a fiercely played game and no one wanted to be the loser. Hard tackles and growling were commonplace, but, at the end, all were still friends. The Bellevues were victorious, 21–13, with Lambeau, Wheeler, Wagner, and Riggie's brother Dutch Dwyer as stars for the victors, while Ladrow, Dalton, and Rosenow were standouts for the Mills team.

The real winner was, of course, Riggie, who a few days later was presented with a check for $4,053.02 by Packer Manager Neil Murphy. Murphy, as the spokesman for the benefit, was quoted,

> In behalf of the Packers, I want to thank everybody for their splendid assistance. It's cooperation of this kind that helps make life worth living.
> I could name hundreds who did their bit towards "putting it over" and I take this means of thanking everybody who came across and helped swell the fund for Riggie.

To underscore the tragedy and triumph of Riggie Dwyer, an article from the December 3 *Press-Gazette* spoke to the true brutality that was indeed present on the football field. "FOOTBALL EXACTED TOLL OF 11 DEATHS DURING '20 SEASON," glared the headline. The writing mentioned that, of the deaths, most were due to Tom Silverwood's old demon, the improper training and conditioning of the athletes involved. Only two of the fatalities were at the collegiate level, the vast majority of incidents occurring in the high school ranks. The causes of death were of the following variety: broken neck, broken skull, spinal injury, crushed chest, and death due to nonspecific injury. Protective equipment was still far from being the norm, and players needed to be prepared and ready to protect one another for these dire consequences.

The fun and frivolity would soon go out of professional football in Green Bay. In 1921, it would become a business, and much less of a citywide affair. Lambeau and friends would take the team to a league and cease to play any of the area teams that had so well provided opposition over the past 25 years.

1921 AND BEYOND

"A YOUNG CLOUDBURST"

Neighborhood team, amateur team, town team, intracity team, city team, semipro team, professional team. It had been an alphabet soup of labels and a ragtag existence for football in Green Bay since Fred Hulbert first kicked the whole thing off in the fall of 1895. But Green Bay's story was a classic, not unusual, and mirrorlike, replicated in every big city and small town that had ever endeavored to field a football team outside the cozy walls of its high school or college.

For every town team that went from someone's fancy to actual existence, there were the struggles of attracting willing players, followed by the struggles of fielding a winning team, followed by the struggles of attracting paying fans, followed by the struggles of maintaining a winning team, followed by the struggles of coordinating schedules with nearby communities that had managed to do the same. Autumn after autumn, it was a juggling act with just two hands and an unpredictable number of balls. All over the area, the process had been repeated again and again with varying degrees of success.

By 1921, football in Green Bay was an established fact. Countless games had been played on dozens of fields and hundreds of men had played in them. Still more had played the game in their imaginations—a well-dressed grown-up screaming along the sidelines or a day-dreaming kid gazing out the September window of his mathematics classroom.

This year, that local football phenom, Lambeau, was pulling together his team for its third season representing Green Bay to the football world. But the stakes had been raised dramatically. This year would see the Packers passing by the other crack squads in their immediate area and, as members of the American Professional Football Association, facing other professional aggregations worthy of national standing. The emphasis here was on "professional" and "national." There would be no more pounding on local, amateur athletic clubs and having it count.

Meanwhile, intracity play had not disappeared from the scene, and those teams were also getting ready to play. The Green Bay football landscape still featured teams like the South Sides, now called the South Sider Merchants; the South Side Maroons; and elevens representing De Pere and West De Pere. Theirs was simply a different gridiron venue.

Jimmy Crowley, another Green Bay football lad and "one of the greatest gridiron warriors ever turned out at the Hilltoppers' institution," according to the *Gazette*, was headed off for the start of an outstanding career at Notre Dame. There was already talk as to whether he would come back to play for Lambeau's Packers. He and Lambeau were often linked in the same sentence in those days; their careers at Green Bay's East High School had run so parallel. At Notre Dame, under Knute Rockne's tutelage, Crowley became one of the legendary Four Horsemen. And the prognosticators were right on this time. Crowley returned to his hometown for a brief one-season stint with Lambeau's team after graduating from Notre Dame in 1925.

Besides directing the on-field fortunes of the Packers, Lambeau assumed the athletic director's post at East High School, where he had also been coaching football since 1919. The game of football had been addressed up and down and sideways in this little town of 31,650 people, and the entire world seemed right. The nation itself was crawling out from a small economic downturn following the end of World War I. Things were indeed looking up!

Getting here, in football terms at least, had been an uneven evolution, not an event, and its steps had been as variable and subtle as the shifting of sand. By 1899, the East River neighborhood aggregation had struck a profile, and the eleven calling itself the "town team" wasn't the prima donna anymore. After just five seasons, the sport had gained that much in popular acceptance. By 1905, town team football in Green Bay had flourished long enough to become passé and risk oblivion in the face of the much simpler world of off-the-cuff, intracity competition.

By 1910, a whole generation of new footballers had learned the game and loved it to the point where, not only did a town team once again emerge, but intracity teams were plentiful enough to accommodate all the willing players. Sunday football games were so commonplace that organized games could be found on the same afternoon at the White City grounds on the way to Bay Beach, at Hagemeister Park or the Wisconsin-Illinois Baseball League field at the end of Walnut Street, at either Jackson or Whitney Parks near downtown, at Zeger's Field in Allouez, at the Saint Norbert College campus in De Pere, and at Union Park or West High School's practice grounds back on Green Bay's west side!

By 1919, the game had emerged so surely out of the football tradition in Green Bay, that the mightiest team and most irrefutable tradition in the history of football was birthed on the company practice field of the Indian Packing

Company on what was then the city's far east side. That team, the Green Bay Packers, remains the third-oldest active member in today's National Football League. But through its 80-plus years of feast or famine it has amassed more championships than any other NFL franchise and achieved what today looks like a nearly impossible task of winning not one, but two triple-year championships.

Most important, the Packers, like the Bears and the Cardinals, can trace their roots to the town team era and, therefore, represent a striking tie to the game's earliest days of mass-line plays, pneumonia jackets, and long hair. That fact may not be foremost on the mind of a new football recruit in a brand-spanking-new millennium or even on the tip of the tongue of a life-long, die-hard Packer fan, but it sure is a part of the aura and mystique that surrounds the body and soul of this story whenever and wherever someone says the words, "Green Bay Packers."

CLINTONVILLE—HOW WOULD THEY HAVE DONE?

What do Clintonville and Chicago have in common? Their town teams were also company teams. In Chicago, that team, of course, was the Bears, who had started their football life as the Decatur Staleys, fielded with the money of A. E. Staley, a starch maker. In Clintonville, they were known as the Truckers or the FWDs because of their sponsorship by the Four-Wheel-Drive Company, which supplied vehicles to the military. Like Staley, the bigwigs at the FWD company were looking for the live action and portable advertising that a football aggregation could provide. Football gave the company's workers something to do and it gave the community some entertainment.

In 1919, the Truckers were listed as a possible opponent for the Green Bay Packer machine, though such a contest never actually took place. While the Truckers were a respectable member of a league with teams from De Pere, Kaukauna, Little Chute, New London, Marinette, Racine, Rhinelander, Shawano, Two Rivers, and Wausau, their chances against Curly Lambeau's crew probably weren't that great. That year, the Packers outscored their opponents for an average of 57 to 0 and the Clintonville Truckers' opponents from New London fit right in there on the losing end of a 54–0 battle. But still, it's fun to wonder.

Professionalism had been toyed with all during the transmutation between town team and NFL membership. It had promised better teams and better turnout by fans, and, ironically enough, it had nearly ruined the possibility of fielding a team at all. Tom Skenandore, the commanding running back from Oneida, was the first professional football player in Green Bay, Wisconsin. With a promise of $20 per game over a five-game season in 1897, his significance in Titletown cannot be overstated. Other paid players came and went over the duration, some for just one key contest and others for a season or two. Jonas Metoxen and Charles Waldron were other paid players in the earliest gridiron days in Green Bay. Such players were usually outside the team's organizational structure but vital to its success. But in 1905, the whole professional issue hit the wall in Green Bay, and it was a vacuous five years before a declared town team would crawl out of the destruction.

Early team leaders in Green Bay saw that elevating a team out of the amateur and neighborhood ranks was a necessary step toward short-term viability and long-term survival. Fred Hulbert, resuming his managerial duties for the team in 1904, understood that paid players and the formation of a league were both important touchstones for keeping a successful organization alive. Tod Burns's effort to field a semipro team in 1905, meaning, in that case, that just some of the players were paid, proved just why the whole thing was such an uphill battle.

There is no doubt that both Hulbert and Burns, through the pages of the *Green Bay Gazette* and word-of-mouth, were cognizant of the dynamic football developments occurring in Pennsylvania at the same time as their own efforts in Green Bay. In the shadow of the much-heralded and better-dressed college game, semipro seemed to be the way to go to promote the sport across the rest of the country but, man, what a headache!

Of course, the term *semipro* had at least two shades of grey in it. In some cases, like Burns's squad, it meant that the best players, the game breakers, would be paid, while the others would volunteer their injuries. It had been exactly that way in 1897 when Skenandore was the only compensated player. On that squad, Hulbert and T. P. Silverwood were far more than yeomen footballers put on the field to round out the eleven. Both of them could have easily earned a handful of cash if it had been available to them. But it wasn't, and they understood the immeasurable value of a game breaker like Skenandore, whose name could even show up in the pages of Lawrence College's yearbook for his on-field exploits.

In other cases, semipro meant that all the boys would split the proceeds of the game, more or less evenly, by divvying up the "hat" money after covering expenses. Whether the pot had been accumulated through actually passing the hat or charging the usual 25 cents for admission, it usually didn't amount to a whole lot when spread out among the open, grimy palms present.

In nearly all cases, semipro also meant that you weren't going to make enough to live on playing ball, and you'd best find yourself another job, a "real" job. Sometimes, as in the case of the Niagara Badgers or the Clintonville Truckers, the company sponsoring the team would take care of that little tidbit of life for you, which meant that you probably did have a full-time job playing football, as it were. In this arrangement, you were expected to show up for work at approximately the same time as everyone else and work about as hard as they did. But your importance to the company football team also often tempered the pressures of your contribution to its work force.

This was still the case when the Packers, sponsored this year by the Acme Packing Company, put their hat in the ring of the American Professional Football

NIAGARA—FOOTBALL PLAYERS, MILL WORKERS, OR BOTH?

The original linchpin for Niagara football was player and manager Jim Manci, who brought a joint Niagara–Iron Mountain team home to roost in Niagara in 1933. Manci, a flamboyant owner of a supper club called The Riverside, lured players to the border city with promises of a job at the local paper mill. This was an effective arrangement that even drew former Packer players Al Serafini to town as a coach and Gus Rosenow as its treasurer. It also attracted one of the U. P.'s legendary stars, Joe Zukowski, out of Iron Mountain.

In the two years that the team existed, 1933 and 1934, it lost only one game, at Shawano. According to Zukowsi, "they beat us 7–6. Every time we got down to the twenty yard line the refs gave us a penalty." Zukowski mentioned that "Stambaugh, Michigan was our biggest rival. There was always a battle at Stambaugh and we always beat them."

After the 1934 season the aggregation dissolved. A number of factors contributed to its demise, but one, according to Zukowski, was that the unionization of the paper mill eliminated "the hiring of men for sports."

Association (APFA) in 1921. Were the 1921 players actually "professional" football players? No! Everyone held other jobs outside of their Sunday afternoon commitment. Several of the players, besides Lambeau, worked at the packing company. Wally Ladrow is listed in Wright's 1921 Green Bay City Directory (the yellow pages in town before there was such a thing) as a foreman at the Indian (soon to be Acme) Packing Company.

So, besides setting some of the guys up with jobs, the packing company sponsored the team for uniforms and other football gear and, if you were good enough a footballer, you were pretty much taken care of for other living needs. To keep you in town and in the fold, the team would see to that.

In July of 1934, the *Green Bay Press-Gazette* reported that this was a tradition carried on even to that date. "Ever since its organization," the paper wrote, "the Football corporation has attempted to place the Packer players in positions here. An all year round residence enables the gridders to catch the Green Bay spirits and the old civic pride helps a lot when a team is battling to keep its door step clean." It went on to cite the case of Verne Lewellen, a back from Nebraska in 1924, as a classic example. Lewellen, a law school grad, had been "taken in" by a Green Bay law firm "and soon after passed the state bar examination."

As far as making money purely as a footballer went, you could pretty much forget it. The APFA was struggling to get its feet off the ground, and most franchises were living hand-to-mouth just to stay in queue. In its first year of operation, the league had lost four teams and found itself reorganizing for 1921.

Mike Michalske, a guard who came to Lambeau's team in 1929 when the New York Yankees football club folded, said money wasn't the real motivator for these professional players in his day. "The only reason ninety percent of them played football," he stated in *The Grandstand Franchise* video in 1983, "is because they liked it. That's the only reason. I could have made more money driving a truck than I could playing football."

But this was the first time in Green Bay's now 27-year-old pigskin annals that football, and not another job, was the team's as well as each individual's priority. And, in that sense, they were "professionals." Football was their primary vocation, and the other thing, work at the packing company or wherever, was now an avocation, a little thing to be tended to but not to get in the way of the game.

It's clear now that this had been Lambeau's vision all along, to field a professional team manned with players who did not miss the train to an away game because they had to work that day or the next. Maybe somewhere on the hallowed ground of Notre Dame, the fantasy had once and for all been sealed for him. He wasn't looking to field a juggernaut city team, nor a powerhouse semipro team. Earl Louis "Curly" Lambeau wanted into the big time and he was willing to take the steps necessary to get there, even from little old Green Bay, Wisconsin. He would have to make some concessions along the way, no doubt. But what he had, along with a good lot of football métier, was a vision. And he was eyeing membership in the APFA as the first step toward making that vision a reality.

Football leagues had come and gone in Green Bay and all across the United States. Hulbert himself had promoted the formation of a league, the Northern State Football League, in 1904 and been elected its first (and only) president. It consisted of teams along the newly constructed interurban electric railroad from Fond du Lac to Green Bay and connected, by regular rail, with cities as far north as Marinette and Escanaba, Michigan. The idea at the time was, according to the *Green Bay Gazette*, to "encourage big attendances from Fond du Lac and all cities and towns this side." Team managers were said to be "scouring the state during [the] past several weeks in the endeavor to get the best of men and very nearly every football man is in the ranks of some team or other." The league folded after just one year because it was still unable to elevate the game to a full-time proposition. The Wisconsin-Illinois Baseball League, of which Green Bay was a perennial member, had fought the same battle year after year, though to a much greater level of success.

But the actual roots of league play as well as semipro and pro football organization can be traced rather directly to the states of Pennsylvania and, later, Ohio. It is from the lineage of the later leagues in Ohio that the National Football League of today can trace its lifeblood. Robert W. Peterson, in *Pigskin: The Early Years of Professional Football*, points out that "the first fully professional teams grew out of rivalries between the athletic associations that proliferated in America's cities during the late nineteenth century." Peterson also avers that the evolution of the athletic association arose from a rather shady social position that gave "ambitious young men a toehold on the social ladder by putting them in touch with well-connected men who also enjoyed sports competition." But it was a delicate little parlay, a tightrope walk between sweaty athleticism and starchy social acceptance, and a lot of athletes just couldn't cut it.

The origin of football in Green Bay was no different. "The team has not yet been fully organized," reported the *Green Bay Sunday Gazette* on August 18, 1895, "but practice games are being played as often as the boys can be gotten together, with a view of picking out the best men for the various positions. Fred Hulbert, trainer of the West Side Athletic association, has the matter in hand, and will captain the team." The citizens of old Green Bay, reading the account of the team's organization from their Astor Park parlors, were no doubt shaken the day that news item appeared. At a minimum, eyebrows snuck upward in trepidation; some toughs from "that" side of the river were going to organize an all-out brawl and dress it up it as sport.

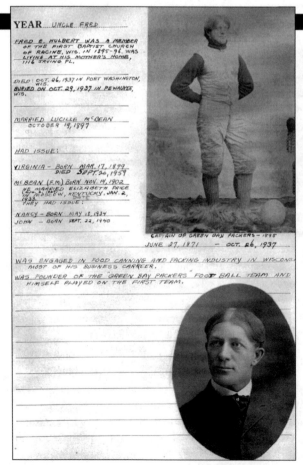

YEAR UNCLE FRED

FRED E. HULBERT WAS A MEMBER OF THE FIRST BAPTIST CHURCH OF RACINE, WIS. IN 1895-96. WAS LIVING AT HIS MOTHER'S HOME, 1116 IRVING PL.

DIED: OCT. 26, 1937 IN PORT WASHINGTON, WIS. BURIED ON OCT. 29, 1937 IN PEWAUKEE, WIS.

MARRIED LUCILLE McGEAN OCTOBER 19, 1897

HAD ISSUE:

VIRGINIA — BORN MAR. 17, 1899 DIED SEPT. 20, 1959
McGEAN (F.M.) BORN NOV. 14, 1902 HE MARRIED ELIZABETH PRICE IN MOSCOW, KENTUCKY, JAN. 2, 1933. THEY HAD ISSUE:
NANCY — BORN MAY 18, 1934
JOHN — BORN SEPT. 22, 1940

CAPTAIN OF GREEN BAY PACKERS — 1895
JUNE 27, 1871 — OCT. 26, 1937

WAS ENGAGED IN FOOD CANNING AND PACKING INDUSTRY IN WISCONSIN MOST OF HIS BUSINESS CAREER.
WAS FOUNDER OF THE GREEN BAY PACKERS FOOT BALL TEAM AND HIMSELF PLAYED ON THE FIRST TEAM.

In 1919, when the Green Bay team became the Packers, 26 football seasons had come and gone since Fred Hulbert had started it all. Although he had relocated to the southern part of Wisconsin to begin a career in the canning industry, his creation remained and grew ever stronger. Here is a page from his family's photo album. Obtained from and used with permission of Hulbert's great-niece, Ethel Evrard, Milwaukee, Wisconsin.

But Hulbert was a man of unquestionable repute, a Baptist, college-educated, and a teetotaler. He was an outsider, sure, born in Chicago and raised in Racine. But he had come from Wayland Academy to start a career and a family in Green Bay, and his drive toward those life goals was primary. Football was an enhancement to those ends. But the recruits on his very first squad were not all cut from that same impeccable cloth. Taverns, such as the Broadway House run by Constantine McGinnis and Fred Gross and J. P. Juenger's Saloon on Broadway, figured prominently into the early days of football, either as gathering places or as sources for team material.

But it was men like Hulbert and, two years later, Tom Silverwood, who gave the athletic associations any kind of upward movement in the first place. These were "good" men, and they liked physical activity too. Without them, organized sports would have gone the way of the overnight lockup and the railroad ride out of town. After all, as every well-bred person knew, along with sports came those social abominations like drinking, excessive laughing, sweating, gambling, growing long hair, missing church on the Sabbath, and sex for pleasure. Instead, thanks to the character of men like Hulbert and Silverwood, these athletic clubs were able to gain a foothold and, then, acceptance, even to the point of reaching out to the community for financial and other support.

A quick history of football leagues arising out of these athletic associations can be gleaned from the pages of the National Football League's own *Record and Fact Book*. In the section, "Chronology of Professional Football," the league recognizes its earliest roots beginning with the 1869 Rutgers and Princeton "college soccer football game, the first ever."

As early as 1892, the Allegheny Athletic Association (AAA) and the Pittsburgh Athletic Club (PAC) are credited with playing an imperative role in the salad days of professional ball. The AAA, of course, was the first to hire a professional football man, William "Pudge" Heffelfinger, who was paid $500 for one game against the PAC. That, of course, was somewhat under the rug. In 1899, a team was formed, which still, to this day, operates as a member of the NFL. It began as the Morgan Street Athletic Club, a neighborhood eleven, and is now the Arizona Cardinals. But it was right after the turn of the century that serious attention was paid to organizing and coordinating "league play" in the Keystone and Buckeye States.

In 1902, two baseball clubs, the Philadelphia Athletics and the Philadelphia Phillies, started football teams and hooked up with the Pittsburgh Stars to form a league called the National Football League. That year also saw what the modern NFL calls the "first World Series of pro football." It was a five-team tournament. Syracuse took the honors, with Glen "Pop" Warner in its lineup at guard. Baseball players turned footballers in that small league also included pitchers Christy Mathewson and Rube Waddell.

As a small aside, that year also saw the first night and indoor games, at least as the official NFL book sees it. Night games had been proposed in Green Bay as early as 1899, and indoor baseball was a matter of record at about the same time. So, to suggest that no night game or indoor contest ever took place before 1902 may just be a matter of missing input from other sectors. Also, to put things in further geographic context, Stambaugh, Michigan, fielded a team that same year and lined up against aggregations from across the U. P. and northern Wisconsin. So, while Pennsylvania was making headlines and being etched into the historical record as a hotbed for early football action, there was plenty going on elsewhere, even in what some might call that day's version of the "frozen tundra."

But that was all Pennsylvania news. In 1903, the Massillon Tigers of Ohio drew four pros west for their last game of the season against Akron, and the epicenter of professional football and league play moved with them. By the following year, Ohio was boasting seven or more professional elevens, and the Tigers ended the year as "Ohio Independent Champions." Team managers were now confronting the inevitable strife and gamesmanship that came with competing for top players and began negotiations for the formation of a statewide league. Skyrocketing salaries became a manageable thing, and universal rules ironed out some of the on-field wrinkles. The league never actually materialized.

In 1905, Canton, Ohio's athletic association fielded, for the first time, a professional football squad. Eventually this aggregation would evolve into the now legendary Bulldogs. For the next 13 years, the cradle of professional football rocked back and forth primarily between Massillon and Canton. In 1906, the two teams toed up twice and ended with a split decision, but the Tigers hauled off the Ohio League Championship. A little tomfoolery involving a betting scandal and a little trouble meeting player salaries put the flame on low for a while.

In 1912, the flame was rekindled in Canton, and three years later Massillon answered their archrival's defi on the field. In 1916, Jim Thorpe left the Pine Village Pros in Indiana to tear it up as a member of the Canton aggregation. With former Carlisle teammate, Pete Calac, at his side, Thorpe led the Cantons to a 9-0-1 record and the Ohio League Championship. The next year, they did it all over again, even though Massillon tarnished their crown with an upset victory. The Bulldogs won another league title in 1919, and it was pretty clear that if there was a sure thing in professional football, they were it. It was out of this success and the vitality of their rivalry with the Massillon team that the National Football League of today blossomed.

These were also pivotal years in the football story of Green Bay. Titletown struggled along without a declared town team from 1906 to 1909, with one or another of the neighborhood or intracity teams assuming the role of town team in order to defend Green Bay's honor against opposing communities. Then, in 1910, a declared town team finally reemerged and began a decade of unyielding football activity that resulted directly in the formation of the Green Bay Packers. Some sportswriters who have dabbled in pre-Packer history would like to suggest that there was no town team in 1916 and that year alone. Most of them also like to convince their readers that there was a town team in every year of Green Bay football history except for that one. They are wrong on both accounts, and those issues have been addressed year-by-year previously in these pages.

In 1920 the spark that was the Canton-Massillon rivalry resulted in an explosion of universal proportions. While the ongoing contention between the Bulldogs and the Tigers was strong enough to draw lots of attention, it wasn't potent enough to produce an entire league. It could, of course, serve as its spiritual nucleus. According to Peterson, the Ohio League was "not really a league at all; it was more a state of mind. Its membership fluctuated somewhat from year to year as the strength of various teams waxed and waned." That was the unique nature of town team football molded into ragtag league formation.

It seems clear that Canton would become the site of the National Football League Hall of Fame because of its gridiron prominence just prior to World War I, because of its serving as the locale of the first league meeting, and because of its emergence as the survivor of that whimsical Ohio League. But it could almost as easily have been Massillon, if Massillon had just hung on a little longer and made it to the organizational meetings.

At the time, professional football in Ohio was facing the same prototypical issues plaguing town teams and semipro teams, to one extent or another, all across the nation. The NFL's *Record and Fact Book* cites three such issues: "Dramatically rising salaries, players continually jumping from one team to another following the highest offer, and the use of college players still enrolled in school." If these were problems in 1920, it's amazing to see how only the third one seems to have been addressed to date.

With this backdrop, an organizational meeting was held at the Jordan and Hupmobile auto showroom in Canton on August 20, 1920, in an effort to form the American Professional Football Conference. Represented at the meeting were the Akron Pros, the Canton Bulldogs, the Cleveland Indians, and the Dayton Triangles. Of course, another organizational meeting of parallel significance had occurred the previous year at the offices of the *Green Bay Press-Gazette*, during which the Green Bay Packer team had been formed. An organizational meeting represented the matins of every town team and league ever formed.

A second meeting, in Canton on September 17, proved that this league had more inertia than many similar efforts, and, this time, teams from four different states were represented: Akron, Canton, Cleveland, and Dayton represented the old Ohio League; the Hammond Pros and Muncie Flyers came from Indiana; the

Rochester Jeffersons were in attendance from New York; and the Rock Island Independents, Decatur Staleys, and Racine Cardinals sojourned from Illinois. Indicating just how things had shifted from the earliest days, Pennsylvania had no representation. But neither did Wisconsin, which had also been a hub of football activity since the mid-1890s and had seen its earliest teams formed in the very late 1880s.

At this second meeting, the name was changed to the American Professional Football Association (APFA), and this would be the league's name until June 24, 1922, when it became the National Football League (NFL) once and for all. League membership was a solid $100 per team, though no team ever actually wrote a check. Jim Thorpe was elected figurehead president, mostly, according the *Record and Fact Book*, "hoping to capitalize on his fame." Universal rules were one of the new league's primary goals.

The attendees at that meeting were joined at various points during the ensuing season by the Buffalo All-Americans, the Chicago Tigers, the Columbus Panhandles, and the Detroit Heralds. The teams were granted total autonomy in scheduling their games, and, according to the official NFL record, "there were wide variations, both in the overall number of games played and in the number played against APFA member teams."

By Thanksgiving Day, the traditional end mark for football at that time, most of the APFA teams had played their games for the season. Two, the Chicago Tigers and the Detroit Heralds, had disbanded and had their franchises shut down by the league. Akron, Buffalo, Canton, and Decatur were in it for championship honors,

The stories of Johnny "Blood" McNally's antics—on and off the field—have reached mythical proportions. Deservedly so! Blood was the classic "tramp" or, more politely, "vagabond" athlete. He would don his cleats in any town where he could find wine, women, football, and a paycheck to make it all go. His love-hate relationship with Curly Lambeau could fill a chapter itself. Obviously there was something about football that could draw characters as disparate as "Blood" and Fred Hulbert. Photograph from the Stiller-Lefebvre Collection.

however, and looking to decide who was boss. Several games were played between them, and Akron came out undefeated, assuming the first APFA title. The official record reports that it was at one of these late-season games that the Pros sold their star tackle, Bob Nash, to the All-Americans for $300 and 5 percent of gate receipts, sealing the first APFA player trade.

It was into this league that Lambeau brought his Packers, at this point the paragon town team, in 1921. It proved to be a wonderful fusion of young Lambeau's vision with a framework for making that vision a reality, the slipshod structure of the fledgling APFA.

Lambeau's teams had tuned up nearly all comers over the previous two years, and they had, in doing so, risen to some degree of national notoriety. Curly's stint at Notre Dame hadn't hurt either, having put him in touch with many movers and shakers, both on the field and on the sidelines, in the young league. But dominating in the town team ranks wasn't his plan. Curly had enough savvy, even at 23 years of age, to know that he couldn't keep whipping opponents by an average score of 57 to 1, as he had done in 1919, and still keep getting worthwhile opponents on the schedule. He didn't want to. He was staring at the same old house of cards, which indicated that the next level would be reached against stiffer competition and the resulting increase in the number of fans lined up at the ticket window. Everything told him to "take the next step," and the entire tableau said, "the time is now. Let the football fly."

For sure, by 1921, the game was no longer exclusively a running event, though the further away from the influence of the APFA you got, the less likely a team was to practice the forward pass or be able to defend against it. Rule changes in 1906 and 1912 had opened up the game for throwing the pigskin, ostensibly to cut down on the injury and death that the early game had offered up on an all-too-regular basis. But, even as a kid growing up on Cherry Street, Lambeau had, according to early Green Bay Packer historians Arch Ward and Chuck Johnson, been a passing fanatic. The kid weighted his salt-sack football with gravel "to give it direction," suggested Johnson. Independent direction was unnecessary, of course, in a football carried under a runner's arm. But for tossing the thing, direction was the absolute name of the game.

The pass attracted Curly. It was flashy and it allowed a cocksure young kid to taunt neighborhood brutes bent on destroying "the little sucker" once they got their grubby mitts on him. They all wanted a piece of him anyway. As an eighth grader, he and his buddies at Whitney Grade School had whipped up East High's freshman squad 18–0. That little upset hadn't gone unnoticed and was told with a good helping of spit every time it was passed around at the high school. Worse yet, this curly headed razz seemed to delight in it. There they would be, just about to jump the kid and put his face into the Saint Claire Street dirt and he'd duck out of it and whip the ball to Natey Abrams before they could snag him. Then he'd brush back that wavy hair, crack that grin of his, and walk away.

His career at East was more of the same. He would run around end for a 60-yard touchdown, heave a 25-yard toss into the end zone, and then hit a 45-yard dropkick to win the game. In the process, he would grab most of the headlines while the rest of the hard-toiling crew would be left as a footnote. George Whitney Calhoun's presence on the sports staff of the *Press-Gazette* was Lambeau's spotlight on Green Bay's football stage and "Cal" turned up the light on Lambeau's exploits early and often.

As a freshman on Knute Rockne's Irish team at Notre Dame in 1918, Lambeau's exposure to the pass was amplified and tuned up. Rockne was heralded as one of the game's great innovators for his use of the downfield toss against Army in 1913, just a year after rule changes made the play a practical addition to a team's huddle options. Of course Rockne himself had been rehearsing the pass as early as 1912 when it had first become a practical weapon in the offensive arsenal.

In 1919 and 1920, the Packers were demolishing opponents with regularity and without breaking much of a sweat. But in the Stambaugh All-Stars, they would find a pretty tough group of miners ready for any kind of barroom brawl. They had had plenty of practice in the vacant lot between Modus's Saloon and the Croatian Hall at the southern foot of the big hill in Stambaugh. The only way Lambeau's squad could beat the heavier aggregation of Yoopers would be to finesse the pass; it couldn't have been too dissimilar to his childhood days along the East River. The Miners weren't pulling up in the face of a superior football crew; they just couldn't put on their behemoth brakes in time to stop the pass on either end of the toss. As a result, Lambeau and his crew would emerge from out of the pileup and join up with the rest of the APFA teams who, each in their own way, had similarly emerged from the town team battles.

Lambeau's star was rising quickly, and it burned hot and bright for nearly 30 years. But not so very far down the road, Lambeau's youthful sassiness would turn to arrogance in the eyes of many Green Bay football fans, and, by the early 1930s, the indictment of "Curly's gone Hollywood" would echo in the city's diners and bars as well as along the sidelines of its football field. By 1949, the imputations would no longer be whispered and Lambeau would, almost literally, be ridden out of town on a rail.

What the plaintiffs didn't realize at that late date was that it was exactly Lambeau's haughtiness that left Green Bay where it is today, owner of a coveted National Football League franchise with little chance of it ever being taken away. And, no matter the love-hate-love relationship between the man whose name graced the stadium in huge yellow letters and the city he made his name in, the Packers did not go the way of every other town team to ever play in the area.

By the time his star burst in supernova fashion, he had alienated a lot of people, fans and players alike. But their denunciations were often mixed with grudging praise. Johnny Blood and Clarke Hinkle played for Lambeau in his heyday, the late 1920s and early 1930s. Both had football credentials that were unimpeachable. Blood could fill one book with his football derring-do and another with his off-field capers. Hinkle was a punishing fullback who was awarded All-Pro honors before the legendary Bronko Nagurski. Blood and Hinkle seem to echo one another in their mixed feelings toward Lambeau.

In his recollections of Lambeau in Richard Whittingham's *What a Game They Played*, Blood said, "I got along pretty well with Curly, for a while anyway. I was one of the only ones who did, most didn't like him at all." Hinkle, by his own account, was one of the ones who "didn't":

> Then there was Curly Lambeau himself. He was the one who gave Green Bay the Packers. The drama of that franchise is spectacular; how a town of 45,000 could get a franchise in the National Football League and maintain it when all the other teams later represented much larger cities. It's an institution now. Curly Lambeau was the founder, creator, and the coach. But I never liked him. Not really respected him either, but he was paying me and I gave him a thousand percent every time I played football for him. Lambeau was the first coach to use the forward pass as a basic offense. His running game was a threat, but he introduced passing as a major part of offensive strategy. He's one of the first who would pass from behind his own goal line on a first down, for example. He himself had been a forward passer in high school and then when he went to Notre Dame for one year.

Obviously, Hinkle's indictment of Lambeau didn't come from the same carefree and forgiving spirit as Blood's. Of course, Blood had had to beg his own share of absolution from Lambeau, and that may have explained a bit of his temperament toward his former coach.

Hinkle did, however, go on to suggest that Lambeau infused his football aggregation with an unusual sense of class for the day. "But Lambeau, whenever we went out on the road, he'd make us wear suits, coats, and ties. If we were in Green Bay, he wouldn't let us smoke in public because the people might think less of us." One can label this "going Hollywood," but to a fairly sober footballer like Hinkle, it made an impression even if it didn't make him like or respect his coach in other ways.

He saw Lambeau as more of a motivator than a good down-after-down coach, a charge made by several other early Packer players. "He believed in pep talks," Hinkle remembered on the Packer historical video *The Grandstand Franchise*, "and he would inspire us. And before we went out on the field, he'd have us jumping through the windows and I ate it up. I was ready to kill people."

When it came to "killing" people, Lambeau's players were also capable of directing some malice toward Curly himself. According to a popular story, it was 1929, Lambeau's last year as a player-coach. The rest of the players had had it with his swearing, frantic cajoling before the snap, and his dressing them down for their failures, especially the guys in the line who could never clear enough traffic for the curly haired one. "Let's open the gates on Curly, fellows," Cal Hubbard, a 6' 5", 250-pound tackle, was said to have whispered to his fellow linemen. The ball was snapped, and nary a blocker made the slightest effort to halt the momentum of the oncoming tacklers. Lambeau was pulverized.

But Hinkle also recalled some good times for the team with the coach's permission. "Hell, we'd all get drunk after a game in those days. Lambeau would say, 'The lid's off, boys, but stay out of jail.'" Perhaps more so than Fred Hulbert, the Father of Football in Green Bay, Lambeau understood the material he was working with and tried to affect a reasonable marriage between the brute who played the game on the field and the gentleman the community was hoping to see on its streets. Lambeau, of course, was not free of his own personal skeletons, while Hulbert's closet seems to have held only clothes, family keepsakes, and some ancient football gear stored in an ornate, turn-of-the-century trunk.

By trying to field the very best team he could, Lambeau was booted out of the APFA after the 1921 season because he had used three Notre Dame boys against the Decatur Staleys the Sunday after Thanksgiving. He did his usual escape-and-throw routine, though, and ended up as owner of the team at season's end. By 1923, Lambeau was the only Green Bay player on the Green Bay Packer roster to have come out of the organization's town-team roots. After that, a smattering of Green Bay boys would be welcomed back into the fold *after* they had earned their spurs in the college ranks. Now, the intracity teams would have to suffice for area footballers who wanted to play the game. It was all in the name of putting the very best team on the field and realizing the fantasy that drove it.

Lambeau wanted New York across the line of scrimmage, not Kaukauna, and he wanted Johnny Blood in his backfield, not Joe Green Bay. To close the chapter on the controversy around Lambeau's persona, his first wife, Marguerite, probably said it best of all: "I just think Curly went out to do what he wanted to do." And Titletown would have to learn to live with it. And it did, eventually, whether it could articulate just what had happened or not.

One thing was sure. Even in the early days, Lambeau's flamboyance had captured the city's imagination. A famous picture from the best-known source of early Packer pictures, the Stiller-Lefebvre collection, commonly known as "Railbirds," bears this out. Green Bay football fans, including former intracity players like Buck Anderson, who didn't always have kind things to say about Lambeau and may well have muttered a few things along the sidelines the very day that picture was taken, would turn out in their finest clothes to watch the Packers do battle.

Thanks to Calhoun's reporting from his desk at the *Press-Gazette* offices, football news was already swirling by early September, 1921. In fact, Lambeau had his team grouped together by early August. Cal reported that Cub Buck of Canton Bulldog fame had watched the team practice on Tuesday night, September 6, and gave the following assessment:

> *The team looks good. The players seem blessed with a lot of pep. The winning spirit is there and unless I miss my guess, the Packers are going to have a bunch on the gridiron this fall that won't have to take a back seat to any of the elevens in the professional football association.*

Lambeau was trying to get Buck into the fold even though his contract as an executive with the Boy Scouts had a "no football" clause. Buck's signing would be another signature on the statement that the Packers really were "big time."

Continuing without the Packers, town team news was sharing a page with a predication of a "big future" for the APFA by President Joseph Carr. The Stambaugh

Although they don't look the part, the 1921 Packers, newly ensconced in the American Professional Football Association, were playing national-caliber competition, not the town teams of their past. Note the wonderful throwback to the earliest days of football in the form of a young Buddy Levitas holding a football as the team's mascot. Here is an attempt to pin identifications on the group: (front row, left to right) Rummy Lambeau, Bill DuMoe, Buff Wagner, Norm Barry, Curly Lambeau, Art Schmael, Wally Ladrow, Tubby Howard, Ray McLean, and Emmett Clair; (back row) Herm Martell, Jim Cook, Nate Abrams, "Cowboy" Wheeler, Frank Coughlin, Joe Carey, Jab Murray, Dave Hayes, Cub Buck, Milt Wilson, unidentified, unidentified, Fee Klaus, and Sam Powers. Only six of these fellows were from Green Bay. Photograph from the Henry Lefebvre Collection of the Neville Public Museum of Brown County, Green Bay, Wisconsin.

All-Stars were mixing it up against a half-dozen elevens in Michigan's U. P. In his daily sports column, "Cal's Comments," Calhoun was also reporting the formation of a company team at the Nash Motor company in Kenosha, which would join the "state football circle."

The Packers were practicing each night and holding "blackboard drills," Cal reported. They were being flooded with requests for games, he continued, "from the biggest teams in the country." Some of them were the Moline Tractors, Muncie Collegians, Saint Paul Tigers, and the Cincinnati Celts. The Packers, perhaps in an attempt to grab a security blanket against tougher opponents, were "endeavoring to play all the contests at home with the possible exception of one date late in November."

The Packers had also strengthened their lineup considerably with the addition of Jab Murray from Marinette, who had starred at Marquette University. Other talents were also said to be in the fold for the team's first action against what Calhoun was promoting as a "crack Windy City aggregation" set for September 25.

THE END OF THE ALL-STARS, THE END OF THE STEELERS

The legacy of the Stambaugh All-Stars came to a screeching halt in 1936. The house of cards had tumbled, and the concertina had sounded its last note. Even the orange at half-time became an unaffordable luxury. Stambaugh's Frank Shepich recalled one of the All-Stars' final games:

And things were tough. I mean we played Niagara up here and the gate was eighty dollars. And by the time you paid off the referees, you know, and bought a little tape for taping ankles and stuff, there just wasn't anything there. I said we tried to pay the guys two dollars a game and we couldn't make it. It just wasn't there. Things were tough here, you know. The mines were shut down.

The mines started up again in '37, "but," Shepich lamented, "by that time, the interest [in football] had died." Guys might have been getting back to work, especially a few years later when World War II was putting a brand new demand on the production of iron, but survival was still the name of the game and football was too much a lark for the sobriety of wartime. After 1936, no Stambaugh football aggregation would ever play under the name "All-Stars" again.

Shepich was straightforward when explaining what finally happened to the team, soon to be known as the Steelers. "Not enough financing," he said. "And the young guys got older and got married and the younger fellows coming up didn't have the same fire we used to have either." There were money problems and distractions, plain and simple—and plenty of football to be had with the flick of a button and the spin of a dial.

Town team football was at an end. It had given birth to the All-Stars as well as the Packers. The teams, one defunct and the other magnificently perpetuated, represented why the town team era ended. The All-Stars and its later rendition, the Steelers, displayed all the pitfalls of fielding town teams that would eventually lead to their demise.

The Packers, thanks to the drive of Curly Lambeau, the assistance of a group of business leaders, the promotion of a cigar-chomping newspaper man, "Cal" Calhoun, and a little bit of luck, were able to move from being a town team to being a professional organization within the relative safety of the NFL. They had survived the ups and downs and made it to the promised land, where a television screen and some TV commentators could make them look just as big and just as talented as guys from New York and Los Angeles and, of course, Chicago.

As far as that proverbial house of cards goes, who knows what the future holds? At least for the foreseeable future, those thin and frail elements of the town team world seem to have been pasted into place by the relative stability of the National Football League. Hats off to the All-Stars and every team like them, including many lost chapters of the NFL's own story from Columbus to Milwaukee to Pottsville to Cleveland and back again.

Rumblings from De Pere on Saturday, September 10, said that the purchase of Pine Grove as an athletic park would increase the interest of De Pere citizens in football. Some of De Pere's sports enthusiasts felt such interest had been flagging because "the proximity of Green Bay with a good team has killed the possibility of football interest in a local organization."

Other pre-action news was being tossed about. Joe Hoeffel, a Green Bay footballer who had made a major name for himself at the University of Wisconsin, was said to be in line to "cooperate with Captain Lambeau in building up a winning football machine for the Green Bay Packers" as coach. But Charlie Mathys, an awesome West High School quarterback, who had made a name for himself at the University of Indiana, would not join the team because of job commitments. The Stambaugh Miners, seeking a "pot of gold," were unlikely to fill an open date with the Packers on October 8. "The champions of the Upper Michigan peninsula," reported Cal, "evidently are having a bad attack of frenzied finance and their demands for appearance here will not be met." Lambeau assumed the newly created position of athletic director at East High School.

The Packers maintained a roster of 22 men in accord with APFA regulations, and several of the players, Leaper, Martell, Gavin, Abrams, the Zoll brothers, Schmael, Ladrow, and Rosenow, represented the hometown. In the face of the unknown—a venture into a national arena—everything, including some local boys to shout about, seemed to be in place, for now at least, to be in place.

But running smack dab into a higher level of competition proved to be a lesson for Lambeau's team. Their 1921 regular season ended at a mediocre 3-2-1 mark, with as many losses and ties as they had experienced over 22 games in both 1919 and 1920. The vision was getting a pretty good once-over. If you tossed in their "preseason" games, the season's record looked a lot better, 7-2-1, but that was a fool's paradise because those victories had come against aggregations cut from town team cloth, and it was an exercise that didn't reconcile itself with Lambeau's quest.

In those contests, against four semipro teams in late September and early October, the Packers were their dominating selves. They clipped the Chicago Boosters, 13–0, and then followed up with a couple of their par-for-the-course beatings. They whipped up on Rockford, 49–0, and hammered Chicago-Hamburg, 40–0. Rockford had traveled 16 hours by automobile for the contest and arrived road weary for their game. Lambeau took note and, in 1940, became the first NFL coach to streamline his team's travel through the use of two airplanes.

Their last warm-up would come against the Beloit Fairies, their nemesis for the past two seasons. The embarrassment of losing to a group calling themselves the Fairies, who had plainly been handed the 1919 contest by a hometown ref, Baldy Zabel, had been refreshed with another loss, in what Calhoun saw as a "fair" contest, in 1920. Despite their light-footed appellation, the Fairies had vied with the Packers as the upper class of the Wisconsin town teams over the past two years and weren't to be taken lightly. Besides handing the Packers their only two losses in 1919 and 1920, they had played a reasonable chess-match with young Lambeau's psyche to boot.

Calhoun saw the upcoming rematch and the changes surrounding it as a benchmark:

> The old football bee sure is buzzing merrily throughout the state. Not alone are all the high school and college teams hard at it but many independent organizations are springing up on the gridiron. The professional field is broadening out considerably. In the olden days, the Packers and Beloit Fairies were about the only pro elevens of any caliber. Racine has jumped into the fold with an all state squad. Allan Davey is going to head a team at La Crosse, while Superior is singing the praises of a fast going tribe.

On the same page, Cal suggested that the team from the "Typewriter City" was already "worrying" about facing the Packers. That was on Wednesday, September 28. By the following Tuesday, October 4, he was hedging his bets a little before giving way to his usual ebullience:

> Of course, the Green Bay Packers may bite the dust before the professional season is history but right at the present time, the Packers size up as likely contenders for national gridiron honors. They have downed their first two opponents like champions and if they continue their path to victory, the Staleys and Canton Bulldogs will have to meet their demands for recognition. None of the so-called "big fellows" have made a better showing in opening games than the Packers.

But this year, the Packers would get the Fairy monkey off their backs, defeating the Beloit Fairbanks boys on October 16 before heading into sanctioned league play on the 23rd. As usual, the forward-pass play, this time from Lambeau to Cowboy Wheeler in the first quarter, had done the deed for the Packers. The final score was a slim 7–0 decision. Writing after the game, Calhoun expressed some concern that there was "a screw loose in the Packer machine somewhere."

That was about it. The rest of the contest was "cleanly fought." The final period, reported Calhoun, "was pretty much Beloit." Cal's capricious poetry then described a little drama injected by Mother Nature herself. "During this period," he mused, "there was a young cloudburst and the ball became dangerous to handle but fumbles were far and few between."

APFA league play was about to start with four Packer players on what Cal called the "hospital list," obtained directly from Saint Vincent Hospital. They included Art Schmael with "caved in ribs," Joe Carey with a bum foot, Buff Wagner with a badly bruised arm, and Red Elliott with a busted leg.

For other APFA elevens, "elimination contests" had begun the last Sunday in September and a "series to establish the championship" was slated for the weekend after Thanksgiving. Teams in the league at the outset were New Haven, Connecticut; Chicago, Decatur, and Rock Island, Illinois; Hammond and Evansville, Indiana; Louisville, Kentucky; Detroit, Michigan; Minneapolis, Minnesota; Buffalo, Rochester, and Tonawanda, New York; Akron, Canton, Cleveland, Columbus, Dayton, and Toledo, Ohio; and Green Bay, Wisconsin.

Over 400 contracts had been signed by "former university stars who will play on the nineteen teams which are members of the association," reported the wire services. "Nationally known" college stars such as Charles "Chick" Harley, Frank "Red" Coughlin, Curly Lambeau, Andrew "Rip" King, Gaylord "Pete" Stinchcomb, Cub Buck, Emmett Keefe, Guy Chamberlain, George Halas, and Johnny Scott were listed among them.

Otto Stiller is seen here perched atop the grandstand at Bellevue Park generating photos of the on-field action. Thanks to the Stiller and Lefebvre families, today's Packer fans can stare back into the early days of the legend and celebrate the great thing they have today. Photograph from the Stiller-Lefebvre Collection.

Also off the wire services was the news that many football authorities of the day considered Fritzie Pollard, a "colored star with the Akron Professionals," as the "greatest living football star." Pollard, it was related, was called the "Rubber Man of Football" and was spoken of as the "Three-Legged Back" because of his "strange close to the ground runs. It is said that he touches the ground with one hand throughout his running giving the appearance of running with his feet and one hand . . . He perhaps had more to do with Akron's cinching the league title last year than any individual player." Opposing tacklers had to be as confused by the lack of punctuation in Pollard's running as readers of that description were.

Of course, there was still football on the intracity front in Green Bay. On Sunday, October 2, the South Side Maroons battled the De Pere city team to a scoreless tie. The *Gazette* cited the "line plunging" of Mathys, Dwyer, and Defresne. They were happy, said the paper, to toe it up against any aggregation averaging 150 pounds, and possible candidates could contact J. Getzloff on Green Bay's near west side.

The amateur tradition was still alive and well. It would continue for another 40 years, until the late 1950s, to fill a void that the professional game did not. Lambeau's vision didn't include, nor did it invite, everyone. Some guys, even with a fair degree of football talent, were content to play the game "on the side" and tend to life's other offerings like a job, a wife, children, and community involvement. For them, semipro or amateur town team play continued to be appealing.

While not everyone would live out the vagabond's life of pro ball like Johnny Blood, the professional ranks did call for a different genre of man than did the more staid cosmos of town team ball. For one, family life and football didn't always blend into a harmonious balance. These guys were on the road, away from the watchful eye of wife or mother. Sometimes, surprise surprise, they strayed a bit from the moral properties of their backgrounds and found themselves out late at night getting a bit twisted in the head and spending the night with some football floozy or whorehouse denizen.

In fact, proper little Green Bay achieved some notoriety for catering to just such forays. In *The Pro Football Chronicle*, Dan Daly and Bob O'Donnell pay particular attention to a small town on the APFA map dubbed "Partytown U.S.A." Green Bay football fans and players called it home. Daly and O'Donnell observed, "Green Bay in the '20s was the most popular stop in the league. Visiting players loved the place. Teams made it a point to schedule several days there. It had a bustling bar scene, and its red-light district in the northeast section was famous."

"On Sunday nights after Packer football games . . . two and three bartenders worked at top speed in the Rex, the Office and the National on Pine St., and in Jake Geurtz's place on Cherry St.," R. G. Lynch, a witness to the actual festivities, wrote in 1928. "Late comers had to stand on the steps and wait for a chance to get in."

Prohibition "was just a slight inconvenience" to the city.

Bawdy houses flourished. One of the most popular among the players was known simply as "801 and 803 Reber," which was the duplex-of-ill-repute's address. Its doors were routinely open to visiting teams, and the parties sometimes lasted till dawn.

"The players would go in about 10 at a time," says Bill Swanson, who grew up two doors down and eventually became sheriff of Green Bay. "But no more than 10. That was the limit. The whole neighborhood knew what was going on."

The only team the madam apparently had her doubts about was the Duluth Eskimos, according to Swanson. She once made the mistake of denying them entrance and locking the door. They responded the way you would expect football players to respond, by breaking it down.

Why was Green Bay's northeast side teeming with whorehouses? The answer was simple. That section of town, according to Mary Jane Herber, Local History and Genealogy Librarian at the Brown County Library, "was Preble, outside the jurisdiction of Green Bay police." Not that Green Bay law enforcement was anxious to close the bordellos in its own enforcement area.

To one degree or another, these sorts of shenanigans were replicated in most of the towns across the nation where pro ball was being promoted and played. But, once again, on an entirely different sort of playing field, "small town" Green Bay, a "drinking town with a football problem," was achieving surprising distinction and showing itself to be equal to any football metropolis.

And, here again, the rowdy character of the town team days was still hanging around. While the "professionals" were laying claim to something very different and far better, especially when it came to the incorporation of women of the night into their game strategies, many of the old character traits marking town team play remained firmly in place.

So, even in the reality of the APFA, there was a struggle between affectation and true identity. Games were still scheduled on the fly, and, as in the days of old, they ran the risk of being switched at the eleventh hour. Membership in the APFA also fluctuated directly in proportion to the success and survival of its individual member aggregations. By October 9, Green Bay circles listed the Cincinnati Celts and Muncie Indianans as members, while dropping Detroit, Akron, and New Haven from the roll. By season's end, it was a question of who was in and who was out.

To signal their part in something bigger, the Packers began to issue *The Dope Sheet: Official Program and Publication, Acme-Packer Football Team* with the start of their 1921 season. As football fans poured into old Hagemeister Park for the games, they would grab a copy as they paid admission. "One of the definite purposes in the publication of 'The Official Dope Sheet,'" the October 9 edition explained, "was to further acquaint the patrons of the game with the players on the team."

The third issue of the season, printed for the October 9 game with the Cornell Hamburgs, celebrated Lambeau's role on the current roster as well as his part in Green Bay football history. It also mourned the loss of Wes Leaper, who was leaving the city for Oklahoma, "to begin work as western representative for a Green Bay manufacturer." Leaper was replaced at right end by Green Bay west-sider Herman Martell, a member of the Packer squad in 1919 and 1920, who, the sheet reflected, "has made some interesting football history while he was with the local school."

The same issue also described why Cub Buck, who had now joined the squad, was such a star:

> It is not so much the little cues or the expressions on the faces of the rivals, nor is it snapping up the signals and remembering what every signal means (tho Cub is a whirlwind at that) but it is because football is a game of rules and a science that Cub Buck is known wherever football is played because of his ability to get the dope before the play is started and kill it before it is under way.

The October 9 issue gave "the dope" on Beloit in an article titled, "Here Comes Beloit; Get Out of the Way." The byline implied just how high-tech the publication was willing to go to bring Green Bay football fans the real scoop. "Special By Telephone to 'The Dope Sheet,'" it stated. Again, it picked up on the tension between the Packers and the Fairies created by the Packer losses in 1919 and 1920.

In fact, Beloit remained a pretty good team, despite the dark cloud over their 1919 "victory." They weren't, however, joining the APFA. And, like all the other town teams, they had begun their descent into the lost pages of history, despite their football skills, as a result. The upcoming matchup would still be contentious, though. "Every automobile that can possible [sic] stand the trip is being recruited as a conveyor," reported the *Dope Sheet*, "and there will be few red bloods left in the boundary city toward sundown next Saturday."

Clearly this was 1921's version of getting the gridiron fan "in on" the inner workings of the game, something the *Dope Sheet* had promised to do. In a later issue that year, the *Dope Sheet* stroked its readers and explained its exact purpose:

> The followers of Green Bay's nationally known "Packers" have been in the custom of arriving early for the games. They have watched the visiting elevens at practice and sized up the opponents. Our former programs were entirely inadequate. They simple [sic] informed you of the names of the numbered players. In no way were you to have first hand "dope" on who these players were, where they have distinguished themselves, what their records were, how the "Packers" measured up with the teams whom they

shall meet this season. In a word, the fans were "short on dope" the real "dope" which they wanted and needed to intelligently and interestedly follow the fortunes of this great aggregation of football stars.

The *Dope Sheet* may not have kept its verb tenses straight or known how many words were implied when it said "in a word," but it was definitely a hit with fans who considered themselves a tad more sophisticated than the average sideliner. Harold T. I. Shannon and Associates, "Green Bay's new advertising agency" had been retained by the team to offer up columns and inches in the sheet, and businesses "wishing to be represented in the select few who will speak thru our pages" were supposed to contact them at their offices in the Colonial Theater Building or by telephone No. 50.

The publication also drummed up support for upcoming contests, even though they might be subject to change. The November 6 edition promised Hammond for the following week and a potential return of Rock Island if such a game could be scheduled. Membership in a roughshod league didn't guarantee a schedule that could be printed and hung on the refrigerator, at least not yet in 1921.

That issue also featured a thumbnail on Sammy Powers, who had been imported from the Marinette city team by Lambeau. "If This Kid Had 40 Pounds More Beef" the sheet lamented. But extra beef might have stifled the very 1919 play for which the *Dope Sheet* cited him. In a game against New London, a team "with a bagful of trick plays," Powers had memorized their signal for a "tackle around play" and intercepted the ball from the quarterback the next time it was called. Thirty yards later, Sammy had himself six points and a great story.

The sheet also took to task "the few persons in the city who have satisfied themselves that the Packer team was an unorganized gathering of individual stars" by relating that the team was drilling plenty tough:

> *The team, every man included, goes through scrimmage practice, from one o'clock until dark on Thursdays and Fridays of every week. Signal practice is gone through at the armory on Thursday and Friday nights, Saturday and Sunday mornings and blackboard talks given to the boys.*

The *Dope Sheet* continued to be published during the Packers' earliest years in the pro ranks, with its usual fusion of player news, looks at rule changes and agitation of the fans for upcoming contests. While the sheet represented a step up for the Green Bay Professionals, or "Blues" as they were called in its pages upon their reentry back into the league in 1922, it also gave a clear indication that this was a time of transition between the rudiments of town team football and the new, all-pro game.

Many contests were still being scheduled "on the fly," and contests still could fall apart without warning. Fortunately, league membership assured a bevy of possible opponents, should a projected skirmish go up in smoke. Contracts for games were also negotiated on an individual basis, and matches could be rejected if the terms offered didn't tickle the other aggregation's fancy. Headlines from the November 6, 1921, *Dope Sheet* imply the tentative nature of the schedule. "Hammond to be Here Next Sunday; Rock Island May Return," declared one header on the front page of that issue. On page five, another stated, "Packers Accept Cardinals Bid; Now Up to Them."

But the sheet did celebrate Green Bay's 1921 membership in the APFA. Green Bay then, as now, found itself the "Smallest City in Professional Football." If nothing else, the dope was that Lambeau's dream and the league were a perfect fit:

> *Green Bay may well be proud of its membership in the American Professional Football Association. Such pride is pardonable. To be classed with the foremost exponents of this phase of the great fall game, and at the same time enjoy the distinction of being the smallest city within the select circle, is something to warrant a general expansion of chests.*

Such hyperbole wasn't the only indication that said the professional game had arrived in the bay city. The general scene of game day had been practiced and nearly perfected over the town team years since 1910. More than a little direction had been provided by the organizational know-how of the Wisconsin-Illinois baseball club. In his 1961 team history, *The Green Bay Packers: Pro Football's Pioneer Team*, Chuck Johnson suggested this maturity:

> *The 1920 season was not dissimilar to that of 1919, except that 3,000 seats were put up at Hagemeister Park. Marcel Lambeau built them and also constructed a fence around the field. No longer could passers-by casually watch the games for nothing. Admission now was fifty cents.*

A photo exists of Hagemeister Park, with Model Ts and the like, parked askew just south of the playing field. One's imagination can zoom in and out from there as an invisible spectator just minutes before kickoff on an autumn afternoon: Downtown Green Bay, some eight blocks to the west, would be completely still. The streetcar had hauled its share of fans to Hagemeister along the lines running down Walnut Street straight from the business district, while scores of other fans had carried their game-day accoutrements in hand as they walked toward Hagemeister Park on nearby streets. The entire city seemed to be converging on a scene of historic importance.

Admission money and tickets were exchanged at E. A. "Spike" Spachmann's booth near the gate, and various volunteers served as ushers and bouncers, sometimes all rolled into the form of one person. The *Dope Sheet* was handed out by other volunteers at the gate, and fans, dressed in their Sunday best, had grabbed one before heading to their seats. Kickoff was just seconds away.

BEFORE THEY WERE THE PACKERS

The new seats were nice; they were comfortable. They also ended a lot of the crowd's direct and unsuspected impact on the game. But also gone were the days of the perpetual 50-yard line, where spectators could move up and down the field with the line of scrimmage. Also disappearing were the many spectators watching from atop their cars. A few diehards still remained out there, their view now mostly obscured, refusing to come into the sophisticated fold of the pro game.

Unfortunately, fans were now paying for a professional-caliber game, and increasing distance between them and the players was one of the trade-offs. The days of gathering around the home team in one of the end zones at halftime or surrounding the opposing backfield were also things for the nostalgic minded. Players no longer showed up at the game having dressed at their home or that of a teammate who lived closer to the field. Now, the boys dressed at the Elk's Club shower rooms on the northwest corner of Jefferson and Cherry Streets and traveled en masse to the clubhouse on the northeast corner of the Hagemeister grounds to be incited by one of Lambeau's oral provocations.

Fortunately, a few remnants of the old town team days still remained, kept alive by fresh-faced kids who weren't sophisticated enough to pay heed to the etiquette of the professional game. According to Ray Drossart and his buddy, Nubs Pigeon, those minutes before a game could be sheer bedlam, and a little cyclone fence wasn't going to prevent young fans from seeing the contest. Once the players arrived at the gates of the stadium, one or more of them would usually engulf a youngster, devoid of admission money, in his arms and enter the stadium with the kid in front of him. "I got snuck in more than one time," recalled Drossart. Elsewhere along the rail, it was a scene like rats off a ship as kids who couldn't hook up with a player either climbed the small trees around the field's perimeter and jumped in or weaseled their way under the fence.

Thank God that trait of town team play hadn't ended with a league membership. And, thank God, at least some of its traits remain intact today. In July 1934, the *Green Bay Press-Gazette* suggested that the "'knot hole gang' whose membership is composed of youngsters of the short pants variety" remained a concern of the Packer management. "These boys are admitted to the games at a quarter a head," the paper reported. "Sometimes, the little fellows are allowed to enter two on a ticket." But stories of kids sneaking into City Stadium, even when it had moved to the far west side of Green Bay along Highland Avenue in 1957, would remain as much a part of the Packer mystique as Bart Starr's quarterback sneak across the south end zone in the 1967 "Ice Bowl."

And, finally, thank God for every Packer jacket, sweatshirt, or T-shirt sold, no matter what the team's current fortunes, in a kid's size today. After all, kids are being priced right out of today's game. One fan recently suggested a modern modification of kids' sneaking into games. Ticketless youth would gather outside a designated gate on game day. Whenever a fan was escorted out for bad behavior or for exerting absolutely no cheer for the home team, a kid would be brought in to take his seat. In today's world of hypersensitivity and three-hundred-dollar tickets, this, of course, amounts to blasphemy, making it sound like an even better idea.

In their first official league scrap of 1921 on Sunday, October 23, the Packers edged out the Minneapolis Marines, 7–6, on that hallowed ground of Green Bay football, Hagemeister Park. Jack Rudolph, famed Green Bay historian, chose this as one of the essential moments in Green Bay football history and wrote of it in his *Press-Gazette* column on October 21, 1961. According to Rudolph, the APFA "promoters had doubts about letting Green Bay play in their backyard . . . The story has never been verified—nor denied—but it was generally believed that the Packers' membership in the league was conditional. If they didn't show up well in their first effort against the fearsome Minneapolis Marines, out they went."

If that was the case, it certainly prompted Lambeau to field the very best team he could possibly muster, a hybrid of the town team the Packers had been and the serious professional eleven they would become. The week before their game against the Marines, Lambeau signed Billy DuMoe, a former Syracuse wingman, and Jigger Hayes and Paul Malone, the latter two of Notre Dame. But it was Art Schmael, hometown product, who scored, with time ticking away, to seal the team's very first league-sanctioned victory.

Now the Marines were damn good. They had been together for 12 seasons and had laid claim to "the Midwestern championship" for the last six of those. Like the Packers, they had risen out of the rubble of town team play and joined the ranks of the APFA in 1921. Rube Ursella was their big star, and he was a prime example of the changing times for football. According to Rudolph, he had never attended college "but in a dozen years of the rough and tumble of pioneer pro ball he had established a reputation as one of the canniest signal callers in the business—if you could call it a business."

Lambeau, reported Rudolph, "had been ordered by his doctor not to play." Likewise, Tubby Howard, the regular at fullback, had injured his ankle. Other dents and dings had been reported the week prior and included the aforementioned Carey, Wagner, Elliott, and Schmael. It was David versus Goliath, and David was limping a little, with his arm in a sling rather than carrying one. Carey, Wagner, and Schmael were able to suck it up and take to the field. Elliott's broken leg made the same heroics a bit tougher for him.

The Marines went for a 30-yard field goal shortly after the opening kickoff, and it was pretty clear that the Packers were up against something big. Fortunately, the Minneapolis crew missed the goal. But a series later they were at it again, this time scoring a touchdown. The classic back and forth followed. A blocked punt here for the Packers, an interception there for the Marines. Then, the Packers tossed an incomplete pass into the end zone, and, in accord with the rules of the day, the ball went over to the Minnies. Sampson, Dvorak, and Regnier all tore through the Packer defense for running yardage, and it was looking like another drive of Marine power and execution. But Carey recovered a fumble in the young seconds of the fourth quarter and the Marines were stopped.

Then there was more back and forth until just about six minutes remained in the show, with the Packers down, 0–6. Rudolph said that "the crowd, resigned to just a good try in the big bid, came up roaring" when the Packers snagged a fumbled punt on the Marine 35-yard line. Two running plays into the Minneapolis line produced nothing for the Packers. Then, wrote Rudolph, "Curley [sic] Obliged . . . With fans pleading for the obvious pass, Lambeau—who had been at quarterback most of the way in defiance of Doc Kelly—obliged with a bullet to Wagner. Buff made a circus catch and reached to the Minneapolis 14 before being pulled down."

The Packers were finally moving the ball with some success, but the score still had them at a six-point deficit. Rudolph continued,

> The park was tense and silent as Curly barked his signals over the crouching lines—the huddle hadn't come into use yet. Schmae[h]l took a direct pass from center and disappeared under a huge pileup on the Minneapolis goal line. When the stack peeled off and Art was found across the big stripe with the tying touchdown the crowd went crazy. Hats and cushions sailed into the air and staid business men hopped around like kids.
>
> Lambeau's drop kick between the uprights for the winning point touched off a continuous din that could be heard for blocks. It hasn't stopped yet.

No doubt the din was loudest a few blocks away, where the curly haired wonder had demonstrated his earliest football skills, or over a few more blocks in the other direction at old East High School, where he had honed them. The Packers, thanks once again to Lambeau's golden arm, had successfully joined the pro ranks. The rest of the season may have tempered the din some, but by Thanksgiving, another milestone would be reached.

Just seven days after their Minneapolis success, the Green Bays were put in check, 3–13, by the Rock Island Independents. This was the very first loss at Hagemeister since their founding in 1919. After that, the Packers enjoyed back-to-back victories, once again restoring the sacredness of their home turf at the end of Walnut Street, as well as their confidence. They whipped the Evansville Crimson Giants on November 6, 43–6, and doubled up on the Hammond Pros the following week, 14–7, again at home. Hammond featured another native son, Charley Mathys, at quarterback. Mathys had graduated from Indiana University after leaving his Green Bay alma mater, West High School, and 4,000 flooded the bleachers at Hagemeister to see the contest. By 1922, Lambeau had lured Mathys back to town to display his wares in front of a familiar audience, and he remained in the fold for five seasons.

The following Sunday, they traveled to Chicago, where they experienced the bitter sweetness of a 3–3 tie against the Chicago Cardinals on November 20. The Cardinals had been playing ball since they were one of those athletic clubs of such ill repute back in 1899. Paddy Driscoll was the do-it-all man for the Cardinals, whose name came from some off-color used jerseys sent to them by the University of Chicago. Over 400 fans climbed on passenger cars at the Chicago & North Western station on Green Bay's west side for the $9.69 overnight trip to the Windy City. It was the first time a Green Bay team had traveled to Chicago for a big-time contest, but these train trips would, eventually, become perfected by the football fanatics from the Bay City.

The *Appleton Post-Crescent* observed the fanaticism of Green Bay, its neighbor to the north, saying, "Green Bay sure has a bunch of wild football fans. At least 400 of the bugs will follow the Packers, their professional football team, to Chicago." What those 400 fans would experience en route, as well as in the big city, would have horrified their mothers and, in some cases, their fathers too. Oh, the debauchery . . . there was drinking and all-night hooting and hollering, and that was reported by the people willing to share their stories. At the game they were able to make some real noise though they made up a little less than half the crowd.

But, back home, there was another first under way in honor of the Cardinal game. Because so many fans had stayed home, a re-enactment of the game was set up at Turner Hall on the corner of Walnut Street and Monroe Avenue. The idea, according to Packer historian Larry Names in *The History of the Green Bay Packers: The Lambeau Years Part One*, had come from the game against the Rock Island Independents earlier that season. "The game was telegraphed back to Rock Island," recorded Names, "and recreated by a local personality in front of a pay-ing audience."

According to Green Bay resident Russell Mott, the Gridograph, or "Playograph" as Mott recalled it, achieved varying degrees of success over the years. And, while it may have been as high-tech as could be imagined in 1921, its actual workings would be viewed as nearly barbaric by today's virtual-reality fan.

Mott recalled a wooden board listing the names of the players on the oppos-ing teams listed in two vertical, side-by-side columns. Behind the board a crew of men worked to keep the spectators informed of the game action. One of the men would receive a live telegraph feed of the actual on-field action in the city where the Packers were playing and relay the play-by-play to another man who worked directly behind the board. This man's job was to move a small cutout of a football from player to player, depending on who had passed or handed off the ball to whom. Another football cutout would be moved across a replica of the gridiron to simulate field position and possession. In this state-of-the-art fashion, the hometown fan was kept posted of the boys' exploits.

The Gridograph, while first located at Turner Hall, was later found, said Mott, "on the back side of the legion hall." Over the years various men took their places behind the board, and a number of them, reminisced Mott, had ties to the post office and White City baseball teams of a few years earlier or the earliest Packer elevens. Such men, he said, included "my dad, Walter Ladrow, George Calhoun, Ed Putney, Spike Spachmann, Jim Coffeen and the fellow copying the code and taking the messages was young Gordon Bent."

Like their counterparts years later, Packer fans were eager to hear the latest about their team's exploits. Here, they've gathered to gaze at a gridograph (or playograph), a wooden board that showed in graphic form the progress of a game being played miles away; the information was relayed to the site by telegraph. This piece of state-of-the-art technology (at least by 1921 standards) was located at a couple of different sports in downtown Green Bay. Can you imagine any fan today sitting for two to three hours watching a small football move across a piece of plywood? Photograph from the Stiller-Lefebvre Collection.

In an article two days before the 1922 Packers-Cardinals game, the *Press-Gazette* reporter warned fans who were considering "watching" the game on the Gridograph to get to Turner Hall early or they wouldn't be able to get in at all. The writer suggested that fans in attendance could enjoy "the comfort of the inside of a heated building while the ones who were brave enough to make the trip will probably be wishing that they had put on that extra pair of socks and at the same time be wishing that they had put on three or four overcoats." For the slight price of 50 cents, the fans could also enjoy the "antics" of Mulligan Seroogy, who would be working a megaphone while the other guys moved the pieces on the Gridograph board. With a "little use of the imagination" said the reporter, fans at Turner Hall would likely find "more excitement than if one were present at the game itself."

As game reporting went electronic, things became more "real time." Mott also remembered Jim Coffeen's role as on-field announcer at home games when he would travel up and down the sidelines, reporting the action to the fans in the bleacher via a portable microphone. Names reported that "Russ Winnie did recreations of Packer games over the radio in 1929 and 1930 for Milwaukee station WTMJ. Later in 1930, he did the first live broadcast of a road game in Chicago for that station."

The Packers' next contest, their last of the 1921 season, was another loss, this time on November 27 at Cubs Park in Chicago. But that game commenced the greatest rivalry ever seen in the National Football League. There are, of course, few sure bets. But here's one: The rivalry begun that day, between the Green Bay Packers and the Chicago Bears, will remain the greatest rivalry, over the uneven ebb and flow of time, that the NFL will ever see.

The Chicago story, all things considered, wasn't that much different than the saga of the Packers. Begun in downstate Illinois as a company team called the Staleys, the team moved to Chicago just prior to the 1921 season. They had organized in late 1919 when the young George Halas was beckoned to Decatur by entrepreneur A. E. Staley. Staley had observed an enticing phenomenon among his peers, who had pulled together and sponsored football aggregations as a means of giving their businesses visibility. He liked the idea, and this Halas kid was in a class by himself as a baseball player and footballer. He wanted Halas to display his wares in both venues. Staley's baseball nine was already an established organization, but Halas would be put in charge of the football side of things. This would be a company team, and, according to Richard Whittingham in *The Chicago Bears: An Illustrated History*, Staley told Halas, "Bring in the best players. I'll give them jobs—they'll earn a living here, and they'll play football for us."

And bring in the best players Halas did. Over the summer of 1921, Halas secured Dutch Sternaman, Guy Chamberlin, George Trafton, and Jimmy Conzelman, just to drop a few names. The four of them alone were enough to send a wave of fear across the faces in the opposing huddle, but Halas wasn't done there. By the time he had finished, he was loaded with former college stars, all now employees of the Staley Manufacturing Company.

For the 1920 season, the Staleys, now among the founding members of the APFA, tore through their opponents, scoring a collective 166 points to 14 for their foes. The only blemishes were a 6–7 misstep against the Cardinals, a 0–0 tie with Rock Island, and a 0–0 tie in the last game of the season against the mighty Akron Pros, who hauled home the APFA trophy following the contest.

But hard economic times forced Staley to jettison his team before the 1921 season. As Whittingham reports, Staley told Halas:

BEFORE THEY WERE THE PACKERS

I know you're more interested in football than the starch business, but we simply can't underwrite the team's expenses any longer. Why don't you move the boys up to Chicago? I think pro football can go over in a big way there—and I'll give you $5,000 to help you get started. All I ask is that you continue to call the team the Staleys for one season.

For the 1921 season, Halas decided to add a couple of players who had made a football name for themselves, Chick Harley and Pete Stinchcomb, as if he needed even more talent. It is suggested that Halas's activities triggered Amos Alonzo Stagg, legendary coach at the University of Chicago, to rip the professional game as a "menace" and a "scourge." "Sunday-playing teams," he was quoted, "debauch college sport and athletes." That attack, of course, was nothing all that new.

CHICAGO—DA BEARS

There is only one reason to mention the Bears in a book about Green Bay's early town teams: hate. Oh, okay, call it rivalry, maybe even respect. But the fact is that the teams are nearly mirror images of one another, including the uncanny parallel universes of their early stars, Curly Lambeau and George Halas.

Yes, the Bears began downstate as the Decatur Staleys and got their present moniker when they were adopted by the Cubs' organization after arriving in Blow Town. No matter the ebb and flow of the Packer-Bear rivalry and even though the Minnesota Vikings are even easier to dislike, the rivalry will always *be* the stuff of legends. Despising the Vikings has even become common ground!

In 1921, Halas described the ongoing argument between his Bears and the Packers as "the most fierce rivalry in pro football." It turns out that rivalry may well *be* the National Football League. Red Grange, the man credited with saving the NFL in its formative years, once said, "if it hadn't been for the Bears and the Green Bay Packers I don't believe there would have been a National Football League."

As tribute to their birthplace, the Staleys played their first few games of the 1921 season at Staley Field in Decatur. In Chicago, Halas and his crew basically had been adopted by the long-standing Chicago Cub baseball organization, and now, as the "Bears," they played nine straight home games at Cubs Park. The move signaled the team's rise from the ranks of the town teams, and, like the Packers in Green Bay, it had hung its football fortunes on the drive of one man, George Halas, with a little bit of help from his friends.

The Staleys gave the Packers their final defeat of the year, a 20–0 reality check with a special twist. In an account bylined "By Cal," the Packers were hailed for their spirited play in the face of defeat. "Fighting as only a Green Bay team can fight," Cal had opened his wrap-up of the game. Unlike many of the Packers' town team opponents of the two previous years, the Bears knew a little bit about the forward pass and used it to their own advantage. The game was replete with "'horse shoe' forward passes" and blocked kicks.

For their final score, the Bears rubbed the Packers' nose in it on a touchdown pass to George Halas from the famous Chick Harley, who Cal said, "now looks more like a faded violet." It was the worst loss of the season for Lambeau's troops as well as the worst beating of the team's entire three-year history.

In choppy verbiage, Calhoun accounted for the entire game, play by play. The bottom line seemed pretty clear and marked the fact that the Packers had climbed from the ranks of the town teams onto the professional plane. Seven thousand football fans witnessed those graduation ceremonies at Cubs Park. "It wasn't long before the final whistle blew and the Packers beaten," observed Cal, "but they had won their way into the hearts of the Chicago football fans for their gritty brick."

In a sidebar, Calhoun denounced the idea, reportedly held by "some college authorities," that "there ain't no such thing as spirit in professional football." Green Bay fans who had followed their lads to the Windy City had put on a "remarkable display of spirit" there. Those college authorities and citizens of what Cal called "staid old Chicago" "stood back and gasped as rooters from Green Bay, Wis. took the town by storm Sunday morning and held full sway until the last car of the special excursion pulled out from the Northwestern about three bells Monday morning."

The lumberjack band and some five hundred fans started parading and "whooping things up" the minute they landed in Chicago's Loop. "The Bay rooters," Cal wrote, "trailed up the street from the depot to the Stratford Hotel and let every one know who they were and why they were here." The war whoops continued at the game site, despite the Packers' troubles. "After the final whistle had blown and the Packers players were trailing off the gridiron," Calhoun observed, "the Green Bay band broke forth into an 'On Wisconsin' and the rooters ended it up with a 'U-rah-rah Green Bay.' Spectators who were hurriedly wending their way to the exits stopped in their tracks and a roar of applause swept the field."

Ed Smith, whom Cal called the "dean of Chicago sport writers," was another one of those football prophets, though some modern fans might say he was a bit off in his forecast: "Never in my experience have I ever witnessed a better display of spirit. I have often been told that Green Bay was one of the best sporting towns in the northwest. I believe it now and one thing is sure hereafter whenever a Green Bay team comes to Chicago they will be given a warm welcome."

Well, it hasn't always been a "warm welcome." But the special rivalry that day between the Packers and the Bears has led to countless newspaper and magazine articles, several books, and intense feelings—most often of the acrimonious variety—among players and fans of both clubs. And the movers and shakers in both organizations have not been above the fray. A few times, both teams were about even in posture.

There are the rumors of George Halas running subterfuge against Lambeau and his Packers and other rumors of Halas being the one who, behind the scenes, assured that football would stay forever in the northern city. There is the open warfare, on record, from the Mike Ditka and Forrest Gregg years, into the Eighties when the Bears, riding high on a Super Bowl victory, survived quarterback Jim McMahon's vicious body slam at the hands of the no-good Packers. But it all began, rather lovingly it would seem, that day, Sunday, November 27, 1921.

No two men have ever been more alike in their football skills, their alignment with the game of football, or their significance to their respective team than Halas and Lambeau. Ultimately, Chicago seems to have been kinder to George Halas than Green Bay was, at least at first, to Curly Lambeau. This is not to say that Halas didn't catch his share of words from his team's fans.

The official Packer roster for 1921 included at least seven hometown lads: Nate Abrams, Wally Ladrow, Herman Martell, Ray "Toody" McLean, Art Schmael, Martin Zoll, and, of course, Lambeau. Other players from the area included Sammy Powers and Jab Murray from the Marinette area and Cub Buck from the Fox River Valley. Other Green Bay boys were featured in the preseason but didn't show in sanctioned league play.

End-of-the-year league stats showed the Packers smack-dab in the middle of the ruckus created by the makeshift APFA:

Chicago Staleys	9-1-1	(11 league games played)	.900 %
Buffalo All-Americans	9-1-2	(12 league games played)	.900 %
Akron Pros	8-3-1	(12 league games played)	.727 %
Canton Bulldogs	5-2-3	(10 league games played)	.714 %
Rock Island Independents	4-2-1	(7 league games played)	.667 %
Evansville Crimson Giants	3-2-0	(5 league games played)	.600 %
Green Bay Packers	**3-2-1**	**(6 league games played)**	**.600 %**
Dayton Triangles	4-4-1	(9 league games played)	.500 %
Chicago Cardinals	3-3-2	(8 league games played)	.500 %
Rochester Jeffersons	2-3-0	(5 league games played)	.400 %
Cleveland Indians	3-5-0	(8 league games played)	.375 %
Washington Senators	1-2-0	(3 league games played)	.333 %

Cincinnati Colts	1-3-0	(4 league games played)	.250 %
Hammond Pros	1-3-1	(5 league games played)	.250 %
Minneapolis Marines	1-3-1	(5 league games played)	.250 %
Detroit Heralds	1-5-1	(7 league games played)	.167 %
Columbus Panhandles	1-8-0	(9 league games played)	.111 %
Tonawanda Kardex	0-1-0	(1 league game played)	.000 %
Muncie Flyers	0-2-0	(2 league games played)	.000 %
Louisville Brecks	0-2-0	(2 league games played)	.000 %
New York Giants	0-2-0	(2 league games played)	.000 %

Other end-of-the-year facts weren't that surprising. Lambeau led the team with 28 total points. Bill DuMoe and Art Schmael were in second place with 12

ELEVEN FORGOTTEN NAMES EVERY PACKER FAN SHOULD KNOW

Fred Hulbert—the Father of Green Bay Football and, as a result, the Grandfather of the Green Bay Packers.

T. P. Silverwood—an early star, captain, coach, and organizer of Green Bay's town teams.

Tom Skenandore—an Oneida standout, the first professional football player in Green Bay history.

Jonas Metoxen—another Oneida standout, sought after by every town team in the area.

Andy Muldoon—a player on Green Bay town teams from 1911 and an early Packer.

Jim Coffeen—high school star, town team and Packer player, first announcer of Packer action.

Nate Abrams—Lambeau's childhood buddy, 1918 captain, town team and early Packer standout.

Art Schmael—a "crack player" from Chicago who coached the 1918 town team, played on the 1919 town team (now the Packers), and then returned to the team, at Lambeau's begging, in 1922.

Bill Ryan—the forgotten first Packer coach, often lost in Lambeau's shadow.

George Whitney "Cal" Calhoun—*Press-Gazette* sportswriter who did as much to ensure the success of the early Packers off the field as Lambeau did on it.

Johnny "Blood" McNally, a.k.a. "Johnny Blood"—the original "tramp athlete" who played town team and professional ball in every locale that would tolerate his antics while celebrating his skill.

each. Natey Abrams and Tubby Howard each had six. The Packers, despite their 3-2-1 record, had outscored their opposition by 25 points, 70 to 55. Surprisingly, and indicative of the upper crust in which they were now mingling, they had one passing touchdown against two by their opponents.

As disorganized a team photo as ever existed (see page 250) was taken somewhere toward the beginning of the team's season, just before a practice. The site is likely the practice field north of the packing company. The Packer players stand in as rough a semblance of a line as one can imagine. Only five of them are wearing the official Acme Packers jerseys. Even more interesting is the smattering of spectators who turned out to watch them practice and are forever included in the team photo. At the front is a beautiful reminder of the old days of King Football. It is young team mascot "Buddy" Levitas, and his inclusion harkens back to the 1890s, when teams posed with just such a mascot, often holding a football.

All told, the aggregation was a mixed bag of imports and homeboys, of college players and street toughs, of swift ball carriers and grunts beefing up the scrum line. Twenty-five footballers saw "regular season" action, with another 10 playing in the "preseason" stretch. To man his boat, Lambeau had gone early and often to the well of his "alma mater," with seven players, including himself, hailing from some time in the Irish locker room.

Other area schools were also represented by Cub Buck and Jim Cook from UW–Madison, Roger Kliebhan from UW–Milwaukee, Jab Murray from Marquette, Cowboy Wheeler from Ripon, and Milt Wilson from UW–Oshkosh. Sammy Powers and Buff Wagner joined the team from Northern Michigan University. Eight of the regulars, including most of the hometown lads, had no college experience. Nearly every one of his preseason players put in time before returning to their regular football duties and studies at area colleges.

Ultimately, this menagerie indicated that "Times Have Changed and So Has the Game." It was the Rubicon between the golden age of the town teams and the salad days of pro ball. The average weight of his aggregation was 192 pounds and their average height was a sliver under six feet. At 250 pounds, Jab Murray and Cub Buck bounced people around from their tackle positions like there was no tomorrow. Both took high-class college training into every block and tackle. The lightest man on the squad, Sammy Powers, tickled the scales at a mere 150 pounds, a full sack of grain less than Murray or Buck.

Most important—and unlike the Cincinnati Celts, Tonawanda Kardex, and Muncie Flyers—they had hung together. Lambeau's dream, rising out of Green Bay's strong town team tradition and so steady in the face of similar competition from the area in 1919 and 1920, was a deer in the headlights of stiff national competition in 1921. But it made it off the road safe and sound and better days were ahead.

In a footnote to the season, and, perhaps testimony to their town team roots, the Packers returned to Wisconsin with a couple of encounters with state teams slated to put the lid on the 1921 campaign. The Packers turned their immediate football attention to the Racine Legion eleven at the Brewer ball park in Milwaukee the following Sunday, December 4, "to settle the professional championship of the state."

Racine had a reputation coming into the game, having mixed it up on a level just a notch down from the APFA. During the season, Cal said, "the Racine management has thrown a lot of verbal brickbats at the Packers and the Bay team expects to teach Racine that football championships are won on the gridiron and not in the papers of the state."

WISCONSIN TEAMS THAT MADE IT TO THE NFL
Green Bay Packers, 1921.
Kenosha Maroons, 1924 (only).
Milwaukee Badgers, 1922 to 1926.
Racine Legions, 1922 to 1924.
Racine Tornadoes, 1926 (only).
Kenosha was the only team that did not begin as a town team.

The contest, at what Cal tagged "Otto Borchert's baseball orchard," ended in a 3–3 tie. The game had a little bit of everything and added up to what Calhoun labeled "as good an exhibition of football as could be wished for." APFA play was also finished for the year, with the Staleys nipping the Buffalo All-Americans, 10–7, on the same Sunday.

The Tuesday, December 6, edition of the *Press-Gazette* ended the season with the headline, "Packer Footballers Lay Away Their Togs; Strong Team in Field Next Fall." But the following day a teaser crept across the same pages suggesting that the Packers would again do battle in Milwaukee against a team of Marquette All-Stars. In town team tradition, the opening set would be played between two aggregations who had "made a fine record" in the Milwaukee Area Football Association, the South Side Malleables and the Hagerdorn Electrics.

Milwaukee's role in the Packer story was already zooming clearly into focus. It was a bigger city offering more spectators, and it was closer to the football hub of Chicago. The Wisconsin-Illinois line had become a "blood border" in the football wars, and good contests against great opponents were readily available. The Packers had clearly worn out the bulk of the competition in the northern climes. By the end of Lambeau's tenure as coach of the team in the late 1940s, there was more than raw speculation that he was considering moving the team to the Beer City if he could finagle it. Larger draws at larger venues meant more money, plain

MILWAUKEE—THE GOLD PACKAGE

Milwaukee's role in Green Bay Packer history cannot be ignored. What many people don't know is that Milwaukee has a strong football history of its own, including its own entrant in the fledgling National Football League. Here are just a few of its stories.

Fans Outraged by Doubling of Admission Charge!

Thanksgiving Day 1903 was to feature a contest between Battery A of Milwaukee and an undefeated, unscored-upon squad from Green Bay in a contest touted as "the Championship of the State." The game would be played at Hagemeister Park in Green Bay. In the days just before the contest, a rumor began circulating that, because the Green Bay team was playing a big town, the price for a ticket would increase to 50 cents. The football public was outraged and the rumor was quickly quelled by Fred Hulbert.

Milwaukee Joins the Big Leagues

Early teams such as the Maple Leaf Athletic Club evolved into the Badgers, Milwaukee's entrant into the NFL in 1922. They stayed in the league for five seasons, accruing the following records: 1922, 2-4-3; 1923, 7-2-3; 1924, 5-8-0; 1925, 0-6-0; 1926, 2-7-0. They signed class players like Fritz Pollard and Paul Robeson, two of the first black players in the league. The Badgers also corralled the great Jimmy Conzleman for two games. Later, Johnny "Blood" McNally appeared in town to play with the Badgers. The Badgers battled the Packers twice in '22, coming away with one tie and one loss. But over the years, the Badgers did have problems with the Bays. Their collective record against the Packers after the end of the 1926 season, the last for the Milwaukee Badgers, was 0-9-1.

At the end of the 1925 season, a harbinger of doom came in the form of a late-scheduled game. After the Badgers had called it quits for the 1925 season, they were called upon by the Chicago Cardinals to help pad their record. Because most of the Badger regulars had hung up their cleats for the season, a full team was hard to muster. Manager John Dunn got the bodies he needed from the local high school but still suffered a 59–0 pounding.

At the winter meeting, President Joe Carr dropped the hammer on the Badgers. He had found out about the illegal players and made the following decree: Team owner Ambrose L. McGurk would be fined $500 and ordered to sell the club within 90 days and have no further connection with the league. John Dunn would be stripped of his position and barred from the game. Art Foltz, a Cardinal player responsible for recruiting the high schoolers, would also be summarily banned from football.

Johnny Bryan took over the Badgers, but they were not long in the pro world, playing just one more season. In 1927, Bryan formed a team called the Milwaukee Eagles, which served as part of the prelude for the Packers' 1927 NFL season.

and simple. Of course, Lambeau's hands were tied when it came to moving the team. He didn't own it.

Milwaukee hosted as few as two and as many as four games per season from 1933 on. In 1995, when the Milwaukee games were eliminated, the Packer organization shifted to packages that still accommodate the team's fans from Wisconsin's largest city. And the platonic competition between Green Bay and Milwaukee fans over who pulls hardest for the team still resounds in the stadium.

Despite the usual midweek reports of the Marquette team stacking its lineup with "cracks" from wherever they could dig them up, the contest was never played. The game's promoters had forgotten to consult the weathermen or the almanacs, and lo and behold, December in Wisconsin decided to enter into the equation. The December 11 contest was called off even after the Packers and their fans had ridden the rails to Milwaukee. The game was moved back and forth between Marquette's football field and the Brewer baseball park but never materialized at either locale. Politics seemed to play as much of a part in the cancellation as did the weather, and that seemed to be the end of it.

Rumors of the same matchup resurfaced the following week, but it was already the middle of December, and most athletes had shifted their focus to a much rounder ball on a hardwood floor. Assurances that the contest would be played "despite weather conditions" aside, a blizzard finally ended the 1921 season. The Staleys and the Cardinals had managed to pull off a game on a snow-covered field to settle Chicago's pro football title but left things wide open in front of several thousand shivering rooters with a scoreless tie.

MODERN TECHNOLOGY DOOMS THE TOWN TEAM GAME

For the people of Stambaugh in Michigan's Upper Peninsula, especially after World War II, the automobile made a sojourn to Green Bay to see the Packers in action a very "doable" thing. Train travel was still around, but motoring independently to City Stadium in Green Bay offered far fewer restrictions on personal liberty. Besides, nearly everyone in the U. P. now pulled for the Packers. Sure you could stay in the area and watch the Steelers—they had even gone undefeated in 1949—but there was something a little more glamorous about the Packers.

As early as 1931, the *Iron River Reporter* was stirring up local interest in the Green Bay Packers. Between the lines, the tone seemed to indicate that fans of the All-Stars had a certain stake in the outcome of the Green Bay team. After all, they had toed up at Highland Park field just 10 or so years before, and the All-Stars had given the Packers a decent run for their money. "Many plan annual trek to see Packers play," proclaimed one headline. "Fans from Iron River, Stambaugh, Caspian, Gaastra and Mineral Hills are beginning to scan the southeastern horizon for tidings of the Green Bay Packers 1931 football team and its chances of winning a third-straight title in the national professional grid league."

Yet, the automobile horn did not sound the death knell for town team football on its own. Only those locals who were well-heeled or well-connected enough or had that kind of leisure time could make the trek south. The car would have to be joined by another bit of technological wizardry to do that.

Radio had been introduced into the sport as early as 1930 in Green Bay, but without an actual picture of the gridiron action, it was make-do at best. Television, on the other hand, gave you the picture, the commentary, and the convenience of home. And it eliminated the requisite travel to the game. Essentially, it was free.

It is often suggested that the 1958 National Football League championship signaled that the NFL had cleared the final hurdle in supplanting the college and town team games as the

Both world wars led to an increase in football action. Men returned from the hostilities with a sense of camaraderie, and a little football seemed to fit the bill for action. Great teams were formed all over Wisconsin and the U.P., including Wausau, Oshkosh, Manitowoc, Sault Ste. Marie, Escanaba, and many others. Sadly, town team football in the late '40s and early '50s was not long for this world. The townies still faced all the usual troubles of fielding a team, while the automobile and television were making the NFL's sophisticated brand of football more accessible. Photograph obtained from and used with permission of Frank Shepich and Harold Anderson, Stambaugh, Michigan.

"big show" when it came to football. That contest, played on December 28 between the Baltimore Colts and the New York Giants at Yankee Stadium, is also often called "the Greatest Game Ever Played" because of the on-field action itself as well as its off-field significance. After all, somewhere between 40 and 50 million people watched the Colts nip the Giants, 23–17, on television.

The NFL had been televising its title games since 1951, but by 1958, with the country about to enter a new decade, the end-of-the-year showdown had taken on a new salience. Barry Frank, a former television sports executive, has described that 1958 trophy bout as "a seminal moment for the NFL, maybe *the* seminal moment for the NFL." And the reasons are simple. That game represented the symbiotic coming together of the sport, the players, the fans, the money, the hype, and a living room appliance that would render every town team still playing the game, no matter how well, as obsolete. By 1962, the NFL had secured its first single-network contract with CBS, and football on TV was a sure thing.

The 1921 football season truly was the watershed moment in the history of the Packer franchise, and Lambeau's audacity had gotten the squad—and the city—over the hump. They had made the ultimate town team statement, taking it not only to the best in the immediate area, but also to the best that had emerged from other town venues across the nation. Would it be smooth sailing from here on out? A fair wind forever over the team's shoulder and a shared bottle of rot gut in their hands? No way. The team would face ineptitude and doubt on the field for the rest of its days, despite its unduplicated success. It would also endure the threat of financial disaster at every turn in its course to the present day. In short, the team would become a legend. And the 1921 season would start it wonderfully on its way.

But what of town team football, the phenomenon that had begotten it all? In the early 1920s, the story of Green Bay town team football had, for all intents and purposes, ended. If it hadn't gone the way of the horse and buggy by now, it soon would.

Teams continued to play on the old circuit, representing Green Bay against a new batch of opponents like Clintonville and a resurfaced Kewaunee team. Town team action still had its place, though it was shrinking in size. Games would still draw a gaggle of spectators who might not make the drive to City Stadium to watch the Packers play. But it was the fatuous act of paying more at the small-town grocery when a short trip to the big-city supermarket would have gotten fresher produce for less money. Town team football still had a role to play, but its time on the stage was definitely measured.

In fact, town team football, re-energized by the camaraderie spurred by World War II, remained a possibility into the 1950s, when elevens like the West Iron County Steelers coached by Frank Shepich would battle up against other crews from across the Upper Peninsula and the northern half of Wisconsin. But radio and TV, along with an intensified struggle to maintain a town team financially, would toll the death knell on town team football by the early 1960s.

Yet, the Packers, born out of the town team tradition, would survive. And nearly every man that played on town teams in this area of the world and every fan that knew his name, would become a Packer fan and pass that love down through his family as part of his own legacy. Once, on a relatively balmy Sunday in November 1919, the Stambaugh All-Stars and the Green Bay Packers met on a flat expanse down the hill from the local high school and battled it out as equals. But that game represented a snapshot, a moment frozen in time.

The Packers, on their way to membership in the future National Football League, won that skirmish, and Lambeau would look back and say, "those miners were tough." The All-Stars, who had been around in one rendition or another since at least 1902, blazed across the various leagues of northern Wisconsin and Upper Michigan, but then flickered and died out during the Depression. Their ashes were stirred by returning GIs in the late 1940s, but it was the last fuel meeting the last heat and air.

Today, nearly everyone who remembers the All-Star legend pulls hard for the Packers. And, whether they can put a verbal finger on it or not, it's because they sense that once, measured on similar frozen tundra fields, the Packers were the same as the All-Stars. And the New London Bulldogs, the Kaukauna city team, the Marinette Lauermans, the Oshkosh Arions, the Nighthawks, the Hillsides, or even the Motor Boat Club could all have slugged it out with those gosh-darn Packers. And they did, for a time.

In Green Bay, something different, and, all things considered, something miraculous happened. There, the town team wasn't lost. But only because the man at the helm wasn't steering a vessel he was willing to call a town team. The vision-ary Lambeau didn't have to die for his beliefs. But his story wouldn't end without some stigma either. "The game is played with local boys and we run gloriously into oblivion. No, it's played with the best you can find and we pass, literally, into a new era with or without our fans."

Certainly, the key was for Lambeau to win. And no year was more of a litmus test for that than 1921. That year, he had said, "look at me," and everyone turned their heads. To fall on his face under that scrutiny would have been a personal embarrassment, for sure, but it would also have caused the entire Packer organiza-tion to stumble on a national plane and rejoin the ranks of the town teams, all of which have now disappeared.

The image speaks volumes about a town's love affair with its team. A clutch of boys and at least two full-grown men perch in a long-forgotten tree along the East River to watch their gridiron heroes in action at Old City Stadium. Photograph from the Henry Lefebvre Collection of the Neville Public Museum of Brown County, Green Bay, Wisconsin.

Lambeau accomplished a lot in the 31 years that his name was synonymous with the Green Bay Packers. He would accumulate the team's first triple champi-onship before it had even been a member team of the APFA/NFL for 10 years. He would also lead the team to NFL titles in 1936, 1939, and 1944. More important, his brashness assured the team's ultimate survival. Certainly the "Hungry Five," a group of Green Bay businessmen, and the team's early fans were important. But the All-Stars had taken similar support with them into battle that November day in 1919. Without Lambeau's arrogance at the center, these things wouldn't have been enough and the Green Bay Packers would now be listed with 47 other teams at nflhistory.com as "defunct."

Lambeau's vision has outlived him and surpassed him. Today, the torch, lit by Fred Hulbert, relit by Lambeau, and fired up again by Vince Lombardi, Mike Holmgren, and Mike Sherman, is burning brightly. And the team's fans, always behind their boys, have a right to celebrate and be recognized. Some of them will bare their bodies at home games this winter to consecrate the relationship of this "drinking town with a football problem" and this team. En route to the hospital emergency room, they won't be dismissed as crazy. They've got something special and they know it, even if they couldn't pronounce it at that point. They've got the best story in all of sports history.

An article in *Smithsonian* in 1991 called the Green Bay Packers "the most unusual franchise in all of professional sports . . . Football is, and always has been, more than a game in Green Bay," it continued. "They're also what you might call, for lack of a better term, a living artifact. As the last of the NFL's original town teams, they provide a unique window into the history of a pastime that many believe has supplanted baseball as the nation's favorite." Oakland Raiders Hall of Fame defensive lineman, Howie Long, probably said it best in his induction speech. "Baseball is the country's pastime, but football is its passion."

The fact that the town loves the team is well-documented. But that feeling— given up so willingly to the town team heroes by every kid sneaking into a game, every nervous wanna-be blaspheming along the sideline, or every young maiden swooning over a diving catch—is familiar, heartfelt territory for every fan of every town team that ever took a whack at the game. Today, the Packers are the survivors of the golden age, left to defend the honor of their fallen comrades like the first Green Bay championship team of 1897 or the Stambaugh All-Stars. And, because of their unique status as the only remaining town team, they will remain in Green Bay forever to do just that.

Rule changes and parity, instant replay and corporate names on stadiums, division realignments and logo changes will come and go. But Green Bay and every town that ever fielded a team will have the Packers, like a solid rock in shifting sand.

However simply, a story passed on in the *Smithsonian* article from the team's later years sums up the town-team era's humble roots well. Gary Knafelc, a good-sized receiver, had caught a touchdown pass in a rare victory in the late 1950s and the crowd was carrying him off the field. "This kid reached up and put something in my hand," he recalled. "I didn't realize what it was until I got to the locker room. He had given me 50 cents."

A FEW TOWN TEAMS

DID YOUR TOWN have a football team? Did you attend a college that helped produce a town team? The following are just a few of those towns and colleges that were a part of the town team era.

WISCONSIN
Algoma
Allouez
Appleton
Beloit
Beloit College
Carroll College
Chippewa Falls
Clintonville
Crystal Falls
De Pere
Eau Claire
Fall River
Fond du Lac
Fort Atkinson
Gillett
Green Bay Business College
Kaukauna
Kenosha
Kewaunee
La Crosse
La Crosse Normal School
Lawrence University
Little Chute
Manitowoc
Marinette
Menasha
Middleton
Milwaukee
Neenah
New London
Niagara
Oconto
Oneida
Oshkosh
Oshkosh Normal
Peshtigo
Plymouth
Port Washington
Racine
Rhinelander
Ripon
Saint Norbert College
Seymour

Shawano
Sheboygan
Sheboygan Falls
Stevens Point
Stevens Point Normal
Sturgeon Bay
University of Wisconsin–Madison
Waukesha
Waupaca
Wausau
Wayland Academy
Wisconsin Dells

MICHIGAN'S UPPER PENINSULA

Bessemer
Caspian
Duluth
Escanaba
Gaastra
Gladstone
Gwinn
Iron Mountain
Iron River
Ironwood
Ishpeming
Manistique
Marquette
Menominee
Norway
Ontonogon
Quinnesec
Sault Ste. Marie
Stambaugh

BIBLIOGRAPHY

ARTICLES

Coe, E. D. Letter to the editor. *Whitewater Register*. Reprinted in *Stevens Point Daily Journal*, March 28, 1906.

Editorial. "In Football Armor. The Safety Appliances of the Modern Player." *Marinette Daily Eagle*, September 21, 1895.

BOOKS, BOOKLETS, AND PAMPHLETS

The Ariel. Lawrence University Yearbook. 1897, 1899, 1901, 1902, 1906.

Ashley, Robert Paul, and George H. Miller. *Ripon College: A History*. Ripon, WI: Ripon College Press, 1990.

Beck, Jack. *Escanaba Eskimoes: 100 Years of Football*. Ann Arbor, MI: Ann Arbor Printing, 1996.

Bernhardt, Marcia, comp. *As Time Goes By: A History of the Streets and Plats of Iron River, Michigan, 1881 - 1972*. Caspian, MI: Iron County Historical and Museum Society, 1972.

———*They Came (to Iron County Michigan)*. Norway, MI: Curriculum Development Center, Dickenson-Iron Intermediate School District, 1975.

Billings, Robert E. *As Once We Were: A Pictorial History of Clintonville, Wisconsin*. Iola, WI: Krause Publication, 1993.

Boorstin, Daniel J., and Brooks Mather Kelley. *A History of the United States*. Lexington, MA: Ginn and Company, 1983.

Bruenig, Charles. *A Great and Good Work: A History of Lawrence University 1847–1964*. Appleton, WI: Lawrence University Press, 1994.

Cameron, Steve. *The Packers! Seventy-five Seasons of Memories and Mystique in Green Bay.* Dallas, TX: Taylor Publishing Company and The Green Bay Packers, 1993.

Carroll, Bob, Michael Gershman, David Neft, and John Thorn. *Total Football: The Official Encyclopedia of the NFL.* New York: HarperCollins, 1997.

Caspian: The Caring City 1918-1993. N.p., 1993.

Claasen, Harold "Spike." *The History of Professional Football.* Englewood Cliffs, NJ: Prentice-Hall, 1963.

Coulton, George Gordon. *The Medieval Village.* Cambridge: Cambridge University Press, 1925.

Daly, Dan, and Bob O'Donnell. *The Pro Football Chronicle: The Complete (Well Almost) Record of the Best Players, the Greatest Photos, the Hardest Hits, the Biggest Scandals and the Funniest Stories in Pro Football.* New York: Macmillan, Colliers Books, 1990.

Erickson III, Edward. "Athletics." In *Frames for the Future,* edited by Marcia Bernhardt. Dallas, TX: Taylor Publishing, 1981.

Gard, Robert E. *University Madison U. S. A.* Madison, WI: Straus Printing and Publishing, 1970.

Goska, Eric. *Packer Legends in Facts.* Germantown, WI: Tech/Data Publications, 1995.

Hall, Moss. *Go, Indians! Stories of the Great Indian Athletes of the Carlisle School.* Los Angeles: Ward Ritchie Press, 1971.

Horrigan, Joe. *The Official Pro Football Hall of Fame Answer Book.* New York: Simon and Schuster, Little Simon Books, 1990.

Johnson, Chuck. *The Green Bay Packers: Pro-Football's Pioneer Team.* New York: Thomas Nelson and Sons, 1961.

Johnson, Walter "Bud." "Recreation and Sports." In *The Manitowoc County: Story of a Century.* Manitowoc, WI: Manitowoc County Centennial Committee, 1948.

Jungwirth, Clarence J. *A History of the City of Oshkosh: The Early Years.* Self-published.

Kronenwetter, Michael. *Wisconsin Heartland: The Story of Wausau and Marathon County.* Midland, MI: Pendell Publishing, 1984.

Kuechle, Oliver, and Jim Mott. *On Wisconsin: Badger Football.* Huntsville, AL: Strode Publishers, 1977.

Langill, Ellen. *Carroll College: The First Century, 1846 - 1946.* Waukesha, WI: Carroll College Press, 1980.

Martin, Adrian R. *I Remember As Though it Were Yesterday.* Amherst, WI: Palmer Publications, n.d.

McCallum, John D., and Charles H. Pearson. *College Football U.S.A. 1869 - 1971: Official Book of the National Football Foundation.* New York: Hall of Fame Publishing, 1972.

Morgan, Lewis Henry. *League of the Iroquois.* New York: Citadel Press, Carol Communications, 1962.

Names, Larry D. *Green Bay Packers Facts and Trivia.* Wautoma, WI: E. B. Houchin Co., 1993.

———. *The History of the Green Bay Packers: The Lambeau Years, Part One.* Wautoma, WI: Angel Press of Wisconsin, 1987.

———. *The History of the Green Bay Packers: The Lambeau Years, Part Two.* Wautoma, WI: Angel Press of Wisconsin, 1987.

Nash, Bruce, and Allan Zullo. *The Football Hall of Shame 2.* New York: Simon and Schuster, Pocket Books, 1990.

Neft, David S., Richard M. Cohen, and Rick Korch. *The Football Encyclopedia: The Complete, Year-By-Year History of Professional Football from 1892 to the Present.* New York: Saint Martin's, Sports Products, Inc., 1994.

Noyes, Dr. Edward, and Tom Herzing, eds. *Here to Serve: The First Hundred Years of the University of Wisconsin-Oshkosh.* Oshkosh: The University of Wisconsin Oshkosh Foundation, Inc., 1997.

Peterson, Robert W. *Pigskin: The Early Years of Pro Football.* New York: Oxford University Press, 1997.

Riffenburgh, Beau. *The Official NFL Encyclopedia.* New York: NAL Books, 1986.

Ripon College Sports Records 1882–1976. Pamphlet.

Silfven, Albert K. *Stambaugh, Michigan Centennial: 100 Years on the Hill.* Caspian, MI: Northern Printing and Graphics, 1982.

Springer, George T., comp. *Early History of Foot Ball in Gladstone, Michigan.* Scrapbook.

Stare, Fred A. *The Story of Wisconsin's Great Canning Industry.* Baltimore: The Canning Trade, 1949.

Steckbeck, John S. *Fabulous Redmen: The Carlisle Indians and Their Famous Football Teams.* Harrisburg, PA: J. Horace McFarland Co., 1951.

Stewart, Mark. *Football: A History of the Gridiron Game.* New York: Grolier Publishing, Franklin Watts, 1998.

Svoboda, Jacqlyn, Mary Hanrahan, Donna Alm, Robin Garber, Sandra Braun, and Judie Stuebs. *Kewaunee: A Harbor Community.* Kewaunee, WI: Centennial Book Committee, 1983.

Swisher, Karen Gayton, and AnCyta Benally. *Native North American Firsts.* Detroit, MI: Gale Research, 1998.

Torinus, John B. *The Packer Legend: An Inside Look.* Neshkoro, WI: Laranmark Press, 1982.

Walsh, Christy. *Intercollegiate Football 1869-1933.* N.p., n.d.

Ward, Arch. *The Green Bay Packers: The Story of Professional Football.* New York: G. P. Putnam's Sons, 1946.

Ward, Geoffery C., and Ken Burns. *Baseball: An Illustrated History.* New York: Knoft, Borzoi Books, 1994.

Wittingham, Richard. *The Chicago Bears: An Illustrated History.* Chicago: Rand McNally, 1979.

———, ed. *The Fireside Book of Pro Football: An Anthology of the Best, Most Entertaining Writing About Professional Football.* New York: Simon and Schuster, Fireside Book, 1989.

———. *What a Game They Played.* New York: Harper and Row, 1984.

Wichman, Alton Edward. *The Wayland Story: 1855 to 1955.* Menasha, WI: The George Banta Publishing Company, 1954.

Wright, David C. *A Stroll Through the Village: Fall River, WI 1846-1996.* Portage, WI: The O'Brion Agency, 1996.

Wyman, Walker Demarquis, ed. *History of the Wisconsin State Universities.* River Falls, WI: River Falls State University Press, 1968.

MAPS

Map of Brown County Wisconsin. N.p.: G. A. Randall and J. H. Hinkley, 1875.

BIBLIOGRAPHY

NEWSPAPERS
Appleton Daily Post
Appleton Evening Crescent
Beloit Daily News
Clintonville Tribune
Crystal Falls Diamond Drill
De Pere Journal
De Pere Journal-Democrat
Escanaba Delta County Reporter
Escanaba Delta Reporter
Fond du Lac Daily Commonwealth
Fond du Lac Journal
Green Bay Advocate
Green Bay Gazette
Green Bay News-Chronicle
Green Bay Press-Gazette
Green Bay Review
Green Bay Semi-Weekly Gazette
Iron River Reporter
Ishpeming Iron Ore
Kaukauna Times
La Crosse Leader-Times
Lawrence University Collegian
Lawrence University Lawrentian
Marinette Daily Eagle
Marinette Eagle
Marinette Eagle-Star
Marquette Mining Journal
Menominee County Journal
Menominee Herald
Milwaukee Journal
New London Press-Republican
Oconto County Reporter

BEFORE THEY WERE THE PACKERS

Oconto County Reporter-Enterprise
Oshkosh Daily Northwestern
Ripon College Collegian
Ripon College News-Letter

SCHOLARLY PAPERS
Rasmusson, W. E. "Study of Social Conditions in Appleton, Wisconsin." 1911.

INDEX

MORE GREAT TITLES FROM
TRAILS BOOKS &
PRAIRIE OAK PRESS

ACTIVITY GUIDES

Biking Wisconsin: 50 Great Road and Trail Rides, *Steve Johnson*

Great Cross-Country Ski Trails: Wisconsin, Minnesota, Michigan & Ontario, *Wm. Chad McGrath*

Great Minnesota Walks: 49 Strolls, Rambles, Hikes, and Treks, *Wm. Chad McGrath*

Great Wisconsin Walks: 45 Strolls, Rambles, Hikes, and Treks, *Wm. Chad McGrath*

Minnesota Underground & the Best of the Black Hills, *Doris Green*

Paddling Illinois: 64 Great Trips by Canoe and Kayak, *Mike Svob*

Paddling Iowa: 96 Great Trips by Canoe and Kayak, *Nate Hoogeveen*

Paddling Northern Wisconsin: 82 Great Trips by Canoe and Kayak, *Mike Svob*

Paddling Southern Wisconsin: 82 Great Trips by Canoe and Kayak, *Mike Svob*

Walking Tours of Wisconsin's Historic Towns, *Lucy Rhodes, Elizabeth McBride, Anita Matcha*

Wisconsin's Outdoor Treasures: A Guide to 150 Natural Destinations, *Tim Bewer*

Wisconsin Underground, *Doris Green*

TRAVEL GUIDES

Classic Wisconsin Weekends, *Michael Bie*

County Parks of Wisconsin, Revised Edition, *Jeannette and Chet Bell*

Great Little Museums of the Midwest, *Christine des Garennes*

Great Minnesota Taverns, *David K. Wright & Monica G. Wright*

Great Minnesota Weekend Adventures, *Beth Gauper*

Great Weekend Adventures, *the Editors of Wisconsin Trails*

Great Wisconsin Taverns: 101 Distinctive Badger Bars, *Dennis Boyer*

Sacred Sites of Minnesota, *John-Brian Paprock & Teresa Peneguy Paprock*

Sacred Sites of Wisconsin, *John-Brian Paprock & Teresa Peneguy Paprock*

Tastes of Minnesota: A Food Lover's Tour, *Donna Tabbert Long*

The Great Iowa Touring Book: 27 Spectacular Auto Trips, *Mike Whye*

The Great Minnesota Touring Book: 30 Spectacular Auto Trips, *Thomas Huhti*

The Great Wisconsin Touring Book: 30 Spectacular Auto Tours, *Gary Knowles*

Wisconsin Family Weekends: 20 Fun Trips for You and the Kids, *Susan Lampert Smith*

Wisconsin Golf Getaways, *Jeff Mayers and Jerry Poling*

Wisconsin Lighthouses: A Photographic and Historical Guide, *Ken and Barb Wardius*

Wisconsin's Hometown Flavors, *Terese Allen*

Wisconsin Waterfalls, *Patrick Lisi*

Up North Wisconsin: A Region for All Seasons, *Sharyn Alden*

HOME & GARDEN

Bountiful Wisconsin: 110 Favorite Recipes, *Terese Allen*

Codfather 2, *Jeff Hagen*

Creating a Perennial Garden in the Midwest, *Joan Severa*

Eating Well in Wisconsin, *Jerry Minnich*

Foods That Made Wisconsin Famous: 150 Great Recipes, *Richard J. Baumann*

Wisconsin Country Gourmet, *Marge Snyder & Suzanne Breckenridge*

Wisconsin Garden Guide, *Jerry Minnich*

Wisconsin Herb Cookbook, *Marge Snyder & Suzanne Breckenridge*

HISTORICAL BOOKS

Barns of Wisconsin, *Jerry Apps*

Duck Hunting on the Fox: Hunting and Decoy-Carving Traditions, *Stephen M. Miller*

Portrait of the Past: A Photographic Journey Through Wisconsin 1865-1920, *Howard Mead,*
Jill Dean, and Susan Smith
Prairie Whistles: Tales of Midwest Railroading, *Dennis Boyer*
Shipwrecks of Lake Michigan, *Benjamin J. Shelak*
Wisconsin At War: 20th Century Conflicts Through the Eyes of Veterans, *Dr. James F. McIntosh, M.D.*
Wisconsin's Historic Houses & Living History Museums, *Krista Finstad Hanson*
Wisconsin: The Story of the Badger State, *Norman K. Risjord*

GIFT BOOKS
Celebrating Door County's Wild Places, *The Ridges Sanctuary*
Fairlawn: Restoring the Splendor, *Tom Davis*
Madison, *Photography by Brent Nicastro*
Milwaukee, *Photography by Todd Dacquisto*
Milwaukee Architecture: A Guide to Notable Buildings, *Joseph Korom*
Spirit of the North: A Photographic Journey Through Northern Wisconsin, *Richard Hamilton Smith*
The Spirit of Door County: A Photographic Essay, *Darryl R. Beers*
Uncommon Sense: The Life Of Marshall Erdman, *Doug Moe & Alice D'Alessio*

LEGENDS & LORE
Driftless Spirits: Ghosts of Southwest Wisconsin, *Dennis Boyer*
Haunted Wisconsin, *Michael Norman and Beth Scott*
The Beast of Bray Road: Tailing Wisconsin's Werewolf, *Linda S. Godfrey*
The Eagle's Voice: Tales Told by Indian Effigy Mounds, *Gary J. Maier, M.D.*
The Poison Widow: A True Story of Sin, Strychnine, & Murder, *Linda S. Godfrey*
The W-Files: True Reports of Wisconsin's Unexplained Phenomena, *Jay Rath*

YOUNG READERS
ABCs Naturally, *Lynne Smith Diebel & Jann Faust Kalscheur*
ABCs of Wisconsin, *Dori Hillestad Butler, Illustrated by Alison Relyea*
H is for Hawkeye, *Jay Wagner, Illustrated by Eileen Potts Dawson*
H is for Hoosier, *Dori Hillestad Butler, Illustrated by Eileen Potts Dawson*
Wisconsin Portraits, *Martin Hintz*
Wisconsin Sports Heroes, *Martin Hintz*
W is for Wisconsin, *Dori Hillestad Butler, Illustrated by Eileen Potts Dawson*

SPORTS
Cold Wars: 40+ Years of Packer-Viking Rivalry, *Todd Mishler*
Downfield: Untold Stories of the Green Bay Packers, *Jerry Poling*
Green Bay Packers Titletown Trivia Teasers, *Don Davenport*
Mean on Sunday: The Autobiography of Ray Nitschke, *Robert W. Wells*
Mudbaths and Bloodbaths: The Inside Story of the Bears-Packers Rivalry, *Gary D'Amato & Cliff Christl*
Packers By the Numbers: Jersey Numbers and the Players Who Wore Them, *John Maxymuk*

OTHER
Driftless Stories, *John Motoviloff*
River Stories: Growing Up on the Wisconsin, *Delores Chamberlain*
The Wisconsin Father's Guide to Divorce, *James Novak*
Travels With Sophie: The Journal of Louise E. Wegner, *Edited by Gene L. LaBerge & Michelle L. Maurer*
Trout Friends, *Bill Stokes*
Wild Wisconsin Notebook, *James Buchholz*

For a free catalog, phone, write, or e-mail us.

Trails Books
P.O. Box 317, Black Earth, WI 53515
(800) 236-8088 • e-mail: books@wistrails.com • www.trailsbooks.com